NEW BRITISH INDUSTRIES
IN THE
TWENTIETH CENTURY

NEW BRITISH INDUSTRIES
IN THE
TWENTIETH CENTURY

A SURVEY OF
DEVELOPMENT AND STRUCTURE

BY

ALFRED PLUMMER
B.Litt., M.Sc. (Econ.), LL.D.

HEAD OF THE DEPARTMENT OF ECONOMICS AND SOCIAL STUDIES
IN THE CITY OF BIRMINGHAM COMMERCIAL COLLEGE
FORMERLY VICE-PRINCIPAL OF RUSKIN COLLEGE, OXFORD

LONDON
SIR ISAAC PITMAN & SONS, LTD.
1937

SIR ISAAC PITMAN & SONS, Ltd.
PITMAN HOUSE, PARKER STREET, KINGSWAY, LONDON, W.C.2
THE PITMAN PRESS, BATH
PITMAN HOUSE, LITTLE COLLINS STREET, MELBOURNE

ASSOCIATED COMPANIES
PITMAN PUBLISHING CORPORATION
2 WEST 45TH STREET, NEW YORK
205 WEST MONROE STREET, CHICAGO

SIR ISAAC PITMAN & SONS (CANADA), Ltd.
(INCORPORATING THE COMMERCIAL TEXT BOOK COMPANY
PITMAN HOUSE, 381–383 CHURCH STREET, TORONTO

MADE IN GREAT BRITAIN AT THE PITMAN PRESS, BATH
C7—(B.251)

PREFACE

THE "basic" industries of Great Britain have, I believe, received a disproportionate amount of attention from authors and the public since the end of the Great War. Too frequently one finds that contemporary writers, purporting to deal with British industries, devote many thousands of words to the position, problems, and prospects of coal, cotton, iron and steel, shipbuilding, and the rest of the old industries, but say very little of the new industries upon whose development the degree of our future prosperity will largely depend. Economic progress and rising standards of living may be expected to call for much more expansion of the new industries than of the old, and it is probably not too much to say that the keynote of policy and endeavour in British industry to-day and to-morrow should not be "back to the land," nor even "back to the basic industries," but rather forward to the "tertiary" industries and the luxury trades, and on with the production of goods and services which people have never consumed before. The present work is an attempt to bring in the new to redress the balance of the old.

I should like to take this opportunity of thanking numerous officials of Government Departments, companies, trade unions, and trade associations who have been kind enough to reply to my letters of inquiry and to supply me with information upon various matters. My thanks are also due to my friend and former pupil, Mr. J. A. Hargreaves, for collecting much of the information regarding wages in the passenger section of the road transport industry.

A. P.

RUSKIN COLLEGE
OXFORD

v

CONTENTS

vii

NEW BRITISH INDUSTRIES
IN THE
TWENTIETH CENTURY

CHAPTER I

CHANGES IN DEMAND, INDUSTRIAL TECHNIQUE, AND THE ATTITUDE OF THE STATE

THE student of modern economic and social history cannot fail to be strongly impressed by the contrast between the appalling conditions of life and labour depicted in such works as *The Town Labourer* 1760-1832 and *The Age of the Chartists*, and the corresponding conditions to-day. A century ago the populations of the new industrial "treadmill" towns lived "without leisure, playing fields or amenities of any kind" in "close and overcrowded haunts" so vile and ramshackle that even the jerry-builders and slum landlords of the present day would have recoiled from them in disgust. There was no Saturday half-holiday; other holidays were rare, and annual holidays unheard of. On the contrary, the working classes were enjoined to be continually industrious and thrifty, to abstain from pleasure, and to bear with Christian patience "the inconveniences of a lower station." Even the Friendly Societies, when they tried to bring good-fellowship and a little colour into that drab industrial desert, were criticized "for pursuing social entertainment when they should have been concentrating on thrift." For the new industrial proletariat literature did not exist, and the arts, "instead of helping the complaining and the miserable to forget themselves and their wrongs, were employed to give new lustre to good fortune, to declare the glory of sudden wealth. Leisure was the exclusive privilege of those for whom work was interesting, giving to

I

those engaged in it a bracing sense of power." But this new-found wealth, derived from a vast industrial expansion, was for the few, not for the many.

Immense fortunes were made in cotton, wool, iron and coal, but on the workers in these industries there fell degradation and distress. Not all employers grew rich with the Peels, nor did all the workmen grow poor with the hand-loom weavers, but the general feature of the times was the rise of a class of rich employers and the creation of a large and miserable proletariat.

This remarkable contrast might seem to demand an explanation: it might provoke misgivings about the justice and good government of society, and make people wonder whether there was not some flaw in the structure that was disfigured by such a basis of misery. These doubts and misgivings entered the mind of the working classes and produced, in time, a more or less organized demand for an altered distribution of the burdens and powers of government.[1]

In the end, some political and economic changes for the better were brought about. The struggle to *maintain* a standard of life already very low was at length transformed into a campaign to *raise* it, so that the worker's life should no longer consist of nothing but work, sleep, and "grub." Success came, albeit tardily, from the mid-Victorian era onwards; and, without in the least subscribing to the soothing sophistry that all is now well with the world, one can freely admit that the past century has indeed been a period of industrial *and social* progress.

But no virile modern community ever is content with the levels of economic progress and welfare reached in the preceding generation. To-day, in all the more advanced countries the majority of the inhabitants, having at last tasted the first-fruits of economic progress, very naturally and rightly desire further increases in their real incomes so that they may be able to attain to a "more varied mode of life, and cultivate social and cultural relationships more worthy of a true civilisation."[2] In twentieth-century Britain, despite certain

[1] J. L. and B. Hammond, *The Town Labourer* (1920), Chap. VI; *The Age of the Chartists* (1930), especially Chap. XVIII.
[2] A. G. B. Fisher, *The Clash of Progress and Security* (1935), 3–4.

temporary reverses and certain industrial black spots; despite wars and rumours of wars, a remarkable general rise in standards of life has been achieved. It is, in all probability, less than might have been realized under an *intelligently directed* Socialist economy; but it is impossible to deny that, on the whole, great progress has been made during the past three or four decades. Moreover, the rise still continues, coupled with a widespread desire for still more progress along the same line, including more variety and more leisure.[1] At the same time, standards of public taste and powers of appreciation are being constantly improved and developed by such agencies as the elementary and secondary schools, the adult education movement, broadcasting, and easy access to literature through public and other lending libraries or cheap reprints of good books.

Developments of this kind cannot fail to produce important repercussions in the industrial field. Astonishing changes in the consumption of goods and services by the masses of the population have taken place in this country during the past twenty years; and the industries supplying food, clothing, travel facilities, entertainments, etc., have all been affected in various ways. So far as food is concerned the demand for extra quantities is outweighed in importance by the demand for more variety. Clothing is demanded in greater quantities as well as in greater varieties, especially when the materials are cheap and æsthetically attractive. The further improvement in the status of women has given rise to new and increasing demands not only in the clothing trades but in other parts of the industrial field; for the desire for more leisure, or at least for more freedom from household drudgery, spreading among the women folk, has opened a market for various domestic

[1] Trade unionists argue that "systematic overtime . . . cuts into a man's rightful leisure. It also subjects him to the strains of systematic overwork"; "spasmodic overtime, they say, breaks without warning into his leisure hours and disorganizes his social arrangements and his home life. In either case, the argument goes, he should be well compensated; . . . for the workman has a right to the planning of his spare time beforehand." J. Hilton and others, *Are Trade Unions Obstructive ?* (1935), 315–6.

labour-saving devices and for tinned foodstuffs which require little or no preparation for the table. The quantity of travel "consumed" is mainly a function of its cheapness, comfort and speed : while cheapness and comfort also figure very largely as factors determining the demand for popular entertainments. For all these "secondary" and "tertiary" products—these "comforts and luxuries" as the textbooks used to call them— there exists a highly elastic actual and potential demand. If proof of this is wanted, it is to be found in the relatively recent expansion of industries producing preserved foods, rayon (artificial silk) fabrics, motor vehicles, radio sets, cinematograph films, and similar goods.

Frequently, latent or potential demand cannot become *effective* demand on any scale worth mentioning until means have been found of bringing costs of production and selling prices down to the pockets of the people, so to speak. This result is most commonly achieved by changes in productive technique resulting in new materials, new products, new services ; or in the cheapening of the costs of existing goods or services. It is, indeed, one of the most important functions of inventors and industrialists to study the *general* features of the trend of demand—including intermediate industrial demand as well as final consumers' demand—and to produce appropriate specific materials, articles or services at prices which potential consumers will be willing to pay. The normal sequence is, firstly, the realization or belief that there is a latent or potential demand for a certain commodity or service ; secondly, the invention and perfection of appropriate productive methods, based upon research and the consequent growth of knowledge ; thirdly, the marketing of the new commodity or service. Usually, production is most economical when it is performed on a large scale, and for many commodities the same holds true of marketing. Therefore, prices must be brought low enough to attract consumers in large numbers ; and it is desirable that the reductions of prices should go far enough to release some consumers' purchasing power, so that it may be either saved and invested, or used to purchase other commodities or services.[1] Thus, consumers will be, in effect, placed in possession of higher average real incomes and their standards of life will be raised. In this way, as Professors Gregory and Fisher point out, when, *as a community*, we improve our production, the average level of real income also rises; for "getting an increased income and producing new things are, for a community, identical" processes.[2] "The rise in the standard of living and the shorter working hours which have characterized the progress of industry in the last hundred years were both conditioned by increased productivity. . . ."[3] Such rising real incomes imply not only changes in the relative importance of different kinds of production—primary production declining in importance *relatively* to secondary and tertiary production—but also an increase in the *variety* of productive activities. These changes are not, as some people imagine, a sign of economic decay, but rather a *sine qua non* of continued economic health.[4]

The wealth-producing system of a modern community is not a definite or prescribed set of industries[5] finally settled

[1] For although the elasticity of demand for this or that product will always be more or less limited, there are no limits to the expansibility of demand as a whole.

[2] Fisher, *op. cit.*, 13–14.

[3] T. E. Gregory, in *Economic Journal*, December, 1930, 566.

[4] Professor Fisher argues, against Sir Henry Strakosch, that "it is neither possible nor desirable to have 'an increase of production extending over the whole range of commodities in an orderly and a symmetrical fashion.' A symmetrical increase of production would not, as Strakosch maintains, raise the standard of life of the people, but would . . . lead to instability and depression. In a progressive economy, increases of production must always be asymmetrical." *Op. cit.*, 39.

[5] An industry is a notoriously difficult thing to define and to pin down within precise limits. According to Professor Sargant Florence, an industry is "any kind of transaction (or series of transactions) for exchange (production, distribution, services, etc.) usually specialized in by a group of firms who do not usually perform other transactions. Thus transport or coal-mining is an industry because there are special transporting or coal-mining firms who do not perform much of any other transaction, though they may provide a fraction of hotel accommodation, or coking or gas production." (*The Logic of Industrial Organization* (1933), 4–5.) A similar line is taken by the Census authorities, who state that "the term Industry, which includes service, may be taken as indicative of the class of work collectively performed by all in one employment." Thus a motor lorry driver in the employment of an engineering firm is classified as in the engineering industry. The same

for all time, but, on the contrary, something flexible and subject to change. We may quite legitimately postulate static conditions in a first or early stage of a complex economic analysis, but this can be no more than a method of approach or first approximation. Economic reality is dynamic; and it is, in a sense, misleading to speak of the present era as an Age of Transition, for evolution and transition are features of life—including, of course, economic life—in every age. Always some crafts or industries are expanding while others are shrinking. It is chiefly the speed and scale of modern changes which distinguish the present from previous periods of economic evolution. Yet many of the implications of this rather obvious fact are by no means clearly visualized in relation to British industries to-day. For instance, attempts to grapple with the problems of some of our older, "basic" or "staple" industries, such as coal-mining and cotton manufacture, are often stultified by the idea that the objective must be to restore them to their "former" position, which usually

principle is adopted by the Ministry of Labour in compiling statistics of the numbers of persons employed and unemployed in various "industries."

These broad lines of classification will be followed in this book as far as possible; but we shall, from time to time, find ourselves compelled to make independent decisions in certain circumstances and for certain purposes. It is necessary to decide, for instance, whether the generation and distribution of electricity shall be treated as a separate "industry" or as part of the "electrical industry": or again, whether the canning of food and the manufacture of beet sugar shall be treated as separate industries, or as constituent parts or sections of the "food and drink industry."

Firms sometimes change from one industry to another by expanding their operations in certain directions and contracting them in others; or by doing this in company with other firms they may together form a new industry. Thus, at certain points in their industrial evolution manufacturers of textile goods engaged in making rayon-mixture fabrics from cotton and rayon yarns might still be classified as in the cotton industry; but with equal force it might be argued that they ought to be included as part of the rayon industry.

Lastly, it may be noted that as a matter of practical policy it is sometimes expedient to break through an existing classification and to adopt another, either permanently or for a particular purpose. For instance, it might be desirable to regard drivers of ancillary motor transport (e.g. tradesmen's delivery vans, builders' lorries, etc.,) as belonging to the road transport industry for purposes of wage-regulation, whatever their industrial classification in the records of the Ministry of Labour or the Board of Trade.

seems to mean their size immediately before the war, or their size at the peak of their former prosperity. We ought to free ourselves from such stale and hampering notions, and take a fresh view of the whole industrial situation. A few years ago the late Dr. Cannan discussed this point with characteristic vigour and vision.

. . . with the progress of discovery, invention, accumulation, and civilization generally, the proportion of the labour force of society required to produce the grosser necessaries of life steadily diminishes. . . . Coal has now gone the same way as corn and cattle. . . . The slackening growth of population, the discovery of alternative fuel, and economies in consumption on the one hand, and the opening up of new and more productive mines, as well as improvements in methods of production, have made it unnecessary to keep in employment the additional number of mineworkers who were brought in by temporary circumstances arising out of the war. But is the world grateful for the release of a considerable body of men from a kind of toil which is decidedly less agreeable than most? Not at all. Almost with one accord it declares that some arrangement ought to be made for keeping up the number of mineworkers. . . . The belief that the number of persons employed in the "old" or "staple" industries must be maintained at all costs arises from their being quite justly regarded as "important" and "great" compared with the newer and rapidly growing industries. Greater importance they certainly have in the sense that it is essential for us to have a certain amount of them. We must have a certain amount of the necessaries of life or die, and this makes us think of agriculture or coal-mining as much more important than the manufacture of gramophones and golf balls. But this kind of comparison is not to the point. It is not proposed that we should abandon the production of food altogether, and eat gramophones and golf balls. . . . The actual comparison is not between all gramophones and all food, but between some gramophones and surplus food which would be over and above what we want. . . .

Of course, anyone who wishes to depreciate the newer industries may call them "luxury trades," but they are none the worse for that. We all want luxuries, and though some of us may distribute our expenditure badly between them, very few of us are in the least likely to have more of all of them than is good for us. To think of the "luxury trades" as chiefly serving a few millionaires is ridiculous in the extreme when anyone may go down the back alleys in working-class districts and count up the number of

wireless installations, or sit by the roadside on a Saturday afternoon and observe the cars and combinations and motor bicycles.
It is the small luxuries of the multitude, not the great ones of the
few rich, that really count.[1]

In recent times, new materials (many of which are synthetic),
new sources of power, new modes of transport, and new
methods of entertainment have played a highly important
part, and have come to occupy a prominent place, in industrial
development in this and many other countries. Enterprising
industrialists, seeking profits by trying to transform the
numerous latent or potential demands of the population into
effective demands, through the offer of cheap but novel and
attractive commodities and services, have been aided by many
remarkable discoveries and inventions springing, in the first
instance, from expanding knowledge in the field of chemistry
and physics. And whenever inventors and industrialists score
important successes along this line, a net increase of intermediate industrial demand for other commodities and services
also ensues. Moreover, it often happens that a new commodity or service, when perfected and cheapened, is capable
of supplying two distinct types of demand: (a) the intermediate industrial demand, such as the demand of manufacturers for aluminium or electricity; or the commercial demand
for motor vans or wireless communication; and (b) the final
consumers' demand, such as the demand for private motor
cars, radio sets, and electricity for domestic purposes.

Another highly important recent development has been the
rapid improvement of the art of mass distribution of goods,
through the medium of the fixed-price, department, and

[1] *Manchester Guardian Commercial Annual Review*, January, 1930.
Cf. also Professor T. E. Gregory who says, "No doubt we shall have
to give up the belief that 'national power' is to be measured by a high
percentage of occupied persons in a few 'staple industries'; but just
as we no longer think of measuring our 'national power' in terms of
agricultural output, so we shall gradually see that those countries
which have the highest standards of life *ought* to be those employing the
largest proportion of their populations in the supply of 'luxuries.' All
that stands in the way are economic and ethical standards no longer
appropriate to the tendencies at work."—*Economic Journal*, December,
1930, 566.

co-operative stores, all of which largely eliminate the whole-salers' profits and reduce the retail price *per article or unit*, thus seconding the manufacturers' efforts to bring a greater variety of articles to the notice of the poorer consumers at prices which they can afford to pay.

Lastly, it is essential to notice that not all of these in-dustrial changes have been "natural" and spontaneous. Some of them would have been much retarded, and others would not have materialized at all, had it not been for State assist-ance. In this generation State aid for industry is available on an unprecedented scale; and in various ways the State has not only given support to old industries, but has encouraged and stimulated the rise and growth of new industries, such as air transport, the manufacture of motor vehicles, synthetic dyestuffs, beet sugar, and coal-oil. Why has the State's attitude changed in recent times from a mainly passive interest in industrial developments to positive encouragement and support on a far from negligible scale?

Various motives and forces have been at work to bring about this *volte face* in British economic policy. The Great War demonstrated (*inter alia*), firstly, that Britain was dependent to a dangerous degree upon certain imported commodities, and, secondly, that the State, through various special departments, could perform large-scale economic functions, such as the bulk purchase and mass-distribution of commodities, with a degree of success which the die-hard *laissez-faire* individualists had always maintained was utterly impossible. The arguments and hair-raising pessimistic pre-dictions of the latter were, therefore, largely discredited, and public opinion became more favourable to the prospect of an extension of State "interference" in economic affairs. After the Great War, British trade and industry suffered such an alarming series of severe slumps that in sheer desperation men of all classes and in all industries turned to the Government for help because it seemed to them that nothing less than the full power of the State would be strong enough to cope with the task of economic resuscitation. And this appeal to the

State was reinforced by the malignant march of economic nationalism throughout the world, and its disastrous effects on British economy. In the circumstances, a favourable response from the State was a foregone conclusion, for the Liberal Party having definitely lost its hold on the political machine, the way was open to either the Conservative Party or the Labour Party, both of which were, and still are, committed to programmes involving considerable extensions of the State's economic functions. In Chapter VI we shall examine the importance of this "attitude of increased responsibility" on the part of the State in relation to the rise and development of certain new industries.

From the survey which follows, it will appear that there has come into existence in Britain, mainly in the present century, a rising generation of young industries. The average "life" of an industry is usually a good deal longer than the normal life of a human being and it takes longer to usher a new industry into the world of commerce and manufactures and to bring it to maturity. Therefore the fact that before the opening of the twentieth century any given industry was conceived, brought forth alive and, in due time, made a few early steps along the road of development, does not exclude it from the category of new industries. So long as its rise and progress towards maturity has taken place, or is taking place, mainly in the twentieth century, it may be legitimately regarded as new. The artificial silk (rayon), electrical equipment, and motor car industries are cases in point. They made their experimental beginnings in the nineteenth century, but in all other respects they belong to the twentieth century—and more especially to the last ten or fifteen years. Using the word "new" in this sense, the principal new industries are the generation and supply of electricity, the manufacture of electrical and radio equipment, aluminium, rayon (or artificial silk), synthetic dyestuffs, beet sugar, motor vehicles and aircraft, the canning of foodstuffs, the extraction of oil from coal, the transportation of passengers and goods by road motor vehicles and aeroplanes, and the manufacture and exhibition of cinematograph films.

There are, in addition, certain small, new, subsidiary industries, such as the manufacture of cellophane wrapping material which is an offshoot of rayon manufacture, and the manufacture of solid fuel ("coalite") and fertilizers from the by-products of the coal-oil extraction plants.

CHAPTER II

ELECTRICITY AND NEW DEVELOPMENTS IN ENGINEERING

(i) THE GENERATION AND SUPPLY OF ELECTRICITY

THE growth of knowledge relating to electricity is one of the most revolutionary developments of modern times. If we did not know how to generate, store, and transmit electric power for domestic and industrial purposes, many of our newer industries would be non-existent. The economical production of electricity is fundamental to much of our modern scientific and industrial progress and underlies a great deal of the recent rise of real incomes discussed above.

I

Although the commercial use of electricity may be said to date from the introduction of electric telegraphy during the earlier half of the nineteenth century, "the inauguration of the public electricity supply company did not take place until the early eighties, after a considerable amount of experimental work had produced practicable dynamo-electric machinery and the incandescent lamp.[1] The invention of the telephone in 1876 led to the installation of telephone exchanges at about the same time." Application to traction advanced during the period 1890–1900, and by the end of the century the use of electricity for lighting purposes had become established; but

[1] In 1881 the President of the Institute of Mechanical Engineers would only hazard an opinion that "it is possible, and even probable, that one of the great uses to which Electric Force will be applied eventually, will be the simple conveyance of power by means of large wires." (Quoted by Clapham, *Economic History of Modern Britain* (1932), II, 108.) Another writer says that at "the end of the 'eighties the industry was still (if we exclude the ... Ferranti station at Deptford) represented by a number of small corrugated iron huts clustered around the Metropolitan area and dotted sparsely about the Provinces, fitted with clanking machinery which supplied a few hundred lamps within a radius of not much more than half-a-mile of the 'station'." (*Financial News Electricity Supplement*, 25th March, 1935, p. 9).

the bulk distribution of electricity over wide areas by power companies for power and lighting did not begin to be of importance in Great Britain until the first decade of the present century.[1] The invention of the carbon filament lamp by Swan in England in 1880, and by Edison in America[2] soon afterwards, made possible the use of electricity for lighting; but electric motors for power purposes had not passed from the experimental to the commercial and industrial stage at that date. Thus it is that the earlier Acts of Parliament dealing with electricity supply are described as electric *lighting* Acts. The first of these, passed in 1882, and various subsequent Acts conferred upon private enterprise powers to produce and supply electricity for lighting purposes. But these powers were not unconditional. Parliament hesitated to confer monopolies upon the electric lighting companies because of the danger of exploitation of the consumers, and expressly restricted the association or combination of small undertakings. Also Parliament conferred upon Local Authorities recurrent rights to purchase the company undertakings after a term of years. Thus, immediately, there entered upon the scene the wastes of small-scale operation (which in a public utility industry of this nature can be very great), followed later by much uncertainty regarding future ownership of the undertakings.

At the beginning of the twentieth century, 518 Board of Trade provisional orders authorizing electricity supplies were in force. Of these, 354 were grants to local authorities (mainly in the larger towns and industrial districts) and 164 to companies. Round about the year 1900 the promotion of electric power companies began, under Acts of Parliament embodying the appropriate provisions of the Electric Lighting (Clauses) Act, 1899. "These companies were given powers of supply over wider areas, and could supply energy in bulk to authorized

[1] Committee on Industry and Trade; *Survey of Metal Industries* (1928), 279–80.

[2] For a recent study of the origin, technique and unemployment problem of the United States electric lamp industry, see Bulletin of the U.S. Bureau of Labor Statistics No. 593 (1933), W. Bowden, *Technological Changes and Employment in the Electric-lamp Industry.*

distributors or direct to consumers. Unlike Provisional Order companies, they were not liable to purchase by local authorities; but they could not supply energy in the area of an authorized distributor without the distributor's consent, although provision was made that such consent should not be unreasonably withheld. While their scale of operation was much more consistent with electrical and industrial development, the economic advantages of large-scale supply were definitely limited by the retention of local monopolies in most of the large towns, so that in only a few cases were really comprehensive systems of supply achieved."[1] In a word, Parliament failed to realize the economic necessity of linking monopoly with large-scale operation.

The intense industrialization of Great Britain was based almost exclusively upon the abundance of coal and steam power. The era of electricity was a later phase, and although a great deal of the research work underlying the rise of the electrical industry was done by British scientists, British industries, in their utilization of electric power, lagged behind certain other countries where the intensification of industrial development came later and was, therefore, less closely wedded to steam power, or where, before hydro-electricity came upon the scene, the fuel and power shortage was always so acute as to be a continuous drag upon industrial progress. Another reason for Britain's backwardness in this matter was the scarcity of convenient natural sources of water power for the generation of cheap hydro-electricity.[2] It is, however, easy to over-estimate the importance of this factor.

The presence of water power aids electrical development,

---

[1] Labour Party pamphlet, *The Reorganization of the Electricity Supply Industry* (1932), 4. By the end of the War there were about thirty power companies in operation.

[2] Professor Clapham says that "electricity and dynamos and motors were expensive. British towns had not the 'arrowy Rhone' flowing through them like Geneva. British factories had their steam engines. . . . Trade conditions in the early 'eighties were seldom such as to encourage capital expenditure on novelties. Coal was cheap. . . . The argument for delay was probably sound in more than nine cases out of ten—if a short view was taken." *Economic History of Modern Britain* (1932), II, 109.

but is not essential to it. This is fortunate for Great Britain, for here suitable sources of water power are by no means abundant, unless one is prepared to envisage a number of highly expensive attempts to "harness the tides." But even in the United States, where water power resources are plentiful the output of electricity from fuel-power electric plants exceeds that from water-power electric plants; and in Germany, although the development of the use of water-power has been pressed forward, electricity is still generated mainly by fuel. When all cost items are brought into account hydro-electricity is not invariably the cheapest form of electric power. It is seen to greatest advantage when a steady continuous, night-and-day output is required, provided that the head of water is not liable to fall below a certain minimum; but "if the load is intermittent and variable, the capital cost of the undertaking and the cost per kilowatt-hour generated will be higher." As a general rule the initial capital cost of a hydro-electric generating plant (including dams, reservoirs, sluices, etc.) is higher than that of a fuel-electric plant; but this is counterbalanced by the lower working (or operating) costs of the hydro-electric plant and its slower rate of depreciation. On the other hand, a fuel-electric plant is usually easier and less costly to extend if demand expands. Scarcity of capital and high interest rates will tend to check the construction of hydro-electric plants; but rising fuel prices will have the opposite effect. This point assumes considerable importance where coal supplies are derived mainly from old mines in which unit-costs of production are increasing; but as a set-off against this we have the growing efficiency of the fuel-driven generating plant, which has increased so greatly that a given quantity of electricity can be produced to-day with little more than one-third of the coal that would have been required twenty-five years ago. Water power, unlike coal, is continually renewed by Nature and although in certain places its quantity may fluctuate with the wetness or dryness of the seasons, it is never completely and finally exhausted. Geographical position is also of prime importance, for if electrical energy has to be transmitted long distances from the point of generation, costs are materially increased, and a fuel-electric station erected near to the centre of maximum consumption of electricity may well be more economical than a hydro-electric station many miles away. In certain manufacturing processes, such as the production of aluminium, or of nitrogen from the air, which require large and constant supplies of cheap electricity, it is most economical to erect the factory close to the water power.

Mr. Hugh Quigley asserts that electricity "can supply industry with motive power cheaper and more elastic than any other type of power; it is more efficient with regard to energy actually utilized than steam or gas used for mechanical drive alone and causes a reduction in fuel consumption per unit of manufacture so that coal supplies can be made to last much longer; it is capable of more diversified use than any other form of power, and can be automatically controlled.[1]

Where power costs are a relatively high proportion of total costs, the use of electricity may reduce the latter as much as 5 or 10 per cent; for apart from the cost of electricity per unit, electrical power is highly efficient because it replaces long distance belt and pulley transmission by direct individual drive.

The costs of generating electricity comprise four main items: (a) fuel consumption; (b) interest upon the capital cost of the generating plant and transmission mains; (c) the cost of labour and material for running the plant, repairs, and general maintenance; (d) plant depreciation and obsolescence. "It has been found that the cost per kilowatt of machinery installed decreases fairly rapidly with the size of the generating units, as well as the coal consumption per kilowatt-hour generated, so that the capital cost of a generating station with two machines of 25,000 kilowatts each, is less than that of a station with five machines of 10,000 kilowatts each, or ten machines of 5000 kilowatts each."[2] The addition of one small

---

[1] *Electrical Power and National Progress* (1925), 20–1. Cf. also I. Thomas, *Coal in the New Era* (1934), p. 34, quoting the Coal Conservation Committee, 1918; and *Manchester Guardian Commercial*, 17th May, 1935, Article by Professor Miles Walker.

[2] Quigley, *Electrical Power and National Progress* (1925), p. 56.

machine to another is evidently not the ideal method of expansion.

The electricity supply industry is characterized by the relatively large amount of its fixed capital in the form of specialized equipment; and in this respect it resembles the railways and certain other public utilities, such as gas and water supply. It follows, therefore, that its unit-costs are likely to be lowest if and when the whole of the plant and equipment comprising the various undertakings can be fully employed.

On the generating side, maximum economy is achieved when the production of electricity is concentrated in a relatively few highly efficient, interconnected super-stations each having a steady, high load. For any given generating plant the lower the load factor, the higher the unit costs of the output will be, since many of the cost items, both direct and indirect, do not fall when the load diminishes. This ideal of a steady, high load can never be completely realized. There are bound to be times during each twenty-four hours when the load falls to a low level; e.g. in the "small hours" when both industrial and domestic demands are at a minimum. Also there will be seasonal fluctuations chiefly due to (a) changes in the hours of daylight and in the temperature; and (b) changes in business activity. The more these various daily and seasonal variations "dovetail" into one another, so that a rise in one type of demand compensates for a fall in another, the more economical will be the generation of electric current. As a general rule, the greater the variety of consumers and diversity of uses, the greater the chances of compensating demands. For example, those industrial users who work night shifts help to keep up the load in the "small hours"; while the use of electricity for domestic cooking, heating, vacuum cleaning, and ironing, will tend to even out the load at other times during the day.

During the past twenty-five years the quantity of electricity generated in Great Britain has increased approximately sevenfold. In the year 1907 the number of units (kilowatt-hours) generated by public supply undertakings, railways, tramways, and all non-statutory undertakings (including privately-owned plants, e.g. in collieries and engineering works) was probably less than 2500 millions, or some sixty units per head of the population. By 1925 the estimated aggregate output had risen to approximately 8000 millions of units, or 200 units per head of the population. Although this rate of increase is remarkable, the *per capita* consumption was only two-thirds of the German consumption in the same year, and much below that of the U.S.A., where the total output of public utility plants alone averaged approximately 500 units per inhabitant in 1924; 550 units in 1925, and 615 in 1926. The latest output statistics for various countries indicate further expansion and a great improvement in Great Britain's relative position.[1]

The total amount of electricity generated by all "authorized undertakers" and railway and tramway authorities in Great Britain has increased steadily from 4884 million units in the year 1921-2 to 17,569 million units in the year ended 31st December, 1935.[2] From 1929 to 1935 world consumption of electricity increased by 20 per cent, while British consumption increased by 70 per cent. Production of electricity per head of population in Great Britain is now in the neighbourhood of 440 units, and new consumers are being added at a rate of between 700,000 and 800,000 per annum.

Sales of electricity by authorized undertakers during 1933-4 reached a new high level at over 11,467 millions of units, an increase of 11 per cent over the previous year. In the year 1934-5 the total sales of authorized undertakers exceeded 13,000 million units, and the estimated sales for 1935-6 are put as high as 14,850 million units. Owing to this continued growth in the demand and the progressive utilization of reserve capacity, the aggregate capacity of the generating plant for new stations and extensions of existing stations sanctioned by the Electricity Commissioners during the year ending in March,

---

[1] *Statistical Year Book of the League of Nations*. The statistics for different countries are not *strictly* comparable because some include private generation while others do not. The necessity of estimating certain of the population statistics is another possible source of error.

[2] These figures include the outputs of a few non-statutory undertakings, but generation by private plants is excluded.

1935, amounted to 594,449 kw. compared with 114,096 kw. in the preceding year.

Apart from private plants, railways and tramways, all the principal producers and retailers of electricity in this country are either municipalities, joint electricity authorities, or joint stock companies.

Authorized Electricity Undertakers

Number of Authorized Undertakers (excluding the Central Electricity Board) holding powers to supply electricity on 01st March, 1936—

	England and Wales	Scotland	Total
1. Local Authorities . . .	336	35	371
2. Companies or Persons . .	214	33	247
3. Joint Boards (representative of Local Authorities) . .	4	1	5
4. Joint Electricity Authorities .	3	–	3
Totals . . .	557	69	626

Electricity is not sold competitively by these bodies, but they all have to face, more or less, the competition of substitutes, such as coal, gas, and oil. Such competition, however, is hampered by the technical fact that a change from one source of power to another can seldom be made unless the user is ready to incur considerable capital expenditure. The electricity supply undertakings, therefore, have substantially a monopolistic position. The buyers of electricity are safeguarded, within rather wide limits, not only by the potential competition of other sources of power, light, and heat, but by certain legal maximum prices or limits upon dividends.

"In the case of local authority or Company undertakings, maximum charges for electricity (which are subject under certain conditions to revision at triennial periods) are fixed for each undertaking in the order which authorizes it. For 'power companies' (which are in the nature of wholesalers and have a special position vis-à-vis their several local authorities) a sliding scale comes into operation when dividends amount to 8 per cent (or sometimes 10 per cent); in other cases profits are subject to sliding-scale conditions which in certain circumstances may be reviewed by the appropriate authority; moreover, sliding scales may be imposed in certain circumstances under the Electricity (Supply) Acts, 1922 and 1926."[1]

The actual ruling prices are at present much lower than the legal maximum prices largely because the steady development of output and earnings has been accompanied by reductions of charges. It may, however, be argued that more generous reductions of prices would have brought still greater benefits to consumers without robbing the suppliers; and that prices could have been lower still had the electricity undertakings not been content to continue operations within areas too small to permit highly economical results to be obtained. The administrative area of a local authority, for instance, is not necessarily a suitable electricity supply area; and the existence of over 600 separate areas and undertakings in such a small country as Great Britain is an obvious absurdity, which the formation of *financial* combinations between some of the companies has done little or nothing to remove.[2]

Early in the present century the difficulties of connecting up the numerous and various electricity supply undertakings in this country began to attract more and more attention as the advantages of doing so came to be more clearly recognized. During the war period, 1914–18, heavy calls were made upon the producers of electricity, and although their response was far from negligible (the output of authorized undertakings doubled in four years), it was discovered that *the organization of electricity generation and distribution was in many respects antiquated and inadequate.* This was pointed out by no less than three important war-time investigating committees set up by the Government; *viz.* the Committee on Electrical

---

[1] Report of Liberal Industrial Inquiry, *Britain's Industrial Future* (1928), 73.

[2] The blame must be shared partly by Parliament and partly by the Municipalities. Cf. M. E. Dimock, *British Public Utilities and National Development* (1933), 202 ff., and W. A. Robson, *Development of Local Government* (1931), 117.

Trades, a sub-committee of the Coal Conservation Committee, and the Electric Power Supply Committee, usually called the Williamson Committee.

In 1917 the Committee on Electrical Trades emphasized the unsatisfactory nature of the legislation which then governed the British electricity supply industry, asserting that it had encouraged development upon a local, rather than a national basis. A large number of relatively small, independent supply authorities and generating stations, with a great variety of frequencies and systems of supply, had come into existence, each pursuing its own particular development policy within its limited area of supply.[1] In the following year the Electric Power Supply Committee showed (*inter alia*) that in London alone there were no fewer than seventy generating stations, fifty different systems of supply, twenty-four different voltages and ten different frequencies. It is the old story of private promotion of numerous parochial undertakings during the early experimental, pioneering stages when nobody had vision enough to think in terms of planned development on a national scale. Nor was the position improved by industrial users who installed their own generating plant, "thus extending the wasteful system of generation on a small scale in a multiplicity of small stations." Small-scale production and high operating costs, excessive expenditure of capital, wasteful consumption of fuel, and unnecessarily high charges met the investigators upon every side and pointed them towards the remedy—"a well-planned scheme of reconstruction involving the concentration of generation in a relatively small number of large power stations." The Williamson Committee recommended a national scheme of electrification under a central authority empowered to create regional electricity authorities.[2]

The first step towards this ultimate objective was taken in 1919 when Parliament passed the Electricity (Supply) Act, which provided for the appointment by the Minister of Transport of a body of Electricity Commissioners, not exceeding five

---

[1] *Committee on the Position of the Electrical Trades after the War.* (*Cmd.* 9072, 1918.) Cf. *Coal Conservation Committee's Report*, 1917.

[2] *Cmd.* 9062, 1918.

in number, to regulate, supervise and promote the supply of electricity throughout Great Britain; to exercise certain powers under the Electric Lighting Acts; and to divide the country into large districts or regions and prepare schemes to improve electricity supply in each of them. This first attempt to tackle the problem systematically and on a national scale was undoubtedly an advance in the right direction; but it may truly be said that so many of the provisions of the original Bill fell victims to the onslaught of vested interests that, in the end, insufficient powers of compulsion were given to the Electricity Commissioners. Although provision was made for the creation of electricity districts to be administered by advisory boards or joint electricity authorities under the control of the Electricity Commission, neither the Commission nor the district boards received any real powers to compel fundamental changes. The Commissioners could plan the generation and distribution of electricity in the districts, but their plan could be carried into effect only with the consent of the separate undertakings in the area, and the Commissioners had no power to control or coerce any undertaking which refused to enter the scheme. New projects for electrical development came under the eye of the Commissioners, and new power stations, extensions, and additions to generating plant could not be erected without their consent; but they were powerless to abolish the uneconomical system of small monopolies, or to compel high-cost producers of electricity to take bulk supplies from more efficient generating stations. The Commissioners had powers to hold inquiries for the purpose of extending existing areas of supply or granting new areas by means of Provisional or Special Orders, but no positive powers to co-ordinate the whole industry. The formation of joint electricity authorities had to wait upon voluntary amalgamations, and from 1919 to 1925 only one such authority was formed.[1] In short, the Act of 1919 "tended to perpetuate the *status quo*

[1] H. G., *The Socialization of the Electrical Supply Industry* (1934), 12. The Electricity Commissioners have "judicial" powers to decide disputes regarding the prices to be paid for generating stations and main transmission lines; the rights and obligations of owners of selected

and made the electricity district a congeries of existing under-takings who might or who might not fall in with the proposals of the Commissioners. . . ."[1] Seven years after the Act came into force, the Minister of Transport told the House of Commons that over practically two-thirds of the country "there are small undertakings with territorial rights strong enough to prevent large enterprises being established in their areas, but incapable themselves of generating electricity on a sufficiently large scale and at a price low enough to encourage large-scale consumption. In our rural areas only about one-tenth are afforded even the semblance of a supply."[2]

The meagre results of the appeal to voluntary co-operation soon proved that compulsory powers would be essential to the co-ordination of generation on a comprehensive scale. Consequently, yet another committee (the Weir Committee) was appointed; and its recommendations, published in 1925, were (a) that generation should be concentrated in fifty-eight selected power stations (including fifteen new stations); (b) that 432 stations should be closed; (c) that the selected stations and existing regional transmission systems should be inter-connected by a high-tension main transmission system; and (d) that a central electricity board should be created to carry out this work. On the strength of this report, supported by a survey prepared by the electricity Commissioners, the Electricity (Supply) Act, 1926, was passed. This Act created the Central Electricity Board and may be said to have socialized the British wholesale trade in electricity. In general terms the main functions of the Board are to construct main transmission lines (commonly known as "the grid"), to concentrate the generation of electricity at standard frequency in the most efficient stations, to supply electricity in bulk for distribution, and by these means to increase the availability of electricity throughout the country

stations; the cost of altering frequencies; the relative costs where owners of stations do not wish to take an exclusive supply from the Central Electricity Board; and closing of generating stations.

[1] Quigley, op. cit., 148.
[2] Quoted by M. E. Dimock, op. cit., 199.

and reduce the cost of production. The Board is neither a joint stock company nor a government department: it is a body of eight experts appointed by the Minister of Transport after consultation with certain bodies representing various "interests," namely local government, electricity, commerce, manufacturing, transport, agriculture, and labour. Each member of the Board is appointed for a period of five or ten years, as the Minister may decide. "The way in which this Board has been placed outside politics," says Mr. Herbert Morrison, "but is nevertheless a public institution with a real sense of public accountability, constituted a lesson . . . from which much was to be learned."[1] The Board raises all its capital by borrowing at fixed rates of interest, and the stockholders have no control whatever over the conduct of the undertaking. It is endowed with monopoly powers and placed in a key position between the generating stations on the one hand and the *authorized* distributors (retailers) and consumers on the other. The Board, which owns the main transmission system, or "grid," buys the whole output of the selected stations, and sells it to the distributors.

"Broadly, the Board are electricity 'middlemen,' whose task is to buy power from the stations generating most efficiently (and, therefore, cheaply) and to resell it to companies and other distributors by way of main transmission lines erected throughout the country. The application of their powers in the latter respect, however, has no element of compulsion beyond that of efficiency"[2]; the general principle being that the price charged by the Board to authorized distributors may be lower, but shall not be higher than the cost which the latter would have incurred, in generating a like quantity of electricity, if the Act had not been passed.

The first step towards the construction of the grid was the delimitation of supply regions and the preparation of a scheme for each. Great Britain has been divided into ten such regions or areas.

[1] *Socialization and Transport* (1933), 153.
[2] *The Economist*, 30th September, 1933; 17th February, 1934.

The procedure is outlined in the Liberal Industrial Report—

The area to be brought within each scheme has to be determined after very careful inquiry into the geographical and industrial sources of energy and after consideration of the best system of linking up the different parts of the area, the possibility of future interconnexion with other areas, and the efficiency and situation of existing generating stations. The scheme in draft form has then to be sent to the Central Electricity Board, who finally decide the form in which it shall be put into force. It has then to be published and any or all of the numerous undertakings or persons affected may within one month claim to be heard. A right of appeal against the decision of the Central Electricity Board is given in certain cases. . . .[1]

The ultimate objective is elimination of all uneconomical and inconvenient generating plants and the concentration of generation in a limited number of carefully chosen stations. This concentration of production in a small number of large, up-to-date and geographically convenient stations has already enhanced efficiency and reduced the cost of current. The number of selected stations finally left in operation will probably not exceed 135, all interconnected by the "grid," which consists of 4000 miles of high-voltage transmission lines, plus about 270 transforming and switching stations at which it can be tapped by distributors. The "initial" grid, virtually completed in 1933, cost £27 millions; and it is estimated that this expenditure will be, in a sense, recovered within ten years through the economies which a national system will make possible.[2]

The revenues of the Board are derived from the sale of electricity in bulk and from a levy by the Electricity Commissioners under Section 9 of the Electricity (Supply) Act, 1926, on the whole of the electricity supply industry within Great Britain of annual sums equal to the interest and sinking fund charges in respect of money borrowed for the standardization of frequency.[3]

---

[1] *Britain's Industrial Future*, p. 309.

[2] Cf. *The Economist*, 9th December, 1933, and 30th March, 1935.

[3] The Board is charged with the duty of raising the necessary funds and disbursing them to authorized undertakers and owners of "selected stations" who have incurred "standardization" expenditure, but it is the duty of the Electricity Commissioners to recover the annual service

The following schemes have been adopted by the Board under section 4 of the Act—

(1) Central Scotland Electricity Scheme, 1927;
(2) South East England Electricity Scheme, 1927;
(3) Central England Electricity Scheme, 1928;
(4) North West England and North Wales Electricity Scheme, 1928;
(5) Mid-East England Electricity Scheme, 1929;
(6) North East England Electricity Scheme, 1929;
(7) South West England and South Wales Electricity Scheme, 1930;
(8) East England Electricity Scheme, 1930;
(9) South Scotland Electricity Scheme, 1931.

These schemes cover the whole of Great Britain except North Scotland.

Trading on a tariff commenced in Central Scotland and Mid-East England on the 1st January, 1933, and within four years the end of the first stage of electrical development under the C.E.B. was in sight, since the extensions of selected stations decided upon during 1934, and brought into service in 1935–6, have a total capacity approximately commensurate with the annual growth of demand throughout the country.[1]

In fixing a tariff the Board are required under Section 11 of the 1926 Act so to calculate it that, over a period of years to be approved by the Electricity Commissioners, the receipts on income account shall be sufficient to cover the expenditure on income account, including interest and sinking fund charges, with such margins as the Commissioners may allow. The Commissioners have approved 10 years as the period to be taken for the areas for which the tariff has been fixed, except for Central England, in which case the period is $9\frac{3}{4}$ years.

of the loans by a levy on the supply industry, and to hand the proceeds over to the Board. The levy is based on the number of units generated by the industry, and represents a very small percentage of the cost of generation.

[1] P.E.P., *Report on the Supply of Electricity in Great Britain* (1936), p. 31.

To ensure conservative estimates and an economic basis for the tariff, surveys have been made by the Board of the probable increase in demand for electricity in those areas over the tariff period. A tariff of the kind prescribed, applied to a growing industry means that, in the earlier years of a budget period, the outgoings will be more than the income and that, in the later years, there will be surpluses sufficient to recoup the earlier deficiencies and leave a margin, the deficiencies being met meanwhile out of working capital.[1] There still remains a very wide field for growth, and in order to assist more rapid development the Board's tariff provides for progressive reductions in the scale of charges to authorized undertakers as their demands increase.

It is generally admitted that within the sphere determined for them by Parliament, the Electricity Commissioners and the Central Electricity Board have pressed forward British electricity supply development at a speed exceeding all expectations and in marked contrast to previous experience in this country.

In general, technical progress has undoubtedly been immensely more rapid than would ever have been possible under independent private enterprise. British manufacturers have probably now got experience in the manufacture of high-voltage apparatus which is in advance of that of any other country in the world. As regards cost . . . very large economies have been effected merely by the large-scale operations of the Board. Had the grid lines, or their equivalent, been constructed piecemeal by private enterprise, the total cost to the country would inevitably have been very much greater.[2]

During 1935 the Board exceeded all expectations by realizing a trading surplus of over £1,000,000. This sum was sufficient to meet three-quarters of the interest on the £33,000,000

[1] The Central Electricity Board has power to pay interest out of capital for five years on loans raised for the construction of the grid.

[2] H. G., *The Socialization of the Electrical Supply Industry* (1934), 32–3. It was officially estimated that in 1933 between 100,000 and 120,000 workers in the engineering, cable-making, building and contracting, iron and steel, coal mining, cement and pottery industries were directly or indirectly employed upon the construction of the grid and the standardization of frequency. This estimate does not include transport employees or industries subsidiary to those mentioned.

of capital borrowed at an average rate of $4\frac{1}{3}$ per cent to construct the grid. Moreover, the experts estimate that up to the end of 1935 the grid scheme had rendered unnecessary the expenditure of approximately £11,500,000 on new generating plant, while concentration of production in the most efficient generating stations had saved some £920,000 in operating costs during 1935.[1]

But even these remarkable achievements do not mark the limits of concentrated production, for the Board does not yet own the selected stations nor has it any control over generating plants belonging to railways, tramways, or private industrial concerns, such as collieries, which, taken as a whole, probably produce between one-quarter and one-third of all the electricity generated in this country.

The Central Electricity Board's position and powers are by no means entirely satisfactory in certain other respects. For example, the Board cannot force an authorized supply company to cease generating its own current and take its requirements from the grid unless the grid price, *including* capital charges, is less than the company's running costs, *excluding* capital charges. Moreover, the Act of 1926 contains no guarantee that the general public will receive the benefits of any economies effected by the Board, and the latter has no power to force distributing undertakings to adopt a progressive policy and to make supplies available throughout their areas at reasonable prices. This is a serious drawback for both the consumers and the Board, for if any of the retailers do not sufficiently reduce prices—preferring instead high profits on a relatively small output—the Board's expansion and economical working is hindered. Other immediate improvements would be (*a*) the expansion of direct supplies from the Board to railway companies; (*b*) the arrangement of working agreements between the Board and privately owned generating stations not engaged in public supply, so that the grid may take their surplus supplies at cheap rates, while they may

---

[1] *Eighth Annual Report of the Central Electricity Board* (1936).

obtain supplementary supplies from the grid at peak periods.[1]

II

Electricity supply in Great Britain is, as we have seen, mainly based upon coal, which is used to raise steam to drive the turbines or reciprocating engines which turn the dynamos or generators. The coal is brought to the generating stations usually by rail, canal, or river. For the unloading of the coal and the stoking of furnaces mechanical aids such as grabs, travelling belts, etc., are generally used. By such methods much dirty and exhausting labour has been eliminated. According to the Census of Production, 1930, the total number of persons employed by the 477 local authorities and companies making returns was 75,330. Assuming that the remaining 28 per cent of authorized undertakings were below the average size, it seems probable that the number of people employed in the British electricity supply industry at the present time is about 90,000, nearly all of whom are males.

The type of labour employed ranges from highly skilled electrical engineers in charge of a plant, and skilled engine drivers, jointers and other craftsmen, down to semi-skilled cleaners and greasers, and unskilled labourers. There are between fifty and sixty different grades in most districts. Working conditions are, on the whole, healthy and not unpleasant, except that there is a good deal of noise in some sections. Some of the work is dangerous, owing to the high voltage carried by the plant; but the industry is subject to special Home Office safety regulations, and accidents are rare.

"Whitley" machinery, first introduced in May, 1919,[2] is well-developed in the electricity supply industry, in which there are two Joint Industrial Councils. One consists of employers' representatives and representatives of all workers in the industry below the grade of charge engineer; the other, called the National Joint Board of Employers and Members of Staff,

[1] These powers have been conferred upon the C.E.B. by the Electricity (Supply) Act, 1935.
[2] Committee on Industry and Trade, *Survey of Industrial Relations* (1926), 272.

deals with matters affecting charge engineers and employees of higher grade. The workpeople are organized in the following trade unions : Electrical Trades Union, Amalgamated Engineering Union, National Union of General and Municipal Workers, Transport and General Workers' Union. The charge engineers and higher grades are organized in the Electrical Power Engineers' Association and the Associated Municipal Electrical Engineers.

There are thirteen District Joint Industrial Councils which negotiate about wages, hours, and other conditions of employment in their respective areas. District Council No. 1, for example, has jurisdiction in the North-East Coast area. The Council consists of fourteen employers' representatives (eight appointed by electricity supply companies and six by municipal undertakings) and fourteen employees' representatives, chosen by the trade unions in the various branches of the industry. Decisions of District Joint Industrial Councils are subject to ratification by the National J.I.C., to which disputes may be referred by District Councils. The majority of the latter appear to have been tolerably successful in settling disputes and creating uniform conditions of employment throughout the country. Disputes not settled by the National J.I.C. have been, on occasion, referred to the Industrial Court ; but there is no formal arrangement for dealing with such difficulties.

The National Joint Board of Employers and Members of Staff has drawn up a schedule of salaries and has formulated conditions of service for engineers on the staffs of electricity undertakings in Great Britain. There are twelve District Joint Boards. All disputes upon which no agreement can be reached by the District and National Boards are referred to the Industrial Court for arbitration.

Throughout the thirteen districts close upon 1000 different rates of wages are in force, and here it is impossible to do much more than indicate the extremes.[1] The weekly rates of wages

[1] A list of the rates of wages in force in Scotland (District No. 13) will be found in Appendix A. For a selection of London rates of wages see *New Survey of London Life and Labour*, Vol. VIII.

for switchboard and sub-station attendants range from approximately 80s. to 95s. in London, and 76s. to 85s. 6d. in the provinces, down to 64s. to 74s. (London) and 46s. 6d. to 58s. 3d. (provinces). Jointers receive approximately 76s. a week in London, and from 68s. 6d. to 72s. 6d. in the provinces. At the other extreme, coal handlers and tippers, labourers, and jointers' mates receive from 64s. 9d. to 69s. 6d. a week in London, and from 48s. 6d. to 51s. 9d. in the provinces. The Ministry of Labour unweighted average of the weekly rates of wages of unskilled labourers in the electricity supply industry in over fifty towns in December, 1934, was 53s. 10d.[1] The wages of other grades fall between these extremes roughly according to the degree of skill and intelligence required for the work.

Forty-seven hours is the normal working week for day men and forty-eight hours for shift workers. When emergencies occur a good deal of overtime may be necessary. Men *temporarily* employed wholly on night work receive ordinary rates of wages plus one-third; and certain classes of unskilled workers permanently engaged on night work receive 3d. per hour above the day rates. Overtime rates are "time-and-a half" up to midnight, and "double-time" after midnight and for work on Sundays, Good Fridays, and Christmas Day. After twelve months' continuous service, day workers are entitled to seven days' holiday and shift workers to fourteen days' holiday, with full pay.

III

We come now to the distribution of the current to consumers. In this sphere there is much room for improvement, and the task should be tackled as energetically as the construction of the grid. There appear to be three main immediate objectives: (*a*) the standardization of voltages and frequencies; (*b*) the standardization of prices; (*c*) reduction of prices.

The Electricity Commissioners' official statistics show that 284 undertakings are distributing alternating current only;

[1] *Labour Gazette*, March, 1935, 88.

279 are distributing both alternating and direct current; 92 are distributing direct current only; and that up and down the country there were not less than 45 different supply voltages between 100 and 480 volts. The Electricity Commissioners have constantly advocated standardization to 230 volts a.c., 50 cycles per sec., and there has been a considerable measure of response from authorized undertakings. It is estimated that over 50 per cent of the distributing authorities are now supplying standard current, and conversion work is still proceeding in various parts of the country.

Price standardization, however, is by no means so far advanced. The systems of charging and the prices per unit vary enormously from one electricity supply authority to another. Some domestic consumers are paying only 2d. per unit, while others are paying anything from 9½d. to 1s. Among industrial charges we find some as high as 6d. or 7d. per unit, and others less than 1d. Even if complete uniformity is not possible—a proposition which still remains to be proved —such wide disparities are neither justifiable nor tolerable.

In *The Reorganization of the Electricity Supply Industry* it is stated that—

The average revenues received by authorized undertakings from the sale of electricity to consumers (excluding inter-sales in bulk) in 1929–30 was 1·38d. per unit, of which about half (0·68d.) represented distribution costs, including capital charges. It will be appreciated that this average includes energy sold in bulk at very low prices for industrial and traction purposes; and actually it is a weighted average of the average revenue received from the following classes of consumers: lighting and domestic purposes 2·86d., public lighting 1·61d., traction 0·81d., and power for industrial and other purposes 0·82d. There are also big variations in the prices charged to consumers in different areas. Of 634 undertakings making 1929–30 returns for lighting and domestic supplies, 143 charged under an average of 3d. per unit, 219 between 3d. and 5d., 138 between 5d. and 7d., 80 between 7d. and 9d., and 54 charged 9d. or over per unit. Of 586 undertakings making 1929–30 returns for power for industrial and other purposes, 134 charged under an average of 1d. per unit, 217 between 1d. and 2d., 188 between 2d. and 4d., 37 between 4d. and 6d., and ten charged 6d. or over per unit.

The average costs of distribution of the smaller distributors are generally much above the national average of 1.38d. per unit, many of them working out at anything from 1·51d. to 2·5d. per unit. Recent statistics show that 369 authorized undertakings, out of a total of 661, are selling less than 100 units per head of the resident population in their supply areas, while many undertakings which have been in operation over twenty-five years have not yet achieved sales averaging 60 units per head. This is more often due to smallness of areas than to poor management.

The character and policy of the undertakings vary enormously. Some undertakings are enlightened, under good technical and commercial management; some have good technicians; some cannot, or do not, pay for first-class staff; some have tariffs based on the doctrine of high charges, good profits, no development, and an easy life; many lack the resources to carry out adequate development. There is no likelihood of any substantial change in the position so long as multiple ownership continues. . . .

Under the national grid scheme, the authorized distributors will obtain electricity in bulk at a low price common to an entire area, and this should largely cut out such part of the differences in price, and such part of excessive prices, as are due to differences and excesses in present generating costs. But generation, as has been shown, accounts for only half the average price to the consumer; and the distribution costs will not be directly affected. Therefore, unless a drastic change takes place in distribution, the consumer will continue to pay an unnecessarily high price in very many areas. For not only are distribution costs, in striking contrast to generation costs, practically standing still, but there can be no substantial reduction while distribution is parcelled out amongst over 600 independent undertakings of all shapes and sizes, some efficient, many quite inadequate. Neither the existing powers to amalgamate, nor the option of local authorities to purchase company undertakings after a certain period, offers any hope of a more rational system.

The argument becomes still clearer if comparison is made with the letter-carrying business of the Post Office. If the collection and delivery of letters were organized upon the basis of local government areas, instead of nationally, it is clear that a much higher charge would have to be made for the service in sparsely-populated areas, or in very poor areas where letter-writing was not so prevalent as in commercial or relatively prosperous districts. The very fact that the charges were higher in some cases would itself discourage the practice of letter-writing in these areas, while there would be a limitation on any reduction of postal rates in the difficult areas, owing to the fixed overhead and main-tenance charges which must be met and the fact that in such areas the traffic could not in any case be developed beyond a moderate point. As it is, everybody, whether living in a town of great population or in a distant rural parish, pays the same rates for inland postage, and it is sound business that this should be so. While charging the same rates for similar classes of electricity supply throughout Great Britain is not immediately practicable, it is nevertheless an aim towards which the industry ought to work.[1]

The systems of charging are almost as diverse as the charges.[2] There is the method of charging a flat rate of so much per unit consumed, with or without the addition of a meter rent. Or there is the method of making a fixed charge plus so much per unit consumed over a certain minimum allowance; the *fixed* charge being based in some districts upon the area of the premises supplied, or upon their rateable value, or the number of rooms occupied; or again, upon the wattage of the lamps installed. Moreover, it seems to be a fairly general grievance in many parts of the country that prices are reduced to industrial users at the expense of domestic consumers; but in the London area one hears a contrary complaint to the effect that the suppliers victimize their industrial consumers in order to sell current cheaply for domestic purposes.

If . . . the grid is to be accounted a national success the domestic load must be stimulated, and with the primary network complete no effort must be spared to establish a complete low-tension network with the aim of making this an electrified country in the fullest sense of the word. Everything depends on the atti-tude of the supply authorities, and the sooner they rid themselves of countless petty restrictions and abandon their take-it-or-leave-it attitude the sooner can they hope to see an expansion in demand.

---

[1] *The Re-organization of the Electricity Supply Industry*, pp. 11, 13–15.
[2] There are "still far too many different kinds of charges and tariffs in force in the various areas of supply throughout the country, and an important measure of simplification could be brought about by a reduction in their number and by greater uniformity in methods of charge." *Annual Report of the Electricity Commissioners*, 1934.

In many areas the price at which electricity is sold is anything up to ten times the rate at which it is supplied to the grid, and consequently the entire benefit of large-scale generation is annulled. Rural electrification schemes have been tested and found remarkably successful, and there is not the slightest ground for supposing that if the supply is available and the price is correct the necessary demand will not be realized. But price is the essential link, and attractive terms must be offered to every potential consumer at once instead of holding out vague hopes of lower prices in the future.[1]

Obviously the rapid progress of the work of the Central Electricity Board creates corresponding opportunities and obligations for the distributors; and it has become increasingly evident that if the expansion of electricity supply is not to be unwisely hindered the rationalization of generation will have to be supplemented or balanced by widespread improvements in, and co-ordination of, distribution.

Discussing the proposed merger of six of the London electricity supply companies in November, 1934, *The Economist* wrote—

Distribution is the bottle-neck of electricity supply. The high-voltage grid constructed and operated by the Central Electricity Board makes possible very great economies for users of electricity, but these economies will not be realized until the distributing concerns are thoroughly co-ordinated. The situation is chaotic enough over the whole country, but is probably worse in London than elsewhere. For electricity supply in London started off on the wrong lines. Competition between companies was encouraged in the 'eighties by granting a franchise to a separate company in every parish, and some parishes were even provided with two companies. At the time when the grid scheme was devised London boasted of some fifty supply undertakings, each with its own generating plant, its own supply voltages and systems. . . . The grid scheme attacked the problem of electricity generation. But the distribution of electricity is still in the hands of the old companies. For these reasons the news of the formation of a Central London Electricity Distribution Committee is welcome. Six companies, all of which take their bulk supply from the London Power Company, have agreed to co-ordinate their distribution systems. How far they will be able to go is not yet

[1] *Manchester Guardian Commercial*, 9th September, 1933.

clear. The aim should be standardization of a 230-volt 50-cycle alternating-current system, and an attractive rate policy which will stimulate increased consumption. There should be no great danger in a considerable reduction of rates, since the potential demand by consumers for electricity is ahead of the capacity of the companies to supply under existing conditions. It is hoped that other companies will join in this scheme, for it offers great benefits to suppliers and consumers. . . . The present scheme for London is evidence that at last some companies are taking steps in the right direction.[1]

On the whole, the present rate of extension of industrial electrification, including electrification of railways,[2] seems to be somewhat slower than the expansion of demand for domestic uses,[3] in spite of the fact that in more than one region the former appears to be partially subsidized by the latter. This is not necessarily uneconomical. Ideally the domestic and industrial uses of electricity should develop in such a ratio as to give not only maximum load, but the most even distribution of the load through time, and, in consequence the lowest possible cost per unit, plus a high degree of immunity from trade slumps.

Electricity is being extensively used for industrial purposes,

---

[1] *The Economist*, 24th November, 1934. The companies in question are the Westminster Electric Supply Corporation, Charing Cross Electricity Supply Company, St. James's and Pall Mall Electric Light Company, Brompton and Kensington Electricity Supply Company, Chelsea Electricity Supply Company, and Kensington and Knightsbridge Electric Lighting Company.

[2] There is a strong case for the electrification of suburban lines in various parts of the country where the traffic is dense or congested. In the opinion of Sir Herbert Walker, "the whole argument for electrification, and the whole criterion for its profitability, depends rather upon its ability to improve the service and so to increase the gross receipts. In congested suburban areas there is a strong presumption that this will be possible. The great superiority of electric traction rests in the quicker acceleration of electric trains, and their more speedy operation in and out of terminal stations, and in the ability to operate economically a much more frequent service than would be possible with steam." The economic advantages of electrifying main lines on which such congestion does not exist, are more doubtful. They certainly cannot be taken for granted. On the contrary, every proposal must be thoroughly examined on its merits with full regard for the particular conditions existing on that line.

[3] Cf. *Thirteenth Annual Report of the Electricity Commissioners* (1933); and *The Economist*, 6th April, 1935. A plan to spend £35 millions on railway electrification was announced in June, 1935.

especially in new and expanding industries, e.g. in factories producing chemicals, vehicles, paper and stationery, hosiery and knitted goods, metal goods, etc. In 1921, 49 per cent of British factories used electricity. In 1929 the percentage was 70, and in 1936 it was nearly 84; the majority of the new factories obtaining their power from public supplies.

The provision of cheap electricity in rural areas depends upon the same principle as in urban areas; viz. the numbers of users and the variety of purposes to which it is applied. The use of electric light and power in the cottages and on the farms of this country is as yet in its infancy; but there are signs that good progress has been made quite recently.[1] If electricity can be supplied to farmers at cheap rates (say, between 1d. and 2d. per unit) so that they can use the electric motor for milking and other dairy operations, threshing, chaff and root cutting, pumping, sawing, etc., it will undoubtedly prove to be a valuable aid to cost-reduction.

The capital costs of supplying a rural area are, of course, higher than those of an urban area, owing to the relative sparseness of rural population; but this fact should point us not in the direction of a fatalistic acceptance of high electricity prices in rural areas, but rather towards the creation of larger "mixed supply" areas containing numerous urban and rural consumers. Within such areas, and as far as possible throughout the whole country, the ultimate objective should be uniformity of prices at the lowest economic level.

Probably the fact is that very appreciable economies are to be made as average mixed urban and rural areas are increased in size up to at least 1000 or possibly 2000 square miles—representing capital investment in distribution of several million pounds. Thereafter the economies are likely to be less as the areas increase in size, but because of the other advantages of uniformity and standardization . . . it may be desirable to have areas considerably greater even than 2000 square miles. . . . The distribution system must be laid down first, and then the load built up by the

[1] Cf. *Manchester Guardian Commercial*, 6th January, 1934, Article on "National Power Planning." The number of electric engines, etc., in use on British farms has quadrupled during the last ten years.

adoption of a low tariff. Such a policy—which means losses in the early years of development, followed by small profits on a large turnover in the later years—is the very antithesis of the policy of many companies.[1]

The Central Electricity Board, on the other hand, has already adopted such a policy, with the consent of the Electricity Commissioners.[2]

(ii) ELECTRICAL AND RADIO EQUIPMENT

I

The increase in the output of electricity has affected, and been affected by, the electrical equipment side of the industry. Obviously there must be the closest reciprocal relationship between the development of electricity supply and the manufacture and installation of electrical equipment. Neither can advance far unless the other also goes forward. If the equipment manufacturers are unprogressive they will be a drag on the extension of the use of electricity; while, on the other hand, lack of initiative and enterprise among the suppliers of electricity will hinder the sale and installation of electrical equipment. Reforms long-delayed, such as the standardization of numerous and widely differing voltages, prevent electrical equipment manufacturers from achieving that high degree of standardization of their products which is essential to economical production.

The phrase—"manufacture of electrical equipment" covers the production of a great variety of goods, heavy and light, simple and complex, ranging from enormous generators, motors and transformers, through submarine cables, switchboards, telegraphic and telephonic apparatus, scientific instruments, domestic appliances for heating, cooking and cleaning, lamps of all sizes, accumulators and batteries,[3] down to wireless

---

[1] H. G., *Socialization of the Electrical Supply Industry* (1934), 49–50; cf. also *Annual Report of the Electricity Commissioners*, 1931, and Chap. VII *post*.

[2] *The Economist*, 16th June, 1934, 1321.

[3] "The increasing demand for dry batteries for wireless, for torch lights and other purposes resulted yesterday in the opening of the eighth London factory of the Ever Ready Co. (Great Britain) Ltd., at

valves and the small "gadgets" familiar to amateur wireless experimenters. There is, of course, a high degree of specialization among the various manufacturers, who are grouped in sections according to the type of product in which they specialize. Thus there are the manufacturers of cable, of telephone equipment, of electric lamps, storage batteries, magnetos, radio sets, and so forth.

The original inventions underlying most of this machinery and apparatus date from the last century, but many remarkable improvements and supplementary inventions have been made within the past twenty years. For example, the telephone dates, as we have already noticed, from 1876; but the automatic telephone "exchange" is an invention of yesteryear. This labour-saving device has enabled the costs and charges for telephone service to be so greatly reduced that a very marked expansion of demand from potential telephone users, hitherto below the margin, is now imminent. One's telephone "pays for its keep" only if a great many other people have the telephone installed also; and although propaganda may do something, not much progress is likely, especially among private residents, in the absence of substantial reductions of charges.

The storage battery section of the British electrical industry was started about fifty years ago, but remained relatively unimportant until the advent of the submarine about the year 1902.[1] Subsequently the section expanded rapidly as the storage battery came to be extensively used in motor cars, railway trains, aeroplanes, and wireless sets, until to-day it ranks with the highly-developed battery manufacturing industries of Germany and the United States. The home market is protected and imports of foreign batteries are small, while, on the other hand, British exports of batteries to the Empire and other overseas markets show an upward tendency, in

Walthamstow. The firm's factories now employ 12,000 people. The ground floor of the new factory is occupied by a mill that crushes 4½ tons of raw manganese dioxide daily." *News Chronicle,* 27th October, 1933.

[1] *Manchester Guardian Commercial Annual Review,* 28th January, 1933, 74.

spite of the keen competition of efficient producers in other countries.

The manufacture of ignition magnetos, used chiefly for motor vehicles and aircraft; and of permanent magnets, used in the manufacture of magnetos, telephone receivers, wireless loud speakers, electricity meters and other electrical instruments, was practically non-existent in Great Britain before 1914. Supplies, which were imported mainly from Germany, were, of course, seriously curtailed at the outbreak of war, and for all practical purposes it is from that point that the manufacture of British magnetos and permanent magnets began to develop. Stimulated by the conditions of war-time demand and the growing manufacture of motor vehicles, and protected by the "McKenna" and safeguarding duties, the manufacture of British magnetos and permanent magnets increased until by 1926 it was possible for British manufacturers to supply the whole of the domestic demand.[1]

II

The development of "radio," or "wireless," and the radio section of the electrical equipment industry is a striking example of a series of inventions capable of awakening and supplying various needs, such as the need for swift communication over long distances and the desire for entertainment and enlightenment at low cost. The perfection of wireless telegraphy has given us the first of these boons; and the development of broadcasting together with the progressive improvement and cheapening of the radio set has provided the second.

As long ago as 1864 James Clerk Maxwell arrived at the conclusion that electromagnetic wave propagation through the ether was a possibility. This theory, based upon purely mathematical investigations, was verified practically during the eighteen-eighties by Hughes (who made a microphone and became convinced of the existence of "aerial electric waves")

[1] *Report on Key Industries, Cmd.* 2631, 1926.

and Heinrich Hertz, who conducted the final series of masterly and quite conclusive experiments (1887-9). Sir Oliver Lodge amplified Hertz's experiments and did valuable pioneer work on coherer methods of detection; and a little later (1896) Capt. (afterwards Sir Henry) Jackson, R.N., succeeded in sending code signals between ships, and noted a fading and subsequent rise in signal strength as the distance between stations increased. His work was quite independent of that of Lodge and Marconi.

These men laid the essential foundations; but the commercial development of radio communication hung fire until after Marconi had completed his pioneer work. His first British patent for wireless telegraphy was taken out in 1896, and in 1897 the Wireless Telegraph and Signal Company Limited was incorporated to acquire Marconi's patents in all countries except Italy and her dependencies. The first wireless stations were erected at the Needles, Isle of Wight, at the end of 1897, and at Chelmsford and Dovercourt in 1899. All modern development is based on Senatore Marconi's "four sevens" patent which he took out in 1900. At that time many sceptics held that radio communication could have only a very limited range, because of the earth's curvature. Marconi set himself to disprove this. In 1901 he received signals at the Lizard from the Isle of Wight (198 miles), and afterwards at Crookhaven, S. Ireland, from Poldhu in Cornwall,

at such great strength that he decided on an immediate transAtlantic experiment and chose Newfoundland as the nearest spot for reception. He determined to use kites and balloons as a means of suspending a receiving aerial and arranged that the letter "s," three dots, should be transmitted from Poldhu at a certain speed and at certain times during the day. Fleming was left in charge of the arrangements at Poldhu while Marconi sailed with his two assistants, Kemp and Paget, to Newfoundland. There they found balloons unmanageable, but succeeded in flying a kite from which was suspended an aerial consisting of 500 ft. of twin wire. The ear was more sensitive than the recorder, so their receiving circuit consisted of a pair of Collier-Marr telephones in a conventional arrangement with a self-restoring coherer. On December 12th, 1901, at 12 p.m., Marconi was able to hear distinctly the three dots being transmitted at intervals from Poldhu. His assistant also heard them.

His claim was met with considerable scepticism, but three months later complete messages were being recorded on tapes in a ship 1500 miles from Cornwall and single letters at distances of over 2000 miles.[1]

Three years later, Dr. J. A. Fleming took out his original patent for thermionic valves, an invention based upon experimental work which he began in 1889.[2]

The Great War gave a tremendous impetus to radio communication and long-distance commercial services were set up in the leading countries including Britain where the Carnarvon, Rugby and Leafield Stations were followed by the English "beam" stations for communication with the Empire.

In America experiments were made in the broadcasting of music and speech. This new form of entertainment caught the imagination of the public and in true American fashion an immense industry came into being without further delay. In Great Britain Marconi's Wireless Telegraph Company at Chelmsford made many improvements in commercial apparatus, and in the years immediately following the war transmissions were carried out from Chelmsford using as much as 15 kw. Regular concert programmes were also sent out. These transmissions were picked up as far away as St. John's, Newfoundland, a range of 2673 miles, while ships 1000 miles at sea overheard the programmes. Successful linking up of wireless telephonic apparatus with the land line telephones was also accomplished, and on 9th August, 1920, a successful connexion was established between a subscriber's instrument in London and an aeroplane in flight on its way to Paris. During 1920 the Department of Scientific and Industrial Research established four sub-committees to assist the Radio Research Board by dealing with the following branches of radio research: the propagation of wireless waves; atmospherics; directional wireless; thermionic valves. After the removal

[1] W. T. O'Dea, *Radio Communication, Part I: History and Development* (*Science Museum Handbook*, 1934), 21–2.
[2] *Ibid.*, 15.

of the wartime restrictions, amateur wireless work made great strides, and even to-day it is not generally realized how much we owe to the enthusiasm and inventive genius of amateur radio workers in this and other countries. The broadcasts from the Marconi station at Chelmsford had aroused such enthusiasm among a large band of experimenters that they united in bringing pressure to bear on the Post Office to such good purpose that a small station of 250 watts was authorized to transmit for half an hour every week in order that these amateurs might have a standard transmission on which to improve and experiment with their receiving apparatus. This small station—the famous Writtle station—began operations in February, 1921, and discontinued early in 1923, when broadcasting had been finally launched.

Broadcasting had now come to stay, and in 1922 the Marconi Company obtained permission to open in London the station 2LO. Towards the end of the same year the first British Broadcasting Company was incorporated. The Board consisted of members from the following companies, Marconi, Radio Communication, Metropolitan Vickers, British Thomson-Houston, General Electric, Western Electric, and Burndept. The revenue of the British Broadcasting Company was to be derived from two sources: (a) they were to receive half of the fee of ten shillings charged by the Post Office for the licence, and (b) a royalty on the sale of instruments by the firms which composed the Broadcasting Company. These instruments were of types approved by the Post Office and had the British Broadcasting Company's trademark. Owing to the rapid development of broadcasting and the increasing difficulties which the Broadcasting Company had to face on account of the almost universal construction of home-made receivers and the large number of persons who neglected to obtain the Government licence, the Government appointed a Committee of Inquiry presided over by Sir Frederick Sykes. Certain recommendations designed to assist the Company were made in the report of the Committee, and it was also proposed that the licence granted to the Company should be

extended for a further term. In 1926, as the result of a recommendation made by another Committee on Broadcasting,
presided over by Lord Crawford, the British Broadcasting
Corporation was established under a Royal Charter, the place
of the Board of Directors of the old Broadcasting Company
was taken by a Board of Governors nominated by the Government, and the original capital of the old Company was paid
out. The ten years' licence of the B.B.C. expired on 11th
December, 1936.[1]

The speed of radio development has been remarkable, even
for modern times. There are probably few, if any, sections of
industry in which so many important inventions and improvements have followed one another in such rapid and regular
succession. Within the space of ten or twelve years the home-
made wireless receiving set has given place to handsome
factory-made sets, which are cheaper and in every way better
than the home-made receiver. Tuning-in and control have been
enormously simplified, the quality of the sound-reproduction
has been greatly improved, and selectivity and sensitiveness
have been rapidly raised to a high level. During the past
decade the manufacturers of radio sets and components have
had the benefit of two types of demand: (a) expansion-demand,
as more and more people decided to acquire their first wireless
sets; and (b) replacement-demand, as more and more people,
becoming dissatisfied with obsolete or obsolescent sets,
decided to buy a new model with all the latest improvements.
This dual demand still exists and will continue so long as new
recruits can be induced to "go in for" wireless, and so long
as the radio manufacturers continue to bring out year by year
models of higher quality at lower prices. Thus, expansion of
demand seems to depend upon six factors: (1) further successful research; (2) further reductions in prices; (3) advertising;
(4) the offer of attractive instalment-purchase terms; (5) the
improvement of public taste and powers of appreciation of

---

[1] For a fuller discussion of the constitution and functions of the
B.B.C., see M. E. Dimock, *British Public Utilities and National Development* (1933), Ch. 8, and H. Matheson, *Broadcasting*.

radio music, etc.; (6) the general acceptance of the idea that no household is properly furnished without a good radio set.

The gramophone and gramophone record trade registered increasing expansion and great prosperity down to 1929, but subsequently the marketing of cheaper and better wireless sets cut into the demand for gramophones. The two forms of mechanical musical intruments have now been combined in the radio-gramophone, and to-day the sales of radio-gramophones are increasing, while the sales of acoustic gramophones are declining.

It has been estimated that the annual turnover of the radio section of the electrical industry increased from £7,800,000 in 1926 to close upon £30,000,000 in 1931; and that the present output exceeds 1,600,000 radio receivers and 150,000 radio gramophones per annum.[1]

British exports of wireless sets—about 60,000 sets a year—accessories and apparatus are more than offset by the imports of foreign sets, etc., which come into this country, chiefly from the U.S.A., in spite of heavy import duties.[2] Export markets are almost everywhere dominated by the American manufacturers.

Since the war the British electrical equipment industry has enjoyed partial protection against foreign competition. The Finance (No. 2) Act, 1915, imposed protective import duties upon (*inter alia*) foreign electrical equipment for motor vehicles; and, in October, 1921, protective import duties were laid upon certain other items of electrical equipment of foreign origin entering Great Britain. The list of goods so taxed includes electric scientific instruments, wireless valves and rectifiers, vacuum tubes, permanent magnets, and arc lamp carbons. These duties have, undoubtedly, benefited the industry, but in no sense can it be said that they created it.

The productive capacity of the electrical manufacturing industry expanded considerably under the abnormal pressure

---

[1] Schonfield, H. J. (ed.), *The Book of British Industries* (1933), 292. *The Economist*, 22nd August, 1936, 359.

[2] Net retained imports in 1934 amounted to 82,000 sets.

of war-time demands, but, happily, the post-war demand for its products did not suffer a contraction to or below the 1913 level. The 1907 Census of Production showed that the value of the output of electrical equipment and electrical contract work (almost the whole of which was produced in Great Britain) was some £14·4 millions. Roughly comparable figures for the years 1913 and 1924 are £30 millions and £39·2 respectively. (The *actual* estimate for 1924 was £65·2 millions; which is equivalent at the general level of wholesale prices of all commodities in 1913 to approximately £39·2 millions).[1] Estimates given in the *Fourth Census of Production*, 1930, indicate that the total value of electrical products in 1924 would be approximately £63 millions if revalued at 1930 prices, and that the volume of production in 1930 exceeded the 1924 volume by about 33 per cent. The recorded figures of employment show an increase of nearly 28 per cent in the same period.

British exports of electrical machinery, cables, lamps, and other electrical goods were fairly stable from 1927 to 1930, averaging £18·7 millions per annum. The figures for subsequent years show a severe fall—

| 1931 | . | . | £11·8 millions | 1933 | . | . | £9·3 millions |
| 1932 | . | . | £9·4 millions | 1934 | . | . | £11·3 millions |

Undoubtedly the major causes of this fall are the general trade depression which discouraged new investment in capital goods, and the general stifling of international trade under the pillow of Protectionism. The shrinkage would probably have been worse but for the use of the Government's export credits guarantee scheme. Retained imports of electrical goods also show a marked decline, so that the British electrical industry may be gaining in the home market what it is losing in overseas markets.[2] *Net* exports of British electrical goods of all kinds

---

[1] The value of British electrical equipment exported in each of the three years 1907, 1913 and 1924 was approximately one-quarter of the value of the total output, if the f.o.b. values of the exports be taken; but a slightly smaller proportion if we take the values *ex* works.

[2] The B.E.A.M.A. index of new orders received by the manufacturers of heavy electrical plant has risen from 60 in 1933 to 117 in May, 1935. This index is based upon the horse-power, not the value, of orders.

exceeded £11 millions in 1930, but the annual average since then has been nearer £7 millions.

The heavy section of the electrical industry, producing generators, motors, switch and control gear, converters and transformers, is normally much more dependent upon export trade than the light section, which relies mainly upon the rate of domestic electrification and the extension of telephone services. British exports of heavy electrical equipment, after reaching 41,212 tons, valued at £6,345,621, in 1930, declined steadily to 17,667 tons, valued at £2,635,985, in 1933. During the next two years there was a recovery in the export trade which, although not large in absolute amount, was very satisfactory when compared with the figures for other important exporters, such as Germany and the United States. For the next five years, however, it seems likely that a high level of activity in the heavy section will be maintained mainly as the result of home demand. The work on the London Passenger Transport improvement scheme, which is to cost £32 millions, and on suburban railway electrification in several other places will give a great deal of employment to the electrical manufacturers; and in this connexion it is interesting to notice the formation of a new company, in May, 1935, called Associated Manufacturers of Electric Traction Equipment, for the pooling of large electrification orders. The shareholders are the British Thomson-Houston Company, English Electric Company, General Electric Company, Metropolitan Vickers, Crompton Parkinson, and Allen West and Company.[1]

III

Not many years ago the units manufacturing electrical equipment were large in number and for the most part small in size. But, more recently, combination has been proceeding, so that now over 30 per cent of the entire invested capital is controlled by four giant concerns. If eighteen of the large cable manufacturers are included, it appears that the twenty-two undertakings together hold half the capital of the industry.

[1] *The Economist*, 10th August, 1935.

Nevertheless, it is estimated that there are still between 300 and 400 relatively small units. In 1930 about 52 per cent of the net output of electrical goods was produced by a small number of large firms, each employing upwards of 1500 work-people. The value of the net output per person employed by these large units was £246 per annum, against a general average of £234.[1]

In the section manufacturing all descriptions of telephone equipment the bulk of the machinery for large exchanges is produced by about half a dozen large units. There are, in addition, ten or twelve companies of medium size, and a considerable number of smaller units producing auxiliary equipment and material.[2] Standardization is well advanced. In 1924 the manufacturers in this section and the suppliers of the raw materials joined hands to form the Telephone Development Association, for the purpose of carrying on publicity designed to popularize the use of the telephone.

The business units in the cable-making section are nearly all large. Over 90 per cent of the productive capacity is owned by fifteen or sixteen large companies, seven of which have each a total capital (including debentures) exceeding £1,000,000. All these large units are closely allied in the Cable Makers' Association which was founded in 1899 to eliminate severe competition and to ensure the maintenance of certain standards of quality. It was thought that persistence in severe internal competition might lead to the loss of the reputation for high quality and reliability which British cable-makers then enjoyed. The C.M.A. has also co-operated with the British Engineering Standards Association, and much economy has resulted. The C.M.A. collects and distributes to its members information relating to the production of cables in Great Britain, and supplies special abstracts of the import and export statistics. The minority of producers not members of the C.M.A. are organized in the Independent Cable Makers' Association. In addition certain of the leading companies have

---

[1] *Fourth Census of Production*, 1930, *Part II* (1934), 283.
[2] Committee on Industry and Trade, *Survey of Metal Industries* (1928), 316.

agreed to conduct research in close association, to pool patents, secret processes and other technical and commercial information, and generally to avoid duplication of effort.[1]

The merger of the Gramophone Company, Ltd. (the ("H.M.V." company) and the Columbia Gramophone Co. Ltd. in 1931 brought under the control of the new concern—Electric and Musical Industries, Ltd.—the fifty assembly units owned by the two companies and their subsidiaries, situated in nineteen countries spread over four continents: thirty-eight in Europe, seven in Asia, three in South Africa, and two in Australia.[2] The new concern has an issued capital of nearly £3,363,000 and it holds over 99 per cent of the share capital of both of the combined companies.[3] It has a joint interest with Marconi's Wireless Telegraph Co. Ltd., in Marconi-E.M.I. Television Co. Ltd., and owns a subsidiary company—H.M.V. Household Appliances Ltd.—formed to market domestic refrigerators made in a department of the E.M.I. factory at Hayes, which is easily the largest gramophone and wireless equipment factory in Great Britain. Another gramophone concern which is not so well known, is the Crystalate Gramophone Record Manufacturing Co. Ltd. This concern has subsidiaries operating in America, France, and Germany, and owns factories in London, Tonbridge, and Berlin. It does a large, specialized business in the cheaper gramophone records. In 1928, it acquired the entire share capital of Regal Record Company Inc. of New York, and this company has since been merged in the American Record Corporation, in which the

---

[1] The cable-making section was described by the Committee on Industry and Trade as "one of the strongest and most consistently successful sections of the British electrical industry." (*Survey of Metal Industries*, 302.) Yet British cable-makers enjoy few natural advantages apart from the abundance of good ports and the shortness of the distances to them from the manufacturing areas. Their final products are exceedingly heavy to transport, and almost all their principal raw materials—copper, lead, rubber, cotton, bitumen and oils—have to be imported. Moreover, the demand for cables is notoriously irregular and intermittent, so that producers owning plants large enough to cope with "peak" demand, often work at other times much below optimum capacity.

[2] *The Economist*, 12th and 19th November, 1932.

[3] *Stock Exchange Year Book*.

Crystalate Company now holds an interest. In 1932, the Crystalate Company acquired the Vocalion Gramophone Company.[1]

In the radio equipment and gramophone trade there are five trade associations. The Radio Manufacturers' Association represents the manufacturers of wireless sets of all kinds, and organizes the various radio exhibitions. The wholesale section is represented by the Radio Wholesalers' Federation, and the retail section by the Wireless Retailers' Association. There is also the Radio Valve Manufacturers' Association,[2] which seeks "to promote the use of British-made radio valves," and a commercial association known as The Association of Gramophone, Radio and Musical Instrument Manufacturers and Wholesale Dealers.

The end of the war may be said to have ushered in a new phase in the evolution of the British electric lamp industry. The post-war period was marked not only by increasing consumption of electricity for lighting purposes, but by the growing demand for wireless valves (the manufacture of which is closely akin to the manufacture of electric lamps), and the closer organization of the majority of the manufacturers in the Electric Lamp Manufacturers' Association of Great Britain, founded in 1919 to obviate the danger of costly litigation regarding patents, to arrange for the inter-licensing of patents between the members of the association, and the pooling of factory experience and the results of research.

The manufacture of electric lamps in Britain is in the hands of a few large makers, the majority of whom produce other kinds of electrical equipment as well. Until quite recently (1932–3) approximately nine-tenths of the output of lamps was made by members of the Electric Lamp Manufacturer's Association; but now several non-combine lamps have made their appearance on the market, heralded by extensive

---

[1] *Stock Exchange Year Book; The Economist*, 12th November, 1932, 887–8.
[2] The British radio valve manufacturers are few in number. They have seven factories in London, one at Rugby, and one at Manchester.

advertisement and commended by lower prices. The combined manufacturers, however, are strongly entrenched both in the manufacturing and the selling sections, and the newcomers will not find it easy to make headway against them.

The members of the E.L.M.A. fix the prices at which their lamps shall be retailed to the public, giving to the wholesalers and retailers rates of discount which vary according to (a) the volume of their sales, and (b) the extent to which the distributors are prepared to restrict their freedom to sell non-combine lamps. The minimum rate of discount of the latter type applies to distributors who decline to tie themselves to the combine in any way; while the highest rate of discount can be secured only if the distributor binds himself never to sell non-combine lamps. A somewhat lower or intermediate rate of discount is allowed to distributors who agree not to advertise or solicit orders for non-combine lamps and not to keep them in stock; although they may obtain them specially for a customer who requests them to do so. By this ingenious device the combine contrives to limit the channels available for the distribution of non-combine lamps and also those available to foreign competitors in the British market.

Foreign competition is further restricted by import duties and by international combination. The duties at the rate of 33⅓ per cent *ad valorem* on foreign tungsten and lamp-blown glass-ware imposed by the Safeguarding of Industries Act, 1921, and confirmed by the Finance Act, 1926, have given substantial protection to the industry. Moreover, imported lamps for use on certain motor vehicles are dutiable under the "McKenna" duties, dating from 1915.

Research is still playing a highly important part in the development of the electric lamp and valve industry. The range of problems is wide, including researches into high vacuum technique, production and purification of rare gases, metallurgy, glass and refractories. In order to keep the average cost of useful results as low as possible, a certain minimum size of research organization and staff must be maintained. This organization should work as a single unit, and imaginative, constructive co-ordination of the work of numerous experts is essential. Standardization, which has already reached a high level in this industry, will be carried still further once the supply voltages have been made uniform throughout the country; and research should, in consequence, become less expensive.

In the incandescent lamp section there have been for many years extensive international combinations, arising from the mutual advantages of sharing the results of scientific research achieved or likely to be achieved, powerfully reinforced by fears of over-production, intense competition, price-cutting and shrinkage of profits due to the rapid growth of productive capacity in all the leading industrial countries. The International Incandescent Lamp Cartel, formed in 1902–3. was originally a sales and price-fixing syndicate of all the German, Austrian, Dutch, Swiss, and Italian producers of carbon filament lamps. In 1911 three leading German manufacturers formed the *Drahtkonzern*, or Filament Trust, under which they agreed to pool their patents. The agreement, apparently, did not extend to prices, and in all other respects also the parties retained their autonomy. The British branches of the members of this combine speedily came to an agreement with the British lamp manufacturers for the mutual use of patents in Great Britain, and similar arrangements were made, in 1912–13, between the German companies and important manufacturers in France, Holland, and Austria. Then came the Great War, shattering people, property, and international political and economic relations.

Immediately after the war, when profiteer-hunting was in full swing in this country, the electric lamp industry was investigated by a Select Committee which found that there was a powerful association—The Tungsten Lamp Association —comprising all the principal British makers of lamps. They also found that unreasonable prices were being charged to the public, and that certain of the most powerful manufacturers were imposing onerous conditions upon other manufacturers in the association. As an example, the Committee cited the limitation of output imposed upon patent licensees, which was against the interests of consumers.[1]

During the war, productive capacity in this industry, as in so many others, expanded enormously. Excessive productive capacity, which the manufacturers had striven to prevent in the pre-war period, became an accomplished fact. World demand for electric lamps immediately after the post-war boom could have been supplied, in all probability, by half the existing plants.[2] In other words, productive capacity had far outstripped effective demand, and this caused a number of leading manufacturers, chiefly in Europe, to take steps to "obviate the possibility of unco-ordinated production and unrestricted competition," which, they feared, would be "disastrous to the industry and the quality of its products." In 1921, a group of German and Central European lamp manufacturers, together with a Dutch company and a Swedish company, formed the International Union for Regulating Prices of Incandescent Lamps (Internationale Glühlampen Preisvereinigung), which delimited territories, fixed common prices and common conditions of delivery and payment. In the following year "the friendly agreement concluded . . . between the American General Electric Company and the Osram Company was of particular importance. Besides an arrangement regarding the exchange of patents and of the results of experimental work, this agreement marked out exclusive sales areas for the two contracting parties, and thus set territorial limits to the competition between these undertakings by applying for the first time the principle of the protection of the home market."[3] This phase of the international combination movement in the electric lamp industry culminated at the close of 1924 in a general Convention for the Development and Progress of the International Electric Lamp Industry, between manufacturers in every country of the

[1] Findings and Decisions of a Sub-Committee on the Electric Lamp Industry (*Cmd.* 622, 1920), 3–4, 14–15.
[2] *Survey of Metal Industries*, 322.
[3] League of Nations *Review of the Economic Aspects of Several International Industrial Agreements* (1930), 70.

world except Canada and the United States. As originally constructed, the convention covered twenty-seven principal companies, including eight lesser combines consisting of thirty-six affiliated companies.

Under the terms of the Convention, each party obtains, during the period of validity of the Convention, the right to utilize the inventions and experiences of the other parties on payment of the usual licence fees. An arbitral tribunal is appointed to decide claims regarding the taking out or infringement of patents. The parties are also bound to allow co-contracting parties to visit their laboratories and workshops at any time. The rationalization of production, stocks and sales is assisted by agreements regarding the standardization of electric lamps and the reduction of the number of varieties. Technical supervision of the firms parties to the Convention is also provided, for the quality of their products is checked. This last-mentioned work is carried on in a special laboratory, to which the parties to the Convention must send samples of their products. Propaganda in favour of the use of electric lamps is carried on on behalf of all the parties through the intermediary of the *Lichtwirtschaft*.

The Convention does not provide for the joint sale of products, nor is price-fixing a condition or an integral part of the Convention. The regulation of prices is left entirely to the members interested in the trade of the various countries. It is facilitated, however, by dividing up the world trade according to countries of origin and common territory.

There is no limitation of output, each party being free to produce as it thinks fit. Production is indirectly regulated, however, by the limitation of sales and the allocation of sales areas—i.e. by sharing the world trade. The sales quotas of the various members are determined by the actual sales during a specified basic year, the various types of lamps being brought to a single basis (unit lamp). Members must also share, in the proportion thus fixed, in any increase in world trade. The aggregate quota is divided into national quotas for the various countries of origin (mainly countries having large electric-light industries) and in national quotas for the rest of the world (common territory). The allocation of quotas to the various members is determined by the actual sales during the basic year. Any firm having no sales at all in a country in the course of that year may sell its products there afterwards. As regards countries in the common territory, a firm may, if it does not reach its full quota in any one country, make up the difference from its sales in another country forming part of the common territory. On the other hand, if a firm does not reach its full quota in its country of origin, it cannot seek compensation in the common territory. If a firm exceeds its quota, it must pay, according to a fixed scale, fees for the benefit of the firms whose quota has not been fully realized. The payment of these fees is secured by the sums deposited with the Phoebus Company by each of the firms parties to the Convention.[1]

"Parts of the world from which British lamp makers were excluded by existing patent or trade-mark rights were opened up to them, and, in return, certain continental makers were granted under royalty the right to sell lamps in Great Britain. Arrangements were also made, and are in full operation, for the interchange of patents, research, and factory experience."[2] The same agreement also set up international committees to promote the use of electric lighting throughout the world; to control the variety of lamps manufactured and to eliminate wasteful overlapping and unnecessary multiplication of varieties; to study manufacturing methods with a view to the improvement of the quality of the product; and to control the combine's testing station at Geneva so as to ensure the maintenance of the highest possible standards. Every member of the Convention is a member of the Phoebus Company, which is the central administrative organization or hub of the whole combine. It is located at Geneva "in order to ensure as far as possible independence of the divergent laws of the various countries."

Many of the leading electrical equipment manufacturers of Great Britain and other countries have developed subsidiary undertakings in various parts of the world. Thus, the British Thomson-Houston Company, which is closely associated with the General Electric Company of the United States, pursues a policy of co-operation with other important electrical companies at home and abroad. In France the Thomson-Houston Company is probably the greatest concern of its kind, for it

---

[1] League of Nations *Review of the Economic Aspects of Several International Industrial Agreements* (1930), 73–4.
[2] Committee on Industry and Trade, *Survey of Metal Industries* (1928), 322.

possesses nine factories, and it has a special arrangement with Schneider of Le Creusot and the Jeumont Company for co-operation in respect of railway electrification schemes. In 1921 it founded, with the International General Electric Company (New York) and the Compagnie Générale d'Électricité, another concern named the Compagnie Générale des Lampes, which embraces several of the chief lamp-making concerns in France and Spain, dominates the French lamp trade, and possesses the manufacturing rights of its three founders in several other countries.[1] The British General Electric Co. Ltd. owns, or is "interested" in, nearly a dozen British companies, and is not only linked financially with the Italian firm of Pirelli through the Pirelli-General Cable Works Ltd., but controls various companies in the British Empire, the continent of Europe, China, and South America. It also has investments in a number of electricity supply companies and a working agreement with the Oerlikon Company of Zurich. These examples could be multiplied many times, but we must be content to conclude by mentioning the English Electric Co. Ltd., which controls a group of British companies manufacturing heavy electrical equipment and allied products, and is associated with companies in Canada, Australia, Belgium, France, and Japan.

In the "wiring and contracting" section, which covers all work connected with the *installation* of electrical equipment in houses, workshops, factories, offices, and ships, the private business units are, in the main, small firms. They are very numerous, but not many employ more than a hundred men.[2] In addition, many of the municipalities have departments which undertake electrical installation work.

Lastly, some mention must be made of the British and Allied Manufacturers' Association, which was founded in 1911 in the belief that voluntary co-operative action by the various firms would go far to meet the economic difficulties which at that time were handicapping the development of electrical

[1] Committee on Industry and Trade, *Survey of Metal Industries*, 332–3, 359.
[2] J. Hilton and others, *Are Trade Unions Obstructive?* (1935), 129–30.

and allied engineering in Britain.[1] Taking "co-operation without the sacrifice of individual initiative" as its basic principle, the Association has progressed until, in 1933, it could claim that its members manufactured 97 per cent of the total value of electrical machinery and apparatus produced in this country. The Association also claims to have done useful work in standardizing designs and conditions of sale, and in extending the export market so considerably that Britain is now one of the leading exporters of electrical machinery and equipment.

IV

In round figures, the number of persons engaged in the British electrical equipment industry in 1911 was 85,000. By 1921 the number had expanded to over 175,000; by 1931 it had reached 211,000, and in July, 1934, it was 257,830. The position at July, 1936, compared with 1923, is shown below.

ELECTRICAL INDUSTRY IN GREAT BRITAIN AND
NORTHERN IRELAND

Section	Nos. insured at		Index of Expansion (1923 = 100)
	July, 1923	July, 1936	
Wiring and Contracting . .	11,870	38,160	321
Cable, Wire, and Lamps . .	72,840	151,830	208
Electrical Engineering . .	62,280	101,700	163
	146,990	291,690	198

On the whole the expansion has been appreciably greater in the southern part of England than in Northern England and Scotland, especially in the section manufacturing cable, wire, and lamps. The index of (net) industrial expansion of all industries together was 116 in 1936. Unemployment percentages in the electrical industry were somewhat lower in 1936 than in 1923; in wiring and contracting the percentage is usually about twice as high as those in the other two sections.

The comparative statistics published monthly by the

[1] B.E.A.M.A., *Twenty-One Years* (1933).

Ministry of Labour show that during the period 1924–34 unemployment in the electrical equipment industry as a whole stood slightly below the general level, and much below that in shipbuilding and many other sections of the engineering and metal trades (e.g. marine, constructional and general engineering; engineers' iron and steel founding, tool making, and bolt, screw and nail making).

Since the end of the war, London has become a leading centre of the manufacture of telegraphic and telephonic apparatus (including automatic telephone machinery), incandescent lamps, cables and flex, volt and watt meters, and electrical merchandise such as stores, lamps, electric irons and kettles, wireless sets and components. A considerable amount of work is also done in Greater London in connexion with ignition machinery, switch gear, accumulators, and primary batteries.[1] The following figures, relating to the year 1931, indicate broadly the localization of the industry in Great Britain—

No. of Insured Workers	Electrical Engineering	Manufacture of Cables, Wire, Lamps, etc.
Greater London	14,700	53,870
Midlands	30,170	13,410
North-west England	21,860	23,650
Scotland	3,430	580
Other districts	21,580	16,740

In the manufacture of heavy electrical equipment (power plant, etc.) London employs 16 per cent of the workers; Birmingham 33 per cent; Manchester and district 24 per cent; and the remaining 27 per cent are scattered over the rest of the country.[2] For lighter electrical equipment (e.g. switches, flex, lamps, etc.) the percentages are: London 50, Birmingham 12, Manchester and District 21, rest of the country 17. Three-fifths of the workers in the radio section are in London and South-east England; and of seven English arc lamp factories, three are in London, and two in Lancashire. Altogether, out

[1] *New Survey of London Life and Labour*, II, 128.
[2] D. H. Smith, *The Industries of Greater London*, 136.

of a total of well over a quarter of a million workers engaged in the electrical equipment industry, nearly one-third are employed in Greater London.

The manufacture of submarine cables has become to a large extent localized on Thames-side at Woolwich, where direct coiling into the holds of ships is possible. Six large cable manufacturers now have works in North and South Woolwich, Greenwich, Erith, and Charlton. "The waterside, which was important, and still remains so, for firms manufacturing submarine cables, has also great advantages in the way of reducing transport charges for makers of other cables, since both the raw materials and the finished products of the industry are heavy to handle."[1]

The large amount of machinery now used in cable making demands a staff of maintenance engineers for its repair and supervision. The repair of breakages of wire or insulating tape also calls for great skill and care. The lighter machines are operated by women and girls, and the heavier by men of varying degrees of skill. Heavy cabling machines and the lead presses which cover insulated cables with lead, work under the control of a highly skilled "driver," assisted by several less skilled men. The semi-skilled men are usually recruited from the ranks of the unskilled by "up-grading." Raw materials are handled, and the finished cables are moved, stored and packed by general labourers. The unemployment percentage in the cable making section is relatively low, and there is little migration to and from other trades.

Most of the work in battery manufacture is unskilled or semi-skilled, and light, though not always pleasant. The majority of the operations are easily learnt and require little more than a combination of care and quickness. Female and juvenile labour is largely employed, e.g. in cutting and bending zinc by machinery, fitting washers, soldering, inserting the contents of the cells and sealing them with wax or tar. Some of these materials must be handled in a hot state, and workers employed in ladling the sealing compound wear

[1] *New Survey of London Life and Labour* (1931), II, 188–9

protective aprons, gloves and leggings. Men are employed for bending the heaviest zincs, grinding, compressing and baking the carbon, and fitting metal terminals into large carbons with molten metal. The manufacture of accumulators is carried out mainly by men, for it is scheduled as a dangerous trade under the Factory Acts because the lead compounds used for the plates are poisonous. The employment of women and juveniles in this department of the trade is confined to the assembling and packing processes. All the work lends itself to payment by results.

In the lamp-making section mass production is now universal and in order to meet continental competition "British lamp makers are adopting automatic machinery and mechanical production methods to a large extent. The male labour employed almost entirely consists of the skilled mechanics and electricians who are required for supervising the machinery. The actual work of lamp manufacture is carried out by female labour, which is remunerated on a piece-work basis. No apprenticeship is served, but the girls achieve a high degree of dexterity, and the most highly skilled are transferred, as opportunity arises, to thermionic valve manufacture in which the pay is higher. . . . the large scale manufacture of thermionic valves for wireless and other electrical communications has only been made possible by the application of scientific knowledge and experience accumulated in connexion with the mass production of lamps."[1]

The structure, parts, and materials of ordinary large lamps are shown in Figs. 1 and 2.[2] The materials are drawn from practically world-wide sources. The filament wire, usually coiled, is mounted on support wires and lead-in wires. The support wires are anchored in a glass rod or stem, which is usually merely an extension of a glass tube used for exhausting air from the bulb. The lead-in wires are for the purpose of connecting the filament with the wires extending from the central station (or source of current) to the socket. A lead-in wire consists of three parts—an outer lead, an inner lead, and

[1] *Survey of Metal Industries*, 320–1.
[2] Taken from W. Bowden, *op. cit.*, by courtesy of the U.S. Commissioner for Labor Statistics.

a seal wire (a weld). It is at this central point, the seal wire, that the lead-in wires are fused with the glass of the stem. At the same point the exhaust tube is fused with the flare. These portions combined (the exhaust tube and the flare, the lead-in wires, the support wires, and the filament) form the mount, the mount minus the filament being called the stem. The

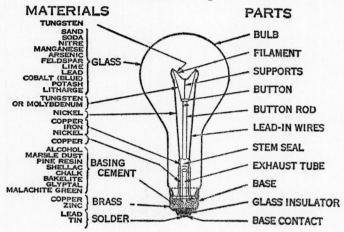

FIG. 1. DIAGRAM OF AN ELECTRIC LAMP

mount is sealed to the neck of the bulb at the flange or enlarged portion of the flare. When the mount and the bulb have been sealed together by fusion of the glass the air is exhausted from the lamp, and if it is a gas-filled lamp, gas is inserted and the exhaust tube is sealed off by fusion of the glass. The base is then cemented on the neck of the bulb with one lead-in wire extending through the eyelet of the base, the other lead-in wire being soldered on the outside of the base.

A number of operations are carried out on machines with rotating tables, attended by girls working in teams, each team-member performing one of a series of operations. The majority of the workers are girls, but men are employed as supervisors and maintenance engineers for the machinery used in preparing the lamp filaments and in assembling the glass and wire components.

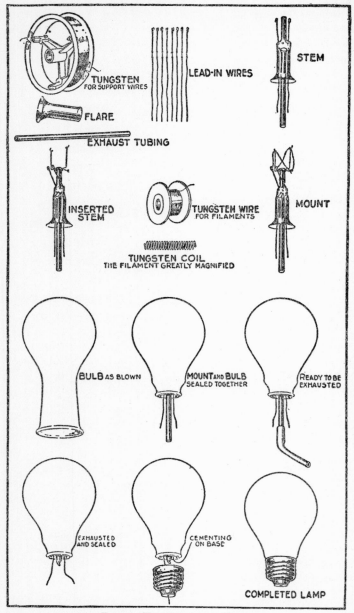

FIG. 2. ELECTRIC-LAMP PARTS.

In the *New Survey of London Life and Labour* it is reported that conditions in the incandescent electric lamp section of the electrical industry were found to be good.

The work is not heavy and most of it is clean. Many of the operations are fine and require good eyesight and neat fingers. Flying glass particles are a danger in some processes, and in some shops the girls consequently wear large plain glass spectacles to protect their eyes. There is no work similar to the press work in which girls are engaged in some branches of engineering. Apprenticeship is unnecessary, as the girls are able to learn most of the processes in two or three months. . . . On the average girls are said to stay at work six or seven years, though there are many cases of women who stay much longer. There is no shortage of labour, though there is little unemployment among the type of worker required for this industry.

The degree of industrial activity in electrical contracting depends upon the expansion of electricity supply, the state of the building industry, and the season. The busiest period occurs in the autumn, and the slackest in the summer. As far as home trade is concerned, the largest firms take contracts in all parts of the country, but the others confine themselves to local work. The operatives must work on the job, and this often means that employees of the largest firms must travel and sleep away from their homes a good deal. The section is an expanding one. At July, 1923, the estimated number of insured persons engaged in electrical wiring and contracting in Great Britain and Northern Ireland was 11,870. To-day, there are over 38,000 insured workers (nearly all males) in this section of the electrical industry, of whom approximately one quarter work for London firms. The labour force employed consists mainly of skilled craftsmen and their "mates," and the employers limit the numbers of unskilled men on any job to not more than one to each skilled journeyman.[1] The trade is recruited mainly by apprenticeship, more or less formal, beginning at the age of 15 or 16 and lasting five years, followed by a period of improvership. Apprentices are encouraged (and

[1] John Hilton and others, *Are Trade Unions Obstructive?* (1935), 129 ff.

in certain cases, required) to attend technical classes. Learners' weekly wages vary from 7s. 6d. to 15s. according to age, and improvers' rates are usually 70 to 80 per cent of the qualified workmen's wage rates. There is little or no piecework. The time rates paid for a 47-hour week tend to vary with the cost of living and are in general higher than the rates for skilled work in the engineering and allied trades.

From a sample inquiry made by the Ministry of Labour in 1931 it appeared that the average weekly earnings of men and youths employed in electrical contracting in October of that year were 52s. 1d. in firms employing 10 or more workpeople, and 44s. 3d. in firms employing less than 10; and that the proportion of workpeople on short time was approximately 4½ per cent.[1] The unweighted average of the recognized time rates of wages of wiremen employed by electrical contractors in twelve large towns at the end of December, 1934, was 71s. 5d. per week of 47 hours.[2] This compares with 69s. 5d. at the end of December, 1933.[3] These averages are useful, but they cloak the fact that there is a wage differential of 3d. or 3½d. per hour between London rates of wages and those paid in provincial towns (e.g. Liverpool, Bristol, Southampton).[4] In London the rates of wages are: qualified electricians, 1s. 10½d. per hour or 88s. 1½d. per 47-hour week; auxiliary workers ("mates"), 1s. 6d. per hour or 70s. 6d. per 47-hour week. Overtime rates are "time-and-a-half" up to midnight, and "time-and-two-thirds" after midnight.[5] "Charge hands" (i.e. men placed in charge of jobs) receive an additional 2d. per hour. Fares and time spent in travelling are paid for by the employers, and 1s. a day extra is paid for abnormally "dirty work." In Liverpool and District qualified electricians (journeymen) receive 1s. 7¼d. per hour and in Scotland 1s. 6d. or 1s. 6½d.[6]

Negotiating machinery dealing with wages and working conditions is provided by a Joint Industrial Council, with

[1] *Labour Gazette*, February, 1933.
[2] *Ibid.*, March, 1935.
[3] *Ibid.*, February, 1934.
[4] Cf. P. Ford, *Work and Wealth in a Modern Port* (1934), 42.
[5] *New Survey of London Life and Labour*, II, 187.
[6] *Labour Gazette*, February, 1937, 75.

local sub-committees, on which the employers' National Electrical Federation and the employees' Electrical Trades Union have equal representation.

There is also a Joint Industrial Council for the Electrical Cable Making Industry on which are represented the Cable Makers' Association, the Independent Cable Makers' Association, the Transport and General Workers' Union, the General and Municipal Workers' Union, the Electrical Trades Union, and the India Rubber, Cable and Asbestos Workers' Union. There is very little piece-work. Time rates for a 47-hour week are the rule; but certain firms work a double or treble shift system. The J.I.C. has graded the adult workers, the principal male grades being: (1) general labourers; (2) "process" labourers; (3) drivers of second-grade machines; (4) drivers of first-grade machines. Juveniles and youths are graded according to age. The wage agreements provide for a basic wage, plus a cost-of-living bonus which varies with every movement of $7\frac{1}{2}$ points in the Ministry of Labour cost-of-living index number. With the index between 45 and $52\frac{1}{2}$ the London time-work wages for a 47-hour week are—

					s.	d.		s.	d.	
Males	(21 and over)	.	.	.	52	$10\frac{1}{2}$	to 60	8$\frac{1}{2}$		according to grade.
Females	(18 and over)	.	.	.	26	6	to 30	6		
Youths	(18–20)	.	.	.	35	3	to 43	1		according
Boys	(14–17)	.	.	.	13	$8\frac{1}{2}$	to 23	6		to
Girls	(14–17)	.	.	.	13	0	to 17	6		age.

For piece-workers the wages rates are fixed so that, when bonus additions based on the cost-of-living index have been made, average workers may be able to make weekly earnings above those of time workers in comparable grades. For boys and girls the piece-work earnings appear to exceed time-work earnings by sums ranging from 3s. to 6s. per week; while for adults the differences seem to range between 6s. 6d. and 10s. in favour of the piece-workers, provided, of course, that they are reasonably efficient.

The jointing of cables, a highly skilled operation chiefly connected with cable-laying, is done by plumber-jointers, assisted by semi-skilled mates. For these workers the wages rates, which are fixed by the J.I.C. in the electrical contracting section, are—

| Plumber-jointers | . | . | . | . | 1s. 10¼d. per hour. |
| Mates | . | . | . | . | . | 1s. 5·8d. per hour. |

In the lighter branches of engineering in the London area the ratio of female to male labour rose from 1 : 50 in 1891 to 1 : 5 in 1929, largely as a result of the increase of automatic machinery, repetition work and assembling of small parts. A large number and a large proportion of women and girls are employed in these branches of work in the electrical trades (lamps and instruments), the making of motor accessories, wireless sets, tin box making, and similar occupations. For the London area the basis of wages laid down by the Electrical and Allied Employers' Association for women and girls is a scale ranging from 12s. a week at 14 years of age to 28s. at the age of 21. The trade unions contend that the adult wage of 28s. should be reached at the age of 18 as is the case under many Trade Board scales; but the employers resist this claim[1]. Where the women and girls are paid by results, as many are, they can often earn more than the wage provided by the time-work scale. Girls working in "teams" in the incandescent lamp section are paid on piece rates which vary with the output of the group as a whole, so that a slow worker may keep down the earnings of the quicker workers in the team. These machine workers "can detect the slightest alteration in the speed" of the machines "since they have to co-ordinate their own movements with those of the machine." The earnings vary between 40s. and 60s. a week, the average being in the neighbourhood of 49s.[2] Handwork on the larger lamps, although it is more skilled, yields, on the whole, lower earnings than high-speed work on ordinary lamps.

In battery manufacture the work is usually paid for on a piece-work basis. A London firm gave 25s. as the average weekly earnings of their female employees, the majority of whom were juveniles.[3] Time-work rates of wages where they

[1] *New Survey of London Life and Labour* (1931), II, 19, 134, 143.
[2] *Ibid.*, 165–6.   [3] *Ibid.*, 170.

are adopted are somewhat below the normal scale for women in engineering, and range from 10s. 9d. per week at 14 years of age to 25s. 6d. at and after the age of 21. There is no doubt that earnings vary widely.

In many branches of the radio section and in the making of motor accessories there is now much light repetition work with automatic or semi-automatic machinery, and a good deal of assembling of small and light parts, all of which lends itself to the employment of female labour. In the *New Survey of London Life and Labour* it is stated that the

manufacture of wireless sets is undertaken by some London firms, in some cases as a branch of general electrical merchandize or instrument manufacture, and in others as their sole product. The trade is somewhat speculative owing to constant changes in methods of construction. The components are not usually made by the firm making sets, but are purchased from instrument makers and assembled. The work is therefore mainly assembly, and much of it can in the earlier and simpler stages be performed by juvenile and female labour. As the set nears completion it is taken over by male assemblers. There is usually also a woodworking department in which cabinets are made for the sets, and a shop in which various insulating substances akin to ebonite are worked.[1]

As to wages and earnings, the general conditions of the engineering trades apply with very little variation. Piecework rates or premium bonus systems are more usual than time-rates.

A gramophone consists of two sections ; the wooden cabinet, and the motor, tone-arm and other metal parts. In the early days of the gramophone industry the cabinets were made almost entirely by the hand-labour of cabinet makers working for small masters in tiny rooms or workshops scattered all over London ; while the motors and other metal accessories were usually bought from specialist engineering factories. The so-called gramophone manufacturers were merely assemblers. Most of this assembling work was done by girls, working on a piece-rate system, and supervised by men. The girls earned from 25s. to 30s. in a full week, and the men from 50s. to 60s. When the demand for gramophones declined, the small

[1] Vol. II, 168.

cabinet makers turned on to the production of cabinets for wireless sets. In recent years the small units in all sections of the trade have been disappearing rapidly, and the tendency has been to concentrate the manufacture of wireless sets and radio-gramophones in a few large mass-production plants, making as much use as possible of the conveyor belt.

When the production of cabinets was mechanized, cabinet makers and polishers received up to 1929 the customary minimum rate of 1s. 9d. per hour, later reduced to 1s. 7d. for a 47-hour week. On the introduction of more automatic jigs and saws for the preparation of the parts and a highly subdivided system of assembly utilizing the conveyor belt, many skilled craftsmen with from 12 to 20 years' service were dismissed. Boys, improvers and women took their place under the supervision of the remaining skilled men.[1]

The rates of wages are: women, 8d. per hour; improvers, 1s. 3d. to 1s. 5d. per hour; skilled men, 1s. 7d. per hour or 74s. 5d. per 47-hour week. During the slack season, which occurs in the three months following Christmas, workers are placed on short time or "stood off" until trade revives. "Working conditions and amenities are good, and the workers have organized friendly and social societies controlled and financed by themselves."[2] Modern machinery and methods are now very generally used throughout this trade, and females, juveniles, and young persons are extensively employed upon automatic turning, the machine-pressing of sheet metal for small parts, coil-winding, and the assembling of parts. Whereas the older type of gramophone was composed of about 500 parts, the manufacture of a modern radio set or radio-gramophone involves the assembly of anything from 1000 to 6000 parts, most of them small and delicate.

Gramophone records are made from a copper matrix, which is produced by an elaborate electrolytic process from the original wax master-record made in the recording studio. The copper matrix is placed in a mould containing a plastic substance (largely shellac) and the mould is then put into a steam-heated hydraulic press. The pressing is done by skilled

[1] *New Survey of London Life and Labour*, VIII (1934), 180.
[2] *Ibid.*, 180.

men, and the subsequent polishing is done by women and girls. All work upon a piece-rate system and earnings vary a good deal from one factory to another. In the best factories in 1935 good pressers were earning from 80s. to 120s. in a full week, and polishers from 35s. to 40s. In factories producing low-grade cheap records, earnings are much lower.[1]

The total number of work people engaged in the manufacture of gramophone records, gramophones, radio sets and radio-gramophones in Great Britain is probably between 12,000 and 15,000. Trade unionism is very weak and, apart from cabinet makers and machinists, very few of the workers belong to any union. The volume of employment fluctuates seasonally, from a minimum at midsummer to a maximum in December. On this topic the Chairman of Electric and Musical Industries, Ltd., made some interesting remarks on 16th September, 1934—

Both the radio and gramophone industries are, as you know, to some extent seasonal, and the efforts of the management have been directed towards levelling the output with the principal object of retaining the great majority of our workers during the whole year. Last summer fewer hands were temporarily laid off and in consequence a very much smaller number of new hands was required to be taken on in the autumn. This has added greatly to the efficiency of the workers and there has been a resultant increase in output *per capita*, for experienced hands may always be depended upon to work more efficiently than those who are new and untried.

This policy is equally beneficial to the workers themselves, who feel that once successfully started on their work they may look forward to continued employment. The great dread of the working man to-day is unemployment, and to any critic of the dole who urges that the British workman prefers idleness with a dole to continued employment I would extend a cordial invitation to visit Hayes at moments when the news spreads that we are taking on new hands. He will then see for himself the long queues formed at the doors of our employment bureau, giving adequate proof that workers will stand in line for hours to get work, particularly if it be with a concern where the employment is reasonably steady and continuous and the wages fair.[2]

Section 2 of the Employment of Women, Young Persons

[1] *New Survey of London Life and Labour*, VIII, 181.
[2] *The Times*, 17th November, 1934.

and Children Act, 1920, permits women and young persons of the age of 16 years and upwards to be employed in factories or workshops on a system of two day-shifts, averaging not more than eight hours each, between 6 a.m. and 10 p.m. on week-days and 6 a.m. and 2 p.m. on Saturdays. Before this two-shift system can be introduced in any factory or workshop a joint application by the employer and a majority of the workers concerned must be submitted to the Home Office. This application is reported upon by the Local Inspector of Factories, and if his report is favourable an Order is issued authorizing the system. There are at present some 35,700 persons working under this system, of whom about 20,000 are engaged upon various manufacturing processes connected with radio equipment, rayon goods, hosiery, aluminium, and rubber tyres. In 1935 a Departmental Committee of Investigation reached the conclusion that the system did not seem to affect detrimentally the health and earnings of the women and young persons employed under it, and that, subject to adequate safeguards, there appeared to be no serious objections to its continuance on a permanent basis.[1]

Taking a general view of industrial relations in the electrical industry, one finds that many of the leading employers regard strong trade union organization as useful and, indeed, essential as part of the machinery of the Joint Industrial Councils, and as a bulwark against Communism.[2] In the wiring and contracting section the employers' federation and the trade union act in concert to enforce apprenticeship and to maintain the level of craftsmanship, although it is true that the employers will not go so far as to undertake to employ none but trade unionists. In other sections there is much less insistence upon apprenticeship, and unskilled and semi-skilled workers are employed in large numbers. On the whole, however, industrial relations in the electrical industry, including electricity supply or generation, seem to be more satisfactory year in, year out, than in any other major British industry.

[1] See *Report* (*Cmd.* 4914, 1935).
[2] *Are Trade Unions Obstructive?* 131.

(iii) MOTOR VEHICLES AND AIRCRAFT

Apart from the fundamental discovery of electric power and the various inventions connected with it, perhaps no modern invention has produced deeper and wider economic and social changes than the internal combustion engine. For at least two centuries thoughtful men have realized the existence of a latent demand for a fast road vehicle, cheap to run and easy to control. Certain mechanically-propelled road carriages (marvellous machines!) were actually put upon the highway in the eighteenth century, and it was anticipated that if such vehicles could be perfected they would be called upon to carry not only goods, and passengers bent upon business, but also passengers travelling for pleasure. The great improvements in road-making and maintenance enhanced the possibilities of successful road transport services if only the technical problems connected with the propulsion of the vehicle could be solved. The advent of a rival means of mechanical transport in the shape of the railway was at first a blow to road transport development; but in the long run railway transport probably aided such development by increasing commerce and wealth, and "creating" not only a great volume of traffic, but a travel-habit which has gradually spread through the various strata or economic classes in the community with the rise in standards of life and the increase and cheapening of travel facilities. The recent development of motor car manufacture and its sister industry, road motor transport, is the result of a series of changes in industrial technique coupled with a highly elastic demand, and progressive reductions of vehicle prices and running costs. These forces have created two gigantic industries in less than a quarter of a century.

I

The early obstacles to the manufacture of a successful internal combustion engine were successfully surmounted nearly thirty years ago, and since then the motor vehicle has grown rapidly in perfection and popularity.[1] The people of the United States were most favourably placed for the development of the new motor car industry, for they live in a country where distances are continental in magnitude, and where quick, convenient, cheap transport is, therefore, correspondingly important. The new motor fuel was abundant, American industry was young, receptive, alert, unfettered by well-established but old-fashioned notions and practices, and the average wealth per head of the population was so high as to promise a substantial demand for the new vehicles. The Americans were the first to realize that the motor car is a highly composite product requiring a very large number of components, and that a major portion of the manufacturing process is nothing more than the *assembling* of these parts, provided that they are first carefully standardized. Knowledge of the "interchangeable" method of production had begun to spread, especially in the United States, where it was quickly seen that its application to the manufacture of motor cars would mean low costs and rapid development. While in Europe the motor-car remained for many years a somewhat rare expensive luxury; in America the trend was all in the direction of a large output of standardized vehicles, at "popular" prices.

If Europeans chiefly "invented" the automobile, Americans certainly developed the methods required for its mass production. . . . It is something of an anomaly that the product which represents one of the mechanically finest, the most cunningly devised, and the most delicately fitted of all contrivances which man has ever made is constructed with the exercise of virtually no personal craftsmanship whatever on the part of most workers engaged in its manufacture.[2]

Thus it came about that in the United States in the early years of the twentieth century a small number of motor car

[1] For interesting details of the evolution of the motor engine, see A. P. Usher, *A History of Mechanical Inventions* (1929); Fleming and Brocklehurst, *A History of Engineering* (1925); Carpenter and Diederichs, *Internal Combustion Engines* (1908); R. C. Epstein, *The Automobile Industry*; and *Manchester Guardian Commercial, Road Haulage Supplement*, 23rd July, 1932.

[2] Epstein, *The Automobile Industry*, 30–1.

manufacturers working upon the mass-assembly plan were producing a surprisingly large and constantly expanding output; while in Europe, on the contrary, there were numerous small producers, little or no standardization, and the aggregate output, although high in quality, was small in quantity.

II

From small beginnings, the number of motor vehicles in use in the United Kingdom has increased steadily, year by year, except during the period 1917–19. Reliable records are not available prior to 1912, but it is estimated that in 1907 there were some 65,000 motor cars in use in the United Kingdom. In 1912 the total number of registered private cars, hackneys and motor trucks was 175,734 and four years later it slightly exceeded 275,000. By 1918 the total had fallen as low as 160,222; but by 1920 it had recovered to a new record number of 362,400, and the expansion proceeded unhindered in subsequent years. In 1926 the "million mark" was passed; in 1930 there were over $1\frac{1}{2}$ millions of registered motor vehicles, including tractors used for agriculture and general haulage. The statistics for 1936 (last quarter: Great Britain and Northern Ireland) are—

	Thousands
Private cars	1,560
Goods Vehicles, Tractors, etc.	456
Motor Omnibuses and Motor Coaches . . .	48·2
Taxis and Hire Cars	38·0
Total (excluding motor cycles and trolley buses)	2,102·2

This steady expansion in the use of motor vehicles in the United Kingdom has been accompanied, at least during the last twenty years, by a steady increase in the proportion of British cars to cars of foreign manufacture.[1] It is, perhaps, not generally known that of the 65,000 motor cars in the United Kingdom in 1907, no fewer than 53,000, or nearly 82 per cent were imported. In 1915 the British motor car industry was given the protection of the McKenna duties, and within ten years the proportions of British to foreign cars in

[1] The first, full-sized *British* petrol motor was the Lanchester. H. O. Duncan, *The World on Wheels* (1926), 865.

6—(B.251)

use in the United Kingdom were almost exactly reversed. An *ad valorem* import duty of 33⅓ per cent came into force in September, 1915, upon motor cars and motor cycles (except commercial vehicles and omnibuses), and their accessories and components imported into this country. From September, 1919, one-third of this duty was remitted if the car, cycle or vehicle was of British Empire origin.[1] These duties (subject to the Empire preference and the exceptions mentioned above), remained in force until August, 1924, when they were repealed. They were, however, soon re-imposed (July, 1925); and in May, 1926, the exceptions were abolished, presumably on the ground that an adequate supply of commercial vehicles had become available from factories in Great Britain. A year later the duty was extended to rubber tyres and tubes for motor vehicles.

Although war-time experience of the uses and reliability of the motor vehicle made clear the possibilities of future progress, the effect of the war upon the British motor manufacturing industry was to divert it from its normal course, and while many British firms went over to the manufacture of aero-engines and shells, the Americans rapidly developed a great motor car industry and an enormous export trade until at the end of the war they stood in "a position of unchallenged superiority." Between 1913 and 1920 the American annual output of motor cars rose from 485,000 to 2,205,000. As for the British makers, their output had remained stationary, they "had lost the small export trade which had been developed in the immediate pre-war years,"[2] and their plants had become ill-balanced by reason of their concentration upon aero-engines and munitions of war. Immediately after the war efforts were made—including the raising and spending of large amounts of new capital—to restore the industry to a proper

---

[1] In order to qualify for the preferential rate of duty (22⅔ per cent *ad. val.*) one-half of the cost price must consist of Empire labour and materials. This offers considerable scope to United States motor manufacturers, who are able to supply branch plants in Canada with large amounts of material from the United States and yet legitimately claim imperial preference when exporting cars and parts to Great Britain.

[2] G. C. Allen, *British Industries and their Organization* (2nd Edn. 1935), 176.

peace-time footing. The onset of the post-war slump, however, caused a setback. Many firms were severely shaken, and there followed a year or two of financial anxiety, capital reductions, and the disappearance of the weakest units. It has been estimated that in 1922 there were ninety-one motor car factories in Great Britain, but only sixty-one in 1925. After this purge, the motor industry, with all the resilience of early youth, recovered from the depression much more rapidly than many of the old industries. Costs and prices were reduced, efficiency and quality were improved, and sales began to expand at home and abroad. The estimated British output of private cars was—[1]

    1920: 50,000   1921: 32,000.   1922: 66,000.

The motor cycle trade also advanced rapidly in 1923 and after. The manufacture of commercial vehicles lagged behind until after 1923, largely because of the sale at low prices of some 60,000 lorries and vans by the War Disposals Committee.

The fall in the number of factories did not mean a fall in the total output of vehicles nor in the general magnitude of the industry, for while the least efficient companies were shrinking into bankruptcy, the most efficient were reducing their prices in face of an elastic demand, expanding their plants more and more on mass-production and continuous-assembly lines, and absorbing here and there, on advantageous terms, some of the smaller and weaker units. The expansion of the whole industry which dates from 1923–4 is a new phase, marked by the adoption of "Ford" methods of mass manufacture and "flow production."

In 1907 the British motor industry produced about 10,300 complete private and commercial cars and chassis, valued at some £3,580,000; in 1936 the output figure was 461,350 units, and the estimated value exceeded £65 millions. The number of workpeople in the industry has increased from approximately 30,000 in 1907 to 314,000 in 1936.

The estimated *value* of the total output has not expanded in step with the volume owing to the fact that increased effective

[1] Allen, *op. cit.*, 177. Estimate based upon the licensing figures.

	OUTPUT Complete cars, commercial vehicles and chassis		EMPLOYMENT Nos. of Insured Workpeople.		
			In the Industry	Un-employed	Total Employed
	No.	Estimated Value £'000s.	(1)	(2)	(1)–(2)
1907 . .	10,300	3,585	30,000	Not available	
1912 . .	23,200	7,436	66,000[1]	Not available	
1924 . .	146,600	40,059	203,340	13,618	189,722
1933 . .	286,290	49,000	261,720	44,168	217,552
1934 . .	342,500	50,500	271,530	28,819	242,711
1935 . .	403,720	57,860	285,830	17,150	268,680
1936 . .	461,352	65,600	314,000	19,720	294,280

demand has been created largely by a series of progressive cost and price reductions. With regard to the employment statistics, it should be noted that those for 1907 are estimates only[1] and those for 1924-1936 relate to workpeople insured under the Unemployment Insurance Acts as engaged in the "construction and repair of motor vehicles, cycles and aircraft" in July of each year. Management staffs and other persons not covered by unemployment insurance are not included. If we exclude those engaged in the cycle trade, and include the motor industry management staffs and other uninsured persons, together with all persons engaged in the manufacture of parts, accessories, paints and tyres for motor vehicles, the final number would probably exceed 350,000. As an employment-providing industry motor manufacturing now compares well with such old-established industries as shipbuilding, seafaring and the woollen and worsted manufacture. The estimated numbers of insured persons and the degree of unemployment among them in these four industries in July, 1936, were—

	No.	Percentage Unemployed
Construction and Repair of Motor Vehicles, Cycles and Aircraft	314,000	6·9
Woollen and Worsted Manufacture . .	223,310	11·3
Shipbuilding and Ship Repairing . . .	161,850	30·7
Shipping Service	141,090	22·3

[1] The Census of Production, 1912, gives 78,000 workers engaged in the construction and repair of motor cars, motor cycles, and aircraft.

There are considerable seasonal variations of employment in the motor industry. In August the new season's models are exhibited to the dealers, who begin to place orders immediately. The work begun on these orders is continued and intensified throughout the autumn and early winter, very largely as a result of the business done at the Motor Show in October. From Christmas until late in February there is a lull during which the volume of employment declines, and this is followed by the beginning of the spring boom which reaches its peak in March or April. Afterwards employment declines to its seasonal trough in July or August. In recent years "there has been a distinct tendency for the secondary autumn peak to increase in importance . . . indicating a certain relative expansion of autumn car purchases."[1] The aggregate production statistics, however, conceal the fact that the production of buses is concentrated mainly in the spring and early summer, while production of other commercial vehicles (lorries, vans, etc.) does not show any regular seasonal variation apart from low figures in August–September. Moreover, in "garage and repair service" (including the retailing of petrol), which employs over one-third of the workers in the motor industry, seasonal unemployment is less marked than in the manufacturing section. The Motor Show helps to spread demand and employment through part of the winter, whereas otherwise it would probably be concentrated very largely in the spring months. Exports, are, on the whole, only a little less seasonal than domestic sales, and, while they help to reduce slackness in winter, they do not do so in the summer, and they intensify the spring boom. Excluding years of particularly severe depression, seasonal fluctuations appear to account for between 10 and 20 per cent of the unemployment in the motor industry.[2] Some of the principal manufacturers are now exploring the possibilities of reducing further the seasonal unemployment and under-employment of labour and capital.

The chief occupations of the workers in an assembly plant

---

[1] C. Saunders, *Seasonal Variations in Employment* (1936), 54.
[2] *Ibid.*, 55–7.

are as follows: (*a*) *skilled:* motor mechanics, tool room mechanics, millwrights and maintenance engineers, carpenters; (*b*) *semi-skilled:* car assemblers, body builders, wood-working machinists, metal machinists, painters and enamellers, trimmers (i.e. upholsterers), testers, internal transport workers. Labour in the industry is fairly well organized, but there are certain important gaps. For example, trade unionism is not recognized in any of the Morris plants. The principal trade unions catering for motor workers are the Amalgamated Engineering Union, the Electrical Trades Union, the Amalgamated Society of Woodworkers, and the Transport and General Workers' Union. On the employers' side the negotiating body is the Engineering and Allied Employers' National Federation.

The Society of Motor Manufacturers and Traders publishes an estimate of the average earnings, on a sample basis, of all skilled and unskilled men in the motor manufacturing industry, and an index of average (money) earnings. With the aid of the cost-of-living index number, an index of average real earnings can be constructed. The results are as follows—

	Per week s. d.	Index of Av. Money Earnings 1924 = 100	Index of Av. Real Earnings
1914 .	40 10½	54·6	95·5
1924 .	74 10	100	100
1925 .	74 6½	99·6	99·1
1926 .	76 3½	101·9	103·3
1927 .	80 3	107·2	111·9
1928 .	77 3½	103·3	109·1
1929, March[1]	81 6	108·9	116·2
October	79 9	106·6	113 8
1930, March	77 5½	103·5	114·6
October	72 7½	97·0	107·4
1931, March	72 4¾	96·7	114·7
October	68 11	92·1	109·3
1932, March	74 4½	99·5	120·9
October	73 7½	98·5	120·0
1933, October	77 6	103·6	129·5
1934, October	79 4¾	106·1	131·6
1935, October	80 7¾	107·8	129·6

[1] The figures from 1929 to 1935 are for two of the busiest months of the year, and are, therefore, higher than the yearly average.

Comparison of the number of employed workers with the total output of motor vehicles shows that the productivity per head of workers engaged in the industry has nearly doubled between 1924 and 1935. This is a purely quantitative compari-

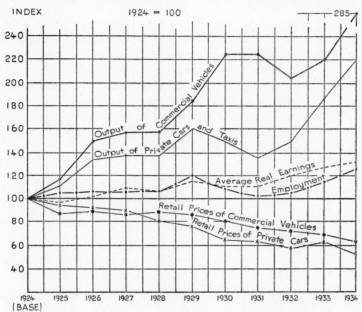

FIG. 3. MANUFACTURE OF BRITISH MOTOR VEHICLES
INDEX NOS. OF OUTPUT, EMPLOYMENT, AVERAGE REAL EARNINGS, AND RETAIL VEHICLE PRICES

son, and takes no account of the probable improvement in the quality of the work done.

A great deal of body-building for cars, motor coaches, omnibuses, and aeroplanes is carried on in Greater London. Wages in this trade are regulated by national agreements between the National Federation of Vehicular Trades and the National Union of Vehicle Builders. The rates are—

Leading hands (men)	.	.	.	.	1s. 7½d. per hour	
Skilled workers	.	.	.	.	1s. 6½d.	,, ,,
Labourers	.	.	.	.	1s. 0½d.	,, ,,

Leading London firms engaged upon special, high-class work, often pay an extra 2d. or 3d. per hour to good workers. Moreover, agreements containing "fair wages" clauses usually govern work done for such bodies as the London County Council and the London Passenger Transport Board. Coach trimmers upholster the vehicle bodies after they have been mounted, complete with doors and windows, upon the chassis. The normal week is 47 hours and the minimum journeyman's rate of wages is 1s. 6½d. per hour, but highly skilled men earn more. Women and girls are being increasingly employed for stitching and stuffing the upholstery.

Apart from occasional cases of dermatitis and lead poisoning in the cellulose painting departments, there appears to be little occupational disease in the motor industry.

III

At the outset the British motor industry was located in the Midlands where, within the first quarter of the twentieth century, the rise of the electrical and motor industries worked a great transformation in the metal trades of Birmingham, Coventry, Wolverhampton, and the surrounding district. "The leading concerns working on Continental patents were all, in 1897, to be found in Coventry . . . on various floors of an old cotton mill."[1] To-day the manufacture of motor cars, parts, accessories and tyres is mainly localized in (a) Birmingham, Coventry, Wolverhampton, and the surrounding district; (b) Greater London; (c) Lancashire and adjacent parts of Cheshire and Derbyshire; (d) Oxford; (e) Luton. The relative importance of Coventry, Birmingham and district in the manufacture of cars is less than it was five or six years ago, but if the making of parts, accessories and tyres is included, it is still easily the leading area for motor manufacture. Of ten new factories set up in the motor industry in 1933, two produce motor bodies, two gears and gear cases, and the rest

[1] Allen, *Industrial Development of Birmingham and the Black Country* (1929), 297.

accessories, side-cars, etc. Nearly all are located either in the Coventry–Birmingham area or in the North-west of Greater London.[1]

The *New Survey of London Life and Labour* outlines the place of London in the industry as follows—

Manufacture of cars is primarily concentrated in the Midlands, but there are several well-known firms within the Greater London area, and others specialize in some particular part or accessory: pistons, gears, windscreens, and radiators being examples. Another associated trade, motor sheet metal work and body building, is carried out by a number of London firms. Garages are like the sand by the seashore in multitude, and vary from roadside stations to large service depots. The making of aeroplanes is confined to one firm in the London area itself, but other firms are engaged in it close to London.[2]

Like the electrical equipment industry, the motor industry does not depend upon supplies of raw materials produced locally. It requires thousands of different products, drawn from a great number of sources. Nearness to a large pool of labour capable of semi-skilled work is a more important consideration. A survey of the geographical distribution of the motor industry in Great Britain, gauged by the numbers employed, shows the Midlands as easily the most important region. Greater London is approximately half as important

---

[1] Board of Trade, *Survey of Industrial Development*, 1933, 12. Dr. K. G. Fenelon has calculated the following percentages, which show the extent of localization in different areas and such relative changes as have taken place between 1923 and 1932.

Area	Percentage of Insured Persons engaged in Construction and Repair of Motor Vehicles, Cycles and Aircraft	
	July, 1923	*July*, 1932
Midlands	44·2	40·1
London	16·7	17·4
Rest of South-east England . . .	11·1	11·6
North-west England . . .	8·9	8·1
South-west ,, . . .	8·0	11·2
North-east ,, . . .	5·3	6·0
Scotland	4·8	4·6
Wales	1·0	1·0
	100·0	100·0

From *Journal of the Royal Statistical Society*, Part II, 1935, 322.

[2] *Vol. II* (1931), 127–8; cf. D. H. Smith, *The Industries of Greater London* (1933).

as the Midlands; North-west England is about half as important as Greater London; and Scotland about half as important as North-west England. Moreover, judged by the same method, the expansion in the southern section of England has been greater than in the northern section.

For basic materials, and for components and accessories, the motor manufacturers depend mainly upon many other industries to which they are welcome customers. The principal raw materials used are cast and malleable iron; forged, bar and sheet steel, and steel alloys; non-ferrous metals (aluminium, copper, brass, lead and lead oxide, tin, zinc alloys and bronze), leather, leather cloths, horsehair, carpet, felt, rubber, wood, paints and glass.[1] The motor industry's consumption of these materials is important and increasing. For instance, it takes nearly one-half of the plate glass produced in this country, and its demand for rubber, mainly in the form of tyres, amounts to nearly two-thirds of the total British consumption.

The motor industry (says Lord Aberconway) is a valuable adjunct to the producers of the finest quality of Sheffield steel. . . . High as the cost may be of these special steels, the extra expense is nothing compared with the losses which may ensue from the breakdown of an engine, an axle, a spring, the steering mechanism or the gear. And to the purchaser of a car its durability, apart from the risk of sudden collapse, counts for much. The value of these steels is demonstrated when the mileage covered over a course of years by a good car is taken into account.[2]

The imposition of the British duties on imported steel, and the inclusion of the British steel makers in the International Steel Cartel, was soon followed (1935) by complaints from the leading motor manufacturers of increases of prices and delay in deliveries of British steel. Austin's, indeed, went so far as to form a new company, Tunstall Steel Ltd., to produce special steels for the Austin works.

[1] The quantities, qualities and proportions of materials used vary with the fashions and designs of different vehicles, and with the increase of competition between the manufacturers.
[2] *The Basic Industries of Great Britain* (1927), 341.

Some motor manufacturers specialize on private cars, and some on commercial vehicles; but others[1] produce a considerable range of models, both private and commercial. Indeed, certain makers, who have come into motor car manufacture *via* the production of pedal cycles and motor cycles,[2] still carry on all three activities simultaneously. But these cases are not common and they are gradually becoming fewer. The predominance of the large mass-manufacturer of cars is now a salient feature of the industry. In 1928 five firms produced 87 per cent of the output of private cars; and, indeed, three-quarters of the total output was produced by three firms only. The small remainder was produced by between 30 and 40 relatively small units. It is important, however, to notice that although the number of cars built by some of these firms is small, the quality and value per unit is high. In other words, in the motor industry, as in many others, there is a place for the smaller unit because of the relatively small, but by no means negligible, demand for goods of a "sports" or "special" type; something different from the main run of standardized products, excellent as these may be in their class.[3] Rileys of Coventry owe their success in recent years largely to the production of a limited range of private cars of high grade but low h.p. The Birmingham Small Arms Co. "whose interests go well outside the motor industry, has successfully tapped a profitable section of the market . . . by bringing a number of hitherto expensive cars into the medium-priced and powered class." Rolls Royce Ltd., the famous makers of high-priced, high-powered, luxury cars and aero-engines, are among the steadiest profit makers in the British motor industry.

[1] E.g. Vauxhall Motors, Ford and Morris produce between them about 70 per cent of the goods vehicles not exceeding $2\frac{1}{2}$ tons unladen weight.

[2] Among the pioneers who passed from cycles to motors one may mention the Sunbeam Company, Singer & Co. Ltd., The Rover Company, and Morris Motors Ltd. The first Wolseley car was made in 1897–8 in the Birmingham Works of the Wolseley Sheep-shearing Machine Co. Ltd. ! *The Book of British Industries* (1933), 251.

[3] The greatly improved performance of ordinary models is now tending to reduce, relatively, the demand for sports cars. Several firms are, therefore, making models which rank between the "popular" and the "luxury" cars.

Some of the smaller companies are actually owned and controlled by the larger ones; and in this category we must include the "branch" plants set up in this country by foreign manufacturers in order to avoid the heavy import duty, e.g. Fords, Vauxhall Motors, and Citroën. Others are really independent, but their number continues to dwindle, chiefly because, sooner or later, they fall under the financial sway of the big companies. Thus, to cite but one instance, the Balfour Committee found that S.T.D. Motors Ltd. owned the share capital of the Sunbeam Motor Co. Ltd., W. and G. Du Cros Ltd., Clement Talbot Ltd., Darracq Motor Engineering Co. Ltd., Heenan & Froude Ltd., and Jones Woodhead & Sons Ltd.; and nearly the whole of the share capital of the Darracq Proprietary Co. Ltd., and a French concern—Automobiles Talbot Soc. Anon.[1] To-day S.T.D. Motors Ltd. is under the control of Rootes Ltd., a holding company which also controls Humber Ltd., the Hillman Motor Car Co., and Commer Cars Ltd.

In addition to the marked tendency towards the elimination of the smaller units, the large concerns continue to acquire "interests" in units which produce the various accessories they need.[2] Thus the typical motor manufacturer does not actually make the whole vehicle from beginning to end; his principal function is the assembly of parts,[3] many of which are made to his own designs and specifications by specialist manufacturers of accessories and components. The strength of the motive to ensure the accuracy and quality of these parts, to say nothing of the desire to reduce costs (e.g. by cutting out the independent suppliers' profits) by gaining control of the units which produce them, is easy to understand. Some of the larger mass-producers have found it economical to manufacture certain parts themselves as an alternative method of getting control over supplies; but they still rely upon specialists for most of their materials, such as pressed-steel bodies, wheels,

---

[1] *Survey of Metal Industries*, 220. The issued capital of S.T.D. Motors Ltd., exceeds £1,000,000.

[2] A similar development has taken place in the United States.

[3] A motor car consists of about 7000 components and it is estimated that its production involves over 100,000 operations.

tyres, lighting sets, castings, and so forth.[1] A great many of
these parts are standardized; but in the motor industry a high
degree of standardization at this stage is "not necessarily in-
consistent with considerable variety in the finished product."
Production of motor cars can be carried to an advanced stage
on a uniform plan, and yet sufficient variation can be introduced in the later stages to make it possible to offer a "range"
of models to the public. Differentiation can take place,
although the majority of the components remain the same.
For example, a variety of bodies, both private and commercial,
can usually be fitted to the same chassis and engine.[2] Some
manufacturers have carried the multiplication of models much
further than others, and it may well be that they are nearing
a point beyond which, as mass-producers, it will be clearly
uneconomical to go. Some, indeed, may have reached this
point already.

This tendency to multiply models is partly due to the
extreme difficulty of estimating the extent of public preference
for any particular make and type of car, the idea being to offer
a range of models in the hope that a least one or two will
"catch on." The multiplication of models is also partly the
result of keen competition between the leading manufacturers.
If one of these brings out a new "Ten-Six" or "Twelve-Six"
model, or something rather special or unusual in vans or trucks,
the others feel that unless they produce something similar
their sales may suffer a setback.

The number of models in production of the ten largest manufacturing groups, controlling over 90 per cent of the market,
increased from 46 in 1929–30 to 55 in 1931–2, 60 in 1932–3, and
64 in 1933–4. The old game continues—everybody endeavouring
to catch the public's fancy with at least one of their range of

[1] Morris Motors Ltd. has its assembly plant at Cowley on the edge
of Oxford, its radiator works in Oxford, and its engines and foundry
branches in Coventry. Also this company owns the M.G. Car Co. which
makes sports cars at Abingdon, and the Wolseley Motor Co. which
makes "Wolseley" cars at Birmingham and performs certain machining
operations for the parent company.

[2] E.g., Morris Motors Ltd., in 1933, was assembling eight types of
car in some thirty different body styles—*The Book of British Industries*,
253.

models and thereby to reap the reward of large sales and high profits. This dissipation of energy undoubtedly makes the motor car dearer than it need be if the speculative element in sales were reduced ; but, so long as popular taste is so fickle, and the industry is so slow in moving towards horizontal integration, it is difficult to see any alternative. The marked trend of demand from the large to the small vehicle renders any scheme for the division of the market by certain firms specializing entirely on large cars, others on medium-sized cars, and others on small cars, particularly difficult ; and in fact the manufacturers of the larger cars, such as Lanchester, Crossley and Vauxhall, have all invaded the small or light-medium markets.[1]

Professor Sargant Florence suggests that the motor industry needs a further dose of rationalization, and that this might be accomplished without depriving buyers of the pleasure and profit of being able to choose from a large range of models.

Of course (he says) motorists want a variety of models to choose from, but why should not the industry be so arranged that each factory specializes in one or a few models instead of duplicating the models of other works ? There would still be plenty of variety in the aggregate output of the whole industry as displayed on the market, and at the same time each works could produce its particular model or models on a large scale. This is what happened in America. Mr. Ford not only makes Fords, he also makes the more luxurious Lincoln cars and the humble tractor; but he makes them in different works, leaving his original plant at Highland Park, Detroit, to concentrate on Fords. Similarly the huge combination of factories known as General Motors makes a wide variety of models but generally speaking each is made at a separate plant and receives the full time, attention and thought of specialists. General Motors as a whole can offer the consumer all the variety of choice he requires while at the same time the individual plants combined with General Motors can concentrate each on one or a few models. Specialization and standardization in production; combination in marketing is here the watchword.[2]

IV

The market for motor cars is, as we have noticed, a highly competitive one. There is competition not only in price, but

---

[1] *The Economist*, 21st October, 1933.
[2] *Logic of Industrial Organization* (1933), 88–9.

in appearance, reliability, speed, and economy of running. Since a motor vehicle is a durable article, which can, at a pinch, be made "to last a little longer" if its owner is unwilling to buy a new one immediately, the motor manufacturer is seriously affected by fluctuations in general business prosperity, while, at the same time, fashion may bestow popularity or the reverse upon his products out of all proportion to their real merits.

The demand for motor cars is a function not only of the prices of the vehicles, but also of the prices of petrol and oil, the cost of motor licences and insurance, and garage rents. In spite of recent increases in the price of petrol and the tax upon it, demand for both private and commercial vehicles has hitherto proved highly elastic. "Expansion-demand" has easily exceeded replacement-demand, a fact mainly attributable to steady reductions of prices. Thus the average factory values of private cars in Great Britain fell from £308 in 1912 to £259 in 1924, £206 in 1930, £156 in 1932, and approximately £130 in 1935-6. At the same time, the British motor manufacturers have constantly striven to increase efficiency, reliability, comfort, equipment, and the general all-round quality of their products, and to reduce the running costs to the owner. They have achieved a great measure of success; and owing to this and various other reasons mentioned below, the British motor industry weathered the catastrophic slump of 1930–2 better than most other industries. But future expansion in the home market may be slower, for although saturation point is not yet reached, new motorists and commercial users will gradually become harder to find or "create." It is doubtful whether prices can be brought much lower.

Owing to the reductions in prices[1] and the increased preference of buyers for smaller cars, the total *value* of cars sold has not expanded to the same degree as the total *numbers*. Some 60 per cent of the new registrations of private cars in the 1932–3

---

[1] The price index for new private cars fell from 100 in 1924, to 59·6 in 1932. In 1933 it rose slightly to 61·4; but it was down to 51·8 in 1934 and 49·8 in 1935.

season were of 10 h.p. or below, compared with about 50 per cent in 1931–2[1] This sudden increase in the popularity of low-powered cars is chiefly due to the introduction of 10 h.p. models by all the leading makers—Austin, Morris, Standard, Rover, Hillman, Lanchester—together with the advent of the new Ford 8 h.p. model. In 1935, 42 per cent of all private cars in use in Great Britain were 10 h.p. or less; and over 60 per cent of the new cars sold were in this class.[2]

Although the prices of commercial vehicles have not fallen, on the whole, so much as those of private cars, the volume of production and sales has been satisfactory considering the severity of the world slump. This applies especially to light vans and goods vehicles of medium-size.

As second-hand cars increase in numbers, their average price will fall and this will tend to slow down the rate of expansion of the demand for new cars. Therefore it is with sound judgment that British motor manufacturers, while still studying and holding the home market, are turning their faces more towards overseas markets where the potential expansion-demand for cars is still enormous.

It is common knowledge that in Great Britain under our dual system of motor taxation, the incidence of the petrol tax is distributed roughly in proportion to the use made of the roads by motorists of all categories. The "horse-power" tax, however, seems *prima facie* to bear somewhat unfairly upon the occasional or pleasure-purposes motorists as compared with the constant commercial users. But this may, perhaps, be justified upon the ground that pleasure or luxury motoring ought to be taxed more highly than business motoring. A more important question is the indirect effects of the horse-power taxes upon the design of British cars and their saleability in export markets where motor taxation is levied on a different basis. One has often heard the complaint that in countries where roads are rough and gradients steep, the majority of British cars, excellent in other respects, are not powerful

---

[1] The corresponding percentage for January–November, 1934, was 57.
[2] *The Economist*, 20th April, 1935, 895.

enough for the work. This is undoubtedly true for some important markets, but it must be remembered that wherever roads are being improved, the more economical British vehicles are certain to prove increasingly attractive to buyers so long as they can be offered at competitive prices, with the prospect of a reasonably efficient after-sales service. But "there's the rub." The motor car manufacturers of the United States were first in the export field and they made the most of their opportunity, so that to-day they are well "dug in" and have an unrivalled and world-wide sales and service organization. There is, moreover, another important respect in which British motor manufacturers stand at a disadvantage in competition with the Americans. Road conditions in the United States are broadly similar to those in regions such as the British Dominions, colonies and protectorates, South America and China. American manufacturers catering for a huge home market can put into production a vast number of cars, knowing that any surplus will be suitable for many important overseas markets. But British manufacturers cannot do this. For many of the overseas markets they must make special models, and the relatively small scale on which these must be produced keeps unit costs of production and selling prices well above the corresponding American costs and prices.

The expansion of British exports of motor vehicles in 1932–3 was due to a fortunate combination of favourable factors, such as the cheapening of British cars in terms of foreign currencies after Great Britain went off the gold standard in 1931 ; and the increased taxation of motor users in other countries since 1930, which has turned attention towards the economical low-powered British cars. The increase in aggregate value and volume of British motor car exports since 1929–30 has been remarkable largely because down to 1933 it coincided with a marked decline in motor exports in the world as a whole. The latter fell from 761,441 vehicles in 1929 to 215,957 in 1931 and 153,224 in 1932 ; the chief losses being sustained by the U.S.A., Canada and Italy. The ratio of U.S. motor exports to British motor exports fell from 13 : 1 in 1929 to little more than 3 : 2 in 1932. But this remarkable eclipse of the American exporters was not permanent; for the devaluation of the dollar, coupled with reviving demand in the United States, has done much to restore their competitive power in overseas markets. Indeed it appears that the recovery of American output and exports is already well advanced. The output of cars in the United States in 1929 was 5,358,000. By 1932 it had fallen to 1,371,000; but in the following year it recovered to 1,959,000[1] and in 1935 it nearly touched 4,000,000 of which 273,000 were exported. The ratio of American to British exports was 3 : 1 in the first half of 1933, 6 : 1 in the first half of 1934,[2] and 4 : 1 in 1935. British exports of commercial vehicles in 1934 continued to show a rather remarkable increase[3]; but there was a distinct slackening of the rate of progress of British exports of private cars. Nevertheless, both volume and value continued to increase. The total value of British motor exports, including parts and accessories, was £11,305,497 in 1934 against £9,373,826 in 1933; but this represented a diminished share of the total world exports, which more than doubled during 1934, the lion's share going to the Americans. The British industry lost heavily in Continental markets (particularly Holland), while even in the British Empire and especially in South Africa and India, the share falling to the British exporters was not maintained. In 1933 foreign markets absorbed 34 per cent of British motor exports and the Empire 66 per cent, while in 1934 the foreign proportion had fallen to 23½ per cent. Taking one year with another, between two-thirds and four-fifths (in value) of British exports of motor vehicles go to countries within the British Empire, where British exporters

---

[1] *Manchester Guardian Commercial*, 7th December, 1934.

[2] *The Economist*, 20th October, 1934, 719; 14th December, 1935, 1195.

[3] The *number* of British commercial vehicles and chassis exported in 1933 was actually very much greater than in the pre-depression years 1928 and 1929, but the total *value* was a good deal less. The average value of all exported motor vehicles fell from £200·8 in 1929 to £130·4 in 1933. In 1936 British motor exports totalled 81,713 units, and the value of all motor vehicles and parts was nearly £17,000,000.

receive tariff preferences. The chief markets for British cars outside the Empire are Belgium, Spain, Sweden, Holland, Norway, Egypt, China, and the Dutch East Indies.

AMERICAN AND BRITISH PRIVATE CAR EXPORTS[1]
(Including chassis)

Year	American Exports	British Exports	British as Percentage of American
1929	340,443	33,792	9·9
1930	153,088	23,210	15·2
1931	82,457	18,992	23·0
1932	41,441	31,805	76.7
1933	64,511	40,956	63·5
1934	145,159	43,937	30·3

During the last five years the competition of imported foreign cars has shrunk to very small proportions in the British market. Net or "Retained" imports (i.e. gross imports, less re-exports) of motor vehicles and chassis into the United Kingdom rose to a peak in 1925 (47,667, valued at £8,158,685), immediately before the re-imposition of the duties, but they have since declined tremendously, especially after 1929. The number for 1933 was only 3,962. In 1934 the retained imports of all kinds of cars into Great Britain rose to 11,087 vehicles, over 60 per cent of which came from the United States, 27 per cent from Canada, and 10 per cent from France. The retained imports in 1935 totalled 15,540, which is still only about 40 per cent of the 1929 imports. On the other hand, it must be noticed that the successful establishment of large factories in this country by companies of foreign origin (e.g. Ford, Vauxhall, and Citroën) has intensified competition from within.

The bulk of the output of the British motor industry is marketed in Great Britain through so-called "agents" or "distributors" and "sub-agents" who are in fact the retailers of the goods within specified areas. If the sub-agents are appointed only by the agents, the "territory" is "closed." If not, the agency is an "open" one. The majority of the agents

[1] Taken from *The Economist*, 20th April, 1935.

represent more than one manufacturer, so that the tendency is for each manufacturer to treat his agents generously in the hope that they will "push" the sales of his particular cars. There are upwards of 20,000 motor car retailers up and down the country, many of whom combine their business in new and/or second-hand cars with the repair of cars and the retailing of spares and accessories. Indeed, the manufacturers prefer to appoint as agents those firms who can render "service" to the buyer after the car is sold.[1] It is quite possible, however, for members of the public to buy direct from the manufacturers, and in the case of commercial vehicles this is very frequently done; but there is no financial advantage to the buyer. The manufacturers fix the wholesale and the retail prices of their cars, and the retail prices are the same whether the purchase is made direct or from a retailer. The "trading in" of old cars, however, is a method whereby retailers can, in effect, reduce somewhat the official list-price of a car by making a large allowance for the buyer's old car. Recently efforts have been made to tighten up the relationship between the manufacturers and their retail outlets, with the object of preventing retailers with limited facilities and low overheads from undercutting the larger firms. In 1934 a scheme was introduced under which the Society of Motor Manufacturers and Traders, to which most of the large car distributors belong, published a list of approved dealers, and all the manufacturers and concessionnaires who supported the scheme undertook not to sell vehicles at trade prices to anyone not named in the list. At the same time retailers were divided into two main classes: (a) stockist dealers who had facilities for displaying cars and contracted to keep at least one in stock, and (b) "casual" traders, equipped to carry out servicing, but not contracting to stock vehicles. The profit margin of these casual traders is now limited to 10 per cent of the price of the vehicle. The

[1] A post-sales service must also be maintained by the manufacturers, and large stocks of spares must be kept for both present and past models. This department is usually expensive, but it is essential, since people will hesitate to buy a car if doubt exists as to the possibility of obtaining future supplies of spare parts.

stockists' commissions are a good deal larger, and the appointed agents probably receive an extra commission and a "quantity discount" as well.

The manufacturers arrange and pay for the bulk of the advertising, usually in the newspapers and popular periodicals, and in the form of pamphlets, illustrated catalogues, posters, and showcards. Also under this head fall the expenses of the annual Motor Show at Olympia, which has become the leading motor fair in Europe. The leading retailers of second-hand cars hold an annual "Used Car Show" at the Agricultural Hall, London.

Cars for export are marketed either through special agents or through subsidiary companies owned by the motor manufacturers. The most satisfactory method for those aiming at any considerable volume of exports seems to be the establishment of a subsidiary marketing company, with power to set up overseas branches and to appoint and control agents in other countries, each branch or agent having a territorial monopoly and working on a commission basis. Such branch offices normally operate a depot carrying a stock of vehicles and parts, and a service station to undertake repairs. "On the whole, it has been found unsatisfactory for an exporter to rely solely on an agent appointed for a foreign market with no branch office to control him. Many of the smaller manufacturers, however, have been compelled to adopt this practice by reason of the limited scale of their operations, and the larger concerns apply it in the less important markets."[1] Hitherto the British manufacturers of cars have been mainly interested in the rapid expansion of the home market, but the time may not be far off when the further development of the industry will depend largely upon adequate facilities for selling British cars abroad.

Since a motor vehicle is a relatively costly and durable article, having a tolerably predictable length of "life"[2] and

[1] *The Economist*, 14th December, 1935, 1195.
[2] Estimated at 7·9 years on the average for private cars, and 8·5 years for goods vehicles. See *The Motor Industry of Great Britain*, 1935.

capable of being identified, the adoption of the instalment purchase system is not surprising. Its spread throughout the trade has, indeed, been described as inevitable. "In some cases the financial arrangements are made by the manufacturers, and in others by retailers. At least one large manufacturing concern has its own financial corporation dealing with time payments; in other cases the risk is undertaken by insurance companies."[1]

V

The profits and dividends of the leading motor car manufacturers vary a great deal from one company to another and from year to year, especially among those manufacturers who concentrate mainly or wholly upon private cars. The fluctuations among the commercial vehicle manufacturers are, on the whole, not so great, for this section of the industry is less subject to the vagaries of fashion and public prejudice, so that the great majority of alterations or innovations are real improvements, not freaks of design introduced in the hope of catching the popular fancy for a season. Thus, the growing popularity of the Diesel lorry and other heavy oil-engined compression-ignition vehicles is based upon substantial economies in operation. Other recent changes in commercial vehicle design have been largely the result of changes in taxation.

The existence of certain combinations of motor manufacturing companies under unified financial control has been noticed above, and it is at least possible that at no very distant date further combinations between other leading companies may be the outcome of intensified competition and wide fluctuations of profits and losses. For when internal organization and technique have been brought near to perfection, and when costs, prices and profits have been reduced in the cut and thrust of competition, the "atmosphere" is favourable to the formation of combines.

[1] Committee on Industry and Trade, *Survey of Metal Industries*, 224. The committee added that "it is significant that by the beginning of 1926 about half the business in new cars was on the deferred or time payment system."

VI

The manufacture of motor cycles is a comparatively new industry of British creation which has grown out of the older pedal bicycle industry. Between 1900 and 1910 it was in its infancy, but it expanded rapidly afterwards. Like the motor car industry it quickly emerged from its post-war difficulties and built up an increasing trade in both home and export markets. Its output increased from 3700 units in 1907 to 120,400 in 1924, and British exports of motor cycles increased from 16,850 units in 1913 to 37,607 in 1924 and 52,805 in 1927.[1] The British makers had the bulk of the world's export trade in motor cycles in their hands, and in the period 1927–9 they exported nearly 40 per cent of their output.

Some of the motor cycle manufacturing concerns are large public companies, but the majority are private limited companies or partnerships. Competition between them is still very active, and there is a much slighter tendency towards amalgamations than is apparent in the motor car industry. Nearly all motor cycle manufacturers make a large proportion of their components in their own factories and it is not considered sound policy to try to go as far in the direction of mass production as the large motor vehicle makers have gone.

In the home market the manufacturers supply motor cycles and motor cycle parts direct to the retailers. The prices are commonly fixed by the manufacturers, the retailers receiving a fixed gross discount ; and the instalment purchase system is in vogue. A good deal of overseas marketing has been done in the past through British merchant houses, but many manufacturers are now seeking direct access to overseas buyers through their own agencies or representatives abroad.

The home demand for motor cycles is a seasonal one, but fortunately the peak demand from export markets comes during the slack season in the home market, and manufacturers

[1] Allen, *Industrial Development of Birmingham and the Black Country*, 401–3.

are thus enabled to maintain tolerable continuity of production although some seasonal unemployment and short-time seem to be unavoidable.

On the whole, the efficiency, quality, output, and home and export sales of British motor cycles increased steadily for ten years after the war; but more recently development has received a check in certain directions. Output declined from 149,000 units in 1929 to about 64,000 in 1935, and exports shrank from 63,776 units (or 43 per cent of total output) in 1929 down to 19,520 units in 1932, 17,100 in 1933, and 16,000 in 1934. In 1936 exports rose to 20,000 units, or about 27 per cent of total output. The total values of exports of motor cycles have also been falling, the figure for 1933 being £670,416, and for 1934 approximately £649,000. The average declared value of each British motor cycle exported was £42 in 1929, and nearly £40 in 1935: yet the British makers managed to secure a larger share of the greatly diminished world export trade. In 1929 they provided 58 per cent of the total of 107,000 motor cycle units exported, and in 1934 their share was 66 per cent of world exports which totalled only 25,000 units. In the same period the number of motor cycles in use in this country at the peak season (August) fell from 735,000 in 1929 to 541,000 in 1933, and to 521,000 in 1935. The fact that under the Road Traffic Act, 1930, the age limit for driving licences was raised from 14 to 16 years, and that third party motor insurance was made compulsory may account for some of this shrinkage; but doubtless a good deal of it is the counterpart of the expansion in the sales of small motor cars new and second-hand. In the August quarter of 1925 the number of motor cars exceeded for the first time the number of motor cycles, and by August 1933 the number of cars was more than double the number of motor cycles.[1] In continental countries, the expansion in the use of motor cycles continues, but British makers do not seem able to secure so large a share of this business as hitherto. Exports of motor cycle engines from Britain to Germany and France have

[1] K. G. Fenelon in *Statistical Journal*, Part II, 1935, 306.

almost disappeared in recent years, while demand from Australia and New Zealand has declined heavily.[1]

VII

There are between twenty and thirty British companies engaged in the manufacture of aircraft and aero-engines.[2] Some of these manufacture the aircraft (or "airframes") and air-screws only; others specialize upon aero-engines; while a few (e.g. the De Havilland Aircraft Co. Ltd.) manufacture both. A small number specialize still further and make airscrews only.

Before 1914 this section of British industry scarcely existed; but by the end of 1918, under pressure of war needs, a great transformation had been wrought. After the war, however, depression settled upon the aircraft manufacturers, who were left with war-time production capacities but an almost negligible demand for their products. But in a few years this phase had passed. Once the superiority of the aeroplane over the airship for the general purposes of air transport was finally accepted, a modest demand began to take shape, and by 1933 aircraft and aero-engine manufacture was giving employment to about 30,000 people.[3] When the last Census of Production was taken in 1930 the value of the output was £8,406,000, against £4,677,000 in 1924.[4] An estimate based upon data extracted from the *Stock Exchange Year Book*, 1935, gives the total capital invested at about £13,000,000, mostly in companies of moderate size; but the figures have doubtless increased a good deal since the beginning of the recent great expansion in air armaments.[5]

[1] Allen, *British Industries and Their Organisation* (2nd Edn., 1935), 184c.

[2] Air Ministry, *Report on the Progress of Civil Aviation*, 1934; cf. *Who's Who in British Aviation.*

[3] H. J. Schonfield (ed.), *The Book of British Industries* (1933), 36.

[4] Excluding airships, balloons, parachutes and parts thereof. *Fourth Census of Production*, 1930. Pt. II, 361.

[5] Mr. Francis Williams asserts that of the total of £7,611,000 of new capital raised from the public for the aircraft industry between March and August, 1935, practically 70 per cent "has gone directly in profits to promoters and Stock Exchange firms." *The Sky's the Limit!* (Labour Publications Dept. pamphlet, 1935).

The financial structure of the aircraft industry shows not only expansion, but a certain tendency towards concentration of control, although as yet it is only at an early stage. Thus the Hawker Siddeley Aircraft Company controls Armstrong Siddeley Motors, Sir W. G. Armstrong Whitworth Aircraft and A. V. Roe and Company, Hawker Aircraft and its subsidiary the Gloster Aircraft Company, Air Service and Aircraft Technical Services, and several small motor car companies. Vickers Ltd. has at least two subsidiary companies in the aircraft industry.

The engine section is, of course, extremely important, and quite a number of British aero-engines are world-famous.

Armstrong Siddeley Motors Ltd. manufacture a range of air-cooled radial engines, having from 5 to 14 cylinders. The Bristol Aeroplane Co. Ltd. produce air-cooled engines which are largely used in the Imperial Airways fleet. Arrangements have been made for the manufacture of Bristol engines under licence in no fewer than sixteen countries outside Great Britain. The De Havilland company makes both aircraft and engines, but the two departments are kept quite separate. De Havilland "Gipsy" engines enjoy a high reputation, and are fitted not only in D.H. aeroplanes, but in various other makes as well. D. Napier & Son Ltd. produce some of the world's finest petrol aero-engines for all purposes, and this company has now acquired from the German manufacturers a licence to manufacture in Great Britain a new Junkers compression-ignition oil engine of unique and successful design. Among the advantages of engines of this type are their great economy, freedom from fire-risk, and mechanical simplicity. Pobjoy Airmotors Ltd. produce a radial engine which is light and extremely compact, and therefore offers to the air transport operator the advantage of higher pay load, because of reduced gross weight and wind resistance or "drag." The engines produced by Rolls-Royce Ltd. are liquid-cooled, and it is urged in their favour that they give high thermal efficiency, low fuel consumption, low drag, and comparatively little noise.

The earnings of all these companies are, of course, drawn

from the repair of aircraft and the supply of parts, as well as from the manufacture of new aircraft and aero-engines.

The supply of accessories, especially instruments for air navigation, is a small but very important section of the industry. S. Smith & Sons (Motor Accessories) Ltd. are said to be the largest manufacturers of aircraft accessories in Europe. They also specialize in the manufacture of clocks, gauges, and other instruments for motor cars. The company owns the entire capital of K.L.G. Sparking Plugs Ltd., and Smith's English Clocks Ltd.; and it has controlling interests in British Jaeger Instruments Ltd., and A.B.E.C. Ltd.

All the raw materials used—alloy and stainless steels in sheets, strips, bars, tubes, and wires—non-ferrous metal alloys,[1] and all the components and accessories, such as wheels, tyres, electrical and wireless equipment, flying instruments, etc., must be very high grade products. Plenty of space is essential in an aircraft factory, for it is necessary to have large-span factory buildings and flying sheds. The use, if not the actual ownership of an aerodrome is also necessary. Relatively large, highly skilled designing and testing staffs must be kept, and a labour force of the best craftsmen obtainable; for the production of aircraft imperatively demands close and expert attention to every detail of every machine.

The workers engaged in this industry are organized by the following trade unions; the Amalgamated Engineering Union, the National Society of Coppersmiths, the United Pattern-makers' Association, and the unions of Vehicle Builders, Boilermakers, Woodworkers, Foundry Workers, Woodcutting Machinists, Brass and Metal Mechanics, Plumbers, and Ship Constructors and Shipwrights. Many of the draughtsmen are members of the Association of Engineering and Shipbuilding Draughtsmen, but those in Government Establishments join the Association of Civil Service Designers and Draughtsmen. A National Council for Aircraft Workers, with local committees in aircraft production areas, has been formed.

[1] Metals, such as thin corrugated high tensile steel strips, have largely displaced wood, even in the construction of seaplanes.

The industry gets its skilled labour chiefly from two sources. Firstly, it draws from the engineering and allied industries some of the best craftsmen, who are attracted by the high quality of the work to be done and the prospects of steady employment; and secondly, it is employing, in increasing numbers, ex-Air Force mechanics, who are particularly valuable by reason of their specialized training and experience.

Progress in the immediate past and the prospects of the near future are well summed up in *The Times Annual Financial and Commercial Review*, 1935—

Taken together, the joint demands from civil and military markets have led to remarkable activity. During the last year over fifty new types of aircraft were produced. How comparatively small is the market for really big types may be seen from the fact that less than one-fifth of these could be described as air liners. The remainder were almost equally divided between the smaller class of aeroplane and military types. The year also produced a promising crop of new engines from the small Pobjoy of about 85 h.p. and the General Aircraft four-cylinder model of 100 h.p. to the 24 cylinder Dagger of the Napier Company, the same firm's adaptation of the Junkers heavy-oil engine, and the two types of sleeve-valve engine produced by the Bristol Company.

The high promise of the year was reflected in the steps taken by aircraft companies to prepare themselves for bigger output. The Hawker Aircraft Company absorbed the Gloster Company and so acquired much additional manufacturing capacity. Airspeed, Limited, allied itself with the shipbuilding firm of Swan, Hunter and Wigham Richardson, and made a public issue to allow for expansion. The Bristol Company built new premises to enable its engine department to increase its output by 25 per cent. Fairey Aviation, Limited, bought new works at Manchester for future use. The De Havilland Company moved into fine new works at Hatfield. The aviation interests of Boulton and Paul were separated from the main engineering firm. General Aircraft, Limited, obtained extra capital and arranged to take bigger premises at Hanworth. The British Klemm Aeroplane Company[1] got fully into its stride.

The upward tendency in the British aircraft industry came with little warning and appears not yet to have been fully realized. It

[1] Since acquired (April, 1935) by the British Aircraft Manufacturing Co. Ltd. (*Financial News*, 10th April, 1935).

has brought with it advances and improvements which should help to encourage it, and there are good prospects of a period of prosperity in the constructing industry and of something approaching prosperity in the operating industry.

Although it is a fact that the average selling price of British aircraft and aero-engines has been considerably reduced during the past ten or twelve years,[1] lowness of price is a secondary consideration. Competition is mainly in excellence of product, and further development of this new branch of manufacture depends not so much upon further reductions of prices, as upon (a) expansion of military demand; (b) extension of regular commercial air services at home and abroad; and (c) increased safety in flight and ease of landing and take-off, which will result in an extension of private civil aviation. Moreover, increased demand in the future may be expected to come not only from the home market, but from export markets, where already British aircraft stand in high repute. The official statistics relating to exports show that the value of British exports of complete aeroplanes, engines, and spares rose from £1,146,000 in 1925 to a peak at £2,159,000 in 1929, and, after a decline to £1,466,000 in 1933, recovered to £1,921,000 in 1934, despite the lower level of prices. The average value of exports for the decade was £1,587,000 per annum.

[1] The average price fell by 35–40 per cent between 1924 and 1930. *Fourth Census of Production*, 1930, Part II, 361.

CHAPTER III

NEW MODES OF TRANSPORT

(i) ROAD MOTOR TRANSPORT

THE road "problem" in Britain at the present time arises almost entirely from the great and rapid increase in the number and variety of road vehicles since the Great War. This remarkable expansion, which may well be described as a second transport revolution, shows how sound was the judgment of the early inventors and *entrepreneurs* connected with mechanical road transport; but, great as their expectations were, it is hardly likely that any of them dreamed of development on so vast a scale, and in such a short time. Indeed, this new transport revolution has already gone so far and so fast that it has become necessary to introduce legislation to suppress and prevent certain serious anti-social consequences.

I

Before 1896 the law of England required that all road engines and similar vehicles should be driven or conducted by at least three persons, one of whom had to walk in front of the vehicle, the speed of which must not exceed four miles per hour. The Locomotives on Highways Act, 1896, permitted "light locomotives" of not more than three tons unladen weight to run on the roads, with or without a trailer, at speeds up to 12 m.p.h. provided that they did not emit "smoke or visible vapour." Within a few years the "light locomotive" or motor car became rather more common; and when the Motor Car Act of 1903 increased the speed limit to 20 m.p.h. road motor transport developed rapidly. Within eighteen months the number of registered motor vehicles rose from 51,549 to 86,638. At the same time motor omnibuses made their appearance and within five or six years they had become an important part of the passenger transport system of London.

In 1919–20 there were about 550,000 motor vehicles[1] in the United Kingdom. Between 1922 and 1930 their number increased from approximately 952,000 (including 378,000 motor cycles) to 2,218,000 (including nearly 700,000 motor-cycles). Goods vehicles numbered 151,000 in 1922 and 334,000 in 1930. At present there are approximately 453,500 goods vehicles in use in Great Britain and N. Ireland, and about 48,200 motor buses and coaches. Private motor cars now number some 1,560,000 and motor cycles 520,000; but not all of them are licensed throughout the year. In no other country in the world is the number of motor vehicles so great in relation to area.[2] It is estimated that the total capital in road motor transport undertakings has risen from £10 millions in 1916 to well over £70 millions at the present time (1935).[3] But in terms of capital goods (e.g. motor lorries and vans), and carrying capacity, the increase is much more than sevenfold. The capital cost of the commercial motor vehicle is now somewhat less than it was in 1914, even if we ignore the fall in the value of money, while efficiency, speed and reliability are to-day much greater.[4] Recent inquiries show that average loads carried, both of passengers and goods, are on the increase, and so is mileage per vehicle.[5] Lastly, we may notice that the aggregate consumption of motor spirit in this country has increased from 101 million gallons in the year 1913 to 1025 million gallons in 1931, and 1291 million gallons in 1935.

The use made of any new advance in industrial technique will, of course, depend upon the price charged, in relation to the efficiency of the commodity or service and the prices of

---

[1] i.e. private motor cars, goods vehicles, motor hackney vehicles and motor cycles.

[2] M. E. Dimock, *British Public Utilities and National Development* (1933), 107.

[3] Figures published by British Road Federation.

[4] A well-known make of 10-cwt. van cost £200 in 1916. In 1935 the same makers were selling a much improved 10-cwt. van for £160. Again, a 1-ton truck cost £180 in 1935: in 1916 the 1-ton *chassis alone* cost £200.

[5] See e.g. *Third Annual Report of the Area Traffic Commissioners* (1934), 4; *Road Traffic Censuses, 1931 and* 1936; *Statistical Abstract for London*; *Final Report of Royal Commission on Transport* (1931), 82.

any available alternatives. And the price charged, under conditions of substantially effective competition, will depend upon production or operating costs.

The costs of road motor transport depend mainly upon six factors—

1. The length of the haul.

2. The volume and regularity of traffic offering, including the extent to which return loads can be obtained.

3. The liability of the goods to damage or pilferage.

4. The nature of the commodity to be transported and the route to be taken.

5. The burden of taxation upon road transporters.

6. The efficiency and keenness of motor vehicle drivers.

1. Length of haul

Road transport is most economical for hauls of moderate length and loads of moderate size. Ideally, it is desirable that the outward and homeward journeys should be completed in one day in order to avoid the expense of accommodation for drivers overnight. Since Great Britain is a small, densely populated country, dotted with many towns, this condition of the haul of moderate length is very largely fulfilled. For long hauls of large loads (e.g. loads which would fill many large lorries) it is broadly true that the railways are superior, though much of their advantage is liable to be cancelled out in cases where the facilities for collection and delivery are poor (e.g. where the consignee has no siding).

2. Volume and regularity of the flow of traffic offering

The road transporter of passengers or goods must, of course, seek to keep all his vehicles in maximum revenue-earning employment; but he can thrive on a quite small volume of traffic provided that it is regular; or, if not, at least the fluctuations should be predictable, so that at slack periods on one route vehicles may be transferred to other routes, or, alternatively, be subjected to thorough overhaul. Thus the proprietor of a rural bus service may ply between different towns and villages on different days (e.g. market days). More-over, a flow of traffic too small to be profitable to a railway, may be quite sufficient to remunerate a road motor operator.

Clearly, ability to obtain adequate return loads falls under this head also, since return loads are all part of the total volume of traffic available, and its regularity or otherwise. The carriage of "returned empties"—crates, jars, baskets, tins, casks, drums, and various other types of containers helps in the solution of this problem.

3. Damage and Pilferage

The liability to damage and pilferage is much reduced if the amount of intermediate handling and transhipment can be decreased or eliminated. Here the road transporters can offer the advantages of a door to door service in the same vehicle under the charge of the same employee the whole time; and the packing and unpacking of the goods can if desirable be carried out by the consignors and consignees respectively upon their own premises. Improvements in the "springing" of road vehicles and in road surfaces, coupled with the use of pneu-matic tyres even for heavy lorries, greatly reduce the risks of damage due to vibration and jolting.

4. The nature of the commodity to be transported, and the route to be taken

These are further factors bearing upon the costs of road transport. Thus, it may be important that a certain kind of perishable produce (e.g. "soft" fruit) should be carried quickly, at a certain time in the early morning from a rural area to an urban market, from which no return loads are available. Or, again, the goods may have to travel at mid-day through several congested areas, in which speed will be slow and petrol consumption high.

5. The burden of taxation upon the road transporters

In Great Britain at present this consists chiefly of the heavy petrol tax, and the annual licence duty levied according to the h.p. or weight of the vehicle.

8—(B.251)

6. The efficiency and keenness of the motor vehicle drivers

It is, generally speaking, false economy to employ low-paid drivers of little experience under bad conditions, especially as to hours of duty, periods of rest, etc. Such a policy—unfortunately much too widespread hitherto in the motor transport industry—means that drivers will take little interest, much less pride, in the mechanical condition of their vehicles, and breakdowns will be more frequent and expensive.

The expenses involved in operating motor vehicles fall into four classes, viz.—

(a) Running costs;   (c) Standing charges;
(b) Wages;   (d) Repairs.

(a) Running costs include tyres, petrol, lubricants, and "wear and tear"[1]; and, taking one month with another, these bear a very close direct relation to the number of miles run.

(b) Wages are not, strictly speaking, a running cost because they do not vary in close proportion to the mileage run; nor are they, on the other hand, a fixed standing charge. More journeys and more miles may be run in busy times than in slack, without any variation in the weekly wages bill, apart from a small amount of overtime occasionally. It is only when some vehicles can be definitely laid up, as in slack seasons, that staffs and wages can be reduced to any appreciable extent. Wages, then, are costs intermediate between running costs and standing charges, but on the whole more nearly akin to running costs.

(c) Standing charges include licence duty,[2] insurance, garaging, and obsolescence (as distinct from wear and tear).

[1] Depreciation consists of two elements: (a) wear and tear, or depreciation due to use, and (b) obsolescence, or depreciation due to the passing of time.

[2] The Budget of 1933, following the recommendations of the Salter Conference, imposed higher scales of motor vehicle duty. As *The Economist* pointed out—

"the new motor vehicle duties increase drastically the taxes paid by the heavier vehicles. Petrol-driven lorries of 5 to 6 tons unladen weight will pay twice as much, and lorries of 8 and 9 tons unladen weight three times as much as they do at present. But the increase to be expected in the costs of carriage by road is not very great.

(*d*) Repairs consist chiefly of the costs of labour and materials. The cost of repairs varies partly in direct ratio to mileage run, and partly in direct ratio to age of the vehicle. A fleet of vehicles of various ages, all in use, with a steady rate of replacement of the oldest vehicles, will tend to show a fairly constant annual repairs cost.

Standing charges or "overheads" have to be met whether the mileage run is much or little, and whether the vehicles are fully loaded, partially loaded or empty. Therefore, the greater the mileage under loads—preferably full loads—the lower the cost per ton-mile or passenger-mile. Hence the economy of return loads. Overhead charges in the motor transport industry, although far from negligible, seem light when compared with those of the railways. In other words, the proportion of running costs in motor transport is higher than on the railways, and therefore it is possible to allocate a substantial portion of total costs against *particular* traffic. Thus a motor transport firm can, if they will, obtain a more exact idea than a railway company of the cost of rendering any particular service. This is largely due to the relatively small capital expenditure necessary to set up a road transport business; while, on the other hand, "the amount of capital sunk in the railways is enormous, and this, as well as a con-

Licence duties make up only a small proportion of the total costs of working a lorry, and, as the duty paid at present is the same (£48 pneumatic-tyred and £60 solid-tyred lorries), for all vehicles of 5 tons unladen weight and over, the heavier the vehicle the lower is the duty in proportion to total costs of working it. The present licence duty is about 6 or 7 per cent of the cost of operating a lorry of 3 to 5 tons unladen weight and 4 to 5 per cent in the case of lorries of 7, 8, and 9 tons. The new duties, high as they are, will increase road carriers' costs by 2 or 3 per cent in the case of vehicles of 3 and 4 tons unladen weight, by 5 or 6 per cent for heavier vehicles of 6 and 7 tons, and by not much more than 10 per cent for the very heaviest lorries of 9 and 10 tons. There are not more than 500 lorries of over 8 tons unladen weight licensed to-day out of a total of 350,000 goods motor vehicles. The Salter Conference estimated that these 500 vehicles carried 55 million of the 4500 million ton-miles of traffic worked annually by road. The Budget imposes higher scales of duty as well on steam wagons and Diesel-engined lorries. No special account need be taken of these. Only Diesel lorries pay more than petrol-driven vehicles, and there are very few of them."—*The Economist*, 29th July, 1933.

siderable portion of the annual expenditure, is incurred for
the sake of the traffic as a whole, not for any particular
service."[1]

Road freight rates are not so elaborately sub-divided and
classified as railway rates. Road hauliers usually quote a rate
per ton which applies to any tonnage of any common commodity. So far as can be ascertained from a small but fairly
representative sample, these freight rates average about 2·3d.
per ton-mile; but the shorter journeys usually cost rather more
than this, and the longer ones rather less. Moreover, it must
be noted that the rates usually quoted do not always vary
directly with the distance, and that special low rates may be
quoted for large quantities or return loads. As a rule, railway
freight rates are higher than road rates except for "low
class" traffic, such as coal, limestone, iron ore, steel, building
materials, etc.

II

The principal sections of the road motor transport industry
are as follows—

A. The Carriage of Passengers in "Public Service
Vehicles"—

1. Town and city omnibuses operating wholly or mainly
within the urban boundaries. As a rule these services are
either municipal monopolies or operated by companies
enjoying a monopolistic position by consent of the
Municipality.[2]

2. Town-country omnibus services, operated by various
undertakings differing greatly in size.

3. Long-distance motor coach services.

4. Motor coach tours, excursions and special contract
journeys.

5. Taxi-cabs.

---

[1] Fenelon, *op. cit.*, 176.
[2] It is very probable that the trackless trolley electric bus will largely
supplant trams in the near future, chiefly because their greater flexibility in traffic helps to relieve congestion. They are faster, quieter, and
more comfortable than trams and there is no rail track to be maintained. Also their routes can be extended at moderate cost.

B. The Carriage of Goods by—

1. Road hauliers and haulage contractors serving urban and rural areas—

(a) Long-distance regular hauliers.

(b) "Free-lance" or "tramp" hauliers, prepared "to carry anything, anywhere."

(c) Local express carriers.

(d) Transport and distribution contractors, who take definite contracts to carry out all transport work for a certain firm or firms for a specified period and within a specified area or areas.

(e) Railway companies' road services.

(f) Specialist carriers, e.g. furniture removers; horse carriers, etc.

2. "Ancillary users"; i.e. in vehicles belonging to the owners of the goods (e.g. retailers' motor delivery vans; farmers' and builders' lorries).

The sorts and sizes of business units in the road motor transport industry vary tremendously. There are municipal services, giant combines, independent (i.e. uncombined) companies, and large and small firms down to units of the one-man-one-vehicle type. The Area Traffic Commissioners' Reports show that there are some 5300 operators of public service vehicles, of whom approximately 42 per cent operate only one vehicle each. Approximately 90 per cent of the firms or companies operate less than ten vehicles each, and own between them only about 28 per cent of the total number of vehicles. But the number of these small operators is falling steadily year by year.[1] At the other extreme where we have undertakings operating upwards of 500 public service vehicles each, twelve undertakings operate more than 25 per cent of the total number of vehicles. The motor transport departments of many of the local authorities are very large units, and so are

[1] In 1931 they numbered 5997; in 1933, 5404, and in 1935 only 4896. *Annual Reports of the Area Traffic Commissioners.*

some of the well-known companies.[1] A great many of these companies are subsidiaries of one or other of the road transport combines, such as Tilling and British Automobile Traction Ltd., Oswald Tillotson Ltd., or Scottish Motor Traction Ltd.[2] On the other hand, there are numerous small firms, companies and local authorities that employ only a dozen or twenty transport workers, and in the goods section of the industry the small unit is at least as universal.[3]

Motor coach services may be roughly divided into (a) suburban, (b) long-distance; and the latter may be subdivided into (i) regular services, and (ii) holiday trips and tours. In all these subsections of the industry the number of small-scale operators is decreasing, and the services are gradually coming more and more into the hands of the large companies, and combines, usually by the process of purchase and absorption of the smaller enterprises.

Another marked change during the past four or five years has been the increase of State regulation and control. After a good deal of discussion and investigation, the Government decided to turn its attention primarily to the passenger side of the industry. The outcome was the Road Traffic Act, 1930, Part IV of which vests the licensing of public service vehicles (motor omnibuses and motor coaches) and their drivers and conductors, as well as the regulation of bus and coach services and fares, and the hours of duty of drivers and conductors, in Area Traffic Commissioners appointed for the purpose and acting under the general direction of the Minister of Transport.[4] No public service vehicle may ply without a licence and

---

[1] E.g. the Corporation of Glasgow employs in its transport department some 530 bus drivers, 500 conductors, 14 petrol lorry drivers, 65 mechanics, 130 cleaners and about 230 other grades. Ribble Motor Services Ltd. operates nearly 900 motor buses, North Western Omnibus Co. over 400, and Hants and Dorset Motor Services Ltd. employs over 700 people.

[2] The combines are discussed more fully in Section VI *post*.

[3] An analysis of a 1931 trade directory for the London area showed that 10 per cent of the firms had only one motor vehicle, and 70 per cent had less than ten. *New Survey of London Life and Labour*, VIII, 44.

[4] There are twelve Traffic Areas; ten in England and Wales and two in Scotland.

a certificate of fitness to carry passengers. Somewhat similar control and regulation of the goods side was introduced three years later.

Turning now to the goods side of the industry, we find that although the modern steam wagon has held its place for a certain limited range of work, the petrol motor van, truck or lorry has advanced in the last fifteen years to a position of paramount importance. Under the abnormal stresses of the war years its utility and reliability were amply demonstrated; and the abundance of vehicles and drivers released for civilian work after the cessation of hostilities, coupled with traffic congestion and high freight rates on the railways, rapidly propelled the motor lorry into popularity. To-day it is by far the most universal type of road vehicle because of its high speed, its cheapness (except where numerous stops are necessary) its fuel-carrying capacity and its ability to climb hills. Moreover, since 1918 much development has taken place in the varieties of motor goods vehicles, ranging from the motor tricycle, or the 8 h.p., 10 or 12 cwt. light van to the 5 ton lorry and trailer or the gigantic six-wheeler of 10 or 12 tons capacity. Recently the variety has been increased by the advent of the compression-ignition or Diesel-engined vehicle running on heavy oil. The number of these vehicles on the roads, while still relatively small, increased rapidly from two in 1928 to 4300 in 1934. Motor manufacturers are making headway with the solution of such problems as high weight in relation to horse-power, noise and disagreeable exhaust fumes; and already quite a range of efficient and reliable Diesel-engined vehicles is available to road transport operators. Hitherto the low running costs have made them very attractive; but the increase of the tax on heavy oil from 1d. to 8d. a gallon (April, 1935) may destroy much of this advantage.[1]

[1] For further details see *Modern Transport*, 17th November, 22nd December, 1934, and 2nd February, 1935; *The Times Trade and Engineering Review*, December, 1934, 39–40; and the *Armstrong-Saurer Bulletin*, November, 1934. Certain local authorities have experimented with town gas as fuel for internal combustion engines. The gas is carried

A rough estimate indicates that the goods traffic carried on
the roads by motor vehicles, expressed in ton-miles, amounts
to between 10 and 11 per cent of the total ton-mileage of goods
traffic carried on the railways. Moreover, the railways carry
a far from negligible proportion of the road goods traffic, for
although the average journey performed by railway road
vehicles is probably shorter than that of other road goods
carriers, their fleet of road vehicles is very large. The railways
are, in fact, the largest owners of motor vehicles in the goods
section of the industry. Between them the four main-line
railways own 6500 motor goods vehicles directly, and 1700
indirectly through railway-controlled transport companies.
Each railway, except the Southern, controls well over 2500
goods vehicles. Very few, if any, other concerns own as
many as this. Indeed, over 39,000 goods motor vehicles are
run by some 9500 concerns owning less than twenty-five
vehicles each. 7000 of these concerns average only two
vehicles each.

The majority of traders and a great many manufacturers
find it more economical to use their own vehicles because the
control is more direct and complete, contact with customers
is closer, quick delivery can be guaranteed with confidence,
and the vehicles afford a cheap advertising medium. Drivers
of delivery vans belonging to firms serving a large area can
deliver goods, and at the same time they can take orders for
future delivery, collect cash and give receipts. It has been estimated that about four-fifths of road-borne goods are carried in
traders' own vehicles or in vehicles working solely for them,
and only one-fifth in road hauliers' vehicles.[1]

in steel cylinders at a pressure of about 3000 lb. per sq. inch, and is fed
to the engine cylinders through a double reduction valve. With gas at
6d. a therm, fuel costs are equivalent to petrol at 9½d. a gall. The
compression of gas into cylinders for use in this manner was the subject
of experiments as long ago as 1811. See Fuel Research Board *Annual
Report to 31st March*, 1933, 59; *Journal of Institute of Fuel*, June,
1934, 291 ff.
   [1] Royal Commission on Transport, *Final Report*, 83. The Licensing
Authorities' Returns do not enable us to check this estimate, mainly
because we do not know to what extent "B" licence holders act as
part-time hauliers.

Road hauliers or general haulage contractors are defined by
the Royal Commission on Transport as "persons or companies
who hold themselves out as willing to carry the goods of others
for hire or reward, although not necessarily holding themselves
out as 'common carriers.' "[1] In evidence before the Royal
Commission on Transport, Sir Maxwell Hicks described the
long-distance road haulage section of the industry (excluding
ancillary users) as comprising (*a*) well-organized companies
owning fleets of vehicles; (*b*) owner-drivers or individuals
operating two or three vehicles; (*c*) clearing houses. The
majority of the companies in the first category obtain their
business mainly through local depots, local agents and can-
vassers; they keep proper accounts of their operating costs
and financial results, and have aimed at securing a regular
flow of traffic by operating efficient vehicles at economic rates.
On the other hand, the owner-driver, according to Sir M. Hicks,
is generally a newcomer to the industry, who has little business
experience and little knowledge of the full costs of running
one or more lorries over a series of years. He lacks an efficient
organization for obtaining traffic, and for return loads in particular he "is almost forced to accept any rate that may be
offered," especially "if his vehicle has been acquired on the
hire-purchase system, under which he has to obtain substantial
cash receipts at any cost in order to meet the instalments as
they fall due." The general result is an attempt to get more
out of both the men and the motors; hence the great disparities between wages and conditions up and down the
country, and the fact that many contractors in most large
centres have constantly complained of undercutting by persons
who do not pay anything like the same rates of wages and
recognize no restrictions as to working hours.[1] The Royal
Commission rightly regarded all this as undesirable, and
recommended that every road haulier (as defined above) should
be required to obtain a licence from the Area Traffic Commissioners, who should be satisfied, before granting a licence,

[1] Royal Commission on Transport, *Final Report*, 84.
[2] *Ibid*., 86.

as to the fitness of the vehicle or vehicles, and the wages and conditions of service of persons employed in connexion with them. On the latter point, it was suggested that the scope of Section 93 of the Road Traffic Act, 1930, should be widened so as to bring road hauliers' employees within the fair wages clause applicable to Government contracts.

According to Sir Maxwell Hicks the introduction of the clearing house system into the road transport industry is good in theory but, so far, very unsatisfactory in practice. He told the Royal Commission that

the theory of the Clearing House is excellent; its purpose is to act as a link between the trader who wishes his goods carried and the haulier who carries the goods, and in particular to save the haulier the time and trouble of canvassing for return loads.

But the fact that anyone is free to open a clearing house of this kind has resulted in much overlapping and various abuses.

It therefore very frequently occurs that unscrupulous persons set themselves up in the Clearing House business (in the City of Liverpool alone there are 27 different Clearing Houses owning no vehicles at all, and similar conditions obtain in most large towns), and obtain their trade by underquoting the organized hauliers and railways and then beating down the owner-driver to the cut rate less the Clearing House commission. The haulier has no option but to accept these terms, return empty, or waste some days in idleness until finally he consents to the dictation of the Clearing House.

The Royal Commission reached the conclusion that "the present unsatisfactory conditions regarding Clearing Houses are due in the main to the equally unsatisfactory conditions of the industry, and that if the latter are removed the former will automatically disappear," and "when once the industry has been placed on a more stable footing, it should itself organize its own Clearing Houses. . . ."[1]

This is probably an unduly optimistic view. It seems to

[1] Royal Commission on Transport, *Final Report*, p. 95. Cf. Report of the Licensing Authority, North-Western Area, 1934–5.

leave too much to the "invisible hand"; and in any case holds out little promise for the immediate future. A better policy would be for the State to prohibit private clearing houses and lay upon Local Authorities, or alternatively the Ministry of Transport, the duty of setting up District Public Clearing Houses for the service of all road hauliers, with the proviso that the charges made should be no more than sufficient to cover the total costs of the services rendered. Now is the time to nip in the bud the wastes and abuses indicated above, and to create a uniform system under public control before vested interests have had time to arise and consolidate themselves in positions from which they can be dislodged only at great cost to the public purse. The establishment of a cheap, efficient and comprehensive clearing house system would help to reduce traffic congestion, for it would increase the quantity of road transport service available, without an increase of the number of vehicles on the roads.

In order to diminish the chaos existing in the goods section of the road transport industry and to meet, to some extent, the railways' complaints of "unfair competition," the Government put through Parliament the Road and Rail Traffic Act, 1933, which provides that every goods-carrying mechanically propelled vehicle, with minor exceptions, can be operated only under licence granted by a licensing authority. The licensing authority is the chairman of the Traffic Commissioners for any Traffic Area within the meaning of the Road Traffic Act, 1930, or his deputy, and the licences are of three kinds, known as "A," "B," and "C" licences.

(a) *The Public Carrier's (or A) licence* entitles the holder to use the authorized vehicles for the carriage of goods for hire or reward and in connection with his business as a carrier of goods but in general for no other purpose connected with the carrying of goods. The normal currency is two years.

(b) *The Limited Carrier's (or B) licence* entitles the holder to use the authorized vehicles for the carriage of goods either in connexion with any trade or business carried on by him or (subject to any special conditions attached to the licence) for hire or reward. The normal currency is one year.

(c) *The Private Carrier's* (or C) *licence* entitles the holder to use the authorized vehicles for the carriage of goods in connexion with any trade or business carried on by him, but for no other purpose connected with the carrying of goods, except in a case of emergency, when the licensing authority may authorize the holder of a C licence to use a vehicle for the carriage of goods for any person to whom he lets the vehicle. Normally, the holder of a C licence will be allowed to charge for delivery of goods sold to a customer in the ordinary course of business, or for delivery or collection of goods which have been, or are to be, subjected to a process or treatment by him (e.g. by a laundry).   A farmer operating under a C licence may, in certain circumstances, make a charge for carrying the produce of a neighbouring farmer. The normal currency is three years.

In general, the use of a goods vehicle for any non-commercial purpose falls outside the scope of the licensing provisions of the Act and these provisions do not affect agricultural vehicles whose restricted use qualifies them for the reduced rates of taxation under the Finance Acts, public service (passenger) vehicles carrying parcels, and vehicles used for certain local authority or police services. Vehicles moved by human or animal power only are not affected by the Act.

When exercising his discretionary powers under the Act, the licensing authority is required to take into consideration the following matters, amongst others, (a) the need for the proposed facilities, (b) the past conduct of the applicant as a carrier, (c) the need for an allowance to cover vehicles under repair, (d) the extent to which the application represents a conversion from horse-drawn to motor transport. In the case of C licences, all applications are granted automatically if the vehicles are mechanically sound and there has been no breach of the law limiting the employees' hours of labour. But considerable restrictions have been imposed upon any expansion of the fleets of A and B licensees, i.e. the whole-time and part-time public carriers. Applicants for these licences must state the facility for the transport of goods intended to be provided, including particulars of the locality in which it is intended that the authorized vehicles will be normally used to carry goods for hire or reward ; and the railway companies as well as other road hauliers have the opportunity of protesting against services which are contemplated between points already, in their opinion, adequately served. Short-term licences may be granted for a period not exceeding three months to enable vehicles to be used temporarily for seasonal business, particular jobs, or any other limited purpose.

Any aggrieved licence-holder, applicant or objector may appeal from the Traffic Commissioners' decision to the Appeal Tribunal constituted under the Act, which consists of three members appointed by the Minister (after consultation with the Lord Chancellor, the President of the Board of Trade and the Secretary of State for Scotland). The Tribunal, which may require the attendance and examination of witnesses on oath, has power to make such Order as it thinks fit on an appeal; and the decision is final and binding on the licensing authorities.

The Act provides that it shall be a condition of *every* licence—

(*a*) that the authorized vehicles are maintained in a fit and serviceable condition;

(*b*) that the law with respect to the limits of speed and weight, laden and unladen, and the loading of goods vehicles is complied with in relation to the authorized vehicles;

(*c*) that in relation to authorized vehicles the requirements of the law regarding the limits of time for which drivers may remain continuously on duty are observed;[1]

(*d*) that the provisions of the Act relating to the keeping of records as to hours of work, intervals of rest, journeys, loads, and greatest weight of goods carried at any one time, are complied with;

(*e*) that in the case of an A or B licence, the conditions of employment of drivers and statutory attendants on the authorized vehicles are not less favourable than those required in respect of Government contracts by the "Fair Wages" Resolution of the House of Commons.

It was intended that the records mentioned in (*d*) should help the authorities to enforce the law more strictly; but their

---

[1] It was estimated (1936) that these hours regulations affected some 80,000 motor drivers and statutory attendants.

value is destroyed if they can be "cooked," either with or without collusion between drivers and owners.

The Area Traffic Commissioners have wide powers and heavy responsibilities, and their duties clearly call for the exercise of judgment, discretion and administrative skill in a high degree, for they have to decide questions relating to the co-ordination, necessity, regularity, adequacy and profitableness of existing and projected goods and passenger transport services; the reasonableness of charges; and the fulfilment of the statutory conditions of employment in the industry.[1] In the interests of public safety and for the protection of the workers employed, they should use strictly and to the full their powers regarding the fitness of vehicles and the wages and hours of the workpeople; but much less rigidly their powers to withhold licences on other grounds, since existing vested interests (of which the railway companies are the chief) will naturally desire to keep the competition of new supplies of motor transport service down to a minimum, and charges up to a maximum. For it must be remembered that although there is now a good deal of State control and regulation in the industry, private profit, not public service, is still the principal incentive and objective.

III

Road motor transport stands high as an employment-giving industry, especially if we include not only the drivers and "mates" of road haulage vehicles and bus drivers and conductors, but all those engaged in operating auxiliary road transport and in supplementary services, such as cleaning, fueling, and repair of vehicles. Estimates based mainly upon the official censuses of occupations and of road vehicles give a total of nearly 802,000 persons in Great Britain occupied as motor bus drivers and conductors, motor van and lorry

---

[1] "One of the most difficult provisions of all states that 'where desirable in the public interest the fares shall be so fixed as to prevent wasteful competition with alternative forms of transport'—a stipulation that pits the railways against almost every new application" for a road transport licence. M. E. Dimock, *British Public Utilities and National Development* (1933), 113.

drivers and mates, taxi drivers, chauffeurs, and motor mechanics. To these must be added the persons engaged in the petrol and oil trades and in road construction and maintenance—probably 140,000 in all.[1] The expansion-rate of road transport has been very high since the War. Between 1923 and 1933 the number of insured workers in road transport service, passenger and goods, increased by about 70 per cent.

Recruitment of labour for road motor transport is largely haphazard. There is no general system of apprenticeship or improvership, and this is hardly surprising seeing that apprenticeship was on the decline before the advent and rise of road motor transport. Some firms take boys from school and employ them about the garages or loading sheds or as van-boys until they attain the age of 17 when they can begin to drive light mechanical vehicles not exceeding $2\frac{1}{2}$ tons unladen weight. Some firms employ these young boys as petrol pump attendants until they reach the age of 18 or so, and then set them to drive light vans. The bulk of the recruitment, however, takes place not at the school leaving age but between the ages of 17 and 20, some firms teaching and training their own drivers, others taking on young men who have first learned to drive elsewhere (e.g. at a motoring school or with the help of friends). In rural districts the recruits come mainly from the farms and the coal mines, attracted usually by the prospects of higher earnings and more regular employment.

It is dangerous to generalize too widely about the incidence of unemployment in the road motor transport industry, since there are considerable variations from one section to another. The fringe of casual labour which at one time gathered around the horse transport industry has been much reduced by the substitution of motor vehicles (since few employers care to entrust an expensive and powerful vehicle and its load to an unknown and possibly inexperienced driver); and in the tramway and omnibus section the unemployment index is

[1] See Appendix B. It was recently found (by sampling) that on Merseyside the average age of motor lorry and van drivers was about 33 years. 35 per cent were between 25 and 34, and less than 4 per cent were over 55.

much below the general average, and is, indeed, among the lowest in the whole of British industry. Unemployment among London passenger transport workers (buses, trams, and tubes) has been reduced to the very low level of about 2 per cent, and casual labour is almost eliminated. In other sections of road transport, however, the incidence of unemployment is far more severe. The fluctuations follow those of the general unemployment index and are usually *above* it.

Trade union organization is seldom strong during the early phases of a new industry. There are no traditions, no precedents, no nuclei of loyal trade unionists from which organization can spread outwards; and when employers are in strong opposition, and employees in the main indifferent and dispersed in small groups over a very wide area, the progress of trade unionism is likely to be slow, and wages and conditions poor and lacking in uniformity. This was broadly the position in the goods haulage section of the road transport industry[1] when, in 1933, the Minister of Labour undertook to deal with the complicated problem of wages, hours, and working conditions.

An attempt had been made, immediately after the war, to establish a joint industrial council for the industry, but the council had failed to function satisfactorily because it lacked statutory powers to make its decisions effective. After the disappearance of the joint industrial council, the industry reverted to local machinery for the fixation of wages and conditions of labour; but the resulting agreements were uncoordinated, and not binding on the majority of the employers, who were not members of the employers' associations. The local agreements, therefore, permitted the existence and persistence of grave disparities. Among the better employers trade union rates of wages in 1932–3 seem to have ranged,

---

[1] Cf. H. Morrison, *Socialization and Transport* (1933), 96. The principal unions catering for road transport workers are Transport and General Workers' Union, Scottish Transport and General Workers' Union, United Road Transport Workers' Association of England, Liverpool and District Carters' and Motormen's Union, Halifax and District Carters, Draymen's and Horsemen's Association, Scottish Horse and Motormen's Association, and the National Union of General and Municipal Workers.

roughly according to the size of the vehicle, from 56s. weekly for drivers of vehicles of 15 cwt. or less in the London and Home Counties area, up to 73s. for drivers of lorries over 2 tons, and 76s. for drivers of six-wheeled vehicles. In the larger provincial towns the corresponding rates of wages appear to have been in the neighbourhood of 57s.–63s.; 57s.–70s.; and 76s. (six-wheelers): and in other areas 49s.–53s., and 59s.–62s. (vehicles over 2 tons). The standard working week was 48 hours, but here again we are looking at the best conditions. Over wide areas where trade union agreements did not exist, or were ignored, wages were generally lower and the working week longer.

After the passing of the Road and Rail Traffic Act, 1933, the Minister appointed an advisory committee, which examined the problem and recommended that a National Joint Board should be established on lines which would constitute it a conciliation board for the purposes of section 32 of the Road and Rail Traffic Act, 1933, and Section 19 of the Road Traffic Act, 1930, "so that its determinations could form a settled foundation on which the administration of the Fair Wages provisions could be based, and variation of the limitation of driving hours effected." The National Joint Board for the Road Transport Industry (Goods) was constituted on these lines in 1934. Representatives from the Transport and General Workers' Union, the Liverpool and District Carters' and Motormen's Union, the United Road Transport Workers' Association, and the National Union of General and Municipal Workers formed the employees' side of the Board, and representatives from the Associated Road Operators (formerly the Road Haulage Association), the Motor Transport Employers' Federation, and the National Road Transport Employers' Federation formed the employers' side.[1] A sub-committee, appointed to examine the problem of wages and working conditions in all its aspects, reported to the full Board on 1st

---

[1] The first and second of these employers' associations embrace haulage contractors and ancillary users; the third, haulage contractors only. The members of the three associations own between them some 120,000 vehicles.

August, 1934, recommending certain national minima of wage rates and hours for various classes of work, "in the belief that every possible means will be taken by the appropriate authorities and others concerned to secure its observance by all A and B licence holders," and with the expectation that the sub-committee's recommendations would also be reflected in the wages and conditions in organized trades where employers own and operate transport ancillary to their main businesses. Moreover, it was clearly stated that the scales recommended were *minima*, and that where superior wages and conditions existed, these should remain in operation, and be changed only by mutual consent.

The National Joint Conciliation Board ratified with one or two minor alterations the sub-committee's suggested scales of wages and conditions of labour, which were published in a document that has been dubbed "the lorrymen's charter." The minimum rates of wages fall into four groups: (a) Long-distance and trunk services; (b) London; (c) Provincial services other than long distance and trunk services; (d) Youths. The weekly wage-rates range from 45s. up to 73s. for drivers and from 48s. to 57s. for statutory attendants and mates, according to the nature of the district and service and the size of the vehicle.[1] Services in group (c) are graded. Grade I rates of wages will apply in important provincial industrial centres and the principal ports; Grade II in other industrial centres; Grade III in rural areas. The actual grading and the work of distinguishing clearly between long-distance and trunk services and other services was delegated to an Area Joint Board in each of the Traffic Commissioners' areas, working in co-operation, if possible, with any existing local joint organizations; all grading to be completed by 1st July, 1935.[2]

Overtime rates were laid down as follows: "time-and-one-eighth" for the first 8 hours in excess of the normal 48 hours and "time-and-a-quarter" thereafter; "time-and-a-half" for

[1] For details of rates of wages, see Appendix A.
[2] An Appeals Committee of the National Joint Board was set up during 1935 to decide disputes regarding grading referred to it by the Area Boards.

Sunday work. Subsistence allowances are provided for, ranging from 5s. to 10s. according to the number of hours of absence from home; and regular employees are to be paid for all statutory and proclaimed holidays, and for one week's annual holiday after twelve months' continuous service. For casual men on long-distance or trunk services a guaranteed minimum of 8½ hours' work or pay was recommended.

For Scotland a separate board has been established. The Interim Agreement for Scotland, dating from February, 1935, makes no distinction between wage rates for long-distance and local services. One flat rate is set for the whole country and is varied according to the carrying capacity of the vehicle.

The new schedules met with little active and open opposition from employers, though some expressed hostility.[1] Others quietly ignored them and took their chance of "getting away with it." The Board has no legal powers to enforce its decisions, but, on the other hand, non-observance of the prescribed rates of wages is a breach of legal licensing conditions, and the efforts of the trade unions to discover and expose evasions are in some cases reinforced by the better employers who resent being placed at a disadvantage in competition with hauliers who pay low wages. The systematic grading introduced by the National Joint Conciliation Board has co-ordinated wages "on paper" throughout the country, but enforcement of these rates upon reluctant and evasive employers is hampered by the difficulty of obtaining evidence (e.g. from workers who fear to lose their jobs), and the cumbersome method of dealing with delinquents which involves referring complaints to the Licensing Authority, the Minister of Labour, the Industrial Court, and finally back to the Licensing Authority. Therefore, the Committee of Inquiry, appointed by the Ministers of Labour and Transport, in July, 1936, suggested that the universal observance of agreed standards of wages by all licence holders should be strictly

---

[1] Cf. *Reports of the National Road Transport Conference*, December, 1934.

enforced by statutory powers; and that C licence holders (ancillary users), who operate at least two-thirds of all the goods vehicles in the country, should be made subject to the same standards, otherwise a great body of employees driving motor vehicles will receive no benefit from the new legislation, while at the same time there is a strong inducement to operate an increasing number of vehicles under C licences, and to give a decreasing amount of work to road hauliers. The "Salter Conference" on Rail and Road Transport considered "that both hauliers and ancillary users should be subject to regulation, enforced through the grant of licences, as regards fair wages and conditions of service and the maintenance of their vehicles in a state of fitness."[1] It is at least equally important in the interests of safety that drivers of vehicles on the public highways should also be kept "in a state of fitness," and this can be done by setting up and enforcing reasonable standards of wages and hours.

There is no national agreement covering the wages and conditions of labour of motor omnibus drivers and conductors employed by municipal authorities and companies. About one half of the municipal authorities apply to their motor bus staffs the terms of the national agreement for the tramways industry,[2] while a number of others pay somewhat higher rates. Under this arrangement wages vary from place to place according to the "grade" of the municipality.[3] Generally speaking, the larger authorities pay the higher wages. Taken as a class, municipal omnibus drivers are the best paid of all the workers operating vehicles in the road transport industry. Typical minimum rates of wages for these men range from 54s. to 61s., and their typical maxima from 58s. 9d. to 64s. 9d., for a 48 hour week. The most usual scales run from about 60s. up to 65s. by increments spread over $3\frac{1}{2}$ to 4 years. Typical

---

[1] Para. 103.

[2] Embodied in the *Decision and Report of the Tribunal for the Tramway Industry* (1924), and the agreement made by the National Joint Industrial Council for the Tramway Industry in February, 1932.

[3] The Ministry of Labour publishes annual unweighted averages of weekly wages rates in the tramway services of forty-five large towns.

minimum rates of wages for adult conductors of municipal omnibuses range from 48s. 3d. to 58s. weekly, and typical maximum rates are around 62s. 9d. The modal scale for conductors is not well marked, but a fairly high proportion of municipal authorities pay from 55s. rising to 63s. per week; while a somewhat smaller proportion pay from 51s. rising to 58s. For junior conductors (18 to 21 years of age), the most typical scales run between 30s. and 45s. for a 48 hour week, but here and there rates are as low as 24s. and as high as 53s. a week.

It must be remembered that the earnings of road transport employees, especially in the passenger section, depend not only upon the rates of pay per hour and the normal working week, but also upon the overtime worked and the rate of pay for it; the rates of pay for work on Sundays, Bank Holidays and other "special days"; whether annual holidays are granted with pay; and, lastly, the nature of the "spread over" arrangements, for where breaks (which may range from a few minutes to several hours) occur between periods of active duty in the same working day, payment, often at special rates, may be made for the time covered by some or all of the breaks.

A comparison of the wage rates paid by (a) local authorities (b) companies, (c) railways in the passenger section of the road transport industry reveals considerable variations from one undertaking to another and from place to place. The weekly wages of drivers in Inner London are 82s. 6d. to 88s. 6d. for 48 hours, and in Outer London 67s. 6d. to 80s; except those employed by the railways, whose rates of wages are a good deal lower. In the provinces the bulk of company bus drivers' wages range from commencing rates of 47s. or 48s. up to maxima as high as 74s. per week. Nearly every large company has an agreement with a trade union, but some of the small, non-trade-union companies pay miserable wages to drivers and conductors and nothing for overtime.[1]

Motor mechanics' weekly wages appear to range from 81s. (Glasgow, night work) down to 59s. 6d. (Manchester, grade

[1] For additional details see Appendix A, pp. 374-5

2 mechanics, day work). Cleaners' wages vary from 30s. a week in a rural area, up to 58s. in Glasgow (maximum rate, day work). There are, of course, a few exceptional cases, but generally speaking the wages paid by the smaller municipalities and companies are below the average for the larger under-takings,[1] especially where the trade unions are not recognized.

A road transport driver's day is usually made up of driving, loading and unloading, and waiting. Owing to the nature of road transport, whether of passengers or goods, it is impossible to work as closely to certain prescribed hours as can be done in factories. The basic or "guaranteed" working week seems to be between 48 and 54 hours, but the actual hours worked probably average between 50 and 60. In many cases, but not in all, extra pay is now received for the extra hours worked on weekdays, Sundays and public holidays. These overtime payments may begin at ordinary time rates or at "time-and-a-quarter," and rise to "time-and-a-half" after a specified number of hours. Such arrangements are most common among the local authorities and larger companies; and the same is true of annual holidays (usually from six to fourteen days) with full pay.

In the passenger section of the industry organization among the workers and employers and the negotiation of collective agreements has reached a more advanced stage than in the goods section, and has been stimulated by the provisions of Section 93 of the Road Traffic Act, 1930, requiring licence holders to establish and maintain wages and conditions not less favourable than those which would have to be paid and observed under the "fair wages" clause of a Government con-tract. Unsettled cases arising under this section may be referred by the Ministry of Labour to the Industrial Court[2]

---

[1] Examples: A small private transport firm in Yorkshire, employing 19 persons in all, was (Jan., 1935) paying bus drivers £2 12s. 6d. per week; conductors £1 4s. up to £1 15s.; lorry drivers £2 12s. 6d.; mates £1 4s. up to £1 15s.; and garage hands £1 15s. During busy periods the lorry drivers are called upon to act as relief drivers on the buses.

[2] A permanent court of arbitration created by the Industrial Courts Act, 1919.

to be settled by arbitration.[1] If the Industrial Court decides that "any person has been guilty of a breach of the provisions of this section, he shall be liable to be dealt with in all respects as if he had failed to comply with a condition of his road service licence."[2]

Under Section 19 of the same statute the drivers of public service vehicles, heavy or light locomotives, motor tractors or motor vehicles carrying goods (other than passengers' luggage) must not drive continuously for more than $5\frac{1}{2}$ hours, or for continuous periods amounting to more than 11 hours in any period of 24 hours, commencing 2 hours after midnight. Every driver must have at least 10 consecutive hours for rest in every 24 hours, unless he is to have 12 consecutive hours in the next period of 24 hours, in which case 9 hours for rest, instead of 10, is sufficient to comply with the Act.[3]

Drivers of ancillary transport are much more numerous than those classified as in the road motor transport industry "proper": e.g. in Greater London the former outnumber the latter by more than 2 to 1. Furthermore, the differences in the wages, hours and nature of the work to be done by ancillary transport drivers are much greater than in other sections of road transport, and trade union organization is far from strong, especially among the drivers of ancillary transport for industries in which the total trade union membership is small. On the whole, the London wages and conditions are superior to those obtaining in other places. This is due partly to the higher cost of living in and around London, and partly to better organization and collective bargaining machinery.

---

[1] *Ministry of Labour Report*, 1932 (*Cmd.* 4281), 80, 43. The efforts of the Industrial Court to put into force the fair wages provisions of Section 93 are much hampered where there are no general wages agreements and no collective bargaining machinery.

[2] Road Traffic Act, 1930, Section 93. This appears to introduce a form of compulsory arbitration in industrial disputes.

[3] Strict enforcement of these rules is important because under the Road and Rail Traffic Act, 1933, the numbers of vehicles can be regulated and limited, but *not the mileage run*. Therefore a stimulus is given towards more intensive working of existing fleets of vehicles and, presumably, their drivers, unless checked by the provisions of the Act of 1930.

For the Retail Distributive Trades section of the road transport industry there is a Joint Council of twelve members; six appointed by the London Employers' Association and the Incorporated Association of Retail Distributors; and six appointed by the Transport and General Workers' Union. These members "hold office during the pleasure of the Organizations appointing them," and their functions are to regulate wages, hours, and working conditions, to provide machinery for the settlement of differences between employers and trade unions in the Retail Distributive Trades Section of the road transport industry; to consider matters arising from existing or proposed legislation; to discuss and make recommendations for the promotion of safety on the roads, the health and welfare of the men employed, and the general efficiency of the industry. It is intended that the Joint Council shall assist the National Conciliation Board in carrying into effect its decisions on wages and working conditions in the road transport industry; but it is well to remember that there are sundry Associations of retail distributors not as yet parties to the Joint Council.

In November, 1934, the Joint Council for the Retail Distributive Trades Section of the Road Transport Industry fixed the following minimum wages and conditions to apply within the London and Metropolitan Police Area.

Drivers of Petrol Vehicles[1]	*Per week of 48 hours exclusive of meal times*	
Up to 15 cwt.	54s.	plus 6d. per day if driving with a trailer.
Over 15 cwt. and up to 30 cwt. . .	60s.	
,, 30 ,, ,, ,, ,, 40 ,, .	64s.	
,, 40 ,, ...	70s.	
Statutory attendants . . .	60s.	

Overtime rates; "time-and-one-eighth" for the first 8 hours, and "time-and-a-quarter" thereafter. Sunday work to be paid for at double ordinary rates, the minimum payment to be 10s. "No temporary or daily man shall be employed or paid for less than 8½ hours on any given day." The agreement

[1] The minimum for drivers of Steam Wagons was fixed at 74s. per week, and their mates, 60s.

also provides (*inter alia*) for minimum lodging and subsistence allowances (5s. a night for a period of rest not exceeding 12 hours); payment for Christmas Day, Good Friday, Bank holidays and proclaimed holidays; and one week's annual holiday with pay for all regular employees.

The London Co-operative Societies pay their motor drivers from 69s. to 76s. a week according to the load capacity of the vehicle.[1] Other London rates of wages are: builders' van and lorry drivers 54s. to 73s. according to load capacity of the vehicle;[1] drivers of railway goods and parcel vehicles, 60s. a week. An important co-operative society in a large Midland city pays its motor drivers 66s. for a 48-hour week; drivers' mates and labourers receive 61s. per week, and deliverers 61s. plus 5s. for taking cash. All the employees receive two weeks annual holiday with pay and full pay for periods of sickness up to a maximum of two weeks in any one year. These rates of wages are representative of those paid by the best employers in large cities; great numbers of van drivers up and down the country are doubtless working longer hours for much lower wages. It is, of course, a fact that drivers who load and unload their own vehicles and come into direct contact with a succession of customers usually receive "tips" which augment their wages; but records are not kept and it is not possible to hazard a guess as to the extent of such additional income, on the average, throughout the year.

Persons working in the taxi-cab section of the road transport industry may be divided into four classes—

(a) The owner-drivers of one cab.[2]

(b) The journeymen drivers.

(c) The non-driving proprietors of cabs.

(d) Garage "hands" employed by (c) to clean, fuel, and overhaul the cabs.

The owner-driver keeps all his earnings, out of which he must

---

[1] *New Survey of London Life and Labour*, VIII (1934).

[2] Judging by the number of hackney carriages having eight seats or less, there are probably some 30,000 taxi-drivers in Great Britain. In London alone the records show 11,400 drivers and 8110 licensed taxicabs. About one-third of the London taxi-drivers are owner-drivers.

pay all the expenses of his cab. The journeyman taxi-driver working "on the clock" pays over to the cab owners 65 or 70 per cent of the takings registered "on the clock" and keeps the remaining 30 per cent or 35 per cent, plus all tips and extra payments for luggage and additional passengers. An alternative method is for the journeyman to pay 10s. or 11s. for the use of the cab for 10 hours, subject to a mileage limit of 60–66 miles. The driver pays for his own petrol, and 2d. a mile or 1s. per hour if he exceeds the 10-hour period or the mileage limit, and pockets all the takings. Many journeymen taxi-drivers aim to acquire a cab of their own (usually on the hire-purchase system), but the cost is over £400, and not a few fail to reach their objective. Taxi-drivers are usually available for hire by the public from 10 to 14 hours a day.

By "keeping moving," as opposed to waiting on the rank, and by carefully anticipating when and where taxis are likely to be required, a driver may earn double as much as one who makes no such effort. Luncheon hours, dinner hours, and the hours at which theatres open and close are among the busy times of a cabman's day. One of the trade journals has recently started a record of social events to assist drivers. But there are limits to efforts made to anticipate business in this way, and luck plays a part of no little importance.[1]

By hard work and in good busy times the London owner-driver can make as much as £5 or £6 a week clear, after meeting all running expenses, insurance, depreciation, etc. But in bad, slack times his surplus may fall as low as £2 a week. It is estimated that on an average journeymen drivers in London are left with 15s. to £1 a day after they have "turned in" the agreed percentage (say 65 or 70 per cent) to the owners. Certain cab companies pay a bonus ranging from 2s. 6d. to 10s. according to the size of the sums "turned in."

In this trade the small "one-man-one-cab" business continues to exist as well as the large-scale cab-owning firm or company. There are three major organizations to which taxi-cab drivers and owners may belong: the Motor Cab Owner-

---

[1] *New Survey of London Life and Labour*, VIII, 97.

drivers' Association, The Motor Cab Trade Protection Society, and the Transport and General Workers' Union.

Chauffeurs may be classified as: (a) in private employment; (b) employed by firms who hire out "private" cars; (c) employed by Government departments, local authorities, banks, and other institutions and organizations. A chauffeur's duties often include certain household duties or gardening, in addition to driving and cleaning the car or cars, and doing running repairs. The weekly rates of wages commonly paid to-day range from 25s. to 40s. with board and lodging; 30s. to 70s. with board only; and 50s. to 80s. without board and lodging. The weekly wages paid by the larger hiring agencies range from 60s. to 80s.; and by the smaller agencies from 50s. to 70s. Chauffeurs employed by firms and institutions usually receive between 60s. and 75s. a week. These are London wages; rates of wages for work exclusively or mainly in the provinces may be somewhat lower. In many instances wages are supplemented by "tips." Chauffeurs are not infrequently "rather snobbish about the cars they drive and the social status of their passengers. They must maintain a smart appearance, be steady and submissive, and avoid alcoholic drinks whilst on duty. As a rule a driver picks up the requisite social graces by watching other chauffeurs. In some posts a chauffeur has to be a person of considerable tact. . . . The hours worked depend upon the social and business life of the employer and the consideration shown by him. Many chauffeurs are on duty a good deal at night and during week-ends. A driver aged over 40 finds difficulty in obtaining new situations on account of the employer's distrust of his strength and vigilance, although his steadiness and training qualify him for posts with funeral undertakers."[1]

IV

Hitherto the road motor transport industry has been highly competitive. But it seems likely to become much less so in

New Survey of London Life and Labour, VIII, 62–9.

the near future. This opinion is based upon two clear tendencies: (*a*) the growth of combinations among road transporters, and (*b*) the integration of the railways and certain of the road transport undertakings. As long ago as 1925 Dr. Fenelon stated that "tacit agreements, combination, association, fusion or other monopolistic tendencies are to be found in many areas. . . . In certain areas, large transport concerns either providing goods haulage or passenger services have attained a practical monopoly as a result of the large scale of their operations, their large capital resources and the moderate use of their monopoly power."[1] It appears that to-day the existence of monopolistic combines is more marked in the passenger section of the industry than among the goods carriers. Early in 1934 *The Economist* published a list of ninety of the principal passenger transport companies[2] concerned in operating a great network of regular omnibus services throughout the country. The total issued capital of the ninety companies, including cross-holdings, but excluding the "parent" companies, exceeded £24 millions, and the total number of vehicles owned by them was in the neighbourhood of 17,650. Not more than a round dozen of these companies, capitalized at some £2,616,000, can be described as "independent." Of the remainder, fifty-six are in the Tilling and British Automobile Traction combine, and ten are controlled by Scottish Motor Traction, which serves virtually the whole of Scotland.

Thomas Tilling Ltd., a company registered in 1897 as road transport contractors, has steadily enlarged its business and sphere of control, particularly during the past decade. Its large London interests have recently been transferred to the London Passenger Transport Board, but its very considerable provincial undertakings remain. British Electric Traction Co. Ltd., registered a year before Thomas Tilling, was originally interested mainly in tramway undertakings. Its great and widespread motor omnibus interests have developed more

[1] Fenelon, *op. cit.*, 183–4.
[2] Excluding the London Passenger Transport Board.

recently with the rapid expansion of the road transport industry. These two companies with their numerous subsidiaries are linked by Tilling & British Automobile Traction Co. Ltd., a giant holding company to which Thomas Tilling Ltd. and British Electric Traction Co. Ltd. "transferred most of their road subsidiaries in May, 1928, to achieve a pooling of forces before the granting of Parliamentary road powers to the railways."[1]

On 12th December, 1934, the chairman and managing director of Thomas Tilling Ltd. outlined that company's interests in other transport companies in the following words—

The main one is our holding of approximately 1¼ million shares in Tilling and British Automobile Traction Ltd., itself a holding company with an interest in over 20 omnibus undertakings in various parts of the country. Then we have the National Omnibus and Transport Co. Ltd., where we hold 93 per cent of the ordinary share capital. This too is a holding company, with a half interest in the equity of each of three provincial omnibus companies. Other important interests are the United Counties Omnibus Co. Ltd., in which we hold nearly the whole of the share capital, and Daimler Hire Ltd., where we own 75 per cent of the ordinary share capital and one-half of the preference shares. In addition, we have the control in H.M.S. Catherwood Ltd., and in two smaller companies engaged in the haulage trade. It will be seen that our interests are spread over more than 30 undertakings and I am right in stating that in every case profits have been earned in the current year after adequate sums have been set aside for depreciation.[2]

To this imposing list must be added a very large holding of London Passenger Transport Board stock, as a result of the acquisition of Tilling's passenger transport businesses in the Greater London area.

The companies associated with the Tilling and Scottish Motor Traction combines own about the same number of vehicles as the "independents," and about two and a half times as many as the London Passenger Transport Board.

[1] *The Economist*, 17th February, 1934, 354.
[2] *Modern Transport*, 15th December, 1934.

Control is further concentrated by interlocking directorates, especially within the Tilling combine. Mr. Chester has recently pointed out that—

> If we take the directors (of the Tilling Group companies) who are on the boards of five or more companies, 21 people have between them 163 directors' seats; in other words, 18·9 per cent of the directors cover 56·9 per cent of the available seats on the companies' boards. It is obvious, therefore, that these people must wield considerable power over policy and especially over the co-ordination of policy between the different companies.[1]

RESULTS OF "GROUP" UNDERTAKINGS [2]

		Thos. Tilling (Dec. 31)	British Electric Traction (Mar. 31)	Tilling and B.A.T. (Dec. 31)	Scottish Motor Traction (Oct. 31)
		£	£	£	£
Paid-up ordinary capital	1930	527,350	184,444	1,600,000	400,000
	1934	1,318,375	490,992	2,500,000	858,434
	1935	2,636,750	540,092	2,500,000	858,434
Total profits	1930	298,152	396,361	272,772	136,306
	1934	322,390	421,272	295,473	278,433
	1935	388,005	465,514	349,731	286,991

		Earned %	Paid %	Earned %	Paid %	Earned %	Paid %	Earned %	Paid %
Ordinary shares	1930	55·4	25	68·3	5	13·0	10	28·6	10
	1934	23·1	15	27·1	5	11·8	10	18·3	10
	1935	13·2	10	34·4	5	13·0	10	19·2	10

Shares in these road transport combines—especially the Tilling and British Electric Traction groups—are eagerly bought up by investors and strongly held because of the combines' high reputations as dividend payers and "an unexampled record of handsome capital bonuses." As a result the market values of the ordinary shares stand very high, and the dividend yields to present buyers are rather low, unless the chances of further capital bonuses are brought into the reckoning. And even then, although neither the combination movement nor the scope for increased cash dividends is yet

[1] D. N. Chester, *Public Control of Road Passenger Transport* (1936), 40–1.
[2] Figures taken from *The Economist*, 15th February, 1936, 367.

at an end, investors may well ask whether it is probable that
future profits will be

. . . sufficiently expansive to permit intermittent share bonuses
for Thomas Tilling and Tilling and British Automobile Traction.
Will earnings continue indefinitely to provide the proprietors of
British Electric Traction with a recurrent 10 per cent capital
bonus? In due course such a policy will presuppose a geometric
annual expansion in earnings.

When in 1928, the four main line railway companies finally
obtained powers to run road transport services on a wide scale
and to invest in road transport undertakings,[1] they found the
passenger side of the road transport industry already partially
monopolized. At first the railways engaged in costly competition with the Tilling combine for control of various
omnibus companies, but in December, 1929, the railways and
the combine agreed to hold equal interests in any operating
company in which they were jointly concerned. Within the
ensuing two years this agreement involved a considerable
reorganization of the areas and services of many of the principal omnibus companies, and the re-arrangement of the
railways' omnibus services. The amount of capital invested
by the railway companies in road passenger transport has
risen from £242,000 in 1927 to well over £9,000,000 at the
present time, nearly all in the form of "subscriptions to
omnibus undertakings." Mr. Gilbert Walker writes—

Now that entry to the business of carrying goods by road has
been made subject to licence, combination among road hauliers
has been stimulated. When the units are large enough, it will be
worth the railway companies' while to obtain a controlling interest
in haulage concerns, as they have already done in the case of bus
and coach undertakings; and there is a lively danger that the
railways and the Traffic Commissioners between them will do for
the carriage of goods by road what they have already done for
the carriage of passengers—namely, establish a level of road
charges not far removed from railway rates.[2]

[1] Under the Railway (Road Transport) Act, 1928, each railway
can operate road vehicles in any district to which its system gives
access, and invest in road transport undertakings or enter into agreements with any municipality, company or other concern.

[2] *Economic Journal*, December, 1936, 673-4.

GROUPING OF ROAD PASSENGER COMPANIES

(T. Thomas Tilling, Ltd., B.E.T. British Electric Traction Company, Ltd. T. & B.A.T. Tilling and British Automobile Traction Company, Ltd. S.M.T. Scottish Motor Traction. Percentages relate to effective voting control.)

THOMAS TILLING CONTROL

1. *United Counties.*—£50,000 pref.; £100,000 ord. T. 100%.
2. *National Omnibus.*—£250,000 pref.*; £250,000 ord. T. 92%.
   2 (a) *Eastern National.*—£350,000 pref.*; £250,000 ord. T. 50%; L.N.E. 25%; L.M.S. 25%.
   2 (b) *Southern National.*—£96,500 pref.*; £350,000 ord. T. 50%; S.R. 50%.
   2 (c) *Western National.*—£1,228,960 pref.*; £567,152 ord. T. 50%; G.W. 50%.
     2 (c) (i) *Bristol Trams.*—£500,000 pref.; £1,000,000 ord. W. Nat. control.

BRITISH ELECTRIC TRACTION CONTROL

3. *Birmingham and Midland.*—£100,000 pref*; £800,000 ord. B.E.T. 50%†; L.M.S. 30%; G.W. 20%.
   3 (a) *Black and White.*—£7,500 ord. (t)
   3 (b) *W. C. Standerwick.*—£6,000 ord. (u)
4. *Hebble Motor.*—£125,000 ord. B.E.T. 50%; L.N.E. 12·5%; L.M.S. 37·5%.
5. *Northern General Transport.*—£300,000 pref.*; £554,053 ord. B.E.T. 44%; L.N.E. 44%.
   5 (a) *Gateshead and District Trams.*—£132,610 pref.; £152,110 ord. N. Gen. Trans. 98%.
   5 (b) *General County.*—N. Gen. control.
   5 (c) *Sunderland and District.*—£100,000 ord. N. Gen. Trans. 100%.
   5 (d) *Tynemouth and District.*—£30,500 pref.; £46,410 ord. N. Gen. Trans. 77%.
6. *Potteries Motor.*—£224,750 ord. B.E.T. 51·6%.
7. *South Wales Transport.*—£179,794 pref.*; £327,906 ord. B.E.T. 96·8%.
8. *Yorkshire (W.D.) E. Trams.*—£220,000 ord. B.E.T. 50%; L.N.E. 16·7%; L.M.S. 33·3%.

NOTES

* Non-voting preference shares. † Through Birmingham and District Investment Trust. (t) Birmingham and Midland control jointly with Bristol Trams and City of Oxford Motor. (u) Birmingham and Midland control, jointly with N. Western Road Car and Ribble Motor.

9. *National Electric Construction.*—£125,000 ord. B.E.T. 100%.

9 (a) *City of Oxford Motor.*—£74,000 pref.*; £141,750 ord. B.E.T. 50%‡; G.W. 50%.

(b) *Devon General.*—£150,000 pref.*; £120,000 ord. B.E.T. 50%‖; G.W. 30%; S.R. 20%.

9 (b) (i) *Fleet Cars.*—Devon Gen. 100%.

9 (b) (ii) *Grey Cars.*—Devon Gen. control.

9 (c) *Rhondda Tramways.*—£100,000 pref.*; £50,002 ord. B.E.T. 23·4%.§

9 (d) *Western Welsh.*—£290,000 ord. B.E.T. 17·2% (r); G.W. 50%.

9 (d) (i) *Eastern Valley Motor.*—West. Welsh control.

9 (d) (ii) *Western Valley Motor.*—West. Welsh control.

9 (e) *Musselburgh and District Traction.*—£50,400 pref.; £51,007 ord. B.E.T. 52%.

Tilling and British Automobile Traction Control

10. *Aldershot and District.*—£200,000 ord. T. & B.A.T. 31·9%; S.R. 31·9%.

11. *Caledonian.*—£125,000 ord. T. & B.A.T. 100%.

12. *Crosville Motor.*—£955,000 ord. T. & B.A.T. 49·9%; L.M.S. 41·9%; G.W. 8·0%.

12 (a) *Western Transport.*—£155,000 ord.

13. *Cumberland Motor.*—£125,000 ord. T. & B.A.T. 33·3%; L.M.S. 33·3%.

14. *East Kent.*—£200,000 pref.*; £350,000 ord. T. & B.A.T. 32·8%; S.R. 32·8%.

14 (a) *London and S. Coast.*—East Kent Control.

15. *Eastern Counties.*—£200,000 pref.*; £672,069 ord. T. & B.A.T. 27·6%(s); L.N.E. 24·3%; L.M.S. 3·3%.

15 (a) *Norwich E. Trams.*—£264,000 ord. E. Counties 98·3%.

16. *East Midland.*—£100,000 ord. T. & B.A.T. 50%; L.N.E. 33·3%; L.M.S. 16·7%.

17. *East Yorkshire.*—£160,000 ord. T. & B.A.T. 49·8%; L.N.E. 49·8%.

18. *Hants and Dorset.*—£150,000 pref.*; £200,000 ord. T. & B.A.T. 38·4%; S.R. 38·4%.

19. *Lincolnshire Road Car.*—£100,000 ord. T. & B.A.T. 39·6%; L.N.E. 31·7%; L.M.S. 7·9%.

* Non-voting Preference Shares.   ‡ National Electric holding through Oxford Trans. Syndicate which is controlled approx. 40% by N.E.C. ‖ N.E.C. control through Torquay Trams directorate. § All directors have B.E.T. interests. (r) Half directors have B.E.T. interests. (s) 43·2% capital held by United Automobile Services (q.v.).

20. *Maidstone and District.*—£200,000 pref.*; £300,000 ord.
    T. & B.A.T. 34·6%; S.R. 34·6%.
    20 (a) *Auto Car Services.*—Maidstone and D. control.
    20 (b) *Chatham and District.*—£45,000 pref.; £106,000 ord.
    Maidstone & D. holds 81·5% capital.
21. *North Western Road Car.*—£450,000 ord. T. & B.A.T. 49·8%;
    L.N.E. 16·6%; L.M.S. 33·2%.
22. *Ribble Motor.*—£200,000 pref.*; £600,000 ord. T. & B.A.T.
    44%; L.M.S. 44%.
23. *Southdown Motor.*—£426,250 ord. T. & B.A.T. 33·2%; S.R.
    33·2%.
24. *Southern Vectis.*—£15,200 pref.*; £55,000 ord. T. & B.A.T.
    50%; S.R. 50%.
25. *Thames Valley.*—£150,000 ord. T. & B.A.T. 48·7%; G.W.
    34·1%; S.R. 14·6%.
    25 (a) *Marlow and District.*—Thames Valley control.
26. *Trent Motor.*—£268,000 ord. T. & B.A.T. 41·2%; L.N.E.
    13·7%; L.M.S. 27·5%.
27. *United Automobile.*—£150,000 pref.; £700,000 ord. T. &
    B.A.T. 44·6%; L.N.E. 44·6%.
28. *West Yorks Road Car.*—£200,000 pref.*; £300,000 ord.
    T. & B.A.T. 49·8%; L.N.E. 24·9%; L.M.S. 24·9%.
29. *Wilts and Dorset.*—£50,000 ord. T. & B.A.T. 25%; S.R. 25%.
30. *Yorkshire Traction.*—£24,350 pref.; £150,000 ord. T. &
    B.A.T. 47·6%; L.N.E. 23·8%; L.M.S. 23·8%.
    30 (a) *County Motors.*—Yorks Traction control jointly with
    Yorks (W.D.) Elec. Trams and Yorks (W.R.) Elec.
    Trams (*q.v.*).
    H.M.S. Catherwood.—£25,000 ord. T. & B.A.T. 100%.

Scottish Motor Traction Group

31. *Scottish Motor Traction.*—£1,000,000 pref.*; £746,078 ord.
    L.N.E. 25%; L.M.S. 25%.
    31 (a) *Central S.M.T.*—£333,750 ord. S.M.T. 99% approx.
    31 (b) *Western S.M.T.*—£500,690 ord. S.M.T. 100%.
    31 (b) (i) *Greenock Motor.*—£42,000 pref.; £57,500 ord.
    W.S.M.T. 100%.
    31 (b) (ii) *Rothesay Trams.*—£10,000 pref.; £81,768 ord.
    W.S.M.T. 100%.
    31 (c) *W. Alexander.*—£200,000 pref.; £700,000 ord. L.N.E.
    25%; L.M.S. 25%.
    31 (d) *Lanarkshire Traction.*—£373,750 ord. S.M.T. 95%.

* Non-voting Preference Shares.

31 (e) *M'Kirdy and M'Millan.*—£4,512 pref.; £7,500 ord.
S.M.T. control.

31 (f) *Peebles Motor.*—£3,240 ord. S.M.T. control.

31 (g) *Pitlochry Motor.*—£25,000 ord. S.M.T. control.

31 (h) *Simpsons and Forresters.*—£100,000 ord. S.M.T. control.

INDEPENDENT COMPANIES

32. *A. Timpson.*—£62,650 pref.; £73,000 ord.

33. *Barton Transport.*—£70,000 pref.; £12,500 ord.

34. *Bath Tramways.*—£40,000 ord.

35. *Belfast Omnibus.*—£144,930 ord.

36. *David MacBrayne* (1928).—£275,000 ord. L.M.S. 50%.

37. *Dublin United Trams.*—£600,000 pref.; £660,000 ord.

38. *Elliott Bros. (Bournemouth).*—£6,321 pref.; £6,963 ord.

39. *Great N. Railway (Ireland).*

40. *Highland Transport.*—£35,000 ord. L.M.S. 50%.

41. *Irish Omnibus.*—£66,130 ord. Gt. Southern Rly. of Ireland.
100%.

42. *J. Bullock* (1928).—£3,985 pref.; £26,793 ord.

43. *Lancashire United.*—£192,878 ord.

44. *Balfour, Beatty and Co.*—Power Securities 100% control.

44 (a) *Cheltenham Dist.*—£24,000 pref.; £72,000 ord. B.B.
control.

44 (b) *Midland General.*—£150,000 ord. B.B. 100%.

44 (b) (i) *Stratford-upon-Avon.*—Mid. Gen. control.

44 (c) *Mansfield and District Omnibus.*—£80,000 pref.; £44,834
ord.—B.B. control.

44 (c) (i) *Mansfield and District Traction.*—£58,000 pref.;
£119,000 ord. Mans. and Dist. Omnibus 100%.

45. *Redcar Services.*—£37,832 pref.*; £12,371 ord.

46. *Red and White.*—£129,335 ord.

47. *Westcliff-on-Sea Motor.*—£99,956 ord.

48. *Yorkshire (W.R.) E. Trams.*—£231,305 pref.; £204,885 ord.

48 (a) *West Riding Auto.*—£80,006 ord. Yorks (W.R.) Trams
100%.

* Non-voting Preference Shares.

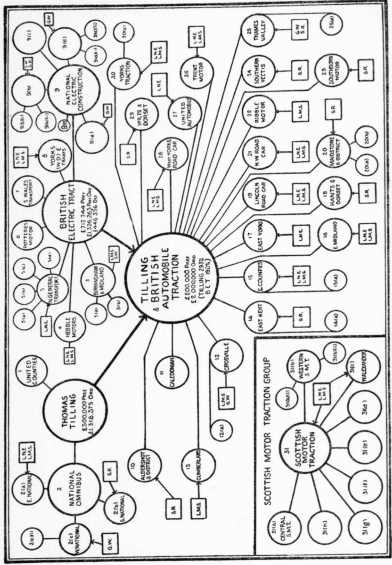

FIG. 4. From *The Economist*, 17th February, 1934, by courtesy of the Editor.

HAULAGE COMPANIES
RAILWAY GROUP

(A) L.M.S.

1. *Joseph Nall.*—£20,000 pref.; £70,212 ord. L.M.S. 50%.
2. *Wordie and Co.*—£100,000 ord. held by L.M.S. ? 100%.

(B) L.N.E.

3. *Currie and Co. (Newcastle).*—£127,500 ord. L.N.E. 50%.

(C) JOINT RAILWAY CONTROL.

4. *Hays Wharf Cartage.*—£138,292 pref.; £211,708 ord. held equally by 4 companies.
    4 (*a*) *Pickfords.*—£52,700 pref.; £155,900 ord. £130,902 formerly held indirectly by Hays Wharf presumed sold to Railways.
5. *Carter Paterson.*—£365,000 pref.; £253,004 ord. held equally by 4 companies.
    5 (*a*) *City and Suburban Carriers.*—C.P. control.

TILLING GROUP

6. *E. W. Rudd.*—£50,000 ord. Thos. Tilling control.
7. *Lon. and S. Counties Trans.*—£8,900 pref.; £30,340 ord. British Electric Traction control through National Electric Construction.

OSWALD TILLOTSON GROUP

8. *Oswald Tillotson* (1929).—£100,000 pref.; £200,000 ord. Joint control with 9.
9. *Bouts-Tillotson Trans.*—£175,000 ord. Joint control with 8.
    9 (*a*) *City Express.*—£3,019 ord. B.-T. 100%.
    9 (*b*) *W. V. Greenwood.*—£2,000 ord. B.-T. 100%.
        9 (*b*) (i) *Same Day Deliveries.*—W. V. Greenwood control.
    9 (*c*) *Mac Carriers.*—£10,000 ord. B.-T. 100%.
        9 (*c*) (i) *Parker and Son.*—Mac Carriers control.
        9 (*c*) (ii) *Lon. and Commer.*—Mac Carriers control.
        9 (*c*) (iii) *Western Rd. Trans.*—Mac Carriers control.
    9 (*d*) *R. V. Morriss.*—£3,000 ord. B.-T. 100%.
    9 (*e*) *Ryburn Un. Trans.*—£64,522. B.-T. 100%.

INDEPENDENT COMPANIES

10. *McNamara and Co.* (1921).—£149,982, ord.
10. (*a*) *Allied Transport.*—£18,000 ord. McNamara control.

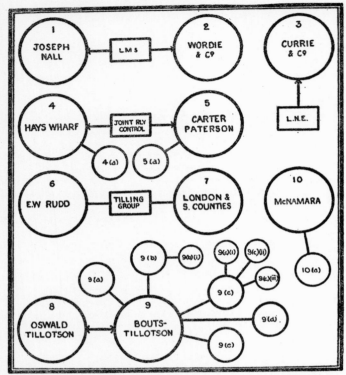

FIG. 5. From *The Economist*, 24th February, 1934, by courtesy of the Editor.

11. *United Service Transport.*—£94,548 pref.; £3,742 ord.
12. *Union Cartage.*—Union Cold Storage 100%.
13. *Mickleover Trans.*—£10,000 ord. United Dairies 100%.
14. *A. G. Gupwell.*—£12,003 ord.
15. *Arthur Pearman.*—£30,000 ord.
16. *Bean's Express.*—£30,000 debs.; £9,034 ord.
17. *Beck and Pollitzer.*
18. *Bristol Haulage.*—Bristol Industries 100%.
19. *Chaplins.*—£33,000 ord.
20. *Convoys.*—£20,000 ord.
21. *E. Tilbury.*—£70,000 pref.; £15,000 ord.
22. *F. J. Timmis.*—£15,015 ord.
23. *Hurst and Payne.*

24. *J. Blake and Co.*—£41,462 ord.
25. *J. Reece, Ltd.*—£5,090 ord.
26. *J. Bennett (Croydon).*—£20,002 ord.
27. *Keith and Boyle.*—£35,900 pref.; £2,500 ord.
28. *M.R.S.*—£75,000 ord.
29. *M. and W. Mack.*
30. *Northern Motor.*—£50,000 pref.; £50,000 ord.
31. *Overseas Motor.*—£50,700 ord.
32. *Samuel Taylor.*—£15,000 pref.; £12,500 ord.
33. *A. Smart.*
34. *Sutton and Co.*—£114,571 pref.; £300,000 ord. ⎱
35. *Sutton and Co. (Manchester).*—£20,000 pref.; £30,000 ord. ⎰ [1]
36. *Southern Roadways.*—£32,166 pref.; £33,089 ord.
37. *Southern Transport.*—£5,000 ord.
38. *Talbot-Serpell Trans.*—£14,893 ord.
39. *W. Clarkson.*—£68,514 ord.
40. *W. E. Chivers.*—£20,000 pref.; £20,000 ord.
41. *Chas. A. Wells.*
42. *Scottish Express Deliveries.*

Among the railways' other road passenger transport interests, one may mention the L.M.S.R. 50 per cent shareholding in David MacBrayne Ltd., whose omnibuses run in conjunction with the L.M.S. steamer services in Scotland; and its 50 per cent interest in Highland Transport Ltd. The L.M.S.R. also has an interest in the Great Southern Railway of Ireland, which has entire control of the Irish Omnibus Co. Ltd., and the G.W.R. has acquired interests in nearly all the principal road passenger transport companies in its area.

For some time past there have been loud and numerous complaints among road hauliers of the unorganized, unco-ordinated, and madly competitive state of their section of the industry. Already there have been amalgamations; and there are four relatively small "groups." Also several associations of road hauliers are now well-established. But even so the relatively unorganized road haulage side of the industry stands in striking contrast to the highly organized passenger transport

---

[1] Sutton & Co. and Sutton & Co. (Manchester) have since been purchased by the railways, through Carter Paterson & Co.

side described above, for there is no single dominating combine, and although many of the companies maintain regular
services, "the bulk of the business is of 'tramp' rather than
'liner' character."[1] The largest single combine is the Bouts-
Tillotson group of companies, capitalized at approximately
£558,000. Oswald Tillotson Ltd., has recently expanded into
the road haulage industry from the manufacture and recon-
ditioning of motor vehicles. In the small Tilling group of
companies (E. W. Rudd and London and Southern Counties
Transport), capitalized at £88,240, we have a link with the
great passenger-carrying Tilling-British Electric Traction
combine. McNamara & Co., Ltd., with their subsidiary company, Allied Transport, operate a general carrying business
(including mail transport contracts with the G.P.O.), originally
established in 1837. So far the railway companies' road goods
services are mainly auxiliary to their rail services. They have
not launched out into the road haulage business to anything
like the same extent as they have on the passenger side of the
road transport industry. It is hard to say whether their joint
acquisition, in July, 1933, of the control of the group comprising Hays Wharf Cartage Co., Pickfords, Carter Paterson,
and City and Suburban Carriers[2] marks the inception of
a more vigorous and expansive policy on the part of the
railways in this section of the road transport industry, or
whether, under the system of State regulation and control
introduced by the Road and Rail Traffic Act, 1933, they
are no longer apprehensive of increased competition in
this field.

No such doubt arises regarding the progress of the combination movement in other parts of the industry. The diagrams on pp. 140 and 142 indicate only the point reached at the
beginning of 1934, not the attainment of a position of comparative stability. The buying up of the "small fry"—bus
and coach companies and goods carriers alike—is still proceed-

---

[1] *The Economist*, 24th February, 1934, 409.
[2] The cost to each of the four railway companies was approximately
£454,000.

ing rapidly and on a large scale,[1] while syndicates are gradually gaining control of the "large fry."[2]

It is probable that the tendency towards combination derives some strength from the licensing provisions of Part I of the Road and Rail Traffic Act, 1933; for although this statute does not affect the numbers of motor vehicle owners who carry their own goods in their own lorries or vans, it places a certain restriction upon the numbers of vehicles and new entrants to the ranks of the road hauliers. Henceforth it is no longer true that anybody with a small capital can put one or more lorries on the road and so intensify or revive competition. The Area Traffic Commissioners in exercising their statutory powers will, as we have seen, take into consideration (*inter alia*) the transport needs of their areas, the existing supply of transport, the degree of traffic congestion on the roads, and any objections made by persons or corporations who are already providing facilities, *whether by road or any other method of transport*. Consolidation and combination of interests seems likely to follow.

The regularization of the haulage industry in respect of hours and wages, and the virtual guarantee provided by the licensing system to established operators against new competition, has brought about a marked tendency for haulers in many districts to "get together" with a view to agreeing scales of charges and eliminating undercutting. This movement has in many districts been sponsored by the Road Haulage Association and the Commercial Motor Users' Association, or by some local association of haulage contractors, but in other areas it has been spontaneous. The difficulties of agreeing scales of charges are considerable, although of course infinitely simpler than a railway classification. It is understood, however, that the Traffic Commissioners look with favour on this movement to stabilize rates, and that firms

---

[1] Not always to the complete satisfaction of the buyers. See e.g. *Motor Transport*, 28th May, 1935, on the absorption of two companies, Ryburn United Transport and Mac Carriers, by Bouts-Tillotson Transport Ltd., a subsidiary of Oswald Tillotson Ltd.

[2] A good example is the acquisition by the Holdsworth-Hanson syndicate of a controlling interest in Oswald Tillotson Ltd. in May, 1935. A perusal of the files of *Modern Transport* and *Motor Transport* reveals the continuous and extensive nature of this aspect of the rationalization of road transport.

which are known to be undercutters may find difficulty in getting their licences renewed. . . .

The rapidity with which it has been necessary for road haulage operators to change from conditions of free and unregulated competition to those of a closely supervised industry under the eye of the Traffic Commissioners has left little time during the past year for amalgamation and concentration of control within the industry, although this may be expected to follow in due course . . .[1]

But before this movement has developed very far, the State may take more positive and extensive action along the line of socialization. Indeed, the first move has already been made.

On 1st July, 1933, the London Passenger Transport Act, 1933, came into force, and the bulk of the passenger transport services of Greater London was combined and placed under the control of a specially appointed public body called the London Passenger Transport Board. The Act in its main outline embodies a scheme originally drawn up by a Labour Minister of Transport (Mr. Herbert Morrison), but was ultimately enacted by a parliament predominantly Conservative. The new combine did not amount to a clear-cut substitution of public for private ownership and control. The ownership of the capital remains partly in the hands of private investors and partly in those of certain local authorities. As to control, the new arrangements mean not only a transfer from private to public enterprise, but also the displacement of various separate local authorities by public control of a very different kind. A huge concentration, with its concomitant promise of better co-ordination, is established; and there is little doubt it has come none too soon. The London Passenger Transport Board now controls the largest passenger transport system in the world. It operates in the London Passenger Transport Area (i.e. within a radius of approximately thirty miles from Charing Cross), a region of nearly 2000 sq. miles containing a population of over 9,000,000, and comprises the Underground group or combine (eighteen railway, omnibus and tramway companies), the

[1] Mr. C. T. Brunner in *The Times British Motor Industry Supplement*, 2nd April, 1935.

Metropolitan Railway, and all the other tramway undertakings and "independent"omnibus companies. The suburban sections of the main-line railways are not taken over, but the services are co-ordinated with those of the Board, and receipts are pooled. In addition to the eighteen Underground companies, the Act schedules sixty other companies and the passenger transport undertakings of fourteen local authorities. Between them these undertakings owned 11,430 vehicles (omnibuses, motor-coaches, trolley-buses, trams and railway coaches), and during their last year they carried 3463 million passengers an aggregate distance of 485 million miles. The employees in all grades number nearly 72,000.

Obviously the choice of the members of the Board is a problem of vital importance, and the solution has been sought along somewhat novel lines. The appointing body is not, as it very well might have been, the Minister of Transport in consultation with certain expert advisers, but a body of Appointing Trustees consisting of the Chairman of the London County Council, the Chairman of the London Clearing Banks, the President of the Law Society, the President of the Institute of Chartered Accountants, a representative of the London Traffic Advisory Committee, elected by the committee, and, after the first constitution of the Board, one of its members nominated by it for the purpose. The first four are *ex officio* members. The Appointing Trustees are convened by the Minister of Transport; three members constitute a quorum, and decisions are made by a majority of the votes of the members present, the chairman having a second or casting vote. For the guidance of the Trustees, the Act stipulates that the chairman and other members of the Board "shall be persons who have had wide experience, and have shown capacity, in transport, industrial, commercial or financial matters or in the conduct of public affairs and, in the case of two members, shall be persons who have had not less than six years experience in local government within the London Passenger Transport Area."[1]

[1] The first Board was appointed as follows—

The members' salaries and allowances for expenses are to be fixed by the Minister of Transport after consultation with the Appointing Trustees and with the consent of the Treasury. The period of office (between three and seven years) is determined in each case by the Trustees, and members are to be eligible for reappointment. No member of the Board may hold or purchase for his own benefit any securities in any passenger transport company or undertaking operating in the London Passenger Transport Area, or any London Transport Stock issued by the Board pursuant to the Act. Failure to comply disqualifies the member; so also does election to the House of Commons, bankruptcy, or absence from the Board's meetings for more than six consecutive months without the consent of the Minister of Transport. Three members form a quorum.

The Act provides an advisory committee by reconstituting the London Transport Advisory Committee which was set up under the London Traffic Act, 1924. The Advisory Committee now consists of forty members (each holding office for three years). Two members represent the Board; the remaining thirty-eight represent various interests, such as labour, the local authorities in and around London, the various police forces in the London Traffic Area, the main-line railways, and the providers and users of other forms of

Name	Qualifications	Term of Present Appointment
Lord Ashfield	⎫ The two full-time members. Experienced in the control of London passenger transport.	7 years
Mr. Frank Pick	⎬	7 years
Sir John Gilbert	(of the London County Council). Experienced in local government within the Area.	3 years
Sir Edward Holland	(of the Surrey County Council).	3 years
Mr. Ashley Cooper	(a Director of the Bank of England) Experienced in finance.	5 years
Sir Henry Maybury	(technical expert representing the London Traffic Advisory Committee, of which he is chairman).	3 years
Mr. John Cliff	(Secretary of the Transport and General Workers' Union, and formerly a member of the London Transport Advisory Committee). Technical knowledge of transport, also representative of the interests of Labour.	5 years

transport in London (e.g. taxi-cabs and horse-drawn vehicles). Representation is not given to stockholders, nor to consumers *qua* consumers. The duties of the Advisory Committee are—

(*a*) to consider, report to and advise the Minister on any matters relating to traffic within the London Traffic Area which in their opinion ought to be brought to the notice of the Minister.

(*b*) to make representations to the Board with respect to any matter connected with the services or facilities provided by the Board in the London Traffic Area.

(*c*) to consider, report to and advise the Minister on any other matters which . . . are referred to them by the Minister.

The Advisory Committee has power to make public inquiries into matters within its scope, and, like a court of law, it can take evidence on oath and compel witnesses to attend and produce documents.

In general terms the Board's duties are to provide an adequate and properly co-ordinated system of passenger transport within its area and from five to ten miles outside according to the needs and circumstances of particular districts; including, possibly, the running of steamboats, motor-boats or other vessels on the River Thames. The Act confers upon the Board a monopoly of the right to pick up *and* set down passengers within the London Passenger Transport Area. Other owners of "stage and express" passenger services may pick up passengers *or* set them down within the Area, but they are prohibited from doing both without the written consent of the Board. It is clearly the intention of the Legislature that the Board shall improve and extend existing services, eliminating and avoiding all "unnecessary and wasteful competitive services," and that it shall charge such fares as will enable it to cover all working expenses, all the interest and sinking fund charges on its capital, and to create an adequate Reserve Fund.

The Board must deposit at the Ministry of Transport complete schedules of the fares in force on 1st July, 1933, throughout the whole combine; and any subsequent proposed alterations of fares must be publicly notified by the Board in conformity with regulations to be made by the Minister of Transport. Furthermore, the

. . . Railway Rates Tribunal established under the Railways Act, 1921, . . . may from time to time . . . by order reduce or increase the fares or any of them charged or chargeable by the Board . . . provided that the rates tribunal in making any order may have regard to the establishment and maintenance of a general basis for fares throughout the London Passenger Transport Area.

Fares so revised are to be unalterable for at least one year, unless the Minister of Transport gives special permission on the ground that "there has been a material change in the circumstances."

In order to arrange the co-ordination of the Board's services with the London suburban passenger services of the four main-line railway companies, a Standing Joint Committee of eight members was set up, four of whom are to be appointed by the Board and one by each of the railway companies. The Joint Committee's duties were to consider and report to the Board measures for co-operation in the services, and it was also charged with the duty of preparing for submission to the Board and the railway companies a scheme for the pooling of the whole of the passenger receipts of the Board and of each of the railway companies on their London suburban lines.

The Act creates five classes of London Transport Stocks, to be issued to the local authorities and the stockholders in the transport companies whose undertakings have been transferred to the Board, in exchange for their holdings in those undertakings on various terms previously agreed upon. In certain specified cases the amount payable in stock and/or cash was determined by arbitration or by agreement confirmed by an Arbitration Tribunal set up under the Act. The Board has no "equity" or common stocks, the nearest approach being the junior or C stock on which the rate of dividend may vary, according to the residue of profits available in any financial year, between zero and a maximum of 6 per cent until 1936–7. After that year the C stock dividends must be not less than $5\frac{1}{2}$ nor more than 6 per cent. Normally no stockholder has any right to participate in the conduct of the Board's affairs; but if the Board makes default in payment of the interest on the A, the L. A. or the B stocks for a period of three months or more, the holders of not less than 5 per cent of the class of stock upon which the interest is in arrears may apply to the High Court for the appointment of a receiver or a receiver and manager. The holders of at least 5 per cent of the C stock have a similar right if, after the initial "years of grace," the Board fails to pay the "standard rate" of $5\frac{1}{2}$ per cent upon that stock. This means, of course, that in the not distant future the whole of the Board, as appointed by the Appointing Trustees, might be superseded by a receiver and manager brought in from outside on the initiative of a minority of the junior stockholders; but, unless the Board had grown exceedingly incompetent, it is difficult to see how this would be likely to make the management more efficient.

In addition to the issue of London Transport stock as consideration for transfer of the various undertakings, the Board has power to borrow up to £10 millions plus the unexhausted statutory borrowing powers of the underground railways taken over. All sums so borrowed are to be repaid within ninety years of the issue of the stock. The Board also has power to borrow temporarily, e.g. by the issue of short-term bonds or on bank overdrafts, but the total amount outstanding at any time must not exceed £3 millions.

To deal with disputes regarding rates of wages, hours of duty, or other conditions of service upon which the Board and the trade unions concerned have failed to reach an agreement, Part VI of the Act sets up (a) a Negotiating Committee consisting of six representatives appointed by the Board and six representatives of the employees (two appointed by the National Union of Railwaymen, two by the Associated Society of Locomotive Engineers and Firemen, and two by the Railway Clerks' Association); and (b) a Wages Board consisting of an independent chairman

nominated by the Minister of Labour, six representatives of
the Board appointed by the Board, six representatives of the
employees (two appointed by each of the three trade unions
mentioned above), one person appointed by the General
Council of the Trades Union Congress, one person appointed
by the Co-operative Union, one by the Association of British
Chambers of Commerce, and one by the National Confedera-
tion of Employers' Organizations. If the Negotiating Committee fails to settle a dispute, it must be referred to the
Wages Board. There is also provision for the establishment
of councils within the Board's undertaking, consisting of
officers of the Board and representatives of the employees.
The functions and constitution of these bodies are not laid
down, but no doubt the intention is that they shall resemble
works councils.

Clearly, the main provisions of this part of the Act stand
foursquare upon the recognition of trade unionism. A very
noteworthy omission from the Act, however, is the name of
the Transport and General Workers' Union. This union has
(or had in 1933) a distinct preference for non-statutory negotiating machinery, which it considers to be more flexible and
therefore more suited to the varying conditions under which
its members are employed; whereas the railway unions have
no such preference and have, indeed, participated for more
than a decade in the statutory scheme for the settlement of
industrial disputes set up by the Railways Act of 1921. In
inter-union discussion of the London Passenger Transport Bill it
was agreed that the respective unions should be free to follow
their own lines; so that it appears that by no means all of the
employees of the London Passenger Transport Board will be
covered by the machinery described in the preceding paragraph.

The position of the consumer or user of the transport
services is safeguarded only indirectly: (a) by the fact that the
clear intention of the Legislature is that, although the Board is
expected to pay its way out of its own earnings, the whole
undertaking is to be run primarily for service and not primarily
for profit; (b) by the fact that the Railway Rates Tribunal has

some control over alterations of fares: and (c) by the right given to local authorities to make representations to the Railway Rates Tribunal as to the adequacy of services or any proposed withdrawal or reduction of services within their areas.

It has been argued that under the Act in its final form there will not be sufficient parliamentary control over the general conduct of the undertaking. Although it is true that Parliament always has power substantially to amend the Act, or to dissolve the Board and appoint another by a different method, or to transfer or lease the whole undertaking to one or more private companies, it is in fact very unlikely to do anything of the kind. So long as the present Act is in force the interposition of "this curious body of Appointing Trustees" has given the London Passenger Transport Board even greater immunity from parliamentary control than the Central Electricity Board and the British Broadcasting Corporation. But, on the other hand, it may be said that the appointment of the members of the Board is not the only channel through which parliamentary surveillance and control can be exercised. Under the provisions of the London Passenger Transport Act, 1933, the Minister of Transport has power (a) to remove any members of the Board for incompetence or misbehaviour; (b) to consult with, and act upon the advice of, the Advisory Committee; (c) to make regulations as to how the Board shall give public notice of proposed alterations of fares. (As we have seen, Parliament has delegated the control of fares to the Railway Rates Tribunal.) Moreover, the Board must make an annual report to the Minister of Transport, "and such report shall be laid before both Houses of Parliament and shall be on sale at a reasonable charge to the public at the offices of the Board"; and the Board must furnish to the Minister "such financial and statistical returns as may be agreed between the Minister and the Board or, in default of agreement, as may be determined by the rates tribunal," and an annual statement of accounts in a form prescribed by the Minister and audited by auditors approved by him.

11—(B.251)

The London Passenger Transport Board's reports for the years ending 30th June, 1934 and 1935, contain a clear and comprehensive review of each year's activities, followed by "accounts with a wealth of detail which leaves no essential fact unknown and no secrets hidden." During the two years the Board absorbed additional undertakings and reorganized its fleet of vehicles, which at 30th June, 1935, numbered 5975 buses and coaches, 2473 trams, 63 trolley buses, 3167 railway passenger vehicles, 820 ancillary railway vehicles (e.g. goods wagons), and 481 lorries and miscellaneous road vehicles.

The passenger receipts of the London Traffic Pool were—

	Years ended 30th June,	
	1934	1935
Originating on—	£	£
Railways	16,980,180	17,847,495
Buses and coaches	14,634,592	15,774,053
Trams	5,895,920	5,932,838
Trolley buses	157,873	163,801
Total	37,668,565	39,718,187
Average per passenger journey . .	2·305d.	2·308d.

(*Note.* Owing to the acquisition of certain undertakings during 1934 and 1935 the figures for the two years are not exactly comparable.)

The Board's share of these pooled receipts for the year 1934–5 was slightly over 62 per cent. Its total traffic receipts (nearly all from passenger traffic) were over £27¼ millions in 1933–4, and over £29 millions in 1934–5, while net profits in those years amounted to £4,956,691 and £5,126,271, after making provision out of income for future renewals to the extent of over £2 millions in 1933–4 and over £2½ millions in 1934–5. Interest at 3½ per cent and 4 per cent per annum was paid on the (junior) "C" stock for the years 1933–4 and 1934–5 respectively, after all interest charges on the senior stocks had been duly met.

(ii) AIR TRANSPORT

I

England has strong claims to the distinction of being the cradle of modern air transport. As far back as 1848 John

Stringfellow and W. S. Henson designed a model aeroplane which actually flew under its own power—a steam engine![1]— but apparently they did not undertake the financial and personal risks of building and trying to fly a full-size machine. Other evidence of British pioneer work in the air is to be found in the records of the Royal Aeronautical Society (founded in January 1866), and the Royal Aero Club, the oldest societies of their kind in the world. F. H. Wenham's first lecture to the Royal Aeronautical Society on "Aerial Locomotion" is a classical exposition of the principles of mechanical flight. But most of those early pioneers experimented with balloons which were lighter than air, not mechanically propelled, and could not be steered. It was not until the first decade of the present century, when men like Farman, Wilbur and Orville Wright Cody, Bleriot, Graham-White, Paulhan and Handley-Page were making "hops" measured in yards and seconds in flimsy contraptions resembling large box-kites, that the outline of the heavier-than-air machines of to-day began to take shape. Progress was already becoming rapid when war came and hurried development on at great speed.

Immediately after the war, Mr. G. Holt Thomas and Mr. F. Handley-Page determined to try to develop British commercial aviation. Mr. Thomas, the head of the Aircraft Manufacturing Co., formed a subsidiary—Aircraft Transport and Travel—and in August, 1919, the first daily air service for passengers and goods in the world was opened between London (Hounslow) and Paris. Others quickly followed, and by January, 1920, three British and two French companies were operating cross-channel services on regular time-tables. The machines then used were quite small.

"I remember quite clearly (says an eye-witness of these early air services) seeing a couple of passengers, resigned but still apprehensive, being packed into one of those small aeroplanes like sardines in a tin. There seemed barely room for them to sit in the tiny cabin facing each other. And then when they had been tucked into their places and seemed

[1] See *Airways and Airports*, November and December, 1934, 306, 350.

incapable of doing more than move their heads slightly, a sort of metal lid was shut down with a clang and fastened into position above their heads."[1] And so they flew to Paris amid such shrieking and roaring of engine, wind and propellor that conversation was utterly impossible. The fare was 20 guineas each.

The same writer tells us how anxiously the company's officials studied the statistics of passenger bookings in the first few weeks of the London-Paris air service. "One would walk into the little office where the clerk concerned with this work was seated and ask: 'How many have you got for to-day?' 'Two,' he would answer, with an air of satisfaction. 'And how many for to-morrow?' . . . 'Three,' he would reply, with an even greater pride."

In 1933 the average number of passengers carried between Great Britain and the Continent by all air lines, British and foreign, was nearly 250 a day.

The years 1920–4 have been well described as the period of trial and error, when the British commercial air transport industry tried "to fly by itself," and proved conclusively that this could not be done in the circumstances and conditions then prevailing, largely because foreign competitors were heavily subsidized and could afford to reduce fares far below the level of profitability for the British companies. Temporary and tentative State grants were given to the London Continental air lines (Handley-Page, Instone and Daimler) but not to other companies.[2] In 1924 pioneer services which had been started to the Channel Islands, from London to Manchester, and from Belfast to England and Scotland, all had to be discontinued owing to lack of support. Even to-day all the improvements in aircraft design and construction, the provision of more aerodromes and airports, and the increase in public interest have scarcely brought commercial aviation within sight of the goal of self-support.

At the beginning of 1924, four companies were in receipt

---

[1] H. Harper, *The Romance of a Modern Airway*, 9–10.
[2] Harper, *op. cit.*, 22–6.

of State subsidy, viz. Handley-Page Transport (London-Paris), Instone Air Line (London–Cologne), Daimler Airways (London–Berlin), and British Marine Air Navigation Co. (Southampton–Channel Islands). In the previous year the Civil Aerial Transport Committee, giving advice upon the best method of assisting air transport for the future, had recommended the establishment of a single organization, to be State-aided by subsidies arranged on a diminishing scale. As a result of this recommendation, Imperial Airways Ltd. was formed in April, 1924, to absorb the four companies then existing, and was charged with the task of developing air transport as rapidly as possible to the point at which it would become a self-supporting industry.

The fleet of aircraft taken over by Imperial Airways from the four pioneer companies consisted of eleven biplanes and two seaplanes capable of carrying from six to fourteen passengers each. Seven of the biplanes (the DH 34's) were single-engined machines built by De Havillands, fitted with a Napier "Lion" water-cooled engine. The crew consisted of the Captain-pilot; an engineer-wireless operator, and a cabin boy. Eight passengers could be carried—a 400 per cent advance upon the capacity of the machines used in 1919–20. The total pay load capacity of this fleet was 23,000 lb. and the total passenger capacity was 112.[1]

After a careful study of past experience the Directors of Imperial Airways arrived (early in 1925) at certain conclusions, viz.—

1. The company's services could never be made profitable if operated on a small scale.

2. The small aircraft was far less economical *as a fleet unit* than the large aircraft.

3. Fleet units must carry more pay load per horse-power unit.

4. Fleet units must fly a greater mileage per annum.

5. The reliability of fleet units must be increased and

[1] To-day both pay load capacity and passenger capacity of the Imperial Airways fleet is six times as large.

their maintenance costs diminished by technical improvements.

6. The most promising main line of expansion was on Empire routes.

By the end of 1926 several of the changes in organization and aircraft necessitated by these conclusions had been carried through. The British route to Amsterdam was discontinued when a German service was begun by the Deutsche Lufthansa under an agreement with Imperial Airways, and the latter company concentrated their European operations on three routes; London–Paris–Zurich; London–Ostend–Brussels–Cologne; and Southampton–Guernsey. The frequency of these services was as follows—

	Summer (May–Sept.)	Winter (Oct.–April)
London–Paris. . . .	Thrice daily	Daily
London–Paris–Basle–Zurich .	Daily	—
London–Ostend . . .	Daily	—
London–Brussels–Cologne .	Twice daily	Daily
Southampton–Channel Islands .	Weekly	Weekly

On these services during 1927 the Company's machines completed a machine mileage of 614,655 and a horse-power mileage of over 543·5 millions. Three big triple-engined air liners—the first of their kind—capable of carrying nineteen passengers and a crew of three were built and put into service in 1926, and in January 1927 the Company forged its first link in the chain of Imperial Air communications by opening a service extending over 1100 miles between Cairo and Basra. With the coming of summer the Cairo–Basra service was run weekly in each direction instead of fortnightly, and the weight of mails carried rose from 856 lb. in January, 1927, to 5560 lb. at the end of the year; or from 214 lb. to 618 lb. per flight on the average. An operating efficiency of 100 per cent was maintained in respect of the commencement and completion of scheduled flights. After two years of successful operation this route was extended eastward to Karachi and westward to Genoa. Genoa and Basle were connected by night train, and at Basle the service linked up with the European air lines.

During 1929 the Southampton–Guernsey service was discontinued but the two services to the Continent were maintained. The frequency of the London–Paris service was increased to four times daily in summer and twice daily in winter, and a winter service was operated from London, *via* Paris, to Basle twice weekly. The London–Brussels–Cologne summer service, on the other hand, was reduced to once daily. The regular flights covered a total of 778,260 miles, representing nearly 840·8 million horse-power miles or nearly double the minimum horse-power mileage laid down by the conditions of the subsidy. The Cairo–Basra weekly service was continued with complete success and it may be said that these services were now regarded as "all in the day's work." The most interesting new departure during 1929 was the linking of England and India by the first of the Empire air services. On 30th March, 1929, the first aircraft on regular service left Croydon with mails and passengers, and the latter were landed at Karachi on 6th April. The experience gained on this service during the summer indicated the necessity of arranging a better and shorter route and making special plans if winter services were to be operated.

During 1930 a London–Birmingham–Manchester–Liverpool service, flying 210 miles in 2 hours 40 min. (including stops) was inaugurated by Imperial Airways. The London–Karachi service was improved and extended to Delhi and operated weekly throughout the year. Plans were also made for beginning an Egypt–Capetown service, and tentative schemes were considered for a weekly service from India to Australia and for a transatlantic service. By the end of January, 1932, the Capetown service was in operation, so that it was possible to travel by air from London to Capetown via Paris, Athens, Alexandria, Cairo, Nairobi and Johannesburg; 8359 miles in eleven days. The economic and technical problems of the proposed England–Australia and the transatlantic services were still under consideration.

General economic conditions were extremely bad in 1931–2 but in spite of this Imperial Airways made substantial progress, particularly in passenger traffic. The total number of passengers passing through Croydon Airport in 1932 was over 40,000 or 12,000 more than in 1931. The passenger traffic on the India and Africa services increased over 200 per cent from 1931 to 1932. New aircraft were put into service, viz. the 13-ton four-engined machines now in use, carrying thirty-eight passengers and a crew of four at 105 miles per hour, and the "Atlanta" class monoplanes with a cruising speed of 120 m.p.h. for the African and Australian services.

During 1933 the Continental services continued to thrive; a twice-weekly service was operated between London and Egypt; the London–India service was extended to Burma, the Federated Malay States and Singapore; and a weekly service was maintained from London to the Sudan, Uganda, Kenya, Tanganyika, Rhodesia, and South Africa. The extension to Singapore opened 8500 miles of the proposed 11,000 mile route to Australia, and in December, 1934, the air mail service was extended to Brisbane by an arrangement between Imperial Airways and its Australian associate, Qantas Empire Airways. The transatlantic service was still the subject of consideration and negotiation with American and Canadian interests. Quite recently Imperial Airways Ltd. has arranged to begin a weekly service between New York and Bermuda in co-operation with Pan American Airways Inc.

The European and Empire services operated by Imperial Airways during the summer of 1935 may be summarized as follows—

EUROPEAN SERVICES

1. Five times daily between London and Paris, and daily between London, Brussels, and Cologne, and between London, Cologne, Leipzig, Prague, Vienna, and Budapest
2. Daily between London, Basle, and Zurich, via Paris. Week-ends and on Sundays

EMPIRE SERVICES

FOUR SERVICES A WEEK—

1. ENGLAND—EGYPT
   Leaving London every Saturday, Sunday, Tuesday, and Wednesday
   Leaving Alexandria every Tuesday, Wednesday, Friday, and Saturday

EUROPEAN SERVICES (*contd.*)

between London and Le Touquet.

3. Twice weekly, carrying mails only, between London, Paris Marseilles, Rome, and Brindisi (the whole journey of 1340 miles being completed in one day during summer).

EMPIRE SERVICES (*contd.*)

TWO SERVICES A WEEK—

2. ENGLAND — EAST AFRICA —SOUTH AFRICA (JOHANNESBURG)
Leaving London every Wednesday and Sunday
Leaving Johannesburg every Wednesday and Saturday

3. ENGLAND — INDIA (CALCUTTA)
Leaving London every Tuesday and Saturday
Leaving Calcutta every Tuesday and Saturday

ONE SERVICE A WEEK—

4. ENGLAND — EAST AFRICA —SOUTH AFRICA (CAPETOWN)
Leaving London every Wednesday
Leaving Capetown every Tuesday

5. ENGLAND — ASIA — AUSTRALIA (BRISBANE)
Leaving London every Saturday
Leaving Brisbane every Wednesday
Singapore — Brisbane section of Australia service for mails only.

The fleet of Imperial Airways and companies working in association on these main Empire and European routes consisted of forty-three air liners, exclusive of a number of machines used by the companies working in association with Imperial Airways on feeder line services in Africa. The staff of Imperial Airways numbered about 1400 in 1935, including 45 pilots, 109 first officers, and 54 wireless operators.

The official (Air Ministry) *Report on the Progress of Civil*

Aviation 1933 contains the following paragraph on general progress—

In the recent growth of traffic on Imperial Airways' routes a striking feature has been the increasing numbers of business men, not only in London, but also in the provinces, who are making regular use of the services to the Continent, and are also, in many cases, taking advantage of the very substantial savings of time to be effected by using the Empire services both for intermediate journeys and . . . between terminal points. . . . It was found possible during 1933 to arrange very considerable reductions in the insurance rates for passengers travelling by the Company's services. The rates are now the same, per day of travel, as for transport by land and sea. The importance of this . . . lies in the recognition that travel by air has now become a normal method of transport.[1]

And, in confirmation of the last sentence, the same *Report* gives details of the new *internal* regular air services.

At the beginning of 1935, seventeen companies were operating air services in the British Isles, mainly between the principal cities—London, Liverpool, Glasgow, Birmingham, and Bristol—or "ferry services" across the English Channel, the Irish Sea, and the principal estuaries.[2] These internal air services include those provided by the railway companies.

The railways' powers to operate air transport were conferred by the Air Transport Act, 1929, which permits them to own and use aircraft to convey passengers and goods in Great Britain and "the Continent and islands of Europe" except east of Long. 20° E. (i.e. approximately east of Warsaw). The first air service provided by a British railway was flown between Birmingham, Cardiff, and Plymouth on 22nd May, 1933, in a time of 2 hrs. 50 min. from aerodrome to aerodrome. In 1934, after negotiations between the railway companies and Imperial Airways Ltd., a new company was established under the name of Railway Air Services Ltd. with a capital of

[1] p. 9.
[2] Flying "for hire or reward" is in the main either the operation of regular scheduled services, or special charter or "air-taxi" work. Some of the companies mentioned above provide special charter services in addition to regular services, and there are thirty or forty air-taxi companies who do not run regular scheduled services.

£50,000, for the purpose of providing such internal air services as the four chief British railway companies might require. Rail-air through-bookings for passengers and goods are now possible, either on the railway air lines or in conjunction with Imperial Airways services.

In the railway annual reports the experimental method can be seen at work. The London Midland and Scottish Railway Company operated a London–Liverpool–Belfast–Glasgow air service with a high degree of regularity at a loss of £7244 in about four months. The Great Western Railway Company operated Liverpool–Birmingham, Cardiff–Plymouth–Birmingham, and Bristol–Southampton–Cowes services also at a loss. In 1934, the company increased its air route mileage by 50 per cent over 1933 and reduced its loss to £5150. The Southern Railway operated the Birmingham–Bristol–Southampton–Cowes line jointly with the Great Western Railway and shared in the London–Isle of Wight and England–Jersey routes at a loss of £4770. The railway companies' losses on air transport in 1935 were: L.M.S., £27,276; G.W.R., £6935; S.R., £8988.

II

The primary advantage and attraction of air transport over other forms of transport is its high speed. Although aerodromes are more distant from the centres of population and business than railway and motor coach termini, this drawback is easily offset on long distance flights by the velocity of transit once the aeroplane is in the air, and the directness of the route which can be taken. Thus both routes and travel times are shortened.[1] But for relatively short flights the danger is that the time taken in going to and from aerodromes may reduce the net time-saving below the point at which it is worth the extra cost of going by air. This fact has so far largely prevented the growth of internal air lines in Great Britain in competition

[1] Aircraft are not *entirely* independent of the nature of the terrain over which they operate. Prevailing weather conditions and the abundance or lack of good landing and fueling grounds may make certain routes preferable to others.

with the railways; but in Germany and the U.S.A. the competition of air transport has been severely felt by the railways.[1]

In the early days of commercial air transport the average cruising speed was about 85 m.p.h. By 1931 it had increased to about 97–100 m.p.h. on the principal air lines of Great Britain, Germany, France, and Holland—not a very striking acceleration. But after that date a considerable "spurt" occurred. Air line companies realized once for all that in order to attract more traffic, faster journeys must be offered, and when ordering new aircraft they made their wishes felt. By the end of 1933 air liners were attaining cruising speeds ranging from 140 up to 200 m.p.h.[2]

Frequency of service, especially on the short air routes, is nearly as important as high speed, and indeed from the traveller's point of view it is, in a sense, part of it. But unless the volume and flow of traffic is large and tolerably steady, it is not possible to give frequent services unless small aircraft are used. The operator, therefore, has to choose between offering a less frequent service with the larger, more economical machines, or a more frequent service with smaller, less economical machines. As a rule he chooses the latter course because it is usually found that the offer of frequent services "creates" traffic; while infrequency of service often produces the opposite effect.

The same is true of regularity of air services. Regular services, flying on weekdays and Sundays alike, and at all seasons, stimulate constant use by the public. Irregular services produce the opposite effect.

The degree of safety and comfort are two other important factors which help to make or mar air transport, just as they do any other form of transport. But it must be remembered that since air transport has come into a world already accustomed to obtain a high degree of comfort and safety from all forms of land and sea transport, it cannot hope to succeed

---

[1] Hallsworth, *Economic Journal*, December, 1934, 547.
[2] *Airways and Airports*, December, 1933, 252

unless it can offer similar facilities, in addition to its other attractions, to help to justify the higher fares charged. For, at least down to the present time, air transport is more expensive than other transport, in spite of the fact that many air lines are in receipt of State subsidies.

Generally speaking, air transport shows clearer advantages over other forms of transport for transit over very long distances, e.g. transcontinental journeys[1]; or when the distance is so long that the journey cannot be completed between morning and evening except by air; or when one or more transhipments (e.g. from railway to steamer, and from steamer back to railway) in a relatively short journey, and/or a sea passage can be avoided by going by air (e.g. the journey from London to Paris, or Brussels); or where transport by other means is extremely difficult, e.g. owing to absence or inferiority of roads or railways. Therefore it is not surprising that the British Air lines which have developed first are those to and from the Continent, and several of the principal parts of the British Empire.

The advantages of regular internal air lines in such vast regions as the United States, Australia, Russia, and even Germany, are almost self-evident, and the remarkable rise and development of air transport in those countries is scarcely surprising. But the successful development and operation of internal air lines in Great Britain is hampered by the relatively short distances to be covered, the high efficiencies of existing road and rail transport services, and the variable weather conditions which militate against punctuality and, in certain circumstances, against safety also. In short, it appears that British internal air lines are most likely to be successful on routes involving a sea passage and/or one or more transhipments; or where aircraft can take much shorter, because more direct, routes between certain points which are separated by long land or sea distances (e.g. the journey from Cardiff to

[1] Provided that the space available for passengers is not too restricted. Ideally, long-distance aircraft should be so large that passengers can move from their seats occasionally, and sleep on board in comfort, if necessary.

Plymouth). Very largely it is a question of relative speed and convenience, and it is probably not far from the truth to say that in order to be attractive to the general run of travellers for business purposes, internal air transport in Britain must include night as well as day flying, and at speeds upwards of 200 m.p.h.[1] This involves (*inter alia*) an accurate weather reporting service and wireless communication with all regular aircraft in flight, together with the necessary instruments, experience and skill which make "blind-flying" not only possible but comparatively safe.

The types of freight most likely to be transported by air are—

(*a*) Goods "in a hurry"—in order to meet sudden and urgent needs, for instance, or to rectify errors, or to appear simultaneously in two or more centres, e.g. Paris fashion garments, or Press photographs.[2]

(*b*) Perishable and very fragile goods such as fruit, flowers and scientific instruments, because of speed and careful handling.

(*c*) Highly valuable goods, because reduction of transit-time is reduction of risk of loss. Insurance companies, indeed, quote reduced preferential premiums for air-borne bullion, expensive furs, and similar articles.

(*d*) Mails.

One cannot stress too strongly the fact that it is chiefly in order to save time that people or goods go by air; and experience of passenger traffic by air shows that speed appeals almost as much to holiday-makers as to travellers on business. The problem for the operator of commercial air transport is to discover how much more revenue he is likely to gain by flying faster, and how much more it will cost him to do so.

The quantity of transport service each aircraft can provide

---

[1] Cf. R. M. Clarkson in *Air Travel*, April, 1934, 112.
[2] The collection of news pictures from distant places for the newspapers is becoming a profitable line of special charter business for the air transport companies.

in a given period depends, in the main, upon four factors, viz.—

1. Net pay load (e.g. in tons).
2. Average cruising speed (m.p.h.).
3. Number of flying-hours in a given period (e.g. one year).
4. Load factor, or average fraction of maximum pay load carried.

These four factors multiplied together give the number of units of transport service in ton-miles per annum.

The net pay load is known when the aeroplane is delivered new; but it has been found that the total weight of all machines increases with age, in spite of all efforts to prevent it. Therefore the net pay load decreases somewhat as the age of the machine increases. An air liner of 10 tons gross weight, capable of carrying from sixteen to twenty-four passengers, will probably have a net pay load of about 22 per cent, the remaining 78 per cent being taken up by the engines, fuselage, wings, fuel and oil tanks, crew and their equipment, and the equipment for passengers. It is probable that as time goes on the gross weight of aircraft may be reduced, e.g. by using lighter materials of the same strength, or improved methods of construction which reduce weight but not strength. For example, it is authoritatively stated that the "monospar" system of construction makes possible a saving of 30 per cent of dead weight without any sacrifice of strength or other safety factors. Furthermore, the shorter the flight-stages, the smaller the amount (and therefore the weight) of fuel that need be carried and the higher the pay load. But against this it must be remembered that frequent stops reduce the flying-hours per annum and tend to *raise* the unit costs of air transport.

In favour of the Diesel-type compression-ignition engine it is urged that it reduces operating costs because less fuel is used per h.p.; that the fuel used is cheaper per gallon than petrol; and that the pay load is increased because the weight of fuel required for a given journey is less than the weight of the necessary quantity of petrol. But against this last advantage must be set the greater weight of the compression-ignition engine compared with the petrol engine.

It is convenient to express the net pay load as a percentage or fraction of the gross weight of the aircraft. This is usually referred to as the "percentage pay load." Hence the maximum payable transport capacity of a given aircraft is its—

Gross weight × percentage pay load × cruising speed.

Cruising speed is a product of three factors, (a) the power or design of the machine, (b) weather (especially wind) conditions, and (c) the amount of subtraction from the maximum possible cruising speed regarded as necessary in order to ensure (i) maximum economy in running costs and (ii) accurate running to time-tables. Some reserve of cruising speed must be kept in hand to be used in unfavourable circumstances, e.g. against strong head winds.

The air speed of a machine and the ground speed are identical only when the air is still. The normal distance an aircraft can travel over the ground in an hour is augmented when it is flying with the wind according to the force and exact direction of the wind, and diminished when flying against the wind. Therefore less time and cost are involved in a flight between two given points if the wind is following, and more if it is a head wind.

Higher average cruising speed may be reached by

(1) increasing the engine power;
(2) improving the fuel-efficiency;
(3) reducing the wing area;
(4) reducing the over-all drag.

Increased engine power usually means greater gross weight (engine *plus* fuel), higher total running costs, and higher costs per unit of transport service because the pay load tends to decrease while total costs increase. Research into fuel efficiency is still proceeding and small improvements are made from time to time; but new and better fuels may cost more per gallon, and it is for the air transport operator to decide whether the additional fuel efficiency is worth the extra expense. Reducing the wing area is equivalent to increasing the wing-loading, i.e. the total weight to be lifted per square foot of wing area. This reduces safety, mainly because the landing speed must be higher if the wing area is reduced, and commercial aircraft pilots have to land in all weathers, and may, on occasions, be forced to land in unfavourable and difficult places. Probably the perfection of the autogiro will overcome this difficulty and, at the same time, make it unnecessary to have *extensive* aerodromes miles away from the centres of the cities they serve. Moreover, the use of the variable-pitch air screw to secure good take-off and high airscrew efficiency in level flight,[1] and the invention of wing-flaps to steepen the angle of glide and reduce the stalling speed when landing, seems likely to make higher wing-loadings possible in the near future without sacrifice of safety.

We are left with the problem of reducing the "over-all drag" or wind resistance. The outstanding line of thought at present, it seems, is that by "cleanness of line" a quite remarkable economy of operation can be achieved, and that this is cheaper and better than increase of engine power. "Giving a greater speed for the same horse-power, it improves the climb, take-off and range, and shortens the time for a given journey . . . the undercarriage must be out of the way, or partly so, when the machine is in flight. After struggling with the design of a retractable undercarriage for a long time, engineers are now finding that it can be achieved. . . . Other surface irregularities are produced by windows, struts, wires, and the abrupt jointings of wing surfaces to the main body. Rounding the contours so that the main wing and tail units merge into the fuselage is found to give improved performance."[2]

The number of flying hours depends upon the speed of the machine, the frequency of the service required, and the

[1] The object of the variable pitch device is to increase the blade pitch *automatically* whenever engine-speed rises above normal, and *vice versa*.

[2] *Air Transport Manual*, 46.

12—(B.251)

number of stops.[1] For maximum economy of working the number of flying hours per machine per annum should be made as high as possible consistent with full safety. Night flying and flying in all weathers and at all seasons help to increase the aggregate number of flying hours and to decrease the unit costs, provided that no serious sacrifice of safety is involved. The perfection of wireless direction-finding and communication with pilots in flight, and the proper illumination of aerodromes at night have already made this possible.

The load factor (whether the load be goods or passengers or mixed) depends mainly upon the "popularity" of the route and machine. With regard to passenger transport, a reputation for safety and reliability, comfort and size of cabins (a large 'plane also suggests greater safety), and relative absence of noise are the principal considerations, other than the speed and the fare.

The costs of operating air transport services may be analysed as follows—

   (a) Running costs which vary with the flying-hours.
   (b) Standing charges which do not vary with flying-hours.

(a) *Running Costs*—
      (i) Fuel and oil.
     (ii) Maintenance (or "upkeep") of aircraft.
    (iii) Maintenance (or "upkeep") of engine.
     (iv) Inspection.
      (v) Wages of pilot and crew.
     (vi) Insurance (part).
    (vii) Landing fees.

High-powered aircraft generally use more fuel and oil per hour than low-powered and slower aircraft of equally good design. Cruising speed should be kept some 20 or 25 per cent below the full-rated speed. This is the optimum cruising speed from the point of view of operating costs, because if machines are run constantly above it, upkeep costs rise rapidly; while

[1] On a "frequent" service each machine normally flies 1500 to 2000 hours per annum.

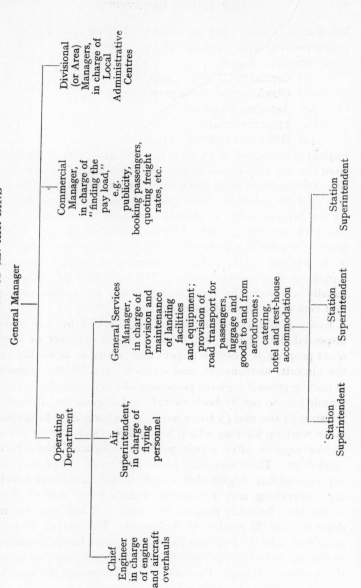

Fig. 6. ORGANIZATION OF AN AIR LINE

General Manager

Operating Department

Commercial Manager, in charge of "finding the pay load," e.g. publicity, booking passengers, quoting freight rates, etc.

Divisional (or Area) Managers, in charge of Local Administrative Centres

Chief Engineer in charge of engine and aircraft overhauls

Air Superintendent, in charge of flying personnel

General Services Manager, in charge of provision and maintenance of landing facilities and equipment; provision of road transport for passengers, luggage and goods to and from aerodromes; catering, hotel and rest-house accommodation

Station Superintendent

Station Superintendent

Station Superintendent

Station Superintendent

below it, they do not fall appreciably. Engine upkeep is more expensive than upkeep of aircraft structure.

(b) *Standing charges—*

    (i) Capital charges (interest).

    (ii) Obsolescence and depreciation.

    (iii) Aerodrome expenses.

    (iv) Insurance (part).

    (v) Office and publicity expenses.

Capital charges and obsolescence, which arise almost entirely from the first cost of the aircraft are the heaviest items in this list. Obsolescence is so much more important than depreciation that the combined item is included as a standing charge. At the present stage of aircraft evolution, obsolescence is a heavy charge, for air liners become obsolescent in four to six years. Insurance falls partly under (a) and partly under (b) as it depends partly upon the number of flying-hours and partly on the "ground risks." The total cost of insurance usually works out at about $12\frac{1}{2}$ per cent per annum on the first cost of the aircraft insured.

Every public transport aircraft is required by law to be inspected daily before flight by a ground engineer or engineers properly licensed to inspect and certify as airworthy (a) the aircraft, instruments, and controls; and (b) the engines. A leading ground engineer possessing the necessary licences to permit him to certify both aircraft and engines usually earns between £4 10s. and £5 10s. a week. A higher grade of engineer is the working foreman who is licensed to certify the air frame and/or engines after repair work or overhauls have been carried out. These men earn about £7 a week. They must be experienced men, highly skilled and reliable, capable of directing, supervising and if necessary carrying out difficult jobs themselves; for other people's lives and their own reputations depend upon the quality of their work. The method of payment may take the form of a basic wage, plus a bonus according to the number of flying-hours achieved by each machine under the foreman's charge. The object is to encourage the man to exert himself to "keep his machines flying."

The rates of wages for other grades of ground workers are approximately as follow—

Engine fitters	£3 to £4 per week	
Engine fitters (apprentices) . . .	£1 " "
Carpenter-riggers	£3 12s. to £4 " "
Carpenter-riggers (apprentices) . . .	£1 " "
Labourers	£2 " "

Messrs. A. V. Roe & Co. Ltd. have published the following estimate of the cost of operating a service of four Avro 642 Commercial Aircraft (three in service, one in reserve), assuming 3750 flying hours per annum at an average speed of 125 m.p.h. The Avro 642 is an up-to-date monoplane driven by two Armstrong-Siddeley geared Jaguar engines. The crew of two is accommodated in a control room in the nose of the fuselage. Immediately behind is the cabin with accommodation for twelve passengers; and behind the cabin is the baggage hold and lavatory. By reducing the petrol storage capacity it is possible to make room for sixteen passengers.

Fixed Annual Costs

		£
(a)	Salaries and wages of staff (4 pilots at £500 p.a., 1 leading ground engineer, 3 ground engineers, 2 engine fitters, 1 carpenter-rigger, 2 apprentices, and 2 labourers	3,924
(b)	Insurance premiums, including operators' legal liability to passengers, and insurance of personnel (£150)	2,650
(c)	Housing and landing expenses at aerodromes, say	900
(d)	Depreciation (20% on £34,000)	6,800
(e)	Miscellaneous expenses	300
		£14,574

Variable costs, per hour of flying-time—

		£	s.	d.
(a)	Fuel, 43 gal. @ 1s. 4d. . . .	2	17	4
(b)	Oil, 2 gal. @ 2s. 6d. . . .		5	0
(c)	Replacements, including requirements at periodic overhauls—			
	(i) Air frame		10	0
	(ii) Engines		15	0
		4	7	4
	Add 5% for non-flying time . .		4	4
		£4	11	8

Therefore, assuming an average of 3750 flying-hours per annum, the total annual operating costs would be (fixed costs

£14,574, *plus* variable costs £17,187) £31,761; and average operating costs, 1s. 4½d. per machine-mile. It will be noticed that fixed costs are as high as 46 per cent of total costs.

III

From a profit earning point of view, the operation of commercial air transport is still a very chancy business unless it is generously subsidized by the State. This has in fact been done for the principal air lines in all the chief countries of the world.[1] There are, apparently, two questions to be answered in connexion with State grants to assist air transport: (a) on what scale, and (b) in what form, shall the subsidies be given?

The main argument against high rates of cash subsidy is the familiar one that they render keen, enterprising action on the part of the operators unnecessary and tend to postpone the time when air transport will be able to "fly by itself." On the other hand, it is argued that low rates of subsidy (a) tend to discourage pioneer enterprise and experiments and so retard the rate of growth of the industry and (b) tend to keep down flying speeds because high speeds mean high costs, which operators are unable to bear in the early stages of development: yet without high-speed services air transport has no chance of attracting a sufficient volume of traffic. It is also urged that if subsidies are meagre, air services cannot be made frequent enough to render them attractive to travellers.

Clearly a parsimonious policy on the part of the State will only waste the taxpayer's money by paying it away in sums insufficient to achieve the objects in mind, and it seems desirable that State-aid should be given rather generously at first, but always subject to the fulfilment of certain conditions.

This brings us to the question of the form State-assistance should take. Two forms present themselves: (a) direct cash subsidies to operators; (b) indirect assistance, e.g. through the establishment, staffing, and maintenance of a system of civil

---

[1] If we take European commercial air services as a whole, about three-quarters of their cost falls upon the State exchequers. (H. Bouché, *Economics of Air Transport in Europe*, [1935], 73.)

aerodromes, fully equipped for flying at night and in bad weather, for the use of air transport at the expense of the State; or through the granting of air mail contracts to air transport operators on generous terms. Any or all of these methods may be adopted. Where it is decided to give cash grants, the basis or formula of the subsidy should depend upon the particular features of commercial aviation which the State wishes most to develop, e.g. high power and speed of aircraft; maximum passenger-mileage or goods-mileage; regularity and frequency of services; night services; Empire services; swift mail transport, or safety. It is essential, however, that the subsidy-conditions, however excellent in other respects, shall not be so framed as to reduce or eliminate elasticity in the development of air transport. This is especially important in the present phase of progress, when enterprise, ingenuity and a high degree of adaptability are demanded on both the economic and technical sides of the industry.

The bulk of the British Government's subsidies in recent years has been paid to Imperial Airways partly in the form of direct cash payments in support of that company's European and Empire air lines, and partly in the form of capital expenditure upon the improvement and equipping of Croydon Airport. Smaller sums of public money have been spent annually upon the staffing and maintenance of civil aerodromes, surveys of air routes and experimental services. It is generally admitted that British air transport has had and is having less assistance from the State than that of any other leading country.[1] For example, the British subsidies have been only about one-third of the French subsidies, whether we look at the total or at the subsidy per ton-mile. Yet the progress of British commercial aviation compares very favourably with the recent progress of French commercial aviation.[2]

[1] The total air transport subsidies for the whole British Empire was only £992,649 in 1932–3, in support of air line routes 30,000 miles in length.

[2] In his report to the League of Nations on the *Economics of Air Transport in Europe*, M. Bouché comments in several places upon the high efficiency of Imperial Airways. See e.g. Final Edition (1935), pp. 16, 18, 70.

At the outset the British Government's cash subsidy to Imperial Airways was paid according to the mileage flown on regular routes, irrespective of the type of machine employed. But as this method did not especially encourage the use of the larger, more economical aircraft, it was modified in December, 1925, and "horse-power miles" instead of "machine miles" became the basis of payment. In order to earn the maximum subsidy a minimum of 425 million horse-power miles per annum must be flown by Imperial Airways machines.[1] These subsidy regulations are naturally an important factor conditioning the policy of the Company when ordering new aircraft for its fleet.

In a recent League of Nations publication,[2] M. Henri Bouché presents some indices designed to show the degree of financial dependence upon State subsidies of the regular European air lines. The first index, $P_1 = \dfrac{\text{Receipts from Customers}}{\text{State Subsidies}}$. For any given air line $P_1 < 1$ when the subsidy exceeds the receipts from customers (i.e. passenger traffic, freight, and mails). If $P_1 > 1$, the service has completed M. Bouché's "first stage, at which subsidies and receipts from customers are equal." Down to 1930 no European air line had advanced so far, although the Dutch were very near, with $P_1 = 0.96$. In 1931 and 1932 the subsidized air lines of three European countries had completed the "first stage"—

	1931 P_1	1932 P_1
United Kingdom	1·05	1·80
Finland	1·25	1·59
Netherlands	1·48	1·43

For Germany, $P_1 = 0.43$ in 1932. The corresponding French index was only 0.26 in 1932; the Polish 0.08, and the Italian 0.07. The average for Europe was 0.35.

The second index is $P_2 = \dfrac{\text{Receipts from Customers}}{\text{Total Revenue}}$. This

[1] In 1934 Imperial Airways flew, on their European services, between three and four times the minimum horse-power mileage necessary to qualify for subsidy.

[2] *Economics of Air Transport in Europe* (Final Edn. 1935), 15 ff, and 67 ff.

shows the degree of financial independence so far attained by
the air lines in question, since if $P_2 = 1$ it means that subsidies
have ceased and the total revenue comes from customers.
None of the subsidized European air lines has yet reached this
stage. The principal ratios are—

	1931 P_2	1932 P_2	1933 P_2
United Kingdom . .	0·512	0·642	0·61
Finland	0·556	0·614	0·70
Netherlands . . .	0·596	0·589	0·76
Germany . . .	—	0·301	0·354
France	—	0·203	0·210
Poland	—	0·073	0·074
Italy	—	0·064	0·087

The average for Europe is about 0.25. Thus, these ratios
indicate that the Dutch lines have gone three-fourths of the
way towards financial independence; the British, not quite
two-thirds of the way; the Germans, a little over one-third, and
the French about two-fifths. Finland is well to the fore, but
Poland and Italy are far behind.

Although these indices are useful as a first line of approach,
they do not carry us very far since they ignore the cost
element; probably because cost statistics are kept secret by
the companies. Moreover, no comparison between, let us say,
Imperial Airways and the Dutch Line is possible because the
latter do not appear to receive subsidies at a fixed rate or
on any pre-arranged scale. The Dutch Government pays as
subsidy the deficit between earned revenue and expenditure,
and in addition to this, the Dutch Line receives what amounts
to a disguised subsidy, because the Dutch Post Office guarantees and pays for a weight of mail which is substantially higher
than the amount carried.[1]

IV

Mails were not entrusted to the early British air lines until
the Post Office was quite convinced that a reliable service could
be maintained. But in less than three months from the inauguration of the London-Paris service the Post Office entered

[1] I am indebted to the Managing Director of Imperial Airways Ltd.
for calling my attention to this point.

into contracts for the regular carriage of mails on the Continental air routes. The first load of mail left Hounslow for Paris on 10th November, 1919. The postage of a letter by air from London to Paris then cost 2s. 6d: to-day the fee is fourpence. In the period 1925–8 British air lines carried an average of 52 tons of mails per annum; and in the period 1929–33 the annual average was 129 tons. 139 tons of mails were carried in 1932, 171 tons in 1933, 250 tons in 1934, and 714 tons in 1935. The bulk of this work was between Britain and the Continent and the British Empire.

Any kind of letter packet can now be sent by air mail. The limits of size and weight are the same as for similar packets sent by ordinary post, but the postage rates are higher, and there are fewer flat rates. Air mail letters can be registered but not insured, except letters and boxes for Holland and Switzerland. Correspondence for countries not directly served by air mail can be sent by air to the nearest point and forwarded thence by ordinary mail, on payment of the appropriate air postage. Messages intended for delivery as air mail letters can be telephoned to most Head Post Offices, or to the Central Telegraph Office, or to Croydon Aerodrome Post Office, in order to catch an outgoing air mail. For certain countries special reduced rates are charged for printed and commercial papers and samples; but where these are not in force, full letter rates must be paid. The general parcel post regulations, e.g. as to weight and dimensions, apply to air mail parcels, except that such parcels cannot be insured if consigned to destinations not in Holland or Switzerland. In addition to the time gained by air transit, air parcels are generally given quick Customs clearance, provided that the proper declarations have been correctly completed.

The rates of postage for letters by air mail to and from Great Britain and all European countries is 4d. for the first ounce, 3d. for each additional ounce, and 2½d. for postcards. Letters from England to the Near East (Egypt, Palestine, Syria, Transjordan, Iran, Iraq, and Sudan) by the Australian or South African air mails cost 3d. per half ounce, and postcards 2d. For other parts of the world most of the postage rates, but not all, vary very approximately according to the distance the letter is carried by air mail. Thus a half ounce letter by air mail to India or South Africa costs 6d., but to Canada only 2d., since there is no air mail across the North Atlantic. A letter to Australia goes all the way by air mail and costs 1s. 3d. per half ounce. On the whole, the air postage rates within the British Empire are much lower than those to places outside. For example, letters to the Argentine cost 4s. per half ounce against only 6d. to Southern Rhodesia or the Malay States.

Where the whole route can be covered by air transport the time saved is very considerable. Air mail letters between London and Paris, Antwerp, Brussels, Cologne, Hamburg, Berlin, and Milan are now delivered as quickly as ordinary letters between London and the chief provincial cities. For air mail services over greater distances the saving of time is even more striking. Thus a letter from London to the Argentine, *via* Germany, reaches Buenos Aires in four days, or from twelve to nineteen days less than if carried by surface transport. Air mails to India reach Karachi in five days; Bombay, Calcutta, or Delhi in six days; and Madras or Rangoon in seven days; the time saved ranging from eight to twelve days. The air mail to Australia (Brisbane) takes twelve days, and saves twenty.

In connexion with air mails within the British Isles the Postmaster-General announced in December, 1934, that, where delivery will be materially accelerated, the Post Office will dispatch, without extra charge, all letters and postcards for destinations in Great Britain by any air service which has a record of regular and punctual operation, provided that the operators of such a service agree to carry the mails at a reasonable price. Tenders were invited and contracts made.[1]

---

[1] E.g. with Hillman's Airways Ltd. for a London–Liverpool–Belfast–Glasgow mail service. Hillman's Airways were built up by Mr. Edward Hillman after he had created a thriving motor-coach business between London and the East Coast. They were the first unsubsidized internal air lines to be operated in the British Isles. The first service was opened in March, 1932. In 1934 this company had an issued capital of £130,000, a fleet of seven aircraft, and two more in course of construction. See *Stock Exchange Year Book*, 1935.

It is likely that before many years are past, all first-class mails will be carried by air throughout the Empire.

Recently the speed of British air mail services, particularly the Empire services, has been adversely criticized. Those in favour of greater speed for Empire Air Mails suggest (1) the separation of passengers from mails; (2) transport of the latter in special *small* high-speed postal aircraft, flying by night as well as by day; and (3) increased frequency in order to give better service to the public and to use the postal aircraft fleet more intensively, thus reducing operating costs.

The arguments on the other side are (a) that experience has proved that on main routes large air liners are more profitable than small ones, and that in order to obtain adequate loads for large air liners a mixed cargo of passengers, mails, and goods must be carried. Furthermore, such a policy seems the most likely to make air services self-supporting. (b) At present the necessary aerodrome facilities are not available. The provision of these by the air lines, *plus* the separation of passengers and mails, would send up costs and therefore make higher fares or larger subsidies essential. But neither the possibility nor the desirability of greater frequency and speed is denied, and by means of a new Empire air transport scheme to be introduced in 1937—

"It is proposed substantially to increase the frequency and speed of the services on the Empire routes . . . and to carry by air all first-class mail between the many parts of the Empire on these routes, the letter rate . . . being if possible a flat rate of 1½d. per half ounce."

V

Whether the progress of British air transport would have been greater under a more generous system of subsidies must remain a moot point; but the extent of progress actually achieved can be measured in various ways. The single-engined aeroplane with which the London–Paris service was begun developed 360 h.p. and carried only 1 lb. of pay-load per horse-power unit. The multi-engined air liners of to-day develop 2200 h.p. and carry over 3 lb. of pay-load per unit of

REGULAR AIR TRANSPORT SERVICES operated by UNITED KINGDOM COMPANIES, INCLUDING ALL INTERNAL SERVICES, UNITED KINGDOM–CONTINENT, LONDON–SINGAPORE, AND LONDON–SOUTH AFRICA SERVICES.[1]

Year or Period	Aircraft Stage Flights		Passengers Carried	Cargo Carried		Mileage		Ton-mileage	
	No.	Average Length		Freight	Mails	Aircraft	Passenger	Freight	Mails
		Miles	*Individuals*	*Tons*		*Thousands*		*Thousands*	
1925 ·	4,000	200	11,000	550		806	2,645	148	
1928 ·	4,800	190	27,300	730	83	916	6,477	178	37
1931 ·	5,800	230	23,500	649	120	1,354	7,009	200	215
1933 ·	23,200	110	79,100	743	171	2,638	21,601	327	406
1934 ·	51,600	90	135,100	1,172	250	4,557	29,162	455	665
Yearly average									
1920–24 ·	3,400	200	10,100[2]	248		693		Not available	
1925–29 ·	4,600	200	20,400	717		896	4,862	204	
1930–34 ·	19,100	120	61,900	783	159	2,312	15,956	286	349

[1] From Air Ministry *Report on the Progress of Civil Aviation*, 1934 (1935), 98.
[2] For 1920–4 the figures represent stage-passengers.

horse-power. They have, in addition, an ampler power reserve, a much higher standard of comfort for passengers, and cruising speeds ranging from 120 to 150 miles per hour. The regularity of services has improved enormously during the past decade. Thus, in 1924–5, 23·25 per cent of services had to be cancelled: in 1933–4, only 1·55 per cent. were cancelled.

In the years 1932–3 the mileage flown by the regular air services of the United Kingdom (including services to and from the British Empire) increased by 47 per cent; the number of passenger-miles increased by 141 per cent; the number of ton-miles of goods traffic increased by 72 per cent, and the ton-miles of mails by 82 per cent.[1] The corresponding percentage increases for European air lines as a whole were, mileage flown, 17 per cent; passenger miles, 25 per cent; ton-miles of goods traffic, $18\frac{1}{2}$ per cent; ton-miles of mails, $16\frac{1}{2}$ per cent.[2] Among the larger European air lines, Imperial Airways (European and London–Egypt services) show the highest co-efficient of utilization of air tonnage offered. The British co-efficients are: 1930 and 1931, 58 per cent; 1932, 62 per cent; 1933, 68 per cent. The corresponding average co-efficients of utilization for Europe as a whole are 37·3, 41·7, 46, and 51·4. Only the French, Finnish, and Swedish lines are above these averages.[3]

At the same time the degree of safety has been increasing. Between 1919–20 and 1933, the number of fatal accidents to British regular aircraft, including Imperial Airways machines at home and abroad, has fallen from one a year, on the average, to three in four or five years; while aircraft-miles flown per annum have increased from 644,000 in 1920 to an annual average of 1,752,000 in the period 1930–33, and the number of passengers carried has increased from under 6000 (1920) to over 60,000 per annum. The number of aircraft-miles flown per accident resulting in death or injury to one or more of the occupants of the aircraft has increased from 1,493,000 in the period 1925–9 to 2,313,000 in the period 1930–4.[4]

---

[1] Calculated from statistics given in *Report on the Progress of Civil Aviation*, 1933 (1934), 98.
[2] Bouché, *op. cit.*, 67.   [3] *Ibid*, 19.
[4] Air Ministry, *Report on the Progress of Civil Aviation*, 1934 (1935).

Although the numbers of regular flights and passengers carried between Britain and the Continent have increased tremendously since 1920, the *proportions* of flights and passengers carried by British aircraft on the cross-channel services have fallen, as the following table shows.

AIRCRAFT FLIGHTS AND PASSENGERS CARRIED BETWEEN GREAT BRITAIN AND THE CONTINENT (EXCLUDING THE CHANNEL ISLANDS)

	British		Total British and Foreign		British Share	
	Flights	Passengers	Flights	Passengers	Flights %	Passengers %
1920 . .	2,854	5,799	3,622	6,383	79	91
1933 . .	4,644	53,483	11,881	90,887	39	59
1934 . .	6,820	58,125	14,682	102,667	46	57
1935 . .	10,181	70,049	18,501	126,739	55	55

VI

The recent increase in the number of internal British air lines has raised the problem of evolving a national plan for our air transport services. The air transport position to-day in this country is, in some ways, not unlike the position reached by the railways nearly a century ago. In September, 1934, about a dozen different companies were operating 3000 miles of air routes, and in two cases there was direct competition on the same routes. It happened that connexions between certain air lines could be made at several points, but no general scheme of development and co-ordination was apparent. By the beginning of 1935 the number of companies was seventeen, and in the summer of that year the Air Minister appointed a committee, in place of the Aerodrome Advisory Board, to advise on the best means of developing civil aviation inside Great Britain. At this point three possibilities presented themselves, viz. (a) voluntary combination between the various air transport companies; (b) permeation, leading eventually to control, of the air transport companies by the railways; (c) compulsory amalgamation of the companies by the State and the subsequent operation of air transport services as a public utility. So far, (*a*) seems more likely to materialize than either (*b*) or (*c*), for in October, 1935, came the announcement of a merger between Hillman's Airways Ltd., United Airways Ltd. and Spartan Air Lines Ltd., with the object of constructing a well-financed and compact organization, called British Airways Ltd., to operate the principal unsubsidized air lines in the British Isles.[1] It was stated that the principal aims were to reduce competition and costs, to co-ordinate services, and to obtain more mail contracts. *Modern Transport* commented upon the merger as follows—

Some idea of the scope and probable effect of the amalgamation can be gained from the fact that at the time of the last return there were 151 machines registered in Great Britain as engaged in air transport. Of these, 42 belonged to Imperial Airways and 9 to Railway Air Services, leaving, therefore, 100 machines operated by companies outside the railway grouping.[2] Of these 100 aircraft 51 were owned by the air lines which will come within the sphere of influence of the new company and its associates. The remaining 49 machines are owned by thirteen different companies. It will be seen, therefore, that the new organization will be by far the largest operator of internal air transport, for the Imperial Airways fleet is mainly engaged in external operation, and the Railway Air Services fleet is small compared with that falling within the ambit of the independent grouping. It is not difficult, meanwhile, to predict that a situation in which 49 aircraft are operated by thirteen different companies is not likely to endure for long. Either of two possibilities then arises : rationalization among these small operators, or their absorption by the new group. The

---

[1] *United Airways*, a recently formed company, has the financial support of Whitehall Securities Corporation and owns a 70 per cent interest in Northern and Scottish Airways and in Highland Airways, operators of the successful Inverness Air Ferry, which was the first internal service to receive a Post Office contract in this country. Whitehall Securities is also financially interested in Spartan Air Lines the third party to the proposed amalgamation, and the pioneer of the London–Isle of Wight air service. Thus five air service companies will be directly affected by the amalgamation, whilst Jersey Airways, pioneer of the London–Channel Islands service, will also be affected indirectly, for it also has the support of Whitehall Securities Corporation.

[2] The regular air services operating in the British Isles had an estimated route mileage of over 5000 in April, 1936. *The Economist*, 25th April, 1936, 189.

probability is that both developments will take place simultaneously, and while some of the small operators will be acquired by the new group, others, in self-defence, will co-operate or amalgamate. . . .

An important feature of the amalgamation is that the financial house mainly interested in the prospective fusion has interests also in two aircraft-construction companies. It will, therefore, be instructive to see how far the merging of the various interests will influence the equipment policy of the air lines involved, which, with the exception of Spartan Air Lines, are at present equipped mainly with De Havilland machines. This also raises the question of whether, in the future, we shall see aircraft-construction companies, in search of wider markets, taking an active part in the developments of air transport.

In July, 1936, the new combine amalgamated with British Continental Airways, Ltd., a company operating air services between England (London and Liverpool) and Lille, Ostend, Antwerp, Amsterdam, and Malmö (via Hamburg and Copenhagen).[1]

Looking to the future and beyond the borders of Britain, it is clear that for obvious geographical reasons this country can never become, like Germany, a *centre* of European air services; but, given a solution of the transatlantic problem, Great Britain may well become (*a*) the principal western terminus of the European "heavy (air) traffic quadrilateral," the four "corners" or extremities being London, Malmö, Marseilles, Budapest—an economically active region which fast aircraft will soon be able to cross in six or seven hours of daytime flying: and (*b*) the principal European end of the long-distance air services to and from Asia, Africa, Australia, and America. This would be no small part to play in the future development of world air transport.

[1] *Report on the Progress of Civil Aviation*, 1935 (1936), 9.

CHAPTER IV

NEW MATERIALS

(i) ALUMINIUM

FOR many years during the progress of the Industrial Revolution, and especially during the first sixty or seventy years of the nineteenth century, iron was the primary industrial metal, while copper and lead occupied a relatively inconspicuous second place. Few industrialists paid much attention to any metal except iron in one or other of its forms—cast iron, wrought iron, steel. They even began to build iron ships, and the "wooden walls of England" gave place to shields of armour plate. But certain scientists, working as it were behind the scenes, were trying to produce a new metal having the advantages of the older metals, without their major disadvantage, namely, great weight in proportion to bulk. Could a very light metal be discovered which also possessed the strength of iron or the conductivity of copper? If so, it would be sure of a wide market, provided always that its cost of production could be brought low enough. To-day we know that the answer to this question has been found in aluminium and its various alloys, produced on a commercial scale by the use of large quantities of cheap electricity.

I

The metal which the English call aluminium and the Americans "aluminum" is a modern product. Normally it is obtained from bauxite, a mineral which is a mixture of oxides, principally oxides of aluminium, silicon and iron in varying proportions according to the locality. In the United Kingdom, bauxite occurs in large quantities in Northern Ireland among the tertiary volcanic rocks of Antrim, especially near Larne and Ballymena, but the chief sources of supplies in use to-day are located in France, Italy, Yugoslavia, British Guiana, the Gold Coast and the United States. Next to silicon, aluminium is the most abundant metal in the world, but in its natural state it exists always in the form of compounds (i.e. in combination with other elements). It is only in quite recent times that it has been possible to isolate and purify the metal and manufacture it in sufficient quantities and at prices low enough to enable it to take its place among the metals of ordinary commerce.

In 1807, Sir Humphry Davy tried to reduce alumina by heating it with potash and electrolysing the mixture, and although he did not succeed in preparing the *metal*, he became convinced that alumina had a metallic base. It was the Danish scientist, H. C. Oersted, who first caused alumina to yield "metal which in colour and lustre somewhat resembles tin"[1]. Simultaneously, Frederick Wohler, a German, was also working on the problem of producing aluminium, and it is upon his experiments and observations that our present knowledge of the various properties of the metal are founded. Partially successful experiments were made by Wohler as early as 1828. In 1845 he published a paper on aluminium in *Annalen der Chymie und Pharmacie* (Vol. 53, p. 422) in which he stated that "We obtain aluminium in a state of grey powder, but on examining the mass closely we find it composed of little melted globules, some of which are of the size of a large pin's head." Sainte-Claire Deville, a French scientist, improved upon Wohler's process and obtained somewhat larger globules of "perfectly pure aluminium." "This metal," he wrote, "is as white as silver, malleable and ductile to the highest degree. . . . We can easily comprehend how a metal . . . which does not tarnish with the air . . . and which has the singular property of being lighter than glass, would be of great service if it were possible to obtain it easily. If we consider that this metal exists in large quantities in nature, that its mineral is

[1] H. C. Oersted, *Oversigt over det Kongelige Danske Videnskabernes Selskabs Forhandlinger* (1824–5), 15–16; quoted in Edwards, Frary and Jeffries, *The Aluminium Industry* (1930), I, 2.

clay, we ought to desire that it may become common. I have every reason to hope that it will be so."[1]

These discoveries inaugurated a period of great experimental activity. Soon the metal could be made, not in particles the size of pinheads, but "in lumps a thousand times greater—say, the size of marbles."[2] The production of aluminium bars and ingots on a commercial scale was in sight. The members of the French Academy contributed 3000 francs towards further research work, a certain number of French scientists and technologists gave their services, and later Napoleon III became interested and offered to bear the expense of further experiments on a larger scale. This work was carried on at the Javel Chemical Works, and some carefully-guarded ingots, made at Javel, were on show in the Paris Exhibition of 1855. This first public appearance of aluminium excited a great deal of curiosity.

In company with three or four other experts, Sainte-Claire Deville commenced the manufacture of aluminium at Glacière, near Paris, in 1856, and in 1857 they began to erect a new plant at Nanterre.[3] In Great Britain aluminium was produced by the Deville process at Battersea, London, in the early 'sixties and at Washington, near Newcastle-upon-Tyne, between 1860 and 1874. In 1885 the world output of aluminium was about 13 tons, or a little more than 29,000 lb.

A promising future lay before the new metal if only its costs of production could be reduced. Sainte-Claire Deville and his associates had worked hard upon this problem, for many years, not without success; and so had Hamilton Castner of New York. Eventually the work of these men was combined, with the result that by the end of the 'eighties aluminium was being produced by the Deville-Castner process in larger quantities and at lower costs than ever before. "The first

---

[1] *Comptes Rendus* (1854), p. 279.

[2] Edwards, Frary and Jeffries, *op. cit.*, I, 4. Cf. H. Sainte-Claire Deville, *On Aluminium and its Chemical Combinations, etc.* (printed by Sir Thomas Phillips from *Comptes Rendus*, 1854).

[3] H. Sainte-Claire Deville, *De l'Aluminium, ses Propriétés, sa Fabrication et ses Applications* (1859).

practical application of the Castner sodium process to the production of aluminium by the Deville process was made by the Aluminium Company Ltd., at Oldbury, near Birmingham, England, where a new works was erected and production started in 1888. During the year, production reached 500 lb. per day, and the metal was being sold at 16s. per lb."[1]

By a remarkable coincidence it was in 1888 that the first works to produce aluminium by a new process—electrolysis—was started at Pittsburgh, U.S.A. Sir Humphry Davy had tried to decompose alumina electrolytically, but he failed to isolate pure aluminium. In 1854, both Sainte-Claire Deville and Robert Wilhelm Bunsen succeeded in producing aluminium by electrolysis, but as they had to obtain the electric current from batteries the method was too expensive to encourage its commercial development in place of the sodium reduction process. Not until 1886 did Charles Martin Hall of Oberlin, Ohio, successfully solve the problem of the production of aluminium by electrolysis and so lay the foundation of an important industry in the United States. At about the same time, Héroult and Kiliani were introducing a similar method in Europe. The direct electrolysis of molten alumina is out of the question owing to the fact that its melting point is over 2000°C. The Hall-Héroult invention consisted of the discovery that a molten fluoride, such as cryolite, will dissolve substantial quantities of alumina at the comparatively low temperature of 900°C., and that the molten solution is capable of being electrolysed. This discovery revolutionized the industry. Whereas previously aluminium had been produced by a costly and laborious chemical process, involving the reduction of aluminium salts by metallic sodium, the new method facilitated the production of aluminium in large quantities and at one-twentieth of the cost.[2] The new process speedily ousted the old, and the production of aluminium by the electrolysis of a solution of purified bauxite or oxide of

---

[1] Edwards, Frary, and Jeffries, *op. cit.*, I, 8, 44.
[2] *Aluminium Production, Properties and Applications* (published by British Aluminium Co. Ltd.). For a detailed account of Chas. M. Hall's experiments, see Edwards, Frary, and Jeffries, *op. cit.*, I, Chap. 2.

aluminium in molten cryolite is now the method universally followed. By the beginning of the present century, world consumption of aluminium had increased to 6000 tons per year, and since then progress has continued until to-day aluminium takes fourth place among the non-ferrous metals in order of magnitude of world production, with an annual output, ranging from 150,000 tons in bad years to upwards of 250,000 in boom years, of which roughly half is produced in Europe and the other half in U.S.A. and Canada. The ratio of increase of production between 1913 and 1929 (a peak year) was over 330 per cent for aluminium against slightly over 100 per cent for copper, 60 per cent for zinc, 40 per cent for tin, and approximately 25 per cent for pig iron.

In Great Britain the modern aluminium industry may be said to date from the formation of the British Aluminium Co. Ltd., in May, 1894. "Prior to this, aluminium was made at the works of the Cowles Syndicate at Milton, Stoke-on-Trent . . . beginning in 1890, but the works closed in 1893. Works were also started in July, 1890, at Patricroft, Lancashire, to operate Hall's electrolytic process, but this plant also ceased operations in 1894."[1] Before the end of the century the British Aluminium Co. Ltd. acquired the British and Colonial rights in the Héroult and Bayer patents[2] and so dominated the new industry in this country. Realizing that ample supplies of very cheap electricity would be essential to commercial success, the Company decided to use hydro-electric power, and, in 1896, they located their first works at Foyers on the Caledonian Canal about twenty miles from Inverness. A power generating plant of some 5000 kw. was installed. In 1907 the Kinlochleven Works, Argyllshire, with 23,000 kw. began operations, and in the following year the Company extended its activities to Stangfjord in Norway. Other plants were established at Greenock, Larne, and Milton (Staffs).

To-day the British Aluminium Company is operating three aluminium reduction plants in Scotland and two in Norway;

[1] Edwards, Frary, and Jeffries, *op. cit.*, I, 44.
[2] K. J. Bayer's patent process was for the production of alumina.

two alumina works—one in Northern Ireland and one in Scotland; two rolling mills in England, and, through a French company, extensive bauxite deposits in the south of France. The British Aluminium Company, which has a total issued capital of £3,500,000, and a similar amount of debenture stock outstanding,[1] owns all the capital of the North British Aluminium Co. Ltd., and the Loch Leven Electricity Supply Co. The Lochaber Power Co. is a subsidiary, and other subsidiary companies manufacture castings, aluminium alloys, hollowware and sheet metal goods. The new Lochaber Works of the North British Aluminium Co., which has cost approximately £5,000,000, is the largest aluminium-producing unit in the British Isles. At one time it seemed likely that a section of the aluminium industry would take root in Wales, but the sale of the Aluminium Corporation's plant to the North Wales Power Co. in 1929 put an end to this development, at least for the time being.

There are five stages, or sections, of aluminium production: (1) mining the ore, (2) chemical treatment of the ore to obtain pure aluminium oxide (Al_2O_3), (3) preparation of the carbon electrodes and carbon linings of the reduction furnaces, (4) reduction of alumina by molten electrolysis and the production of virgin aluminium, (5) rolling, i.e. the manufacture of sheets, strips, extruded sections, wire, etc., in pure or alloy form.[2]

The British Aluminium Company's ore deposits are in Southern France, the Gold Coast, and British Guiana.[3] Since the ore must be imported into Great Britain, the alumina works (stage 2) must be at or near ports capable of accommodating vessels of from 5000 to 10,000 tons: and at the other end of the process the transport of the alumina to the reduction works must present no great difficulties. Moreover, since this process involves the use of large quantities of steam, plentiful supplies of cheap coal are essential. Mr. George Boex has shown that the British Aluminium Company's Burntisland

[1] *Stock Exchange Year Book*, 1936.
[2] See diagram on p. 199, reproduced by the courtesy of the *Manchester Guardian Commercial*.
[3] British Guiana is the chief source of bauxite in the Empire.

Works "are placed close to the vast Fife coal-field, and the harbour deals satisfactorily with the incoming ore and with the outgoing alumina intended for the reduction works of the subsidiary companies in Norway just across the North Sea. It is also well placed for rail transport of the alumina powder by tank wagon to the Lochaber factory at Fort William, . . . belonging to the associated company, the North British Aluminium Company.

"The Larne . . . works were started many years ago using a local deposit, but had to abandon its use. The works are well placed to receive ore from overseas, and to send the alumina by water to the reduction works on the western seaboard of Scotland at Kinlochleven, Lochaber and Foyers, . . . The Company's steamers load the alumina at Larne, deliver it to the three factories in Scotland, then take the metal south to Runcorn for the rolling mills, and afterwards pick up soda ash and other chemicals necessary for the Larne alumina works, and thus complete the triangle."[1]

The British Aluminium Company's carbon production plant is concentrated at Kinlochleven, where the wharf can accommodate vessels bringing the necessary raw materials, chiefly from Glasgow and the U.S.A.

The reduction works are the hub of the whole industry. As we have seen, cheap electric power in great quantities is essential (since it is calculated that about 26,000 Kilowatt-hours are required in the production of every ton of aluminium from alumina), and the cheapest way of supplying this demand is by means of a hydro-electric plant; for although the capital costs are heavy, the running costs are light. The British Aluminium Company generates its current where it is used, so avoiding transmission lines and losses due to conversion from alternating to direct current. In the mountains above the British Aluminium Company's works at Kinlochleven, Argyllshire, a great storage reservoir has been made by building a barrage over 1000 yards long across the valley of the River

---

[1] *Proceedings of Institution of Mechanical Engineers*, Vol. 125 (1933), p. 17

Leven. From this reservoir the water is first carried through an aqueduct $3\frac{1}{2}$ miles in length to a "penstock," and thence it falls through a mile of pipes, each over 3 ft. in diameter, down to the turbines 900 ft. below.

The furnace used for the reduction process consists of a large rectangular, open bath, lined at the sides and bottom with carbon, which constitutes the cathode of the cell. The bath is packed with a mixture of alumina and cryolite. The cryolite is a natural double fluoride of aluminium and sodium which occurs in great abundance in Greenland, but can also be successfully produced synthetically. An electric current passing through the bath fuses the mixture, keeps it in a molten state, and at the same time dissociates the alumina into oxygen and aluminium. The molten metal sinks to the floor of the furnace, whence it is drawn off at intervals and cast into ingots. Normally this reduction process is continuous. Fresh supplies of alumina are added from time to time, and the furnaces do not cease to operate until it becomes necessary to renew the carbon linings. Low unit-costs of production are obtainable only if production is steady, continuous and on a very large scale.

The British Aluminium Company's rolling mills are at Warrington (Lancs), and Milton (Staffs). The final products of the rolling mills are light but bulky; therefore it is better to have the mills less remote from the final consumers than the reduction plants.[1] The degree of purity of the aluminium commonly rolled into sheets and used for the manufacture of cooking utensils, motor car parts and body work and for alloying with other metals is between 99·0 and 99·5 per cent. For electrical work and other special purposes aluminium of a still higher purity is produced. With the exception of aluminium oxide and red oxide the aluminium industry produces hardly any by-products.

The average number of manual workers employed in the

---

[1] About the year 1900 the manufacture of aluminium castings was introduced into the Black Country at Smethwick, where many foundries were already localized. G. C. Allen, *The Industrial Development of Birmingham and the Black Country* (1929), 300.

United Kingdom by the British Aluminium Company Ltd. and its subsidiary and associated companies is probably not far short of 6000. Wages and earnings are low for all grades. The workpeople are chiefly catered for by the National Union of General and Municipal Workers, but so far the British Aluminium Company and its subsidiaries have refused to negotiate with trade union officials.

In its various processes the industry gives employment to skilled, semi-skilled, and unskilled workers, both male and female. Much of the work is done on the shift system, and some of the men are regularly engaged on night work, but others change shift weekly.

Male labourers receive from 10¼d. to 10¾d. per hour in Great Britain and 11½d. in Northern Ireland. At the Warrington works the wages of yard labourers are 10¼d. per hour, or 40s. 2d. for a 47-hour week. Labourers working on 8-hour shifts are allowed half an hour for meals and are paid at the rate of 10¾d. an hour for 7½ hours, or 6s. 8½d. a shift. Those working 12-hour shifts are allowed 1½ hours for meals and receive 10¼d. an hour for 10½ hours, or 8s. 11½d. a shift; but for all hours worked during the week in excess of 47 an overtime rate of "time-and-a-quarter" is paid. This overtime rate applies also to other grades working 12-hour shifts. The grades of workers above the labourers, e.g. doing skilled and semi-skilled work in the rolling mills, casting and press shops, and power-houses, receive from 1s. to 1s. 2d. an hour, except certain men, such as under-firemen, blank shear operators, and a few other grades, who are not described as labourers, but receive only 10¾d. to 11¾d. an hour. "Leading hands" and "charge hands" receive from 1s. to 1s. 3d. an hour according to the process. In Scotland (Burntisland) the rate for male time workers is 1s. 0½d. and for process workers 1s. 2d. an hour. Charge hands receive 1s. 2½d. or 1s. 3d. an hour. Men regularly employed on night shifts, whether labourers or others, receive an additional payment or "compensation" of 5s. 3d. per week. Furnacemen, coolermen, and pressmen receive a small output bonus if the output exceeds a certain quantity.

At Warrington, women workers (over 21 years of age) on shift work receive from 21s. 10d. to 23s. 8d. for 37½ hours, and from 25s. 4d. to 28s. 8d. for 45 hours. There are two shifts—from 6 a.m. to 2 p.m. and from 2 p.m. to 10 p.m. Women on "day" work (i.e. not on shift work) receive 23s. 6d. for a 47-hour week. At Liverpool, girls are employed in the aluminium foil works in two eight-hour shifts between 6 a.m. and 10 p.m. at a wage of 20s. a week. Female charge hands receive 24s. a week.

II

The extent of the use of any material in industry depends chiefly upon suitability and cost, usually in relation to the suitability and cost of available alternative materials. Lightness was, and still is, aluminium's chief industrial and commercial property; and next to this stands its resistance to corrosion and its high thermal and electrical conductivity. Its resistance to chemical attack makes it particularly suitable for use in chemical plants, breweries, dairies, and in the domestic kitchen. The electrical conductivity of aluminium compared with copper is as 61 : 100, but since the corresponding specific gravities are 2·71 and 8·89, it follows that 1 lb. of aluminium is equal as an electrical conductor to 2 lb. of copper. Aluminium is very largely used for overhead transmission lines, by stranding aluminium wires around a core of galvanized steel. The majority of modern high-voltage lines are made in this way, and it is estimated that the British "grid" system used nearly 20,000 miles of steel-cored aluminium overhead conductors, containing some 12,000 tons of aluminium.[1] A further important property of aluminium in the pure form is a remarkable ductility, which is indicated by the almost inconceivable shapes to which it may be worked. As an example, a flat sheet may be spun into a long tube, which afterwards, without annealing, can be drawn back over itself,

---

[1] Cf. Electricity Commissioner's leaflet, *Rural Electrification; Considerations bearing upon the Electrical Development of Rural Areas* (1930), p. 3.

without cracking, until it is completely inside out. The full application of this exceptional workability is rarely called for in practice, yet the property is, nevertheless, of great value in certain applications. It is, for instance, very helpful to the modern motor car body builder, for it gives the designer full scope to obtain the most graceful lines, without being limited by the difficulty of working his material into the shapes required. For this application, the combination of ductility and low weight makes aluminium quite suitable for the whole range, from the stream-lined body of the racing car to the specially shaped body of the trade van designed to represent on a gigantic scale the article dealt in. For the latter purpose, aluminium, in many cases, is the only metal which will admit of a faithful reproduction without excessive weight.[1]

Originally, the softness of aluminium and its low tensile strength were serious hindrances to its use in many directions, but the perfection of several hard aluminium alloys has greatly extended the field of actual and possible uses.

"With the metal magnesium, aluminium forms a valuable alloy called *magnalium* (containing from 1–2% of magnesium), which is even lighter than aluminium itself and is equal to brass in strength; and the construction of airships has been revolutionized by the discovery of the alloy *duralumin*, an alloy of aluminium with copper (4%), magnesium (0·5%), and manganese (0·5%). This alloy, while having a tensile strength equal to or greater than steel, has only one-third of its weight."[2] This fact is important. Bulk for bulk, aluminium is less than one-third the weight of copper and slightly more than one-third the weight of iron, which has a specific gravity of 7·8. Very little of the advantage of lightness is lost when aluminium is alloyed with other metals. The majority of aluminium alloys contain less than 15 per cent of added metals, and have specific gravities ranging from 2·68 to 2·99.

An important method of increasing the strength and hardness of aluminium alloys is heat-treatment, which is a

[1] *Aluminium Production, Properties and Applications.*
[2] Findlay, *Chemistry in the Service of Man* (3rd Edn. 1925) 209.

process of heating and quenching akin to the tempering of steel. The heat-treatment process is, however, a delicate one and must be carried out with much skill and care. The alloy duralumin, discovered in Germany over twenty years ago, is still the most widely used of all the heat-treated aluminium alloys.

During the past ten years the producers of aluminium have been actively extending its uses. According to the *Report* of the Committee on Aluminium Hollow-ware,[1] set up in 1925 under the Safeguarding of Industries Act, very little aluminium hollow-ware was manufactured in Great Britain before the War. A small amount was produced at Birmingham, but the bulk of it was imported from Germany.[2] After the War, however, an increasing number of British firms began to manufacture such goods, and in 1920 1377 tons were produced of which 327 tons were exported. The number of employees in this trade was then about 3500. In the post-war slump the numbers employed fell to 1650 in 1922, while imports of foreign aluminium hollow-ware (chiefly from Germany) rose from 425 tons in 1920, to 713 tons in 1921 and, in anticipation of the imposition of a duty, to 1693 tons in 1922. An import duty was imposed at the end of August, 1922, and remained in force two years during which imports from abroad fell to 536 tons in 1923 and 206 tons in 1924. Meanwhile the numbers employed recovered to approximately 2500 in 1924 and reached 3000 in 1925. The Committee came to the conclusion that the British aluminium hollow-ware trade was carried on with efficiency and economy; that 80 per cent of the home trade was in the hands of the home industry;[3] and that no "safeguarding" duty could be recommended under their terms of reference.

According to the *Fourth Census of Production* (1930) the total value of the British output of aluminium hollow-ware was £616,000 in 1924 (£468,000 at average 1930 values), and

---

[1] *Cmd.* 2530/1925.
[2] G. C. Allen, *The Industrial Development of Birmingham and the Black Country* (1929), 263.
[3] Now localized mainly in the Midlands and Greater London.

£961,000 in 1930; while the average price fell from £372·4 in 1924 to £282·6 per ton in 1930. In 1924 the total value of exports of aluminium hollow-ware was £218,000, and retained imports, £60,000. The corresponding figures for 1930 were £83,000 and £86,000.[1]

Aluminium and aluminium alloys are now largely used for a variety of purposes in the aircraft, motor car and electrical industries; and in the textile industry aluminium alloys are used for warp beams and Jacquard rollers which must be light as well as durable. The economic advantages of using aluminium in connexion with transport, whether by land, sea or air, are easily explained. Since the replacement of heavier metals by aluminium or light alloys reduces the gross weight of the vehicle, if the same load be carried there will be a direct saving in power consumption and other running costs, while for certain classes of road vehicle there is a reduction in taxation because of the lower unladen weight. Of greater importance, however, is the fact that for the same power consumption and for the same maximum laden weight an increased pay load can be carried. On the other hand, aluminium and light alloys are more expensive than wood or steel, so that there is a direct increase in capital expenditure, which will involve increased interest charges. But if these are compared with the increased profit from extra pay load and the reduced depreciation due to the fact that the light alloys are very durable, and have, ultimately, an appreciable value as scrap metal, it will be found that, on balance, it is advantageous to use the light metals.

The same arguments apply to the use of aluminium containers for transport purposes. Certain users of transport have made substantial economies by using duralumin containers. Sling skip containers, having capacities of from 25 cwt. to 3 tons, made of duralumin are used for rail, road, and ocean transport. The tare weight is usually about one-sixth of the load carried, and in certain instances it may be considerably less. Duralumin demountable van bodies, having a

---

[1] *Final Report, Fourth Census of Production, Part II*, 1934, 93–102.

Fig. 7.
PRODUCTION AND MANUFACTURE OF ALUMINIUM

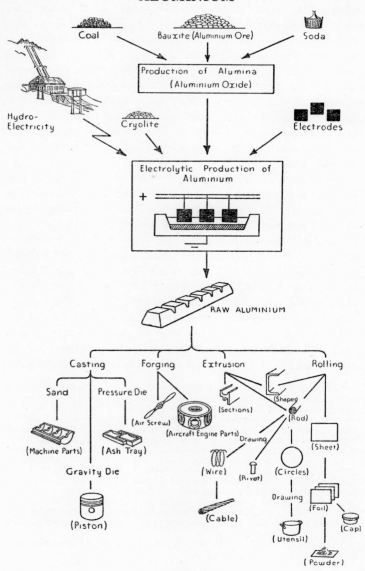

tare of 5 cwt., are in use, capable of carrying approximately 4 tons. The initial cost of duralumin containers is higher than the cost of wooden ones, but this is outweighed by the saving in transport and maintenance charges. In relation to land transport these considerations hold good not only for road vehicles but for railways also. The lightening of railway rolling stock may be effected in numerous ways; e.g. the substitution of aluminium panelling for wood or steel, and the use of high tensile aluminium alloy sections for frame members.[1] The extensive use of aluminium in the construction and furnishing of ships at once reduces weight and increases fire resistance.

Aluminium can be dyed various colours[2] or polished to the brightness of a mirror and it is being used more and more in building construction and decoration. It is beginning to be used for the canning of certain kinds of foodstuffs, and for the manufacture of collapsible tubes to contain toothpaste and many similar preparations. Aluminium cans or "boxes" are slightly dearer than tinplate cans, but this is largely offset by the ease with which the former can be stamped, which saves labels, and their lightness, which reduces freight costs. Moreover, old aluminium cans are useful as scrap. Tin foil, at one time exclusively used for wrapping such goods as chocolates and cigarettes, is now almost entirely superseded by aluminium foil. One pound of aluminium produces more than

[1] It is claimed that the all-aluminium Pullman coach, first exhibited at the Chicago World Fair, 1933, is the last word in design for speed and comfort. It is made of aluminium alloy throughout except for such parts as axles and springs. The coach body weighs only 96,980 lb., which is only a little more than half the weight of the standard steel Pullman of equivalent capacity and equipment, but the aluminium car is equal in strength to the all-steel coach, and the reduction in the cost of haulage is not accompanied by any sacrifice in safety. There is also the special coach constructed for the London & North Eastern Railway, which is built up of aluminium castings. Sides, ends and doors are all cast in silicon aluminium alloy suitably ribbed to give the maximum of rigidity with the minimum of weight, and assembled by riveting to steel side pillars. The roof is of duralumin, but the use of castings for the main portions of the body is a new type of construction which may lead to further development.

[2] Committee on Industry and Trade, *Factors in Industrial and Commercial Efficiency* (1927), 328.

two and a half times as much foil of any given thickness, and as a pound of tin itself costs about two and a half times as much as a pound of aluminium, the economy of aluminium foil is obvious. In the same way, lead foil is also being largely displaced by aluminium foil for the wrapping of tea and the lining of tea chests, though in this case the choice is governed not so much by the economy in first cost as by the large saving in freight costs. "To-day," says Mr. Boex, "the natives of Africa use aluminium pots and pans in place of earthenware, and aluminium wire in place of beaten copper for their rings." Moreover, "it is likely that the desire to reduce weight will in the future lead manufacturers of machinery to employ aluminium to a far greater extent than at present."[1]

III

Without doubt, aluminium is now firmly established as one of the chief industrial metals. The annual consumption of it exceeds that of tin. Between 1924 and 1929 British consumption of aluminium increased 120 per cent; while world consumption increased 62 per cent. Total world output in 1929 approached 300,000 tons. This level was, of course, not maintained during the ensuing years of severe trade depression,[2] but the discovery of new uses for aluminium, together with vigorous and well-directed propaganda, have done much to ease the situation in the industry. But no propaganda is so effective as reductions of prices.

In the early 'eighties the price of aluminium was about £3 per lb., or £6720 a ton; by 1886 it was down to £4400 per ton, and in 1888 a price equal to £1792 a ton is recorded. This marks the end of the period of "primitive" productive methods and high, almost uncommercial, prices. By 1909–10 the price

---

[1] G. Boex, *op. cit.*, 14.

[2] In 1932 the production of aluminium in Europe, Canada, and U.S.A. was only 153,500 tons, distributed as follows: Europe 88,500 tons, Canada 18,000 tons, U.S.A. 47,000 tons. In 1933, the world output was 135,600 tons; but in 1934 it increased to 170,950 tons. In that year, however, Canada produced only 15,500 tons, and U.S.A. only 33,650 tons.

had been brought down to £55 a ton. During the war it rose to the neighbourhood of £225, but by 1924, according to the *Fourth Census of Production*, the average selling values of crude aluminium, ingots, blocks, etc., had fallen to £109·3 per ton, and by 1930 the average was £82·4 per ton. For plates, sheets, bars, sections, etc., the average price was £161·9 in 1924 and £126·8 per ton in 1930   As we saw above, aluminium hollow-ware prices fell by a similar percentage The value of the British output of aluminium and aluminium manufactures (excluding hollow-ware) in 1930 exceeded £6,000,000 [1]

Because it is comparatively new, the aluminium industry has no individualistic traditions. Vertical integration and horizontal combination are among its most marked features. Its development has been in many ways similar to that of other "young" industries, such as the electrical industry, which have been born, as it were, into an age and atmosphere of large-scale production and national and international combination, and have never been organized in any other way. The number of producers of aluminium has always been small, and the preliminary work of bringing most of them together was comparatively easy, especially as they were already "grouped." "The five French participants were firmly organized into a shareholding company, L'Aluminium Française. The other leading European manufacturers, the Aluminium Industry (Shareholding Company), of Neuhausen, did business through four factories in Switzerland, Germany and Austria." The monopolistic Aluminium Company of America controlled a Canadian undertaking—the Northern Canadian Aluminium Company, and had a regional agreement with the Aluminium Industry of Neuhausen until 1912, when the arrangement was dissolved as the result of a prosecution in U.S.A. under the Sherman Act.[2] There were also three undertakings in England and Norway, "all closely connected," and another in Italy. An international convention was arranged

---

[1] *Final Report of Fourth Census of Production* (1930), *Part II*, 1934, 438.
[2] *Journal of Political Economy*, October, 1920, pages 662–3.

as early as 1901, the bond between the various producers
being the exclusive use of the electrolytic patents. But when
these expired in 1905 new competition arose, and the cartel
collapsed in 1908. During its existence the price of aluminium
had risen by about 100 per cent. A new international cartel,
formed in 1912, included all the chief European producers
(French, Swiss, and British), and "it is understood to have
entered into arrangements with the Canadian company producing aluminium, which is believed to be controlled by the
Aluminium Company of America."[1] The Committee on
Trusts stated that the aim of the aluminium cartel was mainly
the regulation of prices.

According to Kossmann the leading aluminium producers
of the world at that time were—Aluminium Industrie A.-G.;
Société Électrometallurgique française, of Froges; Compagnie
des Produits chimiques d'Alais et de la Carmargue; the British
Aluminium Company Ltd.; the Aluminium Company of
America. Out of a total of twelve producers, these five undertakings turned out 90 per cent of the world output, distributed
between them respectively in the following ratios: 60, 60, 25,
45, 120.[2] During the war, of course, the international cartel
was dissolved. The first post-war international agreement
was negotiated in 1923, to be followed in 1926 by a more comprehensive agreement concluded for an initial period of two
years and subsequently renewed. The Aluminium Company
of America, for legal reasons peculiar to the United States of
America, felt obliged to remain outside the agreement, and
"Aluminium Ltd—a company of independent legal status
and which controls all the factories of the same group operating outside the United States . . . felt called upon to adopt
the same attitude."[3] But the great slump which followed the
Wall Street crash in 1929 altered the American attitude, and
it appears that a good understanding now exists between the

[1] *Report of the Committee on Trusts* (1919), p. 41.
[2] W. Kossmann, *Ueber die wirtschaftliche Entwickelung der Aluminiumindustrie.*
[3] League of Nations *Review of the Economic Aspects of Several International Industrial Agreements* (1930), p. 26.

European cartel and the principal American and Canadian producers.[1]

The existing international agreement does not provide for price fixation, but for the control of the sales of members on the basis of a quota allocated to each. The quota covers sales in the home market and export sales, but the agreement does not reserve certain markets to certain producers. All members of the cartel are at liberty to trade wherever they can and at such prices as they choose to accept. It seems likely that during the past ten years aluminium prices have been, on the whole, more stable and higher than they would have been in the absence of a cartel. It is true that aluminium prices have fallen, but it is very doubtful whether they have fallen as much as they would have done under conditions of unrestrained competitive production. Nevertheless, even moderate price reductions stand in sharp contrast to the policies pursued by the international copper cartel before 1931, and by the international tin cartel since that date.[2] Seeing that aluminium can be substituted in many uses for tin and copper, the price policies of the rival groups of producers are of the greatest moment.

After the successful launching of the second international tin restriction scheme in 1931, the cartellized tin producers curtailed world output so drastically as to raise the price of tin within two years from a little over £100 to the neighbourhood of £230 a ton. The wisdom of this price-raising policy has been much questioned, and it has been pointed out that the tin cartel may ultimately be defeated by the use of substitutes, such as aluminium. As to copper, there is no doubt that the copper cartel made a great blunder when for a year (1929–30) they tried to hold the price of copper as near as £10 a ton to the price of aluminium,[3] because this enabled the aluminium producers to "dig themselves in." Within a short time the copper cartel collapsed and copper fell to £28 a ton,

---

[1] *The Economist*, 12th May, 1934, 1036.
[2] See Plummer, *International Combines in Modern Industry* (1934), 92–6, 139–40.
[3] *Ibid.*, 124–5, 149–54.

less than one-third of the price of aluminium. Therefore, it seemed not unlikely that if copper did not rise in price, aluminium might have to be brought down. But now we have a new international cartel of copper producers and, thanks largely to rearmament, copper prices are soaring.

There are two other factors which may have some influence upon the aluminium cartel and its price policy. Firstly, although the cartel comprises many important producers in Europe and seems to have established an understanding with those of North America, there are some important concerns in Europe and elsewhere which are not members, and their numbers and output capacities are increasing. Russia, Japan, Sweden, Hungary, and British India are all actively setting up and developing aluminium industries of their own, much to the surprise and annoyance of the aluminium cartel.[1] Secondly, the German producers recently expressed a firm determination to increase their aluminium output (which was 27,500 tons in 1933), cartel or no cartel: and in 1934 the German quota was increased by the cartel to 55,000 metric tons per annum. This concession has been described as "almost freedom of production"; and had it not been agreed to, there is little doubt that the Germans would have left the cartel.[2]

Almost simultaneously the chief British member of the cartel, the British Aluminium Company Ltd., complained of the increase of foreign competition in the British market. In 1933, while world consumption showed some recovery from previous low levels, the British Aluminium Company's sales "fell somewhat and their production was severely restricted."

The home market sales were especially disappointing, all the more so because of an increase in the home consumption. The decided increase in foreign imports and competition during the closing months of 1932 was progressively evident during 1933, particularly in rolling mills products. Ways and means had been found by importers more than to counteract the entirely inadequate protection of the existing 10 per cent duty on ingot metal

[1] For some interesting details see *Manchester Guardian Commercial*, 28th December, 1934, 505, and *Aluminium Supplement*, 3rd July, 1936. Also U.S.S.R. Trade Delegation *Monthly Review*, July, 1936, 380.

[2] *Manchester Guardian Commercial*, 19th October, 1934.

Table showing the total quantity and declared value of the under-mentioned descriptions of aluminium and manufactures thereof imported into and exported from the United Kingdom during the years 1933 and 1934.

(Abstracted from the published trade returns of the United Kingdom.)

Description	1933		1934[2]	
	Quantity	Declared Value	Quantity	Declared Value
	Cwt.	£	Cwt.	£
Aluminium—	*Total Imports.*			
Crude in ingots, blocks, billets, notch bars, sticks, wirebar, slabs, alloy, and scrap[1] . . .	231,889	996,678	284,432	1,154,343
Plates sheets, bars, sections, tubes, wire, strand, etc. . .	61,169	339,404	64,751	343,488
Vats, tanks, etc., for industrial purposes .	512	2,444		
Hollow-ware, domestic .	322	4,190	22,610	208,019
Other manufactures of aluminium . .	17,817	181,379		
Total . .	311,709	1,524,095	371,793	1,705,850
	Cwt.	£	Cwt.	£
Aluminium—	*Exports of United Kingdom Goods*			
Crude in ingots, blocks, billets, notch bars, sticks, wirebars, slabs, alloy, and scrap . . .	79,436	236,925	30,203	151,231
Plates, sheets, bars, sections, tubes, wire, strand, etc. . .	62,723	401,412	78,194	479,181
Vats, tanks, etc., for industrial purposes .	92	972		
Hollow-ware, domestic .	7,242	69,439	34,305	320,831
Other manufactures of . aluminium . .	20,987	174,637		
Total . .	170,480	883,385	142,702	951,243

[1] Excluding scrap in 1934.
[2] Provisional figures.

and rolling mill products, and the importing countries had set up prohibitive barriers, making retaliation in their territories impossible. In their own countries prices were approximately 25 per cent higher than here, and yet importers sold aluminium products here at less than 70 per cent of their home prices, after having paid freight duty and other incidental charges. This state of affairs was largely brought about by the aid of subsidies granted by foreign Governments to their exporters. The only effective answer was a drastically increased scale of import duties. . . . As to the current year (1934) their (British Aluminium Company's) deliveries to date had been rather better and indications available appeared to point to an increased use of their metal in the home market. If they read those signs correctly, the company should benefit from any such improvements, but only to a limited extent unless the Government took immediate and suitable action to check the ever-increasing flow of importations. Undoubtedly they must look to the home market as the mainstay of their industry.[1]

The Economist's explanation is somewhat different, for it states that the large volume of imports is due to the fact that

the rapid rise in British aluminium consumption has in the past outstripped the British Aluminium group's productive capacity. With the approaching completion of the great North British Lochaber hydro-electric works, however, the group should be able to supply a much greater proportion, if not all, of the domestic market. Meanwhile, the Continental producers (especially the Germans) have had the temerity to expose themselves to the charge of "dumping by sales at prices 30 per cent below the price in their own market, and the Import Duties Advisory Committee is considering the imposition of a duty."[2]

The duty was raised to 15 per cent *ad valorem* from 1st September, 1934.

Foreign imports of aluminium into Great Britain are chiefly in the form of semi-manufactured products from Germany, where the government gives special facilities to exporters in order to stimulate the export trade. Whether the British

---

[1] Press report of Chairman's speech at Annual General Meeting.
[2] *The Economist*, 12th May, 1934, 1936. The British output of aluminium was 13,900 metric tons in 1929, and 12,900 metric tons in 1934. British consumption was 23,000 metric tons in 1934, and probably not far short of 30,000 metric tons in the following year.

Aluminium Company will be able successfully to meet this foreign competition when their new works at Lochaber are in full production remains to be seen.

In conclusion, then, it seems clear that the future fortunes of the British aluminium industry depend partly upon the expansion of existing uses and the discovery of new uses for aluminium and its alloys; and partly upon whether the international cartel continues, and, if so, upon the wisdom of its production policy and the price policies of its members in face of the non-cartellized producers of aluminium, and in relation to the policies of producers of rival metals, such as tin and copper. A fall in the demand for aluminium will follow the completion of the electricity "grid," but this may be offset by the consequent extension of the use of aluminuim parts in electrical equipment of all kinds, by the further expansion of motor manufacture and aviation, and—if the present regretable tendency towards competitive arming continues—by increased consumption of aluminium in the armaments industry. Moreover, there is no reason to think that the discovery of new uses for aluminium and aluminium alloys has reached its limit, especially if the price of the metal is kept low.

(ii) Rayon (Artificial Silk)

The remarkable growth of all forms of communication, including travel and illustrated advertising; the blurring of the hard and fast distinctions between different social classes; the universal increase of personal cleanliness, and the general rise in standards of life, have revealed in Britain and other advanced modern communities an almost insatiable demand for clothing, especially garments for women. In the past this demand had to remain latent so far as the great majority of people were concerned; and if to-day the desire for greater quantities and varieties of clothes; for more comfortable and, at the same time, more elegant garments, has been transformed into effective demand, so that the people of this country, and many others, are dressed far better than ever before in the history of the world, the result is due in no small measure to the development of the rayon (or "artificial silk") industry and to the progressive improvement and cheapening of its products. Once again the vision of early inventors and the judgment of the original industrial *entrepreneurs* have been abundantly justified by subsequent developments in the twin spheres of production and consumption.

I

As long ago as 1734 Ferchault de Réaumur, the French naturalist and physicist wrote: "Silk is only a liquid gum which has been dried; could we not make silk ourselves with gums and resins? This idea, that would appear at first sight fanciful, is more promising when examined more closely. It has already been proved that it is possible to make varnishes which possess the essential qualities of silk. . . . If we had threads of varnish we could make them into fabrics which, by their brilliancy and strength, would imitate those of silk, . . . But how can we draw out these varnishes into threads?"[1] De Réaumur's pregnant question had to wait 120 years for an answer. It had to await the discovery of nitro-cellulose and its special qualities.

About the year 1840 Louis Schwabe, a Manchester silk manufacturer, invented a silk making machine, which he showed to the British Association in 1842; but doubtless this was nothing more than a first rough approximation. In 1855 George Audemars of Lausanne patented a process for transforming dissolved nitro-cellulose into fine threads which he called *soie artificielle*. Important as this is as the beginning of a new phase, it was only after numerous experiments by Count Hilaire de Chardonnet and four or five others working independently in the same field, that artificial silk or rayon was

---

[1] *Memoirs pour servir à l'Histoire des Insectes* (1734–42), I, 154. Mr. M. H. Avram refers to the experiments of a British scientist, Dr. Robert Hooke, c. 1644, and his prophetic declaration that "silk equal to, if not better than, that produced by the silkworm" would eventually be made by mechanical means. See Avram *The Rayon Industry* (1933), 38.

brought from the laboratory to the market place towards the end of the nineteenth century. Chardonnet nitrated cellulose and dissolved the resulting product in a mixture of ether and alcohol. In this way he obtained a viscous liquid which he forced through tiny holes into water. He then converted the filaments or threads so obtained into an amorphous cellulose resembling silk in appearance, by treating them with ammonium sulphide.[1] By 1890 three factories were at work producing artificial silk on a commercial scale by Chardonnet's process.[2]

Mr. Thomas Woodhouse draws attention to the fact that nearly all the original experiments made in the attempt to produce artificial silk thread were made "in the interests of the comparatively new electrical industry,"[3] the object being to discover a suitable filament substance for incandescent electric lamps. Prominent among the group of pioneers mentioned above we find John Mercer (the inventor of "mercerization"—a process of improving, by the use of alkalis, the strength and appearance of textile yarns) who investigated the action of ammoniacal copper oxide upon cellulose; and (Sir) Joseph Wilson Swan who, in 1883, patented a method of forming a continuous thread from a solution of cellulose by a "squirting" process, and anticipated three distinct uses for the product, viz. (a) carbon filaments for electric lamps, (b) threads for electrical insulation, (c) textile threads for ropes, twines and woven fabrics.[4]

Yet another contemporaneous series of experiments, by Messrs. Cross and Bevan, resulted in the invention of the viscose process. They obtained a patent in 1892, and viscose yarn and fabrics were on view at the Paris Exhibition in 1900. Although the experimental period was by no means over, it

[1] Pilcher and Butler-Jones, *What Industry Owes to Chemical Science* (1923), 55–6.

[2] Messrs. Wardle & Davenport, of Leek, claim to be the first British firm to use rayon, for they worked up the first samples of Chardonnet's yarn into braid about the year 1885. *Rayon Record*, May, 1933, 213–4.

[3] *Artificial Silk or Rayon, Its Manufacture and Uses* (2nd Edn., 1929), 6.

[4] For diagrams see T. Woodhouse, *Artificial Silk or Rayon*, 13 ff.

may be said that the foundations of the new rayon industry were well and truly laid by the end of the nineteenth century. Many important technical problems, however, still had to be solved, and it remained to be seen whether an industry of any considerable magnitude could be built up in the present century. In the period 1901–14 the commercial production of rayon and the expansion of demand for it were hindered by certain imperfections which had not been overcome. At that time, however, some progress was being made in France, where the industry first passed from the experimental to the commercial stage, and in Great Britain, Germany, and the U.S.A.

It is in the post-war period that really rapid expansion of the industry took place. This was due mainly to the triumphant solution of various obstinate technical problems and the consequent improvement in quality and attractiveness of rayon fabrics of all kinds. Makers of textile machinery studied the special needs of the rayon manufacturers, and produced machines capable of solving some of their problems. Manufacturers soon found it possible to reduce costs and prices, and by so doing they discovered a demand of very great elasticity. Rayon goods became fashionable chiefly, but not exclusively, among women; and the vogue of the short skirt and the desire for stockings of elegant appearance and in colours harmonizing with the wearer's dress or costume, gave the rayon industry a great fillip. Capital was attracted to the industry in large quantities, both for the establishment of new companies and the extension of the existing, pioneer concerns. Between 1913 and 1932 the rayon output of the world increased more than tenfold.

II

Compared with a textile industry like cotton, the rayon industry is less subject to fluctuations in the supplies and prices of its chief raw material, timber, since this commodity is not an annual crop, nor is it subject to the attacks of insect pests or the vagaries of the weather. Rayon production has now reached a very high level of efficiency. Successful production demands—

1. Easy access to supplies of cotton or suitable timber.

2. A well-equipped factory in a good situation in relation to supplies of raw materials, and markets.

3. Efficient workpeople under capable managers.

4. A group of expert chemists capable of tackling current problems and original research, and a well-developed chemical industry within easy reach.

Briefly, the manufacture of rayon consists in the application of a series of chemical processes to cellulose, a substance which the industry at present obtains either from cotton linters (very short fibres which cling to the cotton seeds—almost a waste product), or spruce wood pulp.[1] Cotton is rich in cellulose (94 to 96 per cent usually) and can be prepared for rayon production in a comparatively short time. Wood pulp, which is produced by boiling wood chips under high steam pressure in a liquor of calcium bisulphite solution together with a certain amount of free sulphur dioxide, requires a long process, but the object is the same, namely the elimination of all non-cellulose substances. This is done by subjecting the pulp to washing, straining, and bleaching processes.

There are four chief kinds of rayon fibre, each corresponding to one of the four principal methods or systems of production used in the industry. These are—

1. The *viscose* method, which has resulted from the original researches of Cross, Bevan, and Beadle, begins with bleached spruce pulp, or cotton linters, or a mixture of both: but pulp is most commonly used. These materials are treated with caustic soda solution, thus forming a compound known as soda cellulose. The excess caustic soda having been pressed out, the soda cellulose is shredded, allowed to "age," and then converted into cellulose xanthate by treatment with carbon bisulphide. The solution which results is viscose, and this, after a "ripening" process is pumped through regulators to the

[1] Flax, cornstalks and straw can also be used. Avram, *The Rayon Industry* (1933), 433.

spinning machine, where it is forced through tiny platinum spinnerets or nozzles, and the filaments so formed are then spun into rayon yarn,[1] each produced by one of the four principal methods or systems of production used in the industry. This is to-day the most important and widely-used method, considerably more than 80 per cent of the world rayon output being made by the viscose process.

2. The *acetate* method, in which a high grade pulp or cotton lint is treated with acetic anhydride and strong acetic acid. The popular "celanese" fabrics are made from acetate rayon.

3. The *cuprammonium* method, in which the chief process is the dissolving of the prepared cellulose in an ammoniacal solution of copper oxide. The rayon produced by this method is said to bear the closest resemblance to real silk.

4. The *nitro-cellulose* or "Chardonnet" method, is the oldest of the four methods, and the fibre made by it is particularly suitable for the production of fine yarns. Dr. Reinthaler is of the opinion, however, that this process "is doomed to become extinct eventually, when works have gradually changed over entirely to the viscose or cellulose acetate processes." The products resulting from these different processes differ from one another as to strength, fineness, lustre and so forth.

Apart from the various chemical treatments, the chief process is the squeezing of the viscous cellulose through small nozzles so that it is converted into continuous filaments, which, after further chemical treatment, can be made into yarn by "doubling." More recently it has become possible and profitable to spin rayon yarn from short lengths of filament, known as staple fibre,[2] and to weave it into attractive, warm and serviceable fabrics.

Staple fibre was a war-time invention. German producers, hard pressed by scarcity due to the Allied blockade, were the first to experiment with it, and to produce it on a large scale. In Great Britain the woollen spinners were the first to take it up; sometimes mixing it with wool, sometimes using it in

[1] Howe, *Chemistry in the World's Work* (1926), 83.
[2] See F. Reinthaler, *Artificial Silk* (1928), Ch. 7.

place of wool with considerable success. Eventually the Lancashire cotton industry tried to spin staple fibre yarns, but for some time they met with little success. Although the rather coarse denier per filament of the staple yarn then available was no obstacle to the wool spinners, it caused great difficulties when attempts were made to spin it on cotton machinery. Moreover, the spinners found (*inter alia*) that the fibre was too straight and so became embedded in the wires of the carding engines, and that thick places often appeared in the yarns. The weavers discovered that owing to the "low wet strength" of the yarn, broken ends frequently occurred during the weaving process. Such difficulties as these naturally caused the cotton men to turn away from staple fibre; but rayon producers continued to study the fibre and its problems from both the chemical and mechanical sides, and in the end they discovered how to simplify and shorten the manufacturing process, and how to impart the necessary curl and extra "wet and dry strength" and fineness to the material. The result has been a revival of staple fibre spinning in Lancashire, chiefly among the firms equipped for spinning good quality Egyptian and superior quality American yarns. The bulk of it is viscose fibre, spun on mules adapted for the purpose.[1] In April, 1934, Courtaulds Ltd., acquired the Arrow Mill, Rochdale, for the purpose of running it as a staple fibre yarn spinning mill,[2] and shortly afterwards they erected a large-scale staple fibre plant at Greenfield, N. Wales. A great fillip was given to the production and use of staple fibre in this country when the excise duty on it was entirely abolished in September, 1935, and its price was so substantially reduced by Courtaulds that it became cheaper than merino and fine crossbred wool tops, and no dearer than medium quality Egyptian cotton. It is expected that staple fibre yarns will come to be widely used to impart a soft, wool-like "handle" to materials, and indeed they are already being used on an

---

[1] *M.G.C. World Textiles Supplement*, October, 1933.

[2] *Manchester Guardian Commercial*, 28th April, 1934. Staple fibre as now used is not a waste product, but is specially prepared and cut ready for spinning. Cf. *The Times Trade and Engineering Review*, December, 1934, p. 46; and *M.G.C., World Textiles*, October, 1936, p. 12.

increasing scale for hosiery, especially the interlock knitting of underwear.[1]

Unlike cotton and wool, the ordinary rayon filament is continuous and smooth; but since it is not so elastic as wool, nor so strong as cotton, it is more liable to damage in sizing, bleaching, dyeing and washing. On the other hand, fabrics woven from rayon yarn are soft and lustrous, and so smooth that they do not readily catch dirt.[2] Although a large volume of rayon yarn is made up into goods which consist entirely of rayon, the major part is used in combination with other materials, chiefly silk, cotton, or wool. This may be done either by weaving or knitting pure rayon yarn with some other yarn (e.g. cotton); or by spinning rayon staple fibre with one of the natural fibres so as to produce a mixed or composite yarn. Thus we find hosiery, dress and underwear fabrics, linings, shirtings, furnishing fabrics, velvets, laces, ribbons and braids being manufactured sometimes entirely from rayon yarn, and sometimes from a mixture. In addition to those manufacturers who concentrate entirely on rayon goods, the latter are being made to an increasing extent by cotton, silk and hosiery manufacturers.

The artificial silk industry has thus placed at the disposal of the cotton and wool textile industries and the hosiery and knit goods industries a new material, the value of which has already been proved. . . . By the use of artificial silk the older textile industries have been enabled to produce new kinds of fabrics and other manufactures, as well as novel designs and original forms of ornamentation; and all such developments are obviously matters of great importance in assisting these industries to extend the market for their products.[3]

Dr. Reinthaler says that "artificial silks have developed . . . along separate lines as textile materials with their own special

[1] See The Times (Annual Financial and Commercial Review), 12th February, 1935; The Economist, Commercial History and Review of 1934; and The Manchester Guardian Commercial Annual Review, January, 1936.

[2] For a technical description (with illustrations) of the properties and uses of various kinds of rayon see Reinthaler, op. cit., Chs. 8 and 12.

[3] Committee on Industry and Trade, Survey of Textile Industries (1928), 283.

uses. They are no longer to be regarded merely as substitutes for natural fibres, for they have acquired their own uses on their merits, and, moreover, can be used in the production of effects which could not be attained with natural silk."[1]

Many of the Lancashire cotton manufacturers have not been slow in grasping the new opportunities. The manufacturers of fashion fabrics, in particular, have taken up new ideas so readily that strictly speaking this section can no longer be regarded as part of the cotton industry. The yarns it uses are quite commonly unions of cotton and rayon, or fine worsted and rayon; indeed the doublers have now succeeded in uniting cotton, rayon and wool, in a single yarn. It has been estimated that 18 to 20 per cent of the active looms in Lancashire (i.e. close upon 90,000 looms) are engaged upon these mixture fabrics, the average rayon content of which is probably about 50 per cent. Exceedingly attractive fabrics can be produced by mixing two types of rayon yarn, e.g. acetate warp and viscose weft. "Staple fibre mixed with continuous filament rayon yarn lends itself to the production of effective and smart woven checks and stripes. One maker, in particular, is obtaining excellent results by the use of continuous filament warp with alternate ends of viscose staple fibre, these being checked alternately with acetate filament weft and viscose staple fibre weft. A fabric so constructed looks charming when cross-dyed."[2]

It has been found that the inclusion of staple fibre yarn improves the draping qualities of the fabrics. Methods have also been perfected for reducing the lustre where a more subdued effect is desired; and of manufacturing a hollow fibre, which bids fair to supplant the solid fibre where extra lightness is considered important.

In such ways as these many original cloths have been evolved, and there are still tremendous possibilities of further progress. Lancashire manufacturers are now using something approaching 60 per cent of the total British output of rayon

---

[1] Reinthaler, *op. cit.*, 223.
[2] *Manchester Guardian Commercial, World Textiles Supplement,* 7th October, 1933.

yarn. Other important centres of rayon manufacture are the West Riding of Yorkshire and the Midlands (Derby, Nottingham, Coventry, Wolverhampton), while factories are also to be found in the Greater London area, at Bristol, in East Anglia and South-west Scotland.[1] Special rayon machinery is made at Manchester, Macclesfield, Leek, Leicester, Nottingham, Keighley, and Bolton.[2]

III

The Ministry of Labour estimate of the number of insured workpeople engaged in the manufacture of rayon yarn at July, 1936, was 30,300, of whom 11,360 were females.[3] These statistics are reliable enough; but when we come to the weaving and knitting of rayon, we are on less solid ground. In publishing the numbers engaged in the weaving section of the industry the Ministry does not distinguish between "silk manufacture" and "artificial silk weaving." The number employed in both of these trades in July, 1936, is given as 49,830 (the females numbering 31,110). Undoubtedly there has been great expansion in the rayon section in recent years, while the majority of silk manufacturers now use large quantities of rayon yarn, some silk and rayon mixtures containing as much as 80 per cent of rayon. Therefore it is permissible to put the number of operatives engaged in rayon weaving at about 40,000. This leaves the knitting and hosiery section to be considered. "Hosiery" in official statistics usually covers the manufacture of stockings, half-hose, underwear, jumpers, pullovers and various other knitted fabrics and garments. The total number of insured persons engaged in this trade is 118,430, of whom 91,740 are females. On the very conservative assumption that, on the average, these people devote a

---

[1] The most important British producers of rayon yarn are Courtaulds (Coventry) and British Celanese (Derby). The advantages of Coventry from the rayon producer's point of view are abundance of young female labour not likely to be drawn off into other employments; its central situation on a main railway line, near coal and the hosiery towns of Hinckley, Leicester and Nottingham; and a good water supply.

[2] Wilmore, *Industrial Britain* (1930), 280–1.

[3] *Labour Gazette.*

quarter of their labour to rayon goods,[1] we shall have to add about 29,600 to the figures already cited. The estimated total is thus—

					Insured Workpeople
Rayon yarn manufacture	.	.	.	.	30,300
Rayon weaving	.	.	.	.	40,000
Rayon hosiery manufacture	.	.	.	.	29,600
					99,900

The manufacture of rayon is a continuous process, and shift work on the three-shift system is the rule among the male operatives. Normally they work six eight-hour shifts per week and the most usual rates of wages are between 9s. 6d. and 11s. a shift. In certain plants rates as low as 10d. or 1s. an hour, or 6s. 8d. and 8s. a shift, are paid, while the best employers pay as much as 13s. 4d. a shift. Men engaged exclusively on day work usually receive somewhat lower wages than those on shift work, while on the other hand, workers who have special skill and/or responsibility (e.g. maintenance engineers) receive higher pay. The average weekly earnings of males under 21 ranged from 26s. (hosiery) to 40s. (rayon spinning) in October, 1935.

Women workers employed upon the twisting, winding, warping, washing and bleaching processes usually work in two shifts (6 a.m. to 2 p.m. and 2 p.m. to 10 p.m.) and their weekly wages range from 28s. up to 35s. 5d. There are close upon 7000 women and "young persons" working on this system in the rayon industry, and about 3400 in the hosiery industry. Women on "day" work (i.e. not on shift work), such as reeling and sorting, receive between 31s. 6d. and 34s. 6d. a week. Girls between the ages of 14 and 19½ years are employed at wages ranging, usually according to age, from a beginner's rate of 13s. up to about 34s. a week of 48 or 48½ hours.[2]

There is little or no uniformity regarding payment for overtime and Sunday work. Some employers pay extra for Sunday work, and agree that overtime rates shall become

---

[1] This assumption is based upon an examination of the statistics given in the *Report on the Import Duties Act Inquiry* (1933), Part I (1935), 69–71.

[2] See also p. 227 *post* for a Note on Wages and Hours.

applicable immediately the normal day or week (e.g. 8 or 48 hours) is exceeded: but others refuse to pay extra for Sunday work no matter how frequently it occurs, and will pay overtime rates only after a certain number of extra hours (e.g. eight) have been worked in any week at ordinary rates.

Trade union organization is somewhat uneven in the rayon industry, being much stronger where rayon manufacture has been grafted on to the cotton industry or the silk industry, as for example at Macclesfield and Leek, where trade unionism has been well established for many years.

Unemployment in the rayon industry has fluctuated very widely in recent years. From a comparatively low level in 1928 and 1929, it rose very rapidly to a high peak, and during the years 1930–1 the level was above the general level of unemployment. But it quickly fell again to relatively low levels in 1934 and 1935. Comparison with the other textile industries shows that in both good times and bad, unemployment in the rayon industry has been lower than in either the cotton industry or the woollen and worsted industry.

A certain amount of time is lost by rayon operatives owing to occupational diseases, chiefly dermatitis and soreness of the eyes. The latter is most common among the spinners. The employers have spent large sums in attempts to remedy these troubles, but without complete success so far.

IV

Some rayon manufacturers produce not only the filaments or fibres, but carry on the spinning processes as well. Others confine themselves to the primary processes, selling the rayon filaments or fibre to spinners in the rayon, woollen or cotton industries, who convert it into yarn. But some of the largest companies in the industry[1] are integrated vertically and manufacture not only rayon and rayon yarns, but also rayon fabrics. The position is similar in Germany, France, Switzerland, and the United States. The rayon industries of Italy

[1] E.g. Courtaulds and British Celanese.

and Holland, however, are mainly concerned with the production of rayon yarns.

Those larger consumers of rayon (e.g. knitting and weaving firms) who do not manufacture their own yarn, buy it direct from the manufacturers or from the sales organizations set up by the combines. Smaller consumers buy from agents or merchants. The finished fabrics and garments find their way to the final consumers *via* wholesalers and the retail shops like other fabrics. A great deal of advertising to the general public is done by the leading manufacturers (e.g. Courtaulds Ltd. and British Celanese Ltd.).

The rayon industry is essentially an industry of large units and extensive combines. It has been so almost from the beginning. Before 1914 Courtaulds Ltd. and the Glanzstoff-Fabriken took the lead in forming an international combine for the control of production and sales.

"The possession of the sole rights of the so-called Müller patents," says Dr. Reinthaler, "placed this syndicate, or at any rate the Glanzstoff-Fabriken in Germany, in such a position of supremacy that the few outside firms gradually fell to some extent into a position of financial dependence. The international relationships were ruptured by the War, but the association has now (1928) become even closer again . . . (and) . . . sooner or later may well lead to the formation of a world trust."[1]

Already we have a remarkable example of a world-wide international combination of national units and combines. It is not merely a large international cartel, but a vast and intricate network of interlacing interests, both financial and industrial, constructed mainly by exchanges of shares, and agreements for interchange and pooling of technical knowledge. "The necessity of finding markets for increased production and the

[1] F. Reinthaler, *Artificial Silk* (1928), 245. Vereinigte Glanzstoff-Fabriken A.-G. was incorporated in Germany in 1899. It owns six factories in Germany, manufacturing rayon by the viscose process. It has a direct controlling interest in American Bemberg Corporation and other rayon companies in Germany, Austria, Czechoslovakia, Japan, and U.S.A.; and joint interests and agreements with Courtaulds, Comptoir des Textiles Artificiels, and Societa Nazionale Industria Applicazione Viscosa (Snia Viscosa). Its issued capital is RM. 76½ millions in ordinary and preferred shares.

imposition of customs duties in many countries have (also) been among the factors which have favoured a movement towards the international syndication of the industry and the extension of the manufacturing activities of large enterprises into other countries. The outstanding tendency, in fact, of the post-war period has been the rapid growth of international arrangements which are extremely intricate and far-reaching, and in this movement British interests have taken a leading part. In Great Britain, Germany, Italy, and the United States (to name only the principal producers) a large part of the domestic production of artificial silk is now in the hands of very large firms, who also control or are associated with producing firms in other countries " In Great Britain the first place is taken by Messrs. Courtaulds Ltd., who produce more than half the British output of rayon, and, with their controlled interests abroad, are also the largest producers in the world. . . . The activities of the company include the production not only of artificial silk but also of manufactured goods (tissues, etc.) made from the material."[1]

Courtaulds' pre-eminent position in the industry has been built up by making industrial agreements with established producers in other countries, by acquiring shares in, or exchanging shares with, foreign undertakings, and by setting up factories in regions where none previously existed. Between 1913 and 1924 the capital of Courtaulds was raised from £2,000,000 to £32,000,000 largely by a succession of capitalized share bonuses. The company's principal interests outside Britain lie in Canada and the United States, where, among other interests, it holds 85 per cent of the share capital of the American Viscose Corporation, an undertaking which produces over one-third of the rayon output of the United States, or approximately 11 per cent of total world output. Courtaulds Ltd. have a working agreement with the rayon producers of France (where Courtaulds practically own La Soie Artificielle

---

[1] Committee on Industry and Trade, *Survey of Textile Industries* (1928), 296. *The Economist* estimates that "about £50 millions are invested in (British) firms making rayon yarns alone." (*The Economist*, 23rd May, 1936.)

de Calais), and an interest in the Asahi Company in Japan. Courtaulds are also "interested" in "Snia Viscosa," the leading Italian rayon producer, which owns several large factories both directly and through subsidiary rayon undertakings. Courtaulds and the Italian concern collaborate in the yarn export markets.[1] Excluding fortuitous profits on the foreign exchanges, and allowing for lower income tax and excise duty, Courtaulds earned 7·6 per cent upon their ordinary share capital in 1934, and 7·5 per cent in 1935, against 6·9 per cent in 1933 and 5·2 per cent in 1932.[2]

Next after Courtaulds, the leading British rayon manufacturing company is British Celanese Ltd. Although the company has nothing like the gigantic proportions of Courtaulds, it owns factories in the United States and Canada as well as in Great Britain, where it is the chief producer of acetate yarns and fabrics.

In Germany the leading company is the Vereinigte Glanzstoff-Fabriken A.-G. which is responsible for over half the total output of Germany. In Italy the principal place is held by the Societa Nazionale Industria Applicazione Viscosa ("Snia Viscosa") of Turin, with a capital of 1000 million lire, or over half the estimated capital of all Italian artificial silk companies.

In 1925, Courtaulds and the Glanzstoff group made "an arrangement for co-operation," and early in 1927 these two giant undertakings entered into an agreement with the Italian company which included an interchange of shares, and was stated to aim at the elimination of wasteful competition and the promotion of co-operation mainly along the line of the pooling of technical improvements and inventions.

Having regard to the previously existing connexion between the three participants in this arrangement with large producers outside their own countries, it is clear that the linking of the companies represents a very important step towards the world-wide inter-connexion of the artificial silk industry. . . . The Glanzstoff concern has international interests extending to the United States, Czechoslovakia, Austria, and Holland; and it is also stated to have agreements with firms in Japan and Switzer-

[1] *The Economist, Commercial History and Review of* 1934, p. 60.
[2] *The Economist,* 2nd March, 1935, 487, and 29th February, 1936, 480.

land. Moreover, it is associated with the other German viscose producers in a combine which was formed in 1926 to standardize and classify viscose silk and to fix uniform prices and terms of delivery. Snia Viscosa has interests in producing concerns in the United States, Poland, Rumania, and possibly other countries.[1]

The Dutch Enka group, which has factories in Holland, Britain and America,[2] has concluded with the German Glanzstoff group "an agreement for close co-operation resembling a merger," generally called the "Aku" or A.K.U. (Algemeene Kunstzijde Unie N.V.), in which Courtaulds hold an interest, believed to amount to about 10 per cent. The A.K.U. group is the second largest rayon-producing combine in the world. The smaller Dutch combine—the Breda group —has interests in enterprises in Britain, France, and Spain. The Breda-Visada Co. Ltd., took over the British Visada, Ltd., as a going concern at the end of 1928,[3] and in November 1933 A.K.U. and Dutch Breda made a joint arrangement relating to technical research and the acquisition and sale of patents and licences, by forming a new and separate company with a capital of 50,000 florins, of which A.K.U. holds 52 per cent and Breda 48 per cent. In Japan, where the industry is making remarkable headway, there are, besides purely national under-takings, factories established by the European combines—the Glanzstoff combine, Courtaulds, and the Comptoir des Textiles artificielles.[4]

The principal export markets for British rayon yarns and fabrics are India, Australia, Canada, New Zealand, and Holland. The position in the Indian market is interesting, for, although the Indians are Britain's largest customers for rayon, they now import much larger quantities of rayon goods from Italy and Japan. In India, as in many other markets, the increase in the imports from Japan is particularly striking.

The rayon industry in Great Britain and elsewhere has had

---

[1] *Survey of Textile Industries*, 297.
[2] British Enka, Ltd., owns one of the largest rayon plants in Great Britain.
[3] *Manchester Guardian Commercial Supplement*, 2nd July, 1931, 30.
[4] League of Nations *Review of the Economic Aspects of Several International Industrial Agreements* (1930), 53.

a truly remarkable growth in the last twenty years. Mr. Samuel Courtauld estimates that from 1907 to 1909 British production of all kinds of rayon averaged 200,000 lb. per annum.[1] By 1936 British production of rayon yarns was in the neighbourhood of 145 million lb. per annum. World production of rayon yarn increased from 440 million lb. in 1929 to 791 million lb. in 1934, and 890 million lb. (plus 160 million lb. of staple fibre) in 1935. The British share of this expanding total has varied between $11\frac{1}{2}$ and 14 per cent in recent years. Among the foreign producers, Japan continues her phenomenal progress, and if her output of staple fibre is brought into account, she is the largest producer of rayon in the world. Next comes the United States, followed by Great Britain, Germany, Italy, and France, in that order. The growth in the British industry has been due very largely to the remarkable expansion of demand in the home market. The export trade in rayon fabrics is a weak spot, and the fluctuations from year to year are considerable.[2] The yarn section of the export trade is more satisfactory and is making steady progress.

From 1925 to 1934 the British rayon industry enjoyed protection in the home market to the extent of the difference between the excise and customs duties set out below—

	Customs Duty	Excise Duty	Difference
	pence per lb.	pence per lb.	pence per lb.
Rayon yarn . . .	24	12	12
Rayon waste . . .	12	6	6
Rayon fabric . . .	42	nil	42

On 7th July, 1934, a reduced scale of duties was introduced—

Rayon yarn . . .	15	6	9
Rayon waste . . .	9	3	6
Rayon fabric . . .	17	nil	17

[1] See *Manchester Guardian Commercial*, 22nd May, 1936, 473.

[2] In 1933 Great Britain's imports of all-rayon fabrics were twice as large as her exports (21·7 against 10·8 million square yards); in 1934 and 1935 exports rose to 16 million and 14·9 million square yards, and slightly exceeded imports. British exports of mixture fabrics exceeded imports by 35 million square yards in 1933, by nearly 43 million square yards in 1934, and by about 30 million square yards in 1935.

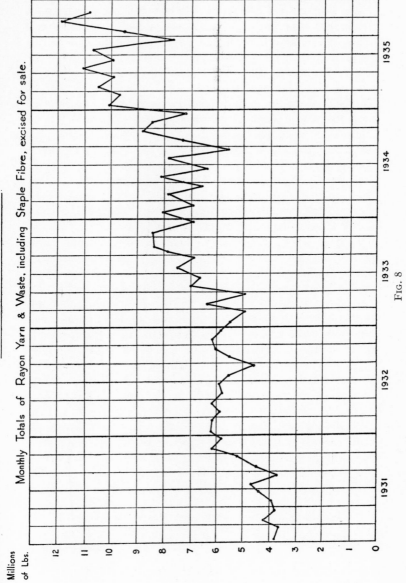

BRITISH RAYON INDUSTRY

Monthly Totals of Rayon Yarn & Waste, including Staple Fibre, excised for sale.

FIG. 8

As soon as the new duties were published Courtaulds announced that, in accordance with a pledge given several years ago, they would immediately pass on the excise reduction to their customers. Other rayon producers, willingly or unwillingly, followed suit, so that all rayon yarn fell in price by 6d. per lb., and rayon waste and staple fibre by 3d. per lb. The changes in the duties also had the effect of reducing the measure of protection given in respect of yarns and fabrics, and it may be argued that as the British rayon industry is no longer an "infant," and in view of the numerous and comprehensive international agreements between British and foreign producers, no protection at all is now necessary.[1] Also it may be urged that even the reduced customs and excise duties upon yarn and the customs duty on waste are objectionable, because they are taxes upon an important raw material.[2]

In spite of protection in the home market, and expanding production and consumption, the dividend records of British rayon producers other than Courtaulds have been far from good.[3] Doubtless the chief reasons for this state of affairs are (a) the fact that expanding demand has been maintained only by frequent and substantial reductions of prices and improvements in quality, and (b) the fact that the rayon market is dominated by Courtaulds both in this country and the United States. When it is a question of making further reductions in costs and selling prices, many of the smaller producers find it difficult, if not impossible, to follow Courtaulds' lead without sacrificing profits. British rayon production to-day is more than double the output in 1927, and prices have been more than halved since that date. Apparently Courtaulds' aim is the creation of a large volume of sales by keeping prices strictly moderate. Thus, although profits per unit of output may fall, they hope to increase their *aggregate* profits without attracting

---

[1] For a general discussion of protective tariffs in relation to international combines see my *International Combines in Modern Industry* (1934), 120–5.

[2] There is now no British *excise* duty upon staple fibre and rayon waste.

[3] For actual figures see *The Economist*, 11th November, 1933, 916.

any new competitors. It is clear, therefore, that both the nature of the existing organization of the rayon industry and its technical processes make the establishment of new independent companies extremely hazardous. A large capital is essential. There may be difficulties regarding existing patents owned by other producers. After the erection of the plant, much money must be spent and many months (perhaps years) must elapse before full continuous production of first grade rayon can be achieved and before dividends can be earned. And last, but not least, there is the dominant influence of Courtaulds, who may at any moment, without warning, announce a new series of price reductions for which the newer and smaller producers are not ready. Yet refusal to follow the leaders is almost certain to result in a serious loss of business. On the whole it seems likely that the future course of development in the rayon industry will be in the direction of still fewer, but larger, business units, possessing world-wide industrial and financial interests, for it is by no means certain that the international combination movement in this industry has yet reached its zenith.

NOTE ON WAGES AND HOURS

From the results of a Ministry of Labour sample inquiry, October, 1935, published in *Labour Gazette*, February, 1937

	All work-people covered by the inquiry	Average weekly earnings of			
		Males		Females	
		21 yrs. and over	Under 21 yrs.	18 yrs. and over	Under 18 yrs.
	s. d.	s. d.	s. d.	s. d.	s. d.
Rayon spinning .	46 3	67 3	39 11	29 9	17 10
Silk throwing and spinning, and silk and rayon weaving	42 7	66 10	30 8	31 1	17 1
Hosiery . . .	37 10	72 3	26 1	35 8	17 6

Rayon spinning, average normal weekly hours, (*a*) day work, 47·7; (*b*) shift work, 44·3 (exclusive of meal-times). In silk and rayon throwing, spinning and weaving, and in hosiery, average normal weekly hours were a little below 48.

CHAPTER V

THE CANNING OF FOODSTUFFS

HIGH or rising standards of life do not, as a rule, mean the consumption of greater *quantities* of foodstuffs, but rather a demand for greater *varieties*. Indeed, where improvements in industrial technique and organization have reduced the amount of heavy work and the length of the working day, the quantity of food consumed by the workers is likely to be reduced also, by reason of the lessening of their output of physical energy. But at the same time they will wish to introduce greater variety into their food budgets. An exhausted and hungry man is mainly concerned to fill himself as soon as may be, and is not likely to complain if the fare be simple, so long as it is sufficient. But suppose him to be much less exhausted by manual toil and, consequently, less hungry; then he will be more critical of whatever is set before him. Dietetic variety, including the consumption of scarce and "out-of-season" foods, has long been one of the signs of high standards of life. The diet of the very poor, in this or any other era, whether in Britain or abroad, in Battersea or Bombay, always lacks variety, even when it is sufficient in quantity.

The majority of foodstuffs are, by their nature, perishable, and in earlier times could be consumed only when in season. Here is a natural obstacle, often resulting in waste and inconvenience, which Man has set himself to overcome. Once again the inventors and the *entrepreneurs* between them had to solve a set of technical and economic problems. Taking a widespread desire for dietetic variety as given, it was necessary to select various attractive agricultural products and to preserve them in such a way that they would be hardly less attractive and no less fit for human consumption at a considerable time—perhaps many months—after leaving the farm, and, at the same time, to be able to sell them at prices low enough to translate desire into effective demand. So far the methods mainly adopted to arrest the decay of foodstuffs have been either to store them at low temperatures or to seal them in specially designed airtight containers.

I

A limited number of methods of preserving certain kinds of food have long been known. The arts of smoking, pickling, and salt-curing fish and meat and the preservation of fruits in the form of jam and of meats and fish "potted" with butter and spices, have been practised for centuries[1]; but beyond this point little progress was made until the nineteenth century. In 1800, the French Government, with an eye upon the needs of Napoleon's armies, offered a prize of 12,000 francs to anyone who could discover any other satisfactory method of preserving foodstuffs. In 1804 the award went to a Frenchman, Nicholas Appert, who managed to preserve fruit, vegetables, meats, soups and milk in glass containers. Appert used the prize-money to set up the first factory for the preservation of food by means of heat. Experiments with tin containers came later, probably between 1810 and 1818. The tin can offered several advantages over the glass container, viz. it was cheaper, lighter, easier to cut, shape, seal, and handle rapidly on mass-production lines, and not liable to break when subjected to heat or steam pressure, or during transport. Tins containing Australian mutton were on show at the Great Exhibition in 1851. It is also on record that tinned meat carried by H.M.S. *Fury* in 1824 was found to be in a perfect state of preservation in 1868. The early commercial manufacture of condensed milk began in America and Switzerland between 1851 and 1860. The great salmon-canning industry of North America was started by two fishermen and a tinsmith on the Sacramento River in 1864, and fruit canning in California began soon after.[2] The needs of the armies in

[1] Cf. e.g. Robert Smith, *Court Cookery* (2nd Edn. 1725), pp. 203–7.
[2] *The Times, British Canning Industry Supplement*, 17th November, 1931, ix.

the American Civil War resulted in a great increase in the output of foods preserved in cans, and from that decade the Americans have led the world in the production and consumption of these goods. In the 'sixties, however, canning in many of its branches was still a somewhat experimental business, and it was not until the late 'seventies that there was any very general consumption of canned meats, meat extracts, and fruits.[1] The bulk of these goods was then manufactured in America or Australia, near the sources of the meat and fruit supplies; but the whole of the tinplate for the cans was made in Great Britain and exported.[2]

The presence of local supplies of tinplate did not produce a canning industry in this country. The British canning industry remained very small indeed during the nineteenth century. Leaving aside the making of jams and potted meats, only three or four pioneer firms, such as John Moir & Sons and Chivers & Sons, were engaged in it, and expansion was extremely slow. The development of fruit-canning in Great Britain appears to have been held back partly by a disbelief in the suitability of British fruits for canning, partly by doubt as to the potentialities of the home market, and partly by certain technical problems connected with the effects of the acids of English fruits upon tin containers. Eventually, this last difficulty was overcome by lacquering the insides of the cans. The British canning industry was still quite small when the outbreak of war in 1914 wrought more harm than good by restricting its supplies of tin plate and causing gradual deterioration of the quality of supplies of fruit. On the other hand, the possibility of a food shortage caused the Ministry of Agriculture, in conjunction with certain other interested bodies, to set up a small committee to investigate methods of conserving home-grown fruit and vegetable crops. This decision had highly important results in the form of an

---

[1] J. H. Clapham, *An Economic History of Modern Britain*, 1932, II, 91.
[2] J. H. Jones, *The Tinplate Industry* (1914), 10–20; cf. Committee on Industry and Trade, *Survey of Metal Industries* (1928), 65–7.

experimental station at Chipping Campden to conduct research into problems connected with fruit and vegetable preservation.

Canning research has two main sides : (a) relating to growing, e.g. the selection of suitable varieties, the correct stage for harvesting, etc., and (b) relating to factory processes. Fundamental research into the scientific principles underlying the technique of canning is carried on at the Low Temperature Station, Cambridge, under the auspices of the Department of Industrial and Scientific Research. Other lines of research have been pursued, with a large measure of success, at the Campden Research Station and the Horticultural Experimental Station at Keston, Lincs. The task of testing scores of varieties of English fruit and vegetables to discover the kinds most suitable for canning has been carried through, and the advice of the Research Stations is available to any cannery. It may be mentioned in passing that by discovering a process for canning peas so that the fresh green colour is not lost, British research workers have placed British canned peas first in all markets.

The resumption of normal production after the war was temporarily checked by the high prices ruling for fruit, and the influx of vast war-time accumulations of Californian and other canned fruits from abroad. The present phase of rapid expansion dates from 1924, when a special commissioner, sent to study fruit canning in Canada and the United States, reported that the development of a large British industry seemed feasible, provided that modern machinery and methods were used. Active co-operation between the South Wales tin-plate manufacturers, the fruit growers, the Ministry of Agriculture and existing canners soon produced remarkable results. A voluntary central organization, called the National Food Canning Council, was formed to give representation to all the interests concerned in canning, and to facilitate the pooling and exchange of knowledge and experience of all branches of the industry. Established canners extended and modernized their plants, and several newcomers erected factories planned and equipped on the most up-to-date American lines.[1] British canners began to raise large amounts of new capital in the money market. A new company, British Canners Ltd., was formed to act as selling agent for several canneries at Hereford, Evesham, and Colchester; and in 1931 the National Canning Company was formed to acquire an existing, up-to-date cannery at Wisbech and to erect and equip other large factories at Spalding, Evesham, Paddock Wood, Ely, and Dundee, each one at the centre of a district which produces fruit and vegetables of outstanding quality. The number of factories canning fruit and vegetables (excluding very small establishments) has risen in eight years from six to eighty.[2]

The canning industry is not concentrated in one or two regions as are so many of our older industries. On the contrary, it is widely scattered. If fish, milk, fruit, and vegetables are to be canned successfully they must be delivered to the canners quickly—within a few hours if possible—after they have been caught or harvested. Costs of transport include not only transport charges, but wastage due to deterioration of the produce in transit. For both technical and financial reasons the distances over which fresh fish, milk, fruit and vegetables have to be transported must be kept down to a minimum. Each cannery is, therefore, built as near as possible to its supplies of produce. Thus we find fish-canneries in the principal herring-fishing ports—Lowestoft, Great Yarmouth, North Shields, Aberdeen, Fraserburgh—since herring is the fish chiefly used for canning in this country. The National Canning Co. Ltd., which cans fruits and vegetables, has recently formed a subsidiary company for the purpose of establishing a "chain" of fish-canneries round the coast of Great Britain. The first of these is at Dundee. The principal British meat

---

[1] In 1922 Mr. S. W. Smedley (now Chairman and Managing Director of the National Canning Co. Ltd.) spent six months in America studying canning factories, their machinery, organization and marketing methods, and in the following year he imported and set up a complete canning plant at Wisbech. Mr. Smedley came into the canning industry from the fruit-buying trade, especially fruit for jam-making.

[2] In 1934 there were 71 in England and Wales, and 9 in Scotland. The corresponding figures for 1930 were 50 and 3. (Imperial Economic Committee, *Canned and Dried Fruit Supplies in* 1934 (1935), 11–12.)

canneries are in or near the great meat-importing centres, like London and Liverpool; and the fruit and vegetable canneries are to be found in the midst of fruit and vegetable-growing areas, like the Vale of Evesham, Lincolnshire, Norfolk, Cambridgeshire, and Kent.

II

Five sections may be distinguished on the production side of the canning industry, viz. (*a*) canning, (*b*) fishing or agriculture (e.g. fruit and vegetable growing), (*c*) the manufacture of tinplate, (*d*) the manufacture of machinery, (*e*) the production of sugar. We will discuss each section in turn.

The canning of foodstuffs varies in detail with each commodity treated, but certain principles are common to all. The produce to be canned must be very fresh and clean; of high quality, undamaged, and of a given size and degree of fitness or ripeness; it must be "packed" in perfectly sealed containers and sterilized after packing at temperatures which have been found to give the best results for each kind of produce and for *each variety* of fish, fruit or vegetable; there must be no discoloration or other action of the contents upon the container, or *vice versa*. This means that every cannery must be controlled by managers possessing ample technical knowledge and experience, aided by the best of modern machinery and by a can-making department or industry of high efficiency. Good organization, also, is essential. By its very nature canning tends strongly to be a seasonal trade, and one of the major problems is how to keep a cannery in full production at optimum speed all the year round. The nearer the factory managers can approximate to this ideal, the lower the unit-costs will be.

One example of canning processes must suffice. At Middleton Junction, near Manchester, the Co-operative Wholesale Society have erected an up-to-date fruit cannery capable of turning out 7000 completed tins of fruit per hour. Continuous, high-speed methods are adopted, and most of the movements of the cans are effected by gravitation. The fruit arrives by road or rail, and is raised by lifts to the packing room on the first floor, where there are girl packers, tables, and two conveyors, moving respectively at about 5 ft. and 3 ft. above the floor level. The fruit is placed upon the tables in front of the packers, empty tins are fed from a balcony on to the upper conveyor, from which they are taken by the packers, filled with fruit, and placed upon the lower conveyor. This conveyor takes them to the syrup filling machines, where syrup, previously prepared from pure sugar, is fed by gravitation from large tanks to the machines. As the cans pass under the filling machines a self-acting device allows a measured quantity of syrup to flow into each. The cans then pass by gravitation over a series of rollers into and across a shallow "exhausting box," measuring about 12 ft. × 6 ft. and containing water kept at a constant high temperature. The hot cans are then carried rapidly by a short belt to the sealing machine, which bends the rim of the lid containing a rubber compound over the lip of the can and then doubles the fold back, so creating an airtight joint. It is absolutely essential to seal the cans while they are hot and to make the joints airtight, so that a partial vacuum will be created inside each can when it cools. The speed at which the cans can be sealed determines the maximum speed at which the whole plant can be run. The final processes are (a) cooking, by passing the sealed cans into a hot-water tank which varies in temperature according to the size and contents of the cans[1]; and (b) cooling, in another tank through which cold water circulates. From this tank the cans are taken by conveyors to the labelling and packing departments, and thence to the stores.

All forms of canning call for close co-operation between the primary producers and the canners. This is especially true of the canning of fruit and vegetables. Canning is a series of factory processes; agriculture is not. In the absence of special adaptation to the canners' requirements, the agriculturists would offer numerous small and dissimilar lots of fruit and vegetables; but, following the modern trend towards stan-

---

[1] 120° C. for 1½ hours is quite usual.

dardization in factory production, the canners are concentrating more and more on standardized grades of each commodity, and their demands are best met by large supplies of a few selected grades of fruit and vegetables. Therefore production for factory consumption should appeal most to large-scale growers. But, whatever may be the scale of their operations, growers of fruit and vegetables for canning must make a special study of the requirements of the canning factories as distinct from those of the fresh produce market. The differences are far from negligible, and the time will soon come when the factories will accept only those varieties which retain their firmness and colour after the heating and sterilizing processes.

In the early days of the canning industry vegetables were not canned so extensively as fruit, but now canned vegetables are becoming more popular. The pea was the first vegetable to be canned successfully on a large scale. Then came canned asparagus, millions of cans of which are now prepared annually. The range of vegetables canned at the present time includes carrots, celery, new potatoes, beetroot, turnips, and parsnips. Not only does canning extend the season during which certain kinds of vegetables are available, but it reduces the labour necessary for their preparation. Here again, only high quality produce is acceptable to the canners, while, at the same time, the costs of production must be kept low by the fullest possible use of machinery so as to provide the market with low-priced products in order that the new home industry may be built up. In America—

Vegetables for canning are grown as "field crops" on a mass production scale. In this way the American grower, using machinery to its maximum, is able to produce large quantities of vegetables for the factories at a small cost; such prices would be considered low by an English market-gardener. The Lincolnshire growers are producing peas for canning factories on mass production lines and there seems no reason why asparagus, beans and other vegetable crops should not be similarly produced in future years. It seems essential, however, that these crops should be grown on a contract basis.[1]

[1] *Fruit and Vegetable Production for Commercial Canning*, Ministry of Agriculture and Fisheries Bulletin No. 45, 1933 (2nd Edn.).

The growing of peas for the canning factories has, indeed, already become an important industry in the eastern counties, particularly in the Holland Division of Lincolnshire, in Huntingdonshire and in the neighbourhood of Wisbech. Peas are also grown for the factories in the Evesham district. Some growers purchase their seed independently, but many buy from the canning factories. Peas should be ready for harvesting within twelve or thirteen weeks from sowing. The pods may be picked by hand, usually by women and girls, as in Gloucestershire and Worcestershire; or the haulms may be mown, and put through a "viner." A small number of growers thresh and shell the peas on the farms with their own viners, but usually the factories own the viners. The shelled peas run into wooden trays and, after a cleaning process, they are weighed and the grower is credited accordingly. The yield ranges from 25 to 45 cwt. of shelled peas per acre; the average being 30 to 35 cwt.

The canned beans marketed in this country are of two quite different types; one is in pod form, the other is the seed. The first are called "stringless" beans (usually known in England as kidney or "French" beans), and the second "baked" beans, generally cooked with tomato sauce. The pods of the well-known runner bean are generally too fibrous for canning. The varieties required for canning are those in which the "string" is lacking or is quite tender, so that the green pod can be packed whole. These stringless "French" beans, or "snap beans," as they are called in America,[1] are as yet little known or cultivated in England and are not extensively canned here. There is undoubtedly an opening for larger supplies of stringless beans, provided that they can be grown near the factories, to enable canning to be done soon after picking.

Considerable interest is now being taken in the canning of new potatoes, not only for home consumption but for export. As new potatoes for canning should be lifted while they are small and immature, it is essential that the crop should be grown specially for the factory. The canners require potatoes

[1] See E. V. Hardenburgh, *Bean Culture* (1927).

of a variety that will retain its "new" flavour in the can, and the potato should be of a waxy consistency, with a smooth unblemished surface and a regular shape.

Milk-canners require that all milk supplied to them shall be clean and of a high fat-content, and they employ farm inspectors to see that the cows are fed and milked in a proper manner. All the milk must be delivered to the cannery quite fresh, and it is canned and sealed the same day. If dairymen and milk-canners were sufficiently enterprising there would seem to be no reason why it should be necessary to import any canned milk into Great Britain.

The British canning industry is so new that the development of methods of securing constant and regular supplies of fruit and vegetables over a period of years, at prices which fluctuate little from year to year, is still in its early stages. In order to ensure some degree of regularity of supplies the system of growing on contract, already evolved in the U.S.A., Canada and South Africa, is being introduced here. Although the British canners, facing the competition of imported canned goods produced by well-established firms, cannot pay high prices for their raw materials, they can offer the growers a less speculative outlet for their produce than the fresh produce market. Certain British growers have in the past supplied a great deal of fruit on contract to the jam factories, and pea crops for the canneries are now invariably grown on a contract basis.

"Sale by contract means the agreement to deliver goods of a certain grade and quality at a certain time in a certain quantity at a stipulated price." By adopting the contract system both grower and canner benefit, for the canner makes his supplies more certain in quantity and quality, while the grower knows in advance the prices his produce will fetch, provided it reaches the agreed grade or standard. For certain crops prices can be stated actually before planting takes place. Thus, if there happens to be an exceptionally heavy crop of peas, "the canning factory which is faced with a carry-over will announce at an early stage the minimum price for the next season's crop, and thus effective control of production by price is exercised in adequate time."[1] The National Food Canning Council and the National Farmers' Union have agreed upon model forms of contract for fruit and green peas, which they recommend growers and canners to adopt.[2] According to the *Bulletin* of the Ministry of Agriculture—

Pea contracts are made by the factories before the peas are sown. Some growers, as in Lincolnshire, arrange with the canning factory to grow a definite acreage of certain varieties. In some areas each canning factory appoints a "field man," often an experienced grower, who undertakes to secure supplies on contract for the factory. He arranges with several growers of peas in the district to plant in such a way that part of the crop is sown in the early and part in the late soils, and in this way he secures a successive maturing. The seed is supplied to the grower by the factory or through an agent who also gives any advice needed on growing the crop. The growers deliver their crop to the factory at harvest time, either the vines complete or the picked pods in bags. The produce is weighed after cleaning and the prices paid according to weight estimated in the factory. . . . Up to the present fruit has generally been bought by "forward buying" much in the same way as it is purchased forward by the jam makers. Sometimes the whole of a grower's crop is bought at a fixed price, or at the average market price for the season. Occasionally three-year contracts are made by which the canneries agree to buy the fruit over the period stated. . . . The quality of the produce must be of a definite standard; in some contracts it is stipulated that not more than 5 per cent waste should be present in the fruit as delivered at the factory, and that any excess over this figure will be paid for at "pulp" prices. . . . The greatest obstacle to be overcome relates to the fixing of prices. Caution, coupled with business acumen, compels the grower to require that the minimum price per ton (or per acre) agreed upon will at least enable him to recover the cost of production; and naturally the canner requires the insertion of a maximum price. The way in which the actual price—between the maximum and the minimum—is fixed must vary with the particular crop selected. For annual crops of vegetables there is no great difficulty at the beginning of the season in coming to an agreement as to the actual price to be paid for that particular year, but for the long-term

[1] Astor and Murray, *The Planning of Agriculture* (1933), 100.
[2] See *Fruit and Vegetable Production for Commercial Canning*, Ministry of Agriculture and Fisheries Bulletin No. 45, pp. 64–70.

contracts for fruit it is obviously difficult to agree on a price to be paid in three, four or five years' time. Realizing these difficulties, the two industries, canning and growing, have arranged in their Model Contract that the price shall be so much above or below the price quoted in the *Agricultural Market Report* of the Ministry of Agriculture and Fisheries for a similar grade and kind of fruit delivered at the same time and sold in a particular market.[1]

While there is much to be said in favour of encouraging growers to conform to the canners' requirements and to adopt the contract system, it is too much to expect growers to do this unless they can look forward to prices which, assuming good husbandry, will afford them a reasonable margin of profit over a term of years. Moreover, it must be remembered that, although special preparations for a vegetable crop may take only one year, preparations for other crops, such as strawberries, loganberries, gooseberries, plums, and damsons, usually take from three to seven years before any appreciable returns are received by growers. Clearly growers need fresh supplies of capital if they are to devote greater acreages to the production of crops for canning. "The canning industry, in effect, is inviting agriculture to add yet another to its many sections—a new section involving the sinking of much capital with, mostly, a long waiting time before any return can be expected." Are these new supplies of capital available to agriculturists at low rates of interest? If not, how can sufficient new capital be turned into this channel? It will indeed be regrettable if the development of the canneries, themselves possessed of ample capital, is held up by the absence of a corresponding development in agriculture. The probable output of the local growers is an important factor limiting the sizes of factories.

One of the greatest needs of the British canning industry in its earlier stages was an adequate supply of well-made cans at low prices. No shortage of first-class raw material was likely, for an industry which had led the world in the manufacture of

[1] *Ibid*, 57–8.

tinplate was already firmly established, chiefly in South Wales. But between 70 and 80 per cent of British tinplate was made for export, and the bulk of the remainder was used at home in the manufacture of tin boxes. Only a very small proportion was manufactured into tin containers for canning,[1] and this on a very small scale. The pioneer firms of canners usually manufactured their own cans or imported them; but in more recent years it has become obvious that large-scale production of cans in this country by up-to-date automatic machinery is the cheapest method, and must accompany any considerable increase in the numbers and sizes of British canneries. Thanks largely to the enterprise of the Metal Box Co. Ltd. the need was speedily met, and no shortage of cheap cans of good quality threatens the canners to-day.[2]

The Metal Box Co. Ltd. was registered in 1921, and during the following decade it secured control of twelve companies manufacturing various kinds of metal containers. To-day the Company has an issued capital of £1,962,000 in ordinary and preference shares, and an outstanding debenture issue of £778,000.[3] It owns practically all the shares in sixteen companies operating eighteen factories in England, and it has also made agreements with two important American can-making companies by which it secures immunity from their competition within the United Kingdom and the benefits of certain American patents and processes. Nearly 90 per cent of the cans used by British canneries are manufactured by the Metal Box Co., which also designs and prints labels, showcards, and other advertising matter. One of the newest can factories, at Worcester, is capable of an output of 1200 cans per minute, or 3,000,000 cans per week. It has an actual average output of

[1] The tinplate used for canning consists of a thin steel sheet covered with a thin layer of tin and, on top of this, a coating of lacquer made chiefly of fossil gums and drying oils.

[2] A tendency for tin-consuming countries to install their own tinplate works has long been evident not only in Europe and America but, more recently, in South Africa and Australia. If the present wave of economic nationalism continues, the British tinplate industry may have to look more and more to the expansion of British canning in order to maintain its total sales.

[3] *Stock Exchange Year Book*, 1936.

over 100 million cans per annum. Another factory at Acton is similarly equipped. Approximately one-third of the British output of tinplate (i.e. 270,000–300,000 tons per annum) is now consumed here.

The recent growth of canning in this country has given to certain engineering firms an opportunity which they have been quick to seize. Complicated automatic machines for can-making and the various processes of canning which only a few years ago had to be imported from America, are now skilfully made in Great Britain. As soon as it became evident that the demand of the British canning industry for machinery of various kinds was likely to be large enough to justify the erection of the appropriate machine-making plants, British engineers studied the American machinery, copied all that was best in it, and, where possible, introduced improvements. British engineering firms can now supply washing and grading machines, band conveyors, exhausters, syrupers, seamers, cookers, coolers, viners, pea-shellers, peelers and corers, to say nothing of machinery for the manufacture of cans and the fibre-board packing cases in which canned goods are usually transported.

An expansion of fruit-canning in Britain will mean an increased demand for sugar, for as much as 20 or 25 per cent of the weight of a can of fruit may consist of sugar. Since research has proved that beet sugar is quite as suitable as cane sugar for canning, it appears, at first glance, not impossible that substantial economies might be effected by integrating the beet-sugar factories with the canneries. The beet-sugar factories operate mainly in the winter, beginning their busy season as the busy season of the jam-makers and canners draws to a close, and *a priori* integration seems to offer a prospect of (*a*) eliminating intermediate profits on sugar used by the canneries, and (*b*) effecting seasonal transfers of labour between canneries and sugar factories. But there are three major obstacles, viz. (*a*) about 90 per cent of a cannery's employees are women, whereas a beet sugar factory employs men only, (*b*) many of the beet-growing areas are not suitable for fruit, (c) the power units of a beet-sugar factory would not be suitable for a canning factory. However, a combination of canners might with advantage arrange to acquire the bulk of the output of a beet-sugar factory, especially if the latter was well-situated in relation to the whole group of canneries.

Official returns of the output of the British canning industry are available in the *Reports* on the Censuses of Production for 1924 and 1930. Some of the latest figures obtainable relate to the output of canned and bottled fruits and vegetables in the year 1932 and are based upon replies to a questionnaire addressed to canning firms by the Ministry of Agriculture and Fisheries. This estimate, which "is necessarily approximate and must be accepted with reserve," is shown below, together with the Census of Production figures for 1924 and 1930. Certain statistics for subsequent years, chiefly 1933, are to be found in the *Report on the Import Duties Act Inquiry, Part I,* 1935.

OUTPUT OF CANNED AND BOTTLED FRUITS AND VEGETABLES
IN GREAT BRITAIN, 1924, 1930 AND 1932

Description	Production				
	1924[1]		1930[1]		1932[2]
	Quantities 'ooo cwt.	Value £'ooo	Quantities 'ooo cwt.	Value £'ooo	Quantities 'ooo cwt.
Fruits—					
(a) In syrup .	58	253	190	557	484
(b) Preserved without sugar .	59	219	125	302	205
Vegetables, dried, canned, and bottled .	40	164	314	768	945[3]
	157	£636	629	£1,627	1,634

Allowing for a possible error of 4 or 5 per cent in the 1932 estimate, it is probably safe to say that the total quantity of

---

[1] Figures for Preserved Foods Trade only. See *Final Report of 4th Census of Production* (1930) *Part III : Food, Drink, Tobacco Trades, etc.* (1934), p. 82.
[2] Estimate.
[3] Does not include dried vegetables.

home-grown fruit and vegetables canned and bottled increased
tenfold between 1924 and 1932. The increase in the fruits
section was less than this, viz. 600 per cent but in the vegetable
section it was much more, viz. 2700 per cent, even if we ignore
the exclusion of dried vegetables from the 1932 estimate. The
increase in total value has, of course, not been so large, because the expansion of output and sales has been achieved
by reducing prices as well as by improving the quality;
but even so the magnitude of the expansion has been of a
high order.[1]

A different picture is presented by the fish and meat
sections of the industry. For the output of preserved fish and
meat products the official figures are—

	1924		1930		1933	
	Quantities '000 cwts.	Value £'000	Quantities '000 cwts.	Value £'000	Quantities '000 cwts.	Value £'000
Canned Herrings	132	321	115	249	104	220
Other fish	19	60	21	78	20	55
Preserved meat in tins, glasses, etc.	172	3,726	116	843	138	988
Meat and fish paste in tins or glasses	—	769	95	1,253	110	1,128
Totals	323	4,876	347	2,423	372	2,391

If we put the missing figure in the first column at, let us say,
45,000 cwt., the general result is a slight decline in the total
quantities in 1930 and a recovery in 1933; but a severe fall in
the total values between 1924 and 1930–3.

The demand for canned and bottled soups is making rapid
headway. The value of canned and bottled soups, soup squares
and powders produced in Great Britain in 1933 is estimated
at £717,000, against £412,000 only three years earlier, and a
further substantial increase is expected.

[1] Official figures which have recently become available show that the
British output of canned and bottled fruit in the year 1933 was
550,000 cwt., valued at £1,354,000, while the output of canned
vegetables was 933,000 cwt., valued at £1,670,000. (*Report on the
Import Duties Act Inquiry, Part I*, 1935.)

III

It is very difficult to arrive at an estimate of the numbers
of workpeople engaged in the canning industry, because canning is not separately distinguished in the official statistics.
Moreover, it is a highly seasonal industry, it is still expanding
rapidly in some sections, and there is a certain amount of
seasonal transfer between canning and other sections of the
food preserving trade. According to the Censuses of Production, the total numbers of persons of all grades employed
in the British preserved food industry as a whole, were 37,036
in 1924 and 42,524 in 1930. The proportion of females to
males was 5 : 3. The workpeople directly employed in canning
in the busy season between June and September total, perhaps, some 15,000, most of whom are women and girls doing
semi-skilled work. This is a very tentative estimate, and it
does not include those indirectly employed in making cans,
cases, labels, machines, etc.

The canning of fruit and vegetables begins early in May and
continues until September. The numbers of workers in the
largest factories during this period vary from 300 to 1000
according to the size of the factory and the point reached in
the season. At the peak of the season, the factories usually
work overtime, and it is claimed that some of the largest
contrive to can from 30 to 50 tons of fruit a day. During the
winter (e.g. from December or January to April) many factories cease their manufacturing operations, keeping only a
skeleton staff to overhaul machinery, and to label, pack, and
dispatch goods as orders come in. Some of the factories provide
a certain amount of winter employment by canning pork and
beans, and winter vegetables. Generally speaking, the more
diversified the output of the factory, the greater the degree of
regularity of employment in it. For example, the Co-operative
Wholesale Society's preserving factories at Middleton Junction, Reading and Acton engage in the manufacture of very
large quantities of jam, pickles, sauces, bottled fruits, mince-
meat, jellies, candied peel, etc., in addition to the canning of

fruit, which is done in a separate department. In the winter season the majority of the fruit canning staff are absorbed into the other departments. At the Society's Lowestoft factory, vegetables, fish and meat products are canned, as well as processed cheese and "table delicacies" in glass containers. Herrings are canned from October to Christmas and peas during June and July, and during these periods it is necessary to engage some 40 or 50 extra workpeople. So far the progress of the plant has been so satisfactory in all sections that it has been possible to transfer the fish and fruit canning staffs, including most of the extra workers, to other departments from January to June and in August and September.

Separate records of wages in the canning industry are not available. For the purposes of the Trade Boards Acts, 1909 and 1918, canning is grouped with sugar confectionery and other forms of food preserving. This means that the legal minimum rates of wages for the lowest grades of experienced adult workers in the canning factories are 1s. an hour for men (over 23 years of age) and 6¾d. for women. The normal working week is 48 hours.[1] Workers of higher grade and greater skill receive somewhat higher wages. The average wage in the preserved food industry as a whole (including canning) in 1930 works out at slightly less than £99 per annum.[2]

IV

Nearly two-thirds of Britain's food supplies are drawn from abroad, and while, doubtless, we shall always be largely dependent in this country upon imported food, few will deny that better use might be made of existing resources and output. The development of the British canning industry will help to make this possible, by preventing wastage of certain perishable foodstuffs. Moreover, with the aid of canning, the population will derive greater utility from a given output because there will be a larger variety of foodstuffs available not at certain seasons only, but throughout the whole year. And

[1] In the C.W.S. factories all employees work a 44-hr. week.
[2] *Final Report of 4th Census of Production, 1930; Part III.*

inquiry shows that such results are not obtained at the expense of the sellers of fresh fish, fruit, and vegetables.

Canned fruit is now an important part of Britain's food supply. British imports of canned fruits preserved in sugar exceed those of any other country, and have risen from a pre-war annual average of 850,000 cwt. to 2,235,678 cwt. in 1926, and 3,229,000 cwt. in 1932; the latter figure representing 89 per cent of all imports of canned fruit. In 1934 a record level of 3,460,000 cwt. was reached.[1] Three-quarters of this imported fruit is tropical or semi-tropical produce and could not be grown in Great Britain. Therefore, the British import duties on canned fruits and vegetables are protective only in respect of the minority of products which compete with similar products canned in this country. Foreign canned fruits preserved in syrup are subject to an import duty of 15 per cent *ad valorem*, with the exception of stoned cherries, which are taxed at 25 per cent *ad valorem*, and apples, on which the duty is 3s. 6d. per cwt. On all these goods there is an additional duty on the sugar content. The duty on foreign canned tomatoes is 10 per cent *ad valorem*, and on all other canned vegetables 20 per cent *ad valorem*. Canned fruit and vegetables consigned from and grown, produced or manufactured in the British Empire (except the Irish Free State) are exempt from British import duties, except a duty, at the preferential rate, on sugar content.

The Empire Marketing Board's inquiry showed that "all of the 100 shops visited stocked peaches and pears, most also stocked pineapples, apricots and fruit salads. Only 34 stocked loganberries, 29 strawberries and plums, and only 5 blackberries."[2] The British fruit canners' task is to expand the home demand for British products either in addition to, or in place of, the present established demand for imported canned

---

[1] Imperial Economic Committee, *Canned and Dried Fruit Supplies in 1934* (1935), 7. The total supply of imported and home-produced canned fruits was estimated by the Committee to be about 4 million cwt. in 1934.

[2] See *The Demand for Canned Fruits*, E.M.B. 37 (1931). Cf. *Fruit and Vegetable Production for Commercial Canning*, Ministry of Agriculture and Fisheries Bulletin No. 45, 2nd Edn. (1933).

fruits. Already some headway has been made, for according to the Census of Production, 1930, the share of the home market held by British canned or bottled fruits (without sugar) was 32 per cent against 12·8 in 1924; and for those in syrup, 8 per cent against 2·7. The British consumer's demand for canned vegetables is mainly a demand for canned tomatoes, "baked" beans, and peas. Until recently the bulk of these goods have been imported, chiefly from Italy, Spain, North America, Belgium and France; but the British output of peas, both "fresh-canned" and "processed," is expanding rapidly, and exports of British canned or bottled vegetables quadrupled in quantity between 1927 and 1932. The share of the home market held by British canned, dried or bottled vegetables was nearly 30 per cent in 1930, against 5 per cent in 1924. The canning of tomatoes and (white haricot) beans in this country awaits the discovery and growth on a large scale of varieties suitable for canning.

Although the home consumption of British canned soups, meats (including tongues, kidneys and entrées), sausages, fish and roast fowls is increasing, the bulk of these goods are exported, especially to tropical countries. A large and growing demand comes from all parts of the British Empire, not only from people of European stock, but from the native populations as well. British canned fruits are also making some headway in overseas markets, where formerly the trade was almost entirely in the hands of American, Canadian, and Australian canners, but this trade is still in its infancy and

EXPORTS OF CANNED AND BOTTLED FRUITS AND VEGETABLES
FROM THE UNITED KINGDOM

Description	1927	1928	1929	1930	1931	1932	1933
	cwt.	cwt.	cwt.	cwt.	cwt,	cwt.	cwt.
Canned or bottled fruit—							
Preserved in sugar	11,917	2,844	2,869	2,672	3,418	4,123	5,110
Preserved without sugar	4,363	5,002	5,037	4,543	4,002	5,669	4,463
Total . . .	16,280	7,846	7,906	7,215	7,420	9,792	9,573
Canned or bottled vegetables: Preserved with no sweetening matter .	3,843	5,033	5,908	7,104	8,175	16,442	20,455

British exports of canned and bottled fruits and vegetables are no more than 3 or 4 per cent of total output.

Exports of canned and bottled vegetables, preserved without sweetening matter, in 1933 were nearly three times the total exported in 1930. The chief increase occurred in 1932, when the total was more than double the quantity exported in the previous year; larger consignments of canned peas accounted for two-thirds of the rise in the total exports. In the following year the increase was less marked, but the aggregate reached the record figure of 20,455 cwt.[1]

The British production of canned herrings in 1930 was 115,000 cwt., of which 86,000 cwt. (or about 75 per cent) were exported.

The fact that most canning factories must get as near as possible to their sources of supplies of fresh produce does not necessarily place all of them at a disadvantage when they come to market their goods. Those who are in or near London have a great home market outside their gates, and are also well situated if they wish to export. Those who are in some other great port, such as Liverpool, Manchester or Hull, are equally well situated. On the whole, it is only the fruit and vegetable canners who are at some disadvantage in the distribution of their goods.

In this country there are two main methods of distributing canned goods. By the older method the canner disposes of his output in large consignments to merchants, who then affix their own labels and supply retailers and exporters from their stocks. While this method is less troublesome to the canners and gives them a quick cash return upon their output, it fails to establish any direct relations between canners and retailers. By the newer method of distribution the canner builds up his own selling organizations through which he establishes direct contacts with grocers and other retailers of canned goods. This method is more troublesome to the canner and requires a much larger capital outlay, and more elastic credit facilities from the banks who "finance the pack"[2] but, on the other

---

[1] Imperial Economic Committee, *Canned and Dried Fruit Supplies in 1934* (1935), 13.

[2] On this point see *Financial News*, 6th July, 1935, p. 6.

hand, it enables the canner to make a much closer first-hand study of the consumers' tastes and preferences, to bring his particular "brands" to their notice, and to establish friendly relations with a large circle of retailers. It is an advantage for canners to have two or more regional headquarters or depots, in which stocks of goods from the canneries can be held in such quantities and varieties as accumulating experience dictates, and from which customers can be promptly supplied.

Fortunately, it has been possible to apply to fruit and vegetable canning the provisions of the Agricultural Produce (Grading and Marking) Act, 1928, which enables the Minister of Agriculture and Fisheries to prescribe, by regulations, grades and grade definitions for canned fruit and vegetables produced in this country.

The use of the standard grades is voluntary on the part of a canner, but if he elects to use them in association with the official grade designation mark, the National Mark, he voluntarily brings himself under a system of supervision and control, designed to ensure the observance of the very high standards of quality laid down in the Minister's regulations for National Mark canned fruit and vegetables. The great majority of the canners have enrolled in the National Mark scheme, and they have been supported by publicity for their products maintained by the Ministry of Agriculture. The results have been very encouraging, for the public soon showed their appreciation of the National Mark graded produce; and the grocers found it easier to handle these standardized products and to sell vast quantities of repeat orders. In its first year of introduction it is reported that 11,000,000 cans of fruit and 6,000,000 cans of peas and beans bearing the National Mark were sold during the season.[1]

By far the most important of the canned vegetables produced in English factories are peas and baked beans. The former include a considerable proportion of fresh-picked peas canned under the National Mark, as well as peas, both fresh-picked and dried, not canned under the Mark. The movement to secure the improvement of the quality of home-grown canned fruits and vegetables by packing to statutory standards under the National Mark continues to progress and, following agreement with the industry, the definitions of quality of National Mark "Select" canned fruits

[1] *The Times, British Canning Industry Supplement,* 7th November, 1931.

have recently been given further precision by the prescription of statutory minimum sizes for strawberries, gooseberries, cherries, plums, damsons, and apples.

Further samples of imported canned fruits examined at the Campden Research Station have confirmed the impression, gained after similar examinations in previous years, that home-grown canned fruits packed to National Mark standards are fully equal, and in some cases superior, to imported kinds. A certain proportion of the pack of canned fruit and vegetables is, however, still packed to standards below the requirements of the National Mark, and there are signs of a movement to secure the compulsory labelling as "Seconds" or "Sub-Standard" of all canned fruit and vegetables falling below a certain minimum, as in the case of the United States, Canada and Australia.[1]

The chances of developing a really large export trade in British canned goods depend upon four main factors, viz. (a) the prices quoted to the overseas consumers, (b) the solution, by research, of problems connected with the transport and storage of canned foods in tropical climates, (c) the production of standardized, "branded" goods of high and stable quality,[2] (d) the creation of an efficient export marketing organization, such as an export cartel comprising all British canners.

In 1933–4 investment and expansion in the British canning industry outstripped the growth of markets. The extraordinary increase in output, coupled with intensified American competition due to the depreciation of the dollar, resulted in a sharp fall of prices, followed by talk of a price and production agreement between British canners. But owing to the unsympathetic attitude of two leading companies, the project came to nothing.

The difficulties mentioned above are probably temporary. In these days it is not unusual for the rate of expansion of a new industry to exceed, for a limited time, the rate of absorption of its products by markets at home and abroad. But such a lack of balance is unlikely to continue for long. The

[1] Imperial Economic Committee, *Canned and Dried Fruit Supplies in 1934* (1935), 12.

[2] The industry is working out standards of weight, size and syrup strength. See *The Times, Trade and Engineering Review*, December, 1934, 41.

demand for canned foods is highly responsive to reductions of prices, and this elasticity, together with a probable weakening of the tendency towards "overcrowding" in the industry and, perhaps, some consolidation of interests, should do much to induce greater stability in the near future. Organization among the canners has recently been improved by the formation of an association, representing the whole of the fruit and vegetable canneries in the country, to work in conjunction with the Food Manufacturers' Association.[1]

[1] *The Times, Trade and Engineering Review*, December, 1934, 41.

CHAPTER VI

STATE ASSISTANCE AND NEW INDUSTRIAL DEVELOPMENT

In Chapter I it was suggested that the principal forces under-lying the development of new industries in recent times are either (1) changes in consumers' demand and in industrial technique, or (2) State action consciously aiming to create or build up certain industries. So far we have been studying the rise and development of new industries illustrating the opera-tion of the first group of causes. Now we must turn to those which illustrate the second group, namely, the manufacture of synthetic dyestuffs, beet sugar and coal-oil, and the production and exhibition of cinematograph films.

The virtual re-creation of the synthetic dyestuffs industry on the initiative of the State and with its financial and legis-lative assistance is the direct result of a determination, springing from war-time experience, to make Great Britain independent of foreign supplies of synthetic dyestuffs. Simi-larly, State assistance to the beet sugar and coal-oil industries is *primarily* the outcome of shortages actually experienced during the Great War, and the fear of future war-time shortages. But there are also secondary considerations which have strengthened the case for State action. Thus, the creation of the beet sugar industry was viewed not solely as a defence measure, but as part of a programme of assistance for British agriculturists; while in favour of the British Hydro-carbon Oils Production Bill it was argued that not only should the nation be made as independent as possible of imported supplies of oil in time of war, but that the development of a domestic coal-oil industry would be a most promising national investment because it would reduce unemployment and help to conserve our natural resources by using coal in a more scientific and economical manner.

In the case of the cinematograph film industry, however, the reasons for State action have been different. Here the problem of national defence does not arise, and the effects of the exhibition of cinematograph films upon the invisible and intangible bonds of empire are extremely obscure. The decision to give State aid to the expiring remnants of the British film industry appears to have sprung mainly from the desire to see British talent making a distinctive contribution to a new and most popular form of dramatic art. It was realized that the history and literature of the British Empire is a rich mine of material for new film "stories," and that there was abundant ability and skill among contemporary British producers, actors, and technicians. The sole obstacle was the powerful and destructive stranglehold obtained by the Americans under entirely abnormal circumstances, and ruthlessly exploited by them to force their, largely inferior, products upon the rest of the world. This situation was exceedingly unhealthy and likely to be fatal to the future of the film as a form of popular entertainment. Artistically (but not, of course, *financially*) it was as deadly to the American film industry as to the British, and the British Government did well to pass the Cinematograph Films Act in 1927.

(i) SYNTHETIC DYESTUFFS

I

The successful scientific researches upon which the modern synthetic dyestuffs industry is founded were carried out chiefly in England in the eighteen-fifties, and for a time it seemed likely that a large and flourishing new industry would be added to the list of important manufactures in which Great Britain led the world. But neither the State nor the industrialists in the chemical trades showed sufficient foresight, energy, and enterprise to make this a *fait accompli*. The alert Germans, on the other hand, were quick to seize the chance of placing the manufacture of synthetic dyestuffs among their young and expanding industries. The result was that the industry passed from British into German hands so completely that—

> . . . in 1913, of the annual consumption of 20,000 tons of synthetic dyes and dyestuffs in the United Kingdom, 18,000 tons valued at £1,890,000 were imported. Of this total over 90 per cent came from Germany and the remainder from Switzerland. The contribution made by British dye-making firms towards supplying the national requirements was therefore trifling, and it has been held that even these flourished only because their existence was tolerated by the great German companies. As regards aniline oil and sulphur black—two comparatively simple but greatly used commodities—British manufacturers had entered into national conventions in which the dominant influence was that of the German companies. The only British makers of alizarine were also members of an international alizarine convention, but here the case is somewhat exceptional in that they were strong enough to force their way into the convention on their own merits. As regards the remainder of the dyes manufactured in the United Kingdom, it would be broadly true to say that the German manufacturers could have driven the British makers out of the market at any time had they chosen to do so.[1]

There were two works in Great Britain owned by German companies, in one of which only the final process was carried out on materials brought from Germany.

At the outbreak of war in 1914 the situation with regard to the production of chemicals in Great Britain was found to be exceedingly unbalanced. The manufacture of heavy chemicals for industrial purposes was efficient and well-established; indeed, "in this branch of manufacture the United Kingdom was probably, on the whole, ahead of any other nation."[2] But the production of "light chemicals," which was not well-developed and lagged behind certain other nations (e.g. the Germans) both in efficiency and in quantity of output, stood in marked contrast to the heavy chemicals; while, as we have seen, the manufacture of synthetic dyestuffs scarcely existed at all.

---

[1] Report on Dyes and Dyestuffs (Cmd. 1370, 1921), 4.
[2] Committee on Industry and Trade, Factors in Industrial and Commercial Efficiency (1927), 445.

The acuteness of the dye shortage which arose in our textile industries when Great Britain went to war with Germany in 1914 can hardly be exaggerated. After prolonged discussions between representatives of the Government and the industrialists concerned, it was decided to form a company, called British Dyes Ltd., for the manufacture of dyes in large quantities. The share capital was subscribed by colour-users, and the Government undertook to lend to the company a sum not exceeding £1,700,000 at a low rate of interest, and to make a special grant to finance research into the production of synthetic dyestuffs. British Dyes Ltd. did not, at first, entirely fulfil the expectations of its promoters, largely because its chief energies had to be diverted almost immediately to the manufacture of explosives. It was able to do little more than produce fairly large quantities of the commoner dyestuffs and limited quantities of a few special ones. Later, however, the company gradually increased its output of dyestuffs and laid the foundation of a large producing plant which would be available when the demand for explosives became less insistent.[1]

In October, 1915, a meeting of dye-users set up a committee "to watch the position of colour supplies for the textile and other industries," and to represent the interests of colour consumers before the Board of Trade or other Government departments, or in negotiations with suppliers. This Colour Users' Committee, which afterwards became the Colour Users' Association, conducted the negotiations prior to the passing of the Dyestuffs (Import Regulation) Act, 1920, and has been the official body representing colour users in all matters arising since.

British Dyes Ltd. (who had acquired the Huddersfield works of Read Holliday & Sons Ltd.) and Levinstein Ltd. were the chief manufacturers of dyestuffs in Great Britain during the war, but several other companies, stimulated by the marked excess of demand over supply and the assured

Committee on Industry and Trade, *Factors in Industrial and Commercial Efficiency* (1927), 417; cf. *Report of the Dyestuffs Industry Development Committee* (*Cmd.* 3658, 1930), p. 2.

market for all their products, were forging ahead. Nevertheless, users continued to complain of both the quality and
quantity of the British output, and in 1918

it was suggested both by the Government and by the principal
colour users that the rate of progress which was being made to
render this country independent of foreign sources of supply of
synthetic dyestuffs was not satisfactory and it was determined that
this object could better be secured by effecting a fusion of interests
of British Dyes Ltd. and Levinstein Ltd. British Dyestuffs Corporation Ltd. was accordingly formed for that purpose and the
majority of the shareholders of the two companies exchanged their
holdings for shares in this Corporation.[1]

For the discharge of obligations taken over from the two
companies and to provide money for future developments, an
issue of £5,000,000 of new capital was made by the Corporation. Since most of this was subscribed by persons not interested in business as colour-users, the composition of the whole
body of shareholders was materially changed. In addition,
the Government subscribed £1,700,000 (£850,000 in Preference
shares and £850,000 in Preferred Ordinary shares) in substitution for the loans previously made or promised to British
Dyes Ltd., and in return the Government received the right
to nominate two directors and to exercise special voting rights
and powers of veto and control over the new Corporation.
Thus an industrial combine was formed which brought under
a single financial control approximately 75 per cent of the
synthetic dyestuffs manufacture of this country. The bulk of
the remainder of the trade was in the hands of five joint-stock
companies. While the British Dyestuffs Corporation had not
a general monopoly, it dominated the industry and had a
monopolistic position with regard to certain products. The
danger to the interests of colour-users was fully realized by
the Sub-Committee on Dyes and Dyestuffs set up by the
Standing Committee on Trusts in 1919, but they hoped that
the presence of the two Government directors would check

---

[1] *Papers relative to . . . British Dyestuffs Corporation Ltd. (Cmd.* 2545,
1925).

any inclination on the part of the British Dyestuffs Corporation to abuse its position.[1] In effect this meant that the Government directors, who controlled a solid block of 1,700,000 votes, were expected to serve three masters—the Dyestuffs Corporation, the colour-users and the general public: and one can well imagine that the more jealously they tried to guard the last two interests, the more unpopular they would become with their fellow directors.

Before the end of 1918, Parliament voted a further £2,000,000 for the development of the industry, but only about £435,500 was actually spent before the scheme ended in 1922. Of this sum, £214,500 was granted in aid of the cost of plant and buildings; £115,260 in aid of the cost of research laboratory buildings and equipment; £14,500 towards annual maintenance costs of such laboratories, and £91,250 by way of loans.

II

At the beginning of the post-war period, then, the British synthetic dye-making industry was still an "infant," and it was feared that, with the return of peace, unless it was carefully protected it would come to a premature end under the weight of German competition.[2] Great Britain had lagged far behind Germany and, indeed, other countries in the industrial application of organic chemistry, particularly in the manufacture of synthetic dyestuffs, synthetic drugs, analytical reagents, developers, tannins, etc.; and the war had revealed in a flash an acute shortage not only of chemical products, but of trained industrial chemists.

To the general argument that the establishment of a larger dye-making industry here was desirable in order to safeguard the textile industries against the ill consequences of dependence on foreign sources for materials which it was not inherently possible to produce here, was added a further argument based on war-time experience . . . dye-making plant is readily adaptable—in some

---

[1] *Cmd.* 1370 (1921), pp. 7–9.
[2] Cf. *Cmd.* 3658 (1930), p. 3.

cases it does not even need adaptation—to the requirements of chemical warfare.[1]

Immediately after the cessation of hostilities the Board of Trade outlined a scheme for the further protection and development of the British dye-making industry.[2] It was clear that for at least several years the home output would be unable to meet even the bulk of the home demand. Imports would have to continue. Therefore it was decided not to impose a general list of protective import duties, but to introduce a system of import licences, issuable by an independent body—called a Trades and Licensing Committee—having a "neutral" chairman and members representing the dye manufacturers and users, "whose duty it would be, while fostering the growth and maintenance of the colour-producing industry, to safeguard the interests of colour users by allowing the importation of foreign dyestuffs where they were of kinds not made in this country but really needed by the using industries, or where the prices of British-produced dyes were unduly high." Towards the end of 1919, however, a judicial decision rendered illegal nearly the whole of the existing import prohibitions, and made it necessary for the Government to introduce legislation, lest the full blast of foreign competition should strike the new industry after all.[3] The Dyestuffs (Import Regulation) Act, 1920, which came into force on 15th January, 1921, prohibited for a period of ten years the importation into the United Kingdom of all synthetic organic dyestuffs, colours, and colouring matters, and all organic intermediate products used in their manufacture, unless authorized by a Board of Trade licence.[4] An advisory committee consisting of five persons concerned in dye-using trades, three persons concerned in dye-making, and three

[1] *Factors in Industrial and Commercial Efficiency* (1927), 418.

[2] *Report of Departmental Committee on the Textile Trades (Cmd. 9070, 1918).*

[3] Committee on Industry and Trade, *Factors in Industrial and Commercial Efficiency* (1927), 418–9.

[4] Imports of synthetic organic chemicals other than dyestuffs, fine chemicals and chemicals manufactured by fermentation processes were not prohibited, but were subjected to a duty of 33⅓ per cent *ad. val.* under the Safeguarding of Industries Act, 1921.

others not directly concerned in either, was set up to assist the Board of Trade in the granting of licences. In general, import licences are issued when the dye required is not made in the United Kingdom, or cannot be obtained from British makers at prices at least as low as those quoted by foreign competitors, "dumping prices" always excepted. The provisions of the Act of 1920 were to remain in force for ten years only, but this period was subsequently extended from year to year.

In addition to the advisory committee on the issue of licences, the Act (Section 2, (6)) set up a Dyestuffs Industry Development Committee consisting of "persons concerned in the trades of dye-maker or dye-user, and of such other persons not directly concerned in such trades as the Board may determine," to advise the Board of Trade "with respect to the efficient and economical development of the dye-making industry."

After the post-war slump the British Dyestuffs Corporation was seen to be in rather low water, a position caused partly by the expenses of pioneering, partly by losses due to the suddenness and severity of the slump, and partly by the Government restrictions upon the Corporation's freedom of action. The upshot was a reconstruction of the Corporation in 1925, which included the writing down of assets and reduction of capital, the purchase of all the Government's shares for £600,000, the disappearance of the two Government directors, and the removal of the Government's special rights of veto and control.[1]

At the end of the decade 1920–30, the Dyestuffs Industry Development Committee issued a report in which they maintained that the main objects of the Dyestuffs Act, 1920, had been achieved. A substantial British dye-making industry had been built up. By the joint labours of chemists and chemical engineers, by expensive but vitally important trials on a semi-works scale and then on a factory scale, and by devising special plant, the complicated problems of the infant industry had

[1] *Cmd.* 2545, 1925.

been very largely solved. Old factories had been extended, new ones had been established, and the total productive capacity had been greatly increased. Whereas before the war "practically no intermediates were made in this country, and the range of colours produced was a meagre one . . . the increase in the output is extraordinary."[1] Vat colours, for example, were not made in Great Britain in 1913; yet by 1928 the British dyestuffs industry was supplying 64 per cent of this country's requirements. And in the manufacture of colours for the dyeing of various types of artificial silk the British dye-makers have led the world. Since the production of such fabrics is still in an early stage, there seems to be good scope for further expansion of this section of the British dyestuffs industry.

UNITED KINGDOM

COMPARISON BETWEEN DOMESTIC PRODUCTION AND
IMPORTS OF DYESTUFFS IN THE YEARS 1913, 1922–33

Year	Brit. Prodn.	Foreign Importn.	Total	British
	lb. millions	lb. millions	lb. millions	per cent. of total
1913 . .	9·1	32·6	41·7	22
1922 . .	23·8	5·5	29·3	81
1928 . .	50·9	3·9	54·8	93
1929 . .	55·8	4·2	60·0	93
1930 . .	42·6	4·2	46·8	91
1931 . .	48·0	5·0	53·0	90
1932 . .	49·3	4·6	53·9	91
1933 . .	52·9	4·8	57·7	91

Over the period 1921–31 the ratio of licences granted to licences refused was approximately 7 : 1, or approximately 5 : 1 if we take the total quantities of dyestuffs involved. According to the Dyestuffs Industry Development Committee the general opinion throughout the colour-using industries is that British dyestuffs now compare favourably with the foreign materials and that there remains little ground for

[1] *Report of the Dyestuffs Industry Development Committee (Cmd.* 3658, 1930), 4–5.

complaint as regards quality. But, so far, although a wide range of dyes not previously made here has now been placed on the market, on the whole, less headway has been made in variety than in quality. The Committee especially drew attention to the "not altogether reassuring" tendency to concentrate on dyestuffs for which the demand is relatively large, "whilst in those cases where consumption is relatively small, the policy appears to have been to leave these to the foreign maker." The inclusion of British dyemakers in an international cartel has strengthened this tendency. It is admitted, moreover, that the progress so far achieved has "laid a serious burden upon the colour-using industries, in the high prices which have been charged to them for dyewares during the early years of the operation of the Act, and by some interference with their access to the world's markets for their wares," and that in the early years of the Act's operation, colour-users were often called upon to use dyes of British manufacture which were not entirely satisfactory in quality in order to give the British dye-makers the necessary experience in production.[1] Our sympathies must surely be with the colour-users who, after tolerating such handicaps and restrictions for ten years, were not only faced, at the end of that time, by an international cartel covering the dye-makers, but forced to accept an extension of the period of protection and licensing as well.

III

A marked tendency towards consolidation has been a feature of the post-war development of the British dyestuffs industry. The great concern, Imperial Chemical Industries Ltd., has taken the lead by acquiring such undertakings as Scottish Dyes Ltd., British Dyestuffs Corporation Ltd., Emco Dyestuffs Ltd., and British Alizarine Co. Ltd.; and although a "fringe" of non-combine dye-makers still exists, "the greater part of the dye-making industry in this country is now under

[1] *Report of the Dyestuffs Industry Development Committee (Cmd. 3658, 1930), 7.*

one control."[1] But this is by no means the limit of the movement, for national boundaries have been passed, and early in
1932 an international agreement was arranged between
Imperial Chemical Industries, the I. G. Farbenindustrie A-G.
of Germany, the Nationale de Matières Colorantes of France,
and three Swiss companies. The Dyestuffs Industry Development Committee report that—

Discussions towards this end have been proceeding at various
times, and in view of the great expansion of dye-stuffs manufacture since 1914, due to the efforts of several countries to establish domestic dye industries and the resultant surplus producing
capacity, some agreement between the principal world producers
was probably inevitable. The terms of the agreement have not
been disclosed, but the Committee have been informed by a
representative of Imperial Chemical Industries, Ltd. that it does
not contain any provision which would impede or restrict the
technical or scientific development of any of the companies concerned, nor does it comprise any selling price arrangements.
Moreover . . . it does not impose any limitation of the British
Colour Users to obtain new products of foreign manufacture. The
main object of the agreement was an endeavour on the part of
the firms concerned to stabilize their share of the world trade in
dyestuffs.

It might be contended that the existence of an international
arrangement between a large section of British and Continental
dye-makers renders protection of this industry unnecessary, but
this contention is unwarranted inasmuch as attack remains possible on the part of the other makers both in the old world and
new. For this reason, the constructive work carried out under
the Dyestuffs (Import Regulation) Act, 1920, might be thrown
away with results that would be disastrous to the industry and
also from a national point of view. Moreover, a continuation of
the present Act is the best means of protecting the industry from
this grave danger of attack. The number and variety of dyestuffs
used by this country is so great that it is essential to have detailed
information made available by the licensing system in order that
the manufacturers in this country may by appropriate discovery
and practical invention keep themselves abreast of the dye-users'
requirements.[2]

[1] *Third Report of the Dyestuffs Industry Development Committee (Cmd.
4191, 1932), 8.*
[2] *Ibid.,* 8–9.

Against this the representatives of the Colour Users' Association contended that—

The agreement reached between Imperial Chemical Industries Ltd., and the Continental Group of dyemakers, constituting as it undoubtedly does a virtual monopoly, removes the necessity for the protection afforded by the Act.

The Dyestuffs (Import Regulation) Act, supplemented by the recently formed international cartel, prejudicially affects the industries represented by the colour consumers (including the textile trade, which is the largest exporting industry of "wholly or partly manufactured goods"). . . .

In view of the statement that the international agreement . . . does not comprise any selling price arrangement, it is conclusive that the British makers cannot substantiate their statement that British users are now being charged world prices, neither for domestically produced colours nor for imported specialities. Further, as the result of this agreement, British users are precluded from competitive buying in approximately 90 per cent of their requirements.

The conclusion of the international agreement was followed almost immediately by substantial increases in the selling prices of domestically made dyestuffs with complete disregard for the precarious condition of many of the consuming industries during a period of national crisis. The experience of users since the formation of the Cartel is definite evidence that the nature of the agreement is such that freedom to obtain foreign quotations is denied to the users except in the case of *new colours*. Full support was given by previous Governments to the claim of the users that territorial restriction would constitute a serious menace to the future of their industries.

. . . although it has been stated that the Cartel Agreement does not comprise any selling price arrangements, it is found in practice that effective quotations for competitive materials cannot be obtained. It may be stated that in comparison with the Board of Trade Wholesale Commodity Index Figure of 102 (*Board of Trade Journal*, September, 1932), the index figure for dyestuffs is 200, an increase of 100 per cent over pre-war.[1]

Whilst the dyeware makers, under the shelter of a Prohibition Act and an international cartel, have no difficulty in increasing their prices, the exporter of textile goods finds it impossible in competition with the world to obtain any better prices; in fact

---

[1] Forty-nine specific examples were given in an appendix. See *Cmd.* 4191, pp. 15–16.

he has to cut prices. Considerable export trade has already been lost owing to prices being too high.

It is a strange anomaly that, whilst the Government have been successful in negotiating terms whereby Lancashire operatives have accepted less wages in order that British textile goods shall be competitive in the world's markets, at the same time the dye-makers by increasing their prices for a major raw material of the textile trade are off-setting the objects of the recent wage cuts.[1]

Attention has been called elsewhere[2] to this international cartel as an example of the complications likely to ensue when international private industrial agreements are superimposed upon national public arrangements for industrial planning and regulation.

The average price of all classes of dyestuffs before the war was approximately one shilling per lb. During and immediately after the war prices were abnormally high, reaching a peak in 1920 when the average worked out at 4s. 4d. per lb. During the next decade a steady decline took place, until the average was little above the pre-war level; but it must be borne in mind that the actual composition of the group of colours has altered considerably since 1913. In 1922 it was agreed between the dye-makers and the dye-users that the latter would not press for the admission (under licence) of foreign dyestuffs *solely* on grounds of price, unless the price of the corresponding British product was more than three times the pre-war price and at the same time higher than the current foreign price. In 1930 the Dyestuffs Industry Development Committee reported that this "price factor arrangement" was still in existence, although the factor *three* had been superseded from time to time by lower factors as the general level of prices moved downwards.

Exports of British dyestuffs are still a comparatively small proportion of total world exports of dyestuffs, but recent progress has apparently given satisfaction to the chief British

---

[1] *Third Report of the Dyestuffs Industry Development Committee* (*Cmd.* 4191), 13–14.

[2] See Plummer, *International Combines in Modern Industry* (1934), p. 116.

producers. Notwithstanding the slump in trade and prices, British exports of dyes and dyestuffs were greater in value in 1932 (£1,182,895) than in 1929 (£1,087,129); and in January, 1933, Sir Harry McGowan stated that—

The dyestuffs industry . . . provides the brightest spot in the exports of chemicals. Indeed the continued success of this post-war industry is one of the most encouraging features of British trade. Over the last three years British dyestuffs have been improving their position in foreign markets. . . . During the first eleven months of 1930 we exported some 197,000 cwt. of dyestuffs products, to the value of £908,976. In 1931, 191,095 cwt. were exported, to the value of £1,008,057, and for the first eleven months of 1932 no less than 253,659 cwt. were exported, to the value of £1,071,205.

Turning to the import figures, it is important to note that these show a decline in total value of just over 26 per cent. . . . Moreover, it is satisfactory to note that . . . . wherever possible imported raw materials are steadily being replaced by those of home manufacture.[1]

This decline in the imports of dyestuffs has continued, while the value of British exports of dyestuffs has now (1937) risen to the neighbourhood of £1,600,000 per annum.

The Act of 1920 not only erected a barrier against foreign imports, but it has had the effect of providing the British dyestuffs industry with information regarding the varying demands for colours, which has been of the greatest service in the formulation of manufacturing policies and schemes of research. Makers and users of dyes have been brought into close contact, and on occasion the British makers have learned at first hand from colour users the exact defects of their products. But, "despite the close-co-operation between the users, the makers and the Licensing Committee, the users undoubtedly have had difficulties" in obtaining supplies of dyestuffs of proved quality and in gaining access to developments and improvements in the world's markets. The licensing system has been lacking in elasticity and rapidity of working. ". . . Samples had to be furnished to the Licensing Committee, thus involving delay which in the case of novelties

[1] *Manchester Guardian Commercial Annual Review*, January, 1933, 16.

was detrimental to the user . . ." and "it seems to have been the rule for applications for licenses for new material to be held up until the makers had reported upon them, and in the rising industries . . . any impediment to the flow of newer products is a serious handicap to the development of their export business."

IV

Dyestuffs for textiles are manufactured mainly at Ellesmere Port, Manchester, Grangemouth, and Huddersfield. The London section of the industry is not concerned with textile dyes, but with printers' inks and colouring matter for food-stuffs, toilet preparations, leather, etc. The materials mainly used are chemical compounds of the aniline group and certain reagents such as caustic soda and sulphuric acid.

The very few firms engaged in this trade in Greater London are old-established businesses re-organized to cope with modern technical and commercial conditions, but not participating in the rationalization schemes which have occurred in many sections of the dyestuffs and chemical industries generally. It is probable that the comparatively small firm is better adapted to handle small and highly specialized lines of product. . . . The London dyestuffs manufacturers can probably look forward to steady business, provided they can hold their own against the combination. But they will only do so by energetic attention to new and specialized lines, as there is a redundancy of dye-making plant in the world.[1]

The number of people employed in the dyestuffs industry is not large, but it is roughly four times the number engaged in it in 1913. The figures obtained by the Dyestuffs Industry Development Committee were—

					Numbers employed	
					1920	1928
Technical staff	.	.	.	.	594	378
Research staff (full time)		.	.	.	120	105
Research staff (part time)		.	.	.	25	28
Administrative staff	.	.	.	.	1075	740
Works staff .	.	.	.	.	5818	5958
					7632	7209

[1] *New Survey of London Life and Labour*, V, 220.

The figure given in the *Fourth Census of Production* for the year 1930 is 7893[1]; and although this is not strictly comparable with the numbers given above, it indicates a slight tendency towards expansion. In addition, two subsidiary industries—pigment colour making and the manufacture of printing inks—have expanded in step with the dyestuffs industry, both in quantity of output and labour employed.

Official statistics relating to wages include the workpeople engaged in the manufacture of synthetic dyestuffs under "Heavy Chemicals." A Ministry of Labour sample inquiry into average earnings in October, 1935, gave the following results for heavy chemical manufacture, including dyes and tar and wood distillation—

Average weekly earnings of—

All workpeople covered by the inquiry	Males		Females	
	21 years and over	Under 21 years	18 years and over	Under 18 years
s. d. 61 10	*s. d.* 66 9	*s. d.* 23 8	*s. d.* 27 1	*s. d.* 14 11

The average weekly hours were 47·2 on day work, and 49·9 (excluding meal-times) on shift work. There is a Joint Industrial Council for the chemical industry on which the National Union of General and Municipal Workers and the Transport and General Workers' Union are represented.

In the London section of the dyestuffs industry, which employs about 800 persons, the processes—grinding, mixing, stirring, decanting, filtering and drying—are carried out with mechanical aids by men working under the direction of trained chemists. The workmen are not skilled in the technical sense, but they must be steady, reliable, and intelligent. Women are seldom employed in productive processes. The time rates of wages are—

Men	per hour	per 47-hour week
Day workers . . .	1s. 3d. to 1s. 4d.	58s. 9d. to 62s. 8d.
Process and shift workers	1s. 5d.	66s. 7d.
Night shift workers .	1s. 6d.	70s. 6d.
Charge hands . .	1s. 6d.	70s. 6d.

[1] *Part III* (1934), 265, 269–70.

There is no piece-work, little overtime, and no seasonal
unemployment. Overtimes rates are "time and a half," and
"double time" for Sunday work. When trade falls slack,
work is stopped on Saturday mornings, and if the slackness
goes further men are discharged.[1]

V

So much for the re-birth of the British synthetic dyestuffs
industry. After weighing the pros and cons the Dyestuffs
Industry Development Committee reached the general conclusion that the type of machinery set up under the Act of
1920 and its administration have been a distinct success.
Indeed, "it may be affirmed unhesitatingly that under no
other form of safeguarding or protection could the same result
have been achieved." In face of this assertion, the Committee's
recommendation to the Government that the Dyestuffs Act,
1920 (with certain amendments), should be continued indefinitely is not surprising. This recommendation was imple-
mented by the Dyestuffs (Import Regulation) Act, 1934,
which made permanent the main provisions of the Act of 1920.
The prohibition upon import now applies to synthetic organic
dyestuffs (including pigment dyestuffs) whether soluble or
insoluble; compounds, preparations, and articles manufactured
from any such dyestuffs, except any which are not suitable for
use in dyeing; and organic intermediate products used in the
manufacture of such dyestuffs. The Dyestuffs Industry
Development Committee is enlarged by the addition of persons
to represent the textile and heavy chemical industries,
chemical science,[2] and any government department which
appears to the Board of Trade to be "specially concerned with

---

[1] Working conditions are, it seems, not ideal. The sheds are unheated,
but there are shower baths and heated cloak-rooms where workers may
change into and out of their working clothes. The dyes are very
penetrating and find their way even to the mess-room tables. Dyes
which are soluble in fat are apt to penetrate the skin and cause temporary poisoning. Cases of dermatitis occur from time to time. *New
Survey of London Life and Labour*, V, 215, 220–2.

[2] This member must be recommended by the Committee of the Privy
Council for Scientific and Industrial Research.

the development" of the dyestuffs industry. The maximum term of office is three years, but reappointment is permitted. If consumers of "substantial quantities" of any prohibited goods complain that their interests are "unduly prejudiced by the prices charged or sought to be charged therefor," it becomes the duty of the Import Duties Advisory Committee to consider the matter and report to the Board of Trade, "and the Board shall . . . lay the report before both Houses of Parliament."

At the beginning of 1935 *The Economist* stated that the revised regulations were working well, "and the recent putting on the tariff Free List of those intermediates used in producing the modern "ice colours" on the fabric has done much to remove the remaining ground of opposition by the organized colour users."[1] The production statistics show that by 1935 Great Britain's output had recovered to the 1929 level, and was inferior only to that of Germany and the United States.[2] According to the latest available information the value of world exports of synthetic dyestuffs is about £22,000,000, of which the Germans supply 55 per cent, and the Swiss 20 per cent. The British take third place with 8 per cent. Owing to the intensification of economic nationalism there is a somewhat widespread tendency to encourage the production of dyestuffs in the consuming countries, and schemes for the erection of new factories are reported in a dozen different places from Copenhagen to Shanghai. Established producers are already actively setting up overseas subsidiary companies to erect factories where "intermediates" supplied by the parent company can be worked up into finished dyestuffs.

(ii) BEET SUGAR

I

It was in the middle of the eighteenth century that the German chemist, Andreas Margraaf, first made sugar from the

---

[1] *The Economist, Commercial History and Review of 1934*, 57.
[2] The German dyestuffs industry, still the largest in the world, produced three times as much as the British industry in 1934.

juice of the sugar beet; but the discovery did not pass beyond the laboratory stage until about 1772 when Franz Karl Achard, one of Margraaf's pupils, having developed research almost to the point of economic exploitation, received from the Prussian Government a grant equal to £8000 and grew 60 acres of sugar beet. After another thirty years of more or less intermittent work, studying and perfecting the production of sugar beet and the sugar extraction processes, Achard was able to set up the first beet sugar factory at Kunern in Silesia in 1801. This achievement created much interest in France. The possibility of producing home-grown sugar, and stimulating agriculture by introducing a new crop which would yield profit, improve the soil and leave as a by-product a valuable feeding-stuff for cattle, greatly appealed to Napoleon, who enlisted the resources of the State with such energy that between 1811 and 1816, 213 small factories were established, with an output capacity of some 4000 tons of sugar per annum.[1] During the first half of the nineteenth century France and Germany were the principal producers of beet sugar, but their example was gradually followed by many other European countries, and in each case the industry was assisted by the State "in much the same way as in Germany, i.e. protected by a high import duty or taxed or controlled in such a way that indirect bounties could be earned."[2] In the United States of America the beet sugar industry dates from 1836, but its first forty years are strewn with failures and, indeed, it made little progress until in 1890 and 1897 it received State support in the form of a bounty on output and a protective tariff.

The developments on the Continent were not entirely without their effects upon the United Kingdom. In the early years of the nineteenth century experiments were made in this country in sugar beet cultivation and beet sugar manufacture; small factories were set up in 1832, 1850, and 1868, but all failed, partly because of technical difficulties and the

[1] Ministry of Agriculture *Report on the Sugar Beet Industry at Home and Abroad* (No. 27, 1931), pp. 18–19.
[2] *Ibid.*, 21.

inexperience of growers, and partly because, in contrast to Continental practice, no assistance was forthcoming from the State. As time went on those who, like the Earl of Denbigh, remained staunch advocates of sugar beet cultivation in Britain, became convinced of the necessity of better organization and education, and Government help. The Cambridge University Department of Agriculture and the Board of Agriculture conducted various experiments and reported favourably upon the prospects of growing sugar beet with a high sugar content in this country. Bodies such as the Sugar Beet Council, the National Sugar Beet Association and the Incorporated English Beet Sugar Pioneer Association of Liverpool helped to organize several factory schemes, which were actually carried through to "various points of development, but not to fruition."[1] The principal obstacles may be summarized thus—

(a) The British investor was unwilling to venture his capital in a beet sugar factory unless he had some assurance that raw material would be forthcoming from growers over a term of years and at prices low enough to enable the factory to show an attractive profit-margin.

(b) The farmer was unwilling to modify his rotation in order to grow a substantial crop of sugar beet over a period of years unless he was assured of a regular market and "fair" prices.

(c) There was, apparently, no prospect of State assistance by way of subsidy or high protection. Although the customs duty on imported sugar was 1s. 10d. per cwt. while, at that time, there was no excise duty, it was thought that, in accordance with prevailing fiscal policy, a countervailing excise duty would probably be imposed as soon as any substantial quantity of home-grown sugar was produced.

At this point foreign enterprise, greatly daring, entered the field. In 1912 a factory was built at Cantley in Norfolk on Dutch initiative and largely with Dutch capital.

The Anglo-Netherland Sugar Corporation Ltd. . . . was made

---

[1] Ministry of Agriculture *Report on the Sugar Beet Industry at Home and Abroad* (No. 27, 1931), p. 30.

possible by a pooling arrangement with a number of Dutch factories. Of the £800,000 of share and loan capital, £170,000 was expended upon the factory and £575,000 was re-invested in shares and debentures in the Dutch allied companies. This arrangement enabled the company to set-off to some extent, by means of dividends, interest and guarantees, its development expenditure and initial losses.[1]

In 1913 eight English agriculturists, registered as the Sugar Beet Growers' Society, managed to obtain the first British Government subsidy to the beet sugar industry, in the form of a grant, not to exceed £11,000, from the Development Fund, to be applied only to the promotion of education and organization. The Society spent the money in demonstrating to farmers in Norfolk and Suffolk foreign methods of beet cultivation (singling, hoeing, harvesting, use of fertilizers, etc.), and incidentally they managed to provide an extra quantity of raw material for the Cantley factory. But even with the Government grant a heavy loss was incurred, the experiment was not repeated, and the Society was wound up. As for the factory, although it managed to secure from growers sufficient beet to allow of manufacture on a modest scale, it ran at a loss for four seasons or "campaigns" (1912–15), and then closed down. Its English assets were acquired by the English Beet Sugar Corporation Ltd., a new company comprising an English group with some leading members of the former Dutch group. But the Cantley factory was not re-opened until 1920.

Meanwhile other important moves were being made. In 1915 the newly-formed British Sugar Beet Society—"an association of prominent agriculturists and public men"— prepared a scheme to bring both the private investor and the State into partnership in the beet sugar industry. The Society proposed that, with the aid of State capital, a beet sugar factory should be erected upon an estate large enough to grow sufficient beet for a manufacturing season of minimum length consistent with economy. At that time the country was facing

[1] Ministry of Agriculture *Report on the Sugar Beet Industry at Home and Abroad* (No. 27, 1931), p. 32.

the prospect of war-time food shortage, and in 1916 the Agricultural Policy Sub-Committee of the Reconstruction Committee (usually called the Selborne Committee) which was set up to consider methods of increasing supplies of home-grown foodstuffs, urged the Government to arrange at once for a complete test on a commercial scale of the possibilities of establishing a beet sugar industry based upon supplies of home-grown beet.

Assuming (said the Committee) that State assistance is offered to promote the establishment of the industry, such assistance can only be given by one of two methods—

(a) Direct—i.e. State factories built, maintained and controlled by the State through a Department of H.M. Government.

(b) Indirect—advances by way of grant or loan to a separately incorporated body on the basis of a partnership between the investing business public and the State.

It is urged that plan (b)—indirect intervention—is the better policy to adopt, but . . . plan (a) is acceptable if it is the only alternative to refusal of State aid.[1]

The outcome of this recommendation was the purchase, with the aid of £125,000 from State funds, of an estate of 5603 acres at Kelham in Nottinghamshire. In 1918 a further loan of £40,000 for working capital was made by the Treasury from the Development Fund. During the war foodstuffs were grown on the estate, but the scheme to grow beet and build a factory was left in abeyance. Early in 1920, however, a company called Home Grown Sugar Ltd., was floated with a capital of £500,000, one-half subscribed by the Government and the other half by private investors.[2] Factories at both Cantley and Kelham were in operation during 1921–2, and both were incurring heavy losses. The excise duty on sugar was first reduced and later (1922) entirely remitted; but by 1924 it was quite clear that nothing short of a substantial

---

[1] *Cmd.* 8506/1917.

[2] British investors, however, were still very shy. Although the Government shares did not rank for dividend for ten years, and on all other shares the Government guaranteed a 5 per cent dividend during the same period, about £65,000 of the public issue was left with the underwriters.

subsidy could keep the beet sugar industry alive.[1] Was it worth preserving on such terms?

The considerations which had weighed with the Selborne Committee in 1916 were now reinforced by other ugent reasons. Between 1918 and 1923 the index number for agricultural produce had fallen from 232 to 157. Arable farming, particularly, was in a depressed state and it was anticipated that the introduction of sugar beet would reduce materially the difficulties in arable districts. Moreover, unemployment had assumed grave proportions and the building and equipment of factories together with the subsidiary trades and industries which would be involved, such as transport, were expected to contribute to the solution of this problem.[2]

The upshot was the passing of the now famous (or notorious) British Sugar (Subsidy) Act, 1925, which guaranteed generous "tapering" subsidies for a period of ten years upon sugar and molasses derived from home-grown beet. Subsidy payments to the factories at the rate of 19s. 6d. per cwt. of sugar for the first four years, 13s. for the next three years, and 6s. 6d. for the period 1932–4 were made conditional upon the sugar manufacturers (a) paying a minimum price of 44s. per ton of beet of 15½ per cent sugar-content during the first four years, (b) buying at least 75 per cent of their plant and machinery from British manufacturers; and (c) paying wages in accordance with the "fair wages clause."

It was expected that the additional security afforded to the industry under the new Act would make it easier to raise capital and build up reserves, to induce farmers to grow more beet, and to make technical improvements on the farm and in the factory. Technical progress would also be stimulated by the diminishing (or tapering) rate of subsidy for which the Act provided. These expectations have been very largely realized. In the last pre-subsidy year (1924) the area under

[1] Before 1925 the acreage under sugar beet in Britain was so small that it did not appear in the annual statistics of agricultural production: ten years later the crop covered 367,000 acres and home-produced beet sugar supplied about 25 per cent of the national requirements.
[2] A. Bridges and R. N. Dixey, *British Sugar Beet: Ten Years progress under the Subsidy* (1934), 8.

sugar beet in England and Wales was 22,440 acres—61½ per cent of the acreage being in Norfolk, Suffolk, and the Isle of Ely, 20½ per cent in Lincolnshire, and the remainder scattered through Essex, Cambridgeshire, and Nottinghamshire. In 1925, the first subsidy year, the sugar beet area increased to 54,750 acres, and five new factories were built—four in the Eastern Counties and one at Kidderminster. In 1926 the acreage increased to 125,800, the number of growers reached 20,000—five more factories opened, and certain districts (e.g. Northamptonshire, Oxfordshire, Wiltshire, and Somerset-shire) grew sugar beet on a much larger scale than before.

A temporary set-back occurred in 1927–8 owing to (*a*) un-favourable weather which reduced both the yield of beet per acre and the sugar-content, and (*b*) the change over to the lower rate of subsidy, beginning in 1928. Expansion was resumed in 1929, and continued in 1930, when the area under beet reached a peak of 347,250 acres; the number of growers exceeded 40,000, and the number of factories was nineteen.

"With 1931 the sugar-beet industry entered upon the final period of the subsidy, when the rate fell from 13s. to 6s. 6d. per cwt. In addition to the effect of this reduction the fac-tories were faced with such low prices for sugar that many of them felt unable to offer farmers a price for their beet which would ensure a sufficient acreage to justify operating the factories."[1] In these circumstances the Government put through the British Sugar Industry (Assistance) Act, 1931, which provided for an advance from the State, repayable under certain conditions, of 1s. 3d. per cwt. for the first 300,000 cwt. of sugar manufactured by each factory during the 1931–2 season, conditional upon the offer by the factories of a firm price for sugar beet high enough to pass the extra subsidy to the growers. Twelve factories accepted the Government's offer and sustained a fall of only 18 per cent in beet acreage in their districts; six factories did not accept the offer, and their acreage fell by approximately 44 per cent. The total beet area declined to 233,200 acres, a decrease of 33 per cent. Once

---

[1] Bridges and Dixey, *op. cit.*, 14–15.

again this proved to be quite temporary, and by 1933 the beet area was the highest on record—365,774 acres.

Technical progress on the farm has also been satisfactory. The sugar-content has always been over 16 per cent and sometimes above 17 per cent. Gross costs of production and transport of sugar beet, so far as they can be ascertained, have been reduced from approximately £24 per acre in 1924 to £17 17s. in 1932; and net costs (i.e. gross costs *minus* residual values) from £22 6s. 6d. per acre in 1924 to £16 5s. in 1932. Net costs of production and transport per ton have been reduced from 43s. 8d. in 1924 to 29s. 4d. in 1932.[1] The yield of beet per acre has increased from an average of 7·3 tons in the period 1924–7, to 8·5 tons in 1928–30, 8·7 tons in 1932 and 9 tons in 1933. This is still from 10 to 30 per cent below the average yields commonly obtained in Holland, Belgium, Czechoslovakia, and Germany; but in Britain cultivation is less intensive, and in the period under review the extension of the margin of beet cultivation together with the accession of new and inexperienced growers must have tended to hold down the general average.

Although British cultivation of sugar beet is less intensive than in most Continental countries, it is one of the most intensive crops grown in the general mixed farming areas of this country, for, broadly speaking, it requires nearly as much labour as potatoes, and three times as much as wheat. The introduction of sugar beet has not increased either the total arable area or the general volume of agricultural employment in this country, nor has it prevented some decrease; but it seems clear that without it a much greater decline of arable and employment in agriculture would have occurred in the Eastern and North-eastern counties.

In addition to the relatively high number of workers employed regularly on farms which grow substantial crops of beet a good deal of temporary or casual labour is also required when the crop reaches certain stages. A survey made in 1933 showed that five farms out of six were employing casual

[1] Bridges and Dixey, *op. cit.*, 62–4.

labour.[1] This extra and occasional labour-demand was at first not readily met; but the difficulty has been overcome by the efforts of the factories, farmers' associations, and Ministry of Labour Employment Exchanges. In 1934 the Employment Exchanges "placed" 7318 workers in field work and 7464 in the factories. For field work it is now usually possible to find sufficient people with experience of work on sugar beet or general agricultural work in the district around each factory. Only 747 of the 7318 workers engaged for field work through the Labour Exchanges in 1934 were brought from other districts.[2] According to evidence submitted to the Greene Committee, the additional agricultural employment due to sugar beet cultivation in 1934 was 32,000 men.

The normal legal minimum rates of wages fixed by the Agricultural Wages Board for adult workers in the principal beet-growing counties are—

	Males		Females	
Norfolk	31s. 6d.	per week[3]	5d.	per hour
Suffolk	31s. 0d.	,, ,,	5d.	,, ,,
Cambridge and Isle of Ely . .	31s. 6d.	,, ,,	5½d.	,, ,,
Lincolnshire				
(i) Holland	34s. 0d.	,, ,,	6d.	,, ,,
(ii) Kesteven and Lindsey .	31s. 0d.	,, ,,	5½d.	,, ,,

These are time rates and generally speaking time work is most usual in British agriculture; but in connexion with sugar beet cultivation piece work is tending to become the rule rather than the exception.

An inquiry amongst 40 beet-growers in different parts of the country in 1933 showed that 32 of them were paying piece-work rates for summer hand work, 10 of them having changed over from time rates, while of the 8 paying day rates only 5 had previously used piece work.

Piece-work rates, in common with all the costs, have declined as experience and skill have been achieved. A farmer in Lincolnshire, for example, now (1934) paying from 60s. to 64s. per acre for all manual operations, chopping out, singling, hand-hoeing, pulling, topping, and heaping, was paying 88s. so late as 1927.

[1] Bridges and Dixey, *op. cit.*, 41.
[2] *Labour Gazette*, April 1935, 134.
[3] 50 hours per week in summer (51 in Kesteven and Lindsey); 48 hours in winter.

Another, in the Fens, is paying 72s. against 125s. in the earlier years. Another in Leicestershire, 60s. against 80s. In Shropshire, 63s. against 78s., and another 70s. against 95s. The average reduction on 25 farms during the last few years has been in the region of 20 per cent. These reductions reflect a general tendency.[1]

Conditional bonuses are paid in many cases as a safeguard against scamped work. At harvest time, individual workers may be paid separate piece-work rates for each process, or a lump sum to cover the whole series of harvest processes. Alternatively, the work may be done by a gang for a stated sum, but since the tasks are diverse, disputes generally arise about the final division of the money among the members of the gang. It is not unusual for piece-work rates to vary according to the weight of the crop, the nature of the soil, the drill widths, and so forth. Haulage costs have declined approximately 36 per cent between 1925–7 and 1931–3, partly by reason of reductions of piece-work rates for loading into carts. Where this is paid for as a separate task the rate ranges from 6s. to 10s. an acre.[2]

It appears that even at the reduced piece-work rates, the workers can earn more for a week's work than they could on or near the legal minimum time rates. Nevertheless, these universal cuts in piece-work rates have obviously deprived the workers of at least part of the benefit of their increasing skill and efficiency.

Beet sugar factories in all countries commonly obtain their beet supplies under a system of contracts (usually annual) with the growers. In Great Britain it is customary to agree upon the contract price for beet some eight months before the actual manufacture of the sugar. The Beet Sugar Factories Committee of Great Britain and the Central Sugar Beet Committee of the National Farmers Union have succeeded in negotiating a standard beet contract. Each year a uniform price for the whole country is agreed upon, which the N.F.U. *recommends* its members to accept. This means that each

[1] Bridges and Dixey, *op. cit.*, 40–1.
[2] *Ibid.*, 52.

factory has still to approach individual growers with the standard contract and the agreed price and each grower decides for himself what beet acreage, if any, he will grow at the price offered. The major considerations influencing the negotiating bodies are the costs of cultivation of the average grower, so far as these are known; the factories' manufacturing costs and capital charges; the anticipated wholesale price of refined sugar, and the amount of State assistance (subsidy, etc.) available. This contract system is advantageous and, indeed, indispensable to both parties. As a rule the grower's only market is the local factory, for costs of beet transportation are too high to permit of resort to alternative markets. Therefore, before undertaking to grow a beet crop, the farmer needs a guarantee that his output will be taken at a price to which he is prepared to agree. For the factory, the contract system secures, within limits set mainly by the vagaries of the weather, an essential certainty of supplies of raw material for each campaign. Thus risks are reduced but not entirely eliminated, for low yield per acre and low sugar-content in bad seasons means reduced total incomes for farmers, and increased unit-costs of production for the factories. Moreover the factories must take the risk of agreeing to a price for beet before they know the acreage which will be grown in response to that price; and also the risk of a falling market for refined sugar after they have made their contracts with the growers.

II

The employment afforded by the beet sugar factories is even more seasonal than that provided by sugar beet cultivation. As the sugar beet cannot be stored for long without marked deterioration, the factories are compelled to turn the whole beet crop into sugar within three or four months of the beginning of the sugar beet harvest. During this period in each year, which is known as "the campaign," the factories aim at running their machinery continuously; the employees inside the factories work in 8-hour shifts, and those outside—the transport and yard workers—usually work overtime throughout the campaign. The average length of the working week during a campaign is between 64 and 69 hours.

The manufacture of sugar beet by modern methods depends for its success upon careful chemical control of the material as it passes through the various processes. The first stage is the reception of the freshly harvested beets at the factory. After the beets have passed over a weighbridge which records the gross weight, samples are taken in order that tare and sugar-content may be ascertained.[1] The beets are then removed from the railway truck or road vehicle into a flume or silo by tipping or forking, or by the force of a stream of water directed from a water-gun. Barges are usually unloaded by a crane grab. The flumes are wedge-shaped troughs through which the beets slide into channels filled with flowing water which partially washes the beets while at the same time it carries them into the factory. Here the beets are more thoroughly cleansed and passed by a screw conveyor and elevator to an automatic weighing machine which, on register-ing a certain weight, discharges them, *via* a trough, down into the cutting mills or slicing machines consisting of rotating drums containing horizontal serrated knives that cut the beets into wedge-shaped pieces, known as "cosettes." The cosettes are then conveyed mechanically to a battery of diffusers where the juice containing the sugar is extracted by successive applications of heat and water under pressure. The cosettes, when exhausted of sugar, are discharged and conveyed to presses which remove much of the water, leaving a by-product called wet pulp. The raw juice, black in colour, is drawn off from the diffuser, subjected to treatment with lime and carbon dioxide gas, and filtered several times to remove all impurities. Next the juice, now thin and much clearer, is converted by evaporation into syrup, which is then pumped through filters into steam-heated pans where it is boiled under vacuum until

[1] At the British beet sugar factories there are growers' representa-tives, appointed by the National Farmers' Union, to verify the factory officials' ascertainments of the weights, tare and sugar content of all beets delivered.

crystallization begins. At the right moment the liquor is passed into centrifugal separators, which, rotating at 900 to 1000 revolutions per minute, fling any uncrystallized liquor through a fine mesh and retain the sugar crystals. The hot, moist white sugar is carried to a granulator to be cooled, dried and screened; after which it is bagged and stored ready for marketing. The final residue of sweet liquor—molasses—is pumped into storage tanks.

The British factories' output of white sugar is sold through London brokers to wholesale dealers and manufacturers of goods containing sugar, the prices being quoted either "ex factory" or "free on rail factory." Buyers have the option of taking delivery from depots in many parts of the country, either at contract price or at varying premiums which do not seem to be definitely related to the distances between depots and factories. The wholesale dealers do not usually "handle" the sugar, but merely give their customers delivery orders upon factories or depots. The Ministry of Agriculture Report on the Sugar Beet Industry (1931) put the average selling expenses of British beet sugar factories at 1s. 4d. to 1s. 6d. per cwt., "of which from 6d. to 8d. represents freight and depot charges, and the remainder quantity rebates, trade and cash discounts and brokerage."

There is in London an important terminal or "futures" market in sugar, which provides facilities for "hedging" and arbitrage operations whereby sugar producers, refiners and traders can avail themselves of a form of insurance against the risks of price-fluctuations.

In actual fact, in proportion to the volume of business negotiated, few tenders of actual sugar are made to liquidate terminal market transactions. In the majority of cases, contracts are liquidated by re-purchase or re-sale, the intermediate seller or buyer losing or gaining on the differences. . . . The transactions on the London Terminal Market are conducted through brokers, who are members of the United Terminal Sugar Market Association, on the terms and conditions of the London Produce Clearing House Ltd.[1]

[1] *Report on the Sugar Beet Industry at Home and Abroad* (1931), 222–5.

Molasses is generally sold to distillers for the manufacture of alcohol and to farmers for stock-feeding. A small proportion is used in the production of yeast and various polishes. By a somewhat complicated process molasses can be "desugarized," and where this is done by the factories a certain amount of employment is provided during the "off" season—February to September. Beet pulp, either wet or dry, is an excellent food for stock. The pulp-drying process provides employment during the off season, and so does the drying of the lime sludge from the filters, which, in the form of lime cake, is a useful manure. Further off-season employment is provided when the factories turn to the refining of imported raw sugar after the beet sugar campaign is over. On the other hand, it is quite possible for beet sugar factories to stop at the raw sugar stage and send the raw beet sugar to be "finished" at sugar refineries; but this is not the practice in Great Britain.

Beet sugar factories, like all others, need to work at or near their optimum capacity in order to secure minimum unit-costs of production. How near any given beet sugar factory can get to this ideal output depends in part upon the effects of the weather upon the beet harvest, and in part upon the area under beet upon which it can draw. Sugar beet is a crop of low value in relation to its bulk, and cannot bear heavy transportation costs. Therefore, although it is not impossible for a factory to draw some beets from a distance by water transport, it has to depend for the bulk of its principal raw material upon the crop grown locally, i.e. within a radius of twenty or twenty-five miles. This means that the best situation for a sugar beet factory is in the middle of a tract of flat, high-yielding land most of which is under the plough. Good transport and unloading facilities and sufficient field and factory labour to meet the fluctuations of productive activity are also essential.

Each beet sugar factory employs between thirty-five and forty-five persons on its "general staff"—managers, superintendents, engineers, chemists, accountants, and fieldmen. During the campaigns of 1932 and 1933 the average number of workmen employed by the factories was between 480 and 500 per factory; the aggregates being 8100 in 1932 and approximately 9000 in 1933. Of these about 20 per cent are skilled craftsmen—fitters, welders, turners, blacksmiths, crane-drivers, and electricians—paid at or above the usual trade union rates; and about 13 or 14 per cent are "general" workers acting as "charge hands." The remainder are classed as "unskilled." As a rule only about one-quarter of the whole staff is required in the off season. Many of the skilled men are retained to overhaul and renew machinery, and the chief incidence of seasonal unemployment falls upon the unskilled workers. The Ministry of Labour reported that in 1933, under special pooling arrangements between certain of the factories in South-east England, "farmers' delivery quotas were extended, and any factory which received a supply of beet in excess of requirements was able to direct it to other factories working at less than full output. These arrangements resulted in a much larger tonnage of beet being handled during the year, and in more regular employment at the factories."[1] Those skilled and unskilled men who are retained after the campaign usually work on the average between 46 and 52 hours per week when refining of imported sugar is in progress; at other times during the off season the working week averages 46 hours only. Those discharged during the off season usually seek employment on road making, building, drainage work, and road transport.

Factories receiving the sugar subsidy must pay rates of wages in accordance with the Fair Wages Clause in general use in Government contracts, except in cases where a rate or rates have been agreed upon by a joint industrial council representing the employer and employees, or where an award has been made by the Industrial Court.[2] In practice the payment of "fair wages" means that all the workers, whether members of a trade union or not, receive the prevailing local trade union rates of wages, so far as these can be ascertained. Approximately nine-tenths of the factory employees work on a time-work basis. Those on piece-work are mainly "outside"

---

[1] *Labour Gazette*, April, 1934, 121.
[2] British Sugar (Subsidy) Act, 1925, Section 3.

workers employed at unloading beet, coal, cake, or limestone, or loading sugar or pulp at so much a ton. The basic time-rates of wages for general labourers range from 9½d. to 1s. 2d. per hour, and earnings range from an average of £3 per week on basic rates to £3 10s. on higher rates. For fitters and welders the basic hourly time rates and weekly earnings range from 11d. to 1s. 6¼d.; and from £3 17s. 6d. to £4 5s. Turners and blacksmiths receive time rates ranging from 11d. to 1s. 5d. per hour, and weekly earnings averaging from £3 17s. 6d. up to £4. Corresponding wage rates and earnings for crane drivers are 11d. to 1s. 4½d. and £3 11s. 3d. to £3 13s. 9d.; for stokers, 11d. to 1s. 5½d. and £3 7s. 6d. to £3 16s. 3d.; and for electricians, 10d. to 1s. 7¼d. and £3 16s. 3d. to £4 3s. 9d. All these rates and earnings are for a normal week of 56 hours and include extra payments for Sunday work as part of the shift-week, but not overtime or bonuses on production. Some factories pay higher rates of wages to individuals of special efficiency or taking increased responsibility. Charge hands are sometimes transferred from an hourly to a weekly basis. Long service is recognized usually by giving to men on the permanent staff from ½d. to 2d. an hour above basic rates for each unbroken year's service over four years. During the off season the working week averages 46–7 hours, and the earnings of those unskilled workers who are not discharged fall to about £2 10s. a week on the average. Corresponding average weekly off-season earnings for fitters and welders are £3 4s.; for turners and blacksmiths, about £3 1s.; for crane-drivers, about £2 16s.; stokers, about £2 14s., and electricians, approximately £3 13s.

Practice regarding overtime rates and Sunday work is not uniform. Some factories pay only ordinary hourly rates; others pay "time and a quarter," or "time and a half," and some, for Sunday work, "double-time." Bonuses on production are also paid to supplement wages, but the basis of calculation—e.g. amount of production per shift, or tonnage of beets put through, or output of sugar—varies widely, and so do the resulting bonuses. "It is impossible to calculate accurately the average additional earnings per man in the form of bonus. During one campaign, the weekly bonus yield at one factory was 4s. 8d. per man; at another, 12s. 3d. per man.

In the majority of the British factories there is no break for meals. Practically all the factories provide a canteen and refreshments are carried round several times during each shift. Where a break for meals is permitted, the relay system applies, each man being allowed from 20 minutes to ¾-hour for lunch and ½-hour for tea. Where a 12-hour shift is worked, 1 hour is allowed for dinner, with a short break in the morning and again in the afternoon. The day workers usually have fixed meal-times. During the campaign, canteens are open day and night, hot water is always available, and the men can buy meals in the canteens or bring food to be heated.

Labour for beet sugar factories is recruited mainly from the unemployed industrial workers in the towns and villages in the vicinity of the factories. The factories prefer to engage "genuinely unemployed" men rather than those who give up less remunerative jobs in order to obtain higher wages at the beet sugar factories. This rules out farm workers already in employment; and it is argued that this is necessary because the beet harvest overlaps the beginning of the manufacturing campaign, and the recruiting of agricultural workers for factory work would seriously interfere with the maintenance of the supply of raw material for the factories. "While there is no evidence of any definite arrangement between factories and farmers to debar farm labourers from being employed at a factory, it is in the interests of factories not to give farmers cause to suspect that the effect of a local factory will be to compete with them for supplies of labour."[1] The factories keep lists of the men employed in each campaign, and these are given the first opportunity of employment in succeeding seasons. In the past this practice has meant that about two-thirds of the seasonal labourers engaged have had previous experience in a beet sugar factory.

[1] *Report on the Sugar Beet Industry at Home and Abroad* (1931),162.

III

When the Kelham factory was built in 1921 the French consultants expressed the opinion that the optimum size for a beet sugar factory was a capacity of 500–600 tons of beet per day. But the British factories, under the stimulus of the subsidy, have developed much larger capacities than this, ranging from 700 tons up to 2500 tons per day. The average capacity is in the neighbourhood of 1300 tons. The construction of factories of this size calls for a large amount of capital, which, as we have noticed, it is not possible to employ fully all the year round, nor can the plant be turned to any other use except raw sugar refining. The major portion of the capital raised by a beet sugar company is spent upon the construction and equipment of the factory. The remainder is used as working capital, chiefly for financing the crop, purchasing fuel, and paying wages. This working capital is generally augmented by short-term bank loans and by placing undistributed profits to reserve. All but one of the British beet sugar factories have been built at prices ruling in the period 1921–9, which means that they have higher burdens of capital charges (annual interest and depreciation) than the majority of the Continental factories built before the War. There is reason to suspect, however, that the higher post-War price-level is not entirely responsible. Mr. J. L. Fairrie, a sugar trade expert, hinted as late as August, 1933, that "a group with constructional interests" had been "endeavouring to make such arrangements as will enable it to proceed with the erection of three new factories—one in South Wales . . . another at Bridgwater or Taunton, and the third in West Sussex . . ." and added that the "receiving of debentures or the like in return for contracting work and the design and supply of machinery inevitably results in inflated capital costs."[1] One is prompted to ask how it is that the Skoda Company holds the whole mortgage debenture issue (£200,000) of British Sugar Manufacturers Ltd.

[1] *Manchester Guardian Commercial*, 19th August, 1933.

None of the British beet sugar factories is owned co-operatively, as are so many of the factories in Germany. The British sugar beet industry "owed its birth to the initiative of certain leading agriculturists and industrialists who believed in its possibilities, with the assistance of leaders in the industry in European countries. It did not develop as a result of the initiative of farmers themselves. It has therefore been built up on the basis of proprietary factories."[1]

The aggregate issued share and loan (debenture) capital invested in the British beet sugar factories exceeds £5,400,000.[2] The capital per factory ranges from £500,000 to £175,000; and the average is approximately £340,000. About one-third of the capital in the industry is owned by foreigners. Of the 2373 shareholders on the register of fifteen of the British beet sugar companies at 31st March, 1930, 135, holding £1,525,165 or 33 per cent of the total share capital, were known to be foreign. The average holding of each foreign shareholder was £11,297, against an average of £1400 for British shareholders. In both cases shareholders include corporations as well as individuals.[3] £336,248 of the £500,000 ordinary shares in the so-called English Beet Sugar Corporation are held by a Dutch concern, the Maatschappij voor Landbauwen Beet Wartelsuiken-Industrie.[4]

In 1936 there were four groups of beet sugar companies in Britain: (a) the Anglo-Dutch group consisting of the English Beet Sugar Corporation, three subsidiaries and one leased

[1] *Report on the Sugar Beet Industry at Home and Abroad* (1931), 165.

[2] i.e. Issued shares and debentures of each Company, *less* investments in subsidiary companies. See Ministry of Agriculture, *Statements in the form of balance sheets transmitted . . . by companies which manufactured in Great Britain in 1933–4, sugar and/or molasses from home-grown beet.* Section I, Factories (1934).

[3] *Report on the Sugar Beet Industry at Home and Abroad*, 175. Down to the middle of 1926 loans to beet sugar companies totalling £1,650,000 had been guaranteed by the Government under the Trade Facilities Acts, 1921–6, for periods of 9, 12, and 13 years. *Factors in Industrial and Commercial Efficiency* (1927), 433.

[4] It is asserted that other large foreign shareholders include Erste Brunnen Maschinenfabrik Gesellschaft, Continentale Gesellschaft für Bank und Industriewerke (Basle), and Hatvaner Zuckerfabrik Aktien-Gesellschaft (Budapest). (*Reynolds's Supplement*, 11th November, 1934.)

factory; (*b*) the Anglo-Scottish or Weir group of three companies operating six factories; (*c*) the Tate & Lyle group of four companies each running one factory; and (*d*) the Lincolnshire group of two companies running factories at Bardney and Brigg. Tate & Lyle Ltd. owns direct controlling interests in Central Sugar Company Ltd., and Shropshire Beet Sugar Company Ltd., and its directorate is interlocked with that of the United Sugar Company, which is connected in a similar way with the Yorkshire Sugar Co. Ltd.

Although two or three of these companies have met with more losses than profits in the past decade, the majority have made large profits which have been in part distributed to shareholders, and in part added to reserve funds. At 31st March, 1934, of the fifteen companies making returns, all had made net profits during the financial year 1933–4 amounting in the aggregate to over £530,000, or nearly 10 per cent upon the whole capital invested; and only two carried forward outstanding debit balances on profit and loss account, the accumulated losses then outstanding being £69,876 and £32,713. In addition, Home Grown Sugar Ltd. sustained net losses of upwards of £64,000 during 1929–33. The Anglo-Dutch group appears to be the most prosperous. In 1924–5 and 1925–6, the leading company in the group, the English Beet Sugar Co. Ltd., paid dividends on its ordinary shares at 12½ per cent per annum; from 1926–7 to 1930–1 inclusive, 20 per cent was paid each year; and in 1931–2 and 1932–3, the dividend was 10 per cent per annum. In the seven years 1927 to 1934 the aggregate profits of the companies in the Anglo-Dutch group (excluding Home-Grown Sugar Ltd., Kelham, which after incurring losses was leased to the group until 31st March, 1935) exceeded £2,700,000; and this sum, together with the group's aggregate accumulated reserves of £990,000, is *more than double the aggregate share and loan capital invested*.

During the same period the manufacturing profits of two of the three companies in Lord Weir's Anglo-Scottish group exceeded £500,000; the other company, however, lost £92,168. In the financial year 1933–4 the three companies made profits totalling £122,217; or approximately 6¾ per cent upon the net capital invested. The accumulated reserves of this group are £59,000. During the same financial year (1933-4) the Tate & Lyle group of companies made a total net profit of £168,000; or 16¾ per cent upon the net capital invested; and their reserves total £210,000. The Lincolnshire group also makes a good showing. From 1928 to 1934 the two factories made total profits exceeding £459,000, and the parent company has a reserve fund of £42,000. These two sums are nearly equal to the net capital invested in the Lincolnshire companies. In the financial year 1933-4 their accounts showed net profits £46,469 or nearly 8 per cent upon the net capital invested.

The most recent dividend distributions of the four companies in the Anglo-Dutch group are not without interest, particularly to the British taxpayer. For the year 1934 the English Beet Sugar Corporation paid a 20 per cent dividend (free of tax) plus a cash bonus of 60 per cent out of general reserve; and in 1935 again a dividend of 20 per cent free of tax. The Ely Beet Sugar Co. paid 15 per cent free of tax in 1935, and in 1934 the same percentage plus a cash bonus of 66.7 per cent (£301,000) from its reserves. The King's Lynn Beet Sugar Co. paid tax-free dividends of 8 per cent in 1934 and 6 per cent in 1935; and the Ipswich Beet Sugar Co. paid 8 per cent free of tax in 1935, and 7 per cent plus a cash bonus of 35 per cent (£140,000) from reserves in 1934.

IV

There is not the slightest doubt that the recent prosperity of the British beet sugar factories is largely "artificial" in the sense that the whole industry is bounty-fed and the existing levels of production and profit are maintained only as a result of constant heavy "injections" of subsidy payments and revenue abatements at the taxpayers' expense. In the decade 1924-34 the beet sugar subsidy payments amounted to over £30 millions and abatement of excise duties to over £10 millions. The subsidy was extended into 1935 by the British

Sugar (Subsidy) Act, 1934, at a cost to the taxpayers estimated at about £3,250,000. Taking a further eleven months' revenue abatement into account, by August, 1935, the grand total of subsidy and revenue abatement was probably not far short of £45,000,000.

In the period 1924–8, when the subsidy payments were at a maximum, the average price paid by the factories to the farmers was 56s. 7d. per ton of beet, while the value of the subsidy alone—ignoring revenue abatements—was equivalent to 56s. 6d. per ton of beet. Revenue abatements totalled £1,737,000; so that the beet sugar factories received their beets *gratis* as a present from the taxpayers, while the Exchequer lost nearly £1¾ millions of revenue. In the second subsidy period, 1928–31, farmers received an average price of 51s. 3d. per ton, while the subsidy worked out at 41s.; and in the period 1931–4 the average price was approximately 40s. and the subsidy about 21s. 4d. In the period 1924–7 when the average wholesale price of white sugar (*cum* duty) in Great Britain averaged 3½d. per lb., the subsidy averaged 2⅓d. per lb. of beet sugar produced; in 1933, the subsidy averaged approximately 1¼d. per lb. with white sugar at less than 2d. per lb. wholesale.

One may well ask whether the game has been worth the candle? What have we to show for such heavy payments? Can it be said that a new industry likely to be a national asset has been firmly established? Or have we, on the contrary, brought into the world a weakling, a national liability clinging precariously to life and likely to live only so long as vested interests can succeed in drawing copious supplies of free "milk" from the State? As two expert agricultural economists have said: "One of the purposes of a long subsidy period was to enable the industry to get a good start and to become efficient. By 1935 the new industry will have completed eleven cycles in growing beet and manufacturing sugar, which may be regarded as sufficient to achieve efficiency. . . . There are now eighteen factories in Great Britain and nearly 40,000 growers supplied beet to them from 365,774 acres in 1933.

The trial, therefore, may be said to have been adequate both in point of size and in the scale of operations."[1]

In favour of the experiment it may be said that the introduction of sugar beet into British farming has improved the soil. The sugar beet is "a biennial plant which develops its stores of sugar in the first year of growth, maturity being reached in about six months. It therefore takes a normal place in a crop rotation and is only one of several products of a farming system. . . . Beet sugar may . . . in a sense be regarded as a by-product rather than a primary product. It is, in fact, largely for its effect on soil fertility that the crop is grown in Europe."[2] Dr. J. A. Venn asserts that "In many respects advantage has been derived from the introduction of sugar beet into the farming economy of this country: more labour has been employed, other crops have benefited, certain by-products (in the shape of tops and pulp) have been rendered available, no serious displacement of the root-break has occurred, nor has the keeping of stock been affected, while the standard of farming has necessarily been maintained in circumstances that would otherwise have witnessed its deterioration . . . this crop has always been more profitable than any possible alternative."[3] Mr. C. S. Orwin's opinion is that "The expectations of the British Sugar (Subsidy) Act, 1925, were realized to the extent that experience in growing the crop has enabled farmers to reduce their production costs to meet the periodic fall in beet prices at the factories, consequent on the periodic fall in the rate of subsidy. They were falsified in that reductions in costs have not sufficed to enable the industry to meet world competition at the prevailing price of sugar."

The growing of sugar beet demands little additional farming capital and, undoubtedly, the insertion of a *cash* crop into the rotation has been a boon to many hard-pressed farmers and has

[1] Bridges and Dixey, *op. cit.*, 83.
[2] Ministry of Agriculture *Report on the Beet Sugar Industry at Home and Abroad* (No. 27, 1931), p. 4.
[3] Venn, *Foundations of Agricultural Economics* (2nd Edn. 1933), 526–7.

helped to stem the decline of arable farming in certain districts. It is difficult to say with any certainty how much of the subsidy has reached the growers. The Cambridge University Department of Agriculture estimated that about two-thirds of the subsidy payments had remained with the factories[1]; but in a recent Oxford University study the authors worked upon the tentative assumption "that 69 per cent of the subsidy is passed on to the farmer."[2] It seems clear, moreover, that increasing experience of beet-growing has brought increased efficiency and has enabled growers' costs to be reduced so that in spite of falling beet prices since 1926, the farmers' profits on the crop per acre and per ton have been maintained.[3]

Although it may be said that some additional employment has been provided by the beet sugar factories, and some decline of agricultural employment has been averted, it can hardly be disputed that this has been dearly bought by the community as a whole. As to the construction and equipment of the factories, a leading British firm of sugar machinery manufacturers, after an investigation involving an analysis of cost and labour sheets by all the contractors and sub-contractors concerned, found that the erection and equipment of a factory with a capacity of 1200 tons of beet per day would provide 393 man-years of employment for skilled labour and 446 man-years for unskilled labour, assuming a normal week.[4] On this basis it appears that the erection of sixteen British factories of an average capacity slightly exceeding 1200 tons, in the years 1925–8, must have provided employment for some 3500 skilled and unskilled workers in each of the four years upon the manufacture and fitting of machinery and the erection of the factories, including the flumes, road approaches, private sidings, and houses for the principal officers. This estimate does not include the manufacture of steel, plates,

---

[1] *Farm Economics Branch Report No. 9.*
[2] Bridges and Dixey, *op. cit.* Cf. the Greene Committee's figures, pp. 298–9 *post.*
[3] Bridges and Dixey, *op. cit.,* 64–5, 83.
[4] Ministry of Agriculture *Report on the Sugar Beet Industry at Home and Abroad,* 144–5.

rails, bricks, cement, etc. The numbers employed by the factories when in full operation rose from an average of 6930 in 1925–7 to 9000 in 1933. The net effects upon employment in agriculture and auxiliary transport (e.g. by rail and water) are very difficult to estimate, but, probably, a figure of 32,000–34,000 workers is not far wrong. It must be remembered, however, that the work is seasonal and by no means all these workers in the beet fields and factories are employed regularly all the year round. The length of the factories' "campaigns" averaged 104 working days in 1925–7, 91 in 1928–30, 64 in 1931, 80 in 1932, and 107 in 1933. For the quite moderate increase of employment here outlined the community paid during the decade 1925–34 at the rate of nearly £3,000,000 per annum in direct subsidy and approximately £965,000 per annum in revenue abatements.

Against the production of home-grown beet sugar it may be argued that Great Britain is not well-suited to the production of sugar. Not only is the yield of beet-sugar per acre very much less than the yield of cane-sugar per acre—for the sun is superior to the subsidy—but the continental yields of beet sugar are greater, in varying degrees, than British yields. Lord Astor contends that British conditions are "not generally suited to this root," and that contemporary improvements in sugar cane cultivation have made beet sugar competition impossible without the help of tariffs and subsidies. "Consequently in 1930–1 we paid £11 millions for home-grown sugar, the equivalent of which could have been imported for £4,703,000. . . ."[1]

The proportion of the subsidy which has reached the farming community is, as we have seen, indeterminate; but whatever it amounts to, it is clear that the benefit has been confined mainly to the large-scale farmers within the areas lying around the factories in the eastern and north-eastern counties. Sugarbeet is essentially a crop for high-yielding soils and large farms. The labour costs of cultivating sugar beet in small fields is much greater than in large fields, ranging from about £11 13s.

[1] *The Planning of Agriculture*, Introduction, XIII (*1933*).

per acre in fields of 5 acres or less, to £9 19s. in fields of over 15 acres; and there is no compensatory difference in crop-yield on the smaller fields.[1]

The farm units most suited to sugar beet are those upwards of 150 acres,[2] yet nearly 88 per cent of British farms are less than 150 acres in extent. "The small holder," says Mr. A. G. Street, "touches none of the Wheat Quota money, and precious little of the Beet Sugar Subsidy,"[3] and the fact is that the Subsidy Act of 1925 has, in effect, transferred well over £40,000,000 from the general body of taxpayers to a relatively small body of large farmers in the Eastern and South-eastern counties and to the (partly alien) owners of the beet sugar factories. The value of sugar beet sold off British farms is even now not more than one-tenth of the value of milk and dairy produce, and less than one-thirteenth of the value of sales of live stock (mainly for meat). Even the humble potato is more than twice as productive of income for the farmers of this country.

World sugar production has risen and prices have fallen tremendously since the British beet sugar subsidy was first voted in 1925. Cane sugar output has expanded surprisingly, largely as a result of successful scientific experiments in sugar cane breeding and cultivation. The price of raw sugar (foreign cane, 96° polarization, quoted C.I.F. United Kingdom) fell from 10s. a cwt. in 1929 to under 4s. a cwt. towards the end of 1934.[4] Of course, it may be pleaded that the advocates of the British beet sugar subsidy could not be expected to foresee such a slump, and that if prices had remained at or near the 1925 level all would have been well. The fact remains, however, that all is *not* well; and the Government has to decide what is to be done next.

There are at least six possible main lines of policy: (a) further

---

[1] R. M. Carslaw's figures, quoted by Astor and Murray, *The Planning of Agriculture* (1933), 6.
[2] Cambridge Department of Agriculture, Report No. 19, *An Economic Survey of Agriculture in the Eastern Counties of England* (1931).
[3] *The Highway*, December, 1933.
[4] *Manchester Guardian Commercial*, 23rd November, 1934, 404.

long-term State assistance, e.g. by subsidies paid to factories or growers, on a more or less lavish scale; or (b) a so-called "sugar-marketing" scheme, under which sugar refiners would receive monopoly powers to tax all consumers and subsidize the beet sugar factories out of the proceeds; or (c) temporary short-term State assistance, ending within, say, five years; or (d) no further State assistance after 1935; or (e) public control of the beet sugar industry as though it were a public utility; or (f) complete socialization of the whole British sugar manufacturing industry and its operation as a public utility under a Public Corporation.

Against further long-term State assistance of sugar production in this country the argument succinctly stated by Sir Arthur Salter in his Foreword to *The Planning of Agriculture* seems to be conclusive—

". . . if permanent State assistance is to be given, it is clearly better that it should encourage the production of those commodities for which we have a natural advantage. The main criterion is obvious. Food that is perishable, that suffers in quality by storage and long transport, has a natural advantage in being produced near its market. Fresh meat is better than chilled; new laid eggs are better than preserved, and so on. The natural field of development for Great Britain is clearly in live stock, dairying, poultry, fruit, flowers, and vegetables. In contrast, wheat and sugar, which are more economically produced in other lands or climates, which are cheaply transported and stored without deterioration . . . are the least suitable for expansion here at the consumer's cost. The choice of exactly these two commodities as the first to receive special help, at the consumers' expense, is a melancholy example of the folly of governments in response to pressure. . . ."[1]

A "sugar-marketing" scheme of the kind put forward by the sugar refiners in 1934, and strenuously opposed by the Co-operative Movement, would be a particularly pernicious grant of a statutory monopoly to certain private profit-making interests and a transformation of a straightforward subsidy

---

[1] Astor and Murray, *The Planning of Agriculture* (1933), pp. viii–ix; cf. a similar argument by the present writer in an article on the British Wheat Act, 1932, in *Quarterly Journal of Economics*, November, 1932.

raised by general taxation into a disguised and heavily regressive tax, politely called a "levy," upon consumers of sugar. Under this proposal, which bears certain striking and sinister resemblances to the existing ingenious, but economically indefensible, disguised taxation of breadstuffs, the British consumer is to be bound hand and foot and delivered over to the gluttonous monster of Private Monopoly. The audacity of this plan to give a legal monopoly of sugar refining to the twenty-two companies who were engaged in it in 1933 is, says *The Economist*, "really enough to take one's breath away. . . . To confer on private interests, with less than the shadow of public control, an absolute legal monopoly for producing an essential foodstuff is in itself an outrageous proposal. But to subsidize this monopoly out of the proceeds of a tax which must inevitably be paid largely by the poor, if indeed this is the Government's intention, would be nothing short of a national scandal of the first order."[1] In short, the scheme is such a transparent attempt to obtain legal power in order shamelessly to exploit the consumers of sugar that no government worthy of the name ought to give it a moment's consideration.

Putting aside for the moment the possibility of treating beet sugar production as a public utility, or of socializing the whole industry, we are left with a choice between temporary State assistance, and none at all. Probably the latter policy would be unreasonably drastic, in view of the fact that the industry has hitherto been heavily subsidized, though at a diminishing rate per cwt. of sugar produced; and it may well be urged that growers and factories, having so far made a good deal of technical progress, should be encouraged to go further in this direction while at the same time they prepare for a

---

[1] *The Economist*, 12th May, 1934, 1022, and 17th November, 1934, 917. It is not likely that the writers of the Ministry of Agriculture *Report on the Sugar Beet Industry* had in mind anything so monstrous when they suggested that since the concerns in Great Britain interested in white sugar production are relatively few, "a closer understanding between the refiners and the beet sugar factories on questions of sale and distribution of sugar, resulting in economies to both parties, should be possible" (p. 226).

total cessation of the subsidy at no very distant date—say not less than five and not more than ten years hence. For example, it would be feasible to continue the "tapering" of the subsidy, preferably by small annual decrements, so that zero could be reached at some prescribed time between 1941 and 1945.

Judging by previous experience the effects of such a decision would probably be an immediate sharp fall in the area under beet, followed by a considerable, if not complete, recovery in subsequent subsidy years. After the cessation of the subsidy a similar fluctuation would probably take place until the acreage under beet finally settled down to a smaller, but more economic figure. It is unlikely that the sugar beet would disappear from the countryside, for, as Dr. Venn points out, it has so abundantly proved its value upon certain soils and in particular localities, that it has become in those places a part of the normal rotation. Even at lower prices, farmers might be able to make further improvements and economies. "Many of the improvements are not yet (1934) complete and few of them have been adopted on a universal scale; others are still out of sight. Most of the farmers consulted in 1933 said they were 'still learning.' One went so far as to say, 'Ten years ago we knew all about it, but we are realizing that we are only now beginning to learn.'"[1] The relative prices of sugar beet and other crops or products which farmers can substitute would also be important, and so would the policy of the beet sugar factories. *Drastic* reduction of the prices paid to growers would hardly be wise, because it would result in a severe shrinkage of the beet acreage, which would cause a shortage of beets, a shorter campaign, and rising unit-costs, since factories would have to work much more below optimum capacity than they do at present. If they shut down certain factories and concentrated production in the others, the internal (factory) economies might be wholly or largely offset by increased transport costs. The factories would naturally strive to keep as much plant in operation as possible, and in

---

[1] Bridges and Dixey, *op. cit.*, 81.

the absence of a rise of world sugar prices it seems that they
would have to overcome the withdrawal of the subsidy wholly
or partly by acquiescing in lower rates of profit; and this the
majority could well afford to do.

Let us now turn to the report of the United Kingdom Sugar
Industry Inquiry Committee[1] (the "Greene Committee"),
published in 1935. The Committee, consisting of Mr. Wilfrid
Greene, K.C. (chairman), Sir Kenneth Lee, and Mr. Cyril Lloyd,
was appointed by the Chancellor of the Exchequer and the
Minister of Agriculture,

To inquire into the condition of the sugar industry in the United
Kingdom, including both home-grown beet sugar and imported
sugar and covering production, refining and distribution and,
having in mind the changes in the structure of the industry which
would follow upon its reorganization under the Agricultural
Marketing Acts, to make recommendations for its future conduct
and in particular as to the application of State aid in so far as this
may be considered necessary.

It appears, from the Committee's investigations, that a little
more than one-quarter of the total sugar consumed in the
United Kingdom has been produced in recent years from home-
grown beet; and for this the public have paid twice, first as
consumers of sugar and *again* as taxpayers. During the ten
years 1924–34, the industry cost the taxpayer £30,112,077 in
subsidy and £10,180,000 in abatement of excise duty, a total
cost of £40,292,077. The total income of the industry from sales
and subsidy was only £66,940,351. The price paid by the
factories for the beet purchased was £40,321,025—almost
exactly the same as the total of assistance, so that, in effect,
the factories received free raw material entirely at State
expense. After meeting manufacturing costs (£15,424,207) the
companies were left with a "trading margin" of £11,195,119,
sufficient to repay nearly 18½ per cent of their capital, to
accumulate net assets equal to about 27 per cent of the remaining capital, to write off approximately 42 per cent of their
expenditure on fixed assets and to pay gross dividends amounting to more than 83 per cent of the share capital outstanding.

[1] *Cmd.* 4871, 1935.

The Committee found that over the whole subsidy period the total factory receipts from sales and subsidy have been divided between farmers and factories in the ratio 3 : 2, but in the last subsidy period (1931–4) the farmers have received about two-thirds, and the factories one-third. Largely as a consequence of this assistance to farmers the arable acreage in the beet-growing areas has declined much less than the arable acreage in England and Wales as a whole, and there is no doubt that in areas within an economic distance of factories the maintenance of the arable area has been greatly assisted by the cultivation of sugar beet. Furthermore, the crops for which beet has been substituted are not only other fallow crops. The very substantial decline in the supply of home-grown fodder has been more than offset by the fodder provided as a by-product of the sugar-beet crop, for the numbers of cattle and sheep have increased. There is, therefore, no indication that the substitution of sugar beet for part, at least, of the normal fodder course in the rotation has had any marked effect on the stock-carrying capacity of farms.

The industry has provided a certain amount of additional agricultural and industrial employment, much of it seasonal in character. In 1934 the aggregate number of such additional workers was about 41,000. Reckoning the annual direct and indirect cost to the State at £7,300,000—which is the Committee's estimate for 1934–5—and ignoring incidental benefits to farmers and factory owners, it appears that the additional employment, whether seasonal or permanent, has been provided at an average cost of about £180 per head per annum.

After discussing at length the case for the continuance of assistance to the beet sugar industry, the possibilities of economies and the scope for reorganization in the industry, and after making suggestions for organization and assistance, the majority of the Committee were "forced to the conclusion, on the evidence presented to us, that the principal value of the industry is that of a relief measure. Stress was laid by nearly all the witnesses who spoke for agriculture on the effect the industry had had in helping farmers in a period of depression, in supplying a cash crop when cash was urgently needed and in maintaining in cultivation land which might otherwise have been abandoned. It is impossible to deny that the assistance given to the industry has resulted in considerable relief to a large number of farmers. Nevertheless, after giving due consideration to the evidence of witnesses in favour of the opposite view, we have come to the conclusion that it has not proved satisfactory as a relief measure."

The majority accordingly recommended the discontinuance of the subsidy, subject to the grant of special interim assistance to help farmers over the transitional period until they have been able to find alternative crops. Occupiers of all farms now growing beet would receive compensation, based on their acreage on the average of the years 1933–5 inclusive, for a period of three years at a tapering rate. The report suggested rates of £3 an acre in the first year, £2 in the second year, and £1 in the third year.

The Committee recognized that these recommendations might not be accepted, and that the Government might decide to continue to assist the industry. In that event, the Committee recommended that a small body of Sugar Commissioners, independent of the industry, should be appointed by the Government, charged specifically "with the duty of considering not only the interest of the sugar industry, but the national interests generally, including the interests of the consumer." The existing factories should be unified in a single Factory Corporation. The price of beet would be negotiated between the Factory Corporation and the Sugar Beet Marketing Board (if such a Board, already proposed by the National Farmers' Union, is set up) and fixed by the Sugar Commission in case of disagreement. The Commission should also fix the rate of assistance, taking into account the cost of beet, fixed charges, depreciation, interest on working capital and a certain "processing margin." The "processing margin" should cover the costs of manufacture and distribution and a margin of profit. It was recommended that in calculating profit "no allowance should be included for goodwill, and a relatively low rate of interest should be allowed on the physical value of the assets, which should be calculated at substantially written-down values." The Committee also urged that assistance should continue to be paid out of the Budget and not out of a levy on the consumption of sugar.

The report was not unanimous. In his minority report, Mr. Cyril Lloyd sets out at some length his reasons for dissenting from his colleagues' views on many points and makes the following recommendations—

That provision should be made for the support, for a further long-term period, of the British beet sugar industry at approximately its present size: that the assistance required should, as far as possible, be provided by the remission of the Excise duty on home-produced sugar and that any further marginal assistance that may be necessary should be provided by means of a fractional levy on all sugar in a manner similar to that adopted in the Wheat Act, 1932; that the growers of sugar beet should be organized under the Agricultural Marketing Acts as contemplated in the Scheme now before the Minister of Agriculture, with possible modifications that the manufacturers of sugar from home grown beet should be required to unify their interests in a single corporation: that a permanent Sugar Commission should be set up to exercise surveillance over the sugar industry as a whole: that the Sugar Commission should have regard to the interests of the sugar industry, and should exercise its powers and functions in such a manner as to secure the maximum efficiency of that industry: that the scale of future assistance for the beet sugar industry should be calculated on the basis of factory performance and related to the price of sugar, leaving a working margin to the discretion of the Sugar Commission: that the fiscal scale applied to sugars of varying degrees of polarization should be revised so as to remove the existing discrimination against the production of white sugar by the beet sugar factories: that the calculation of the rate of assistance should be on the basis of the minimum beet price, which each year is estimated to be necessary to secure the desired acreage of sugar-beet; and that the production and sale of refined sugar should be regulated by a modified industrial agreement, to be approved by the Sugar Commission.

The National Government were unwilling, for agricultural and political reasons, to drop the beet sugar subsidy, so they adopted the alternative scheme outlined by the Greene

Committee, and decided to amalgamate the fifteen beet sugar companies into a single corporation[1] and to continue the subsidy on a basis limited to 560,000 tons of white sugar annually for a "transitional period" of five years, upon a diminishing scale determined by reference to the world price of sugar, the price of beet, and certain other factors. After the first five years the basis of State assistance is to be reviewed triennially. An independent Sugar Commission, consisting of a chairman and not more than four other commissioners, none of whom may be members of Parliament or financially interested in sugar, will supervise the working of the scheme, control the sugar beet acreage, and try in general to implement the Government's policy. It is estimated that henceforth the total subsidy payments from the Exchequer will be somewhat less than in the past, and that the amalgamation of the factories will also yield economies. Obviously much depends upon the capital values at which the various companies, plants and other property are brought into the accounts of the new Corporation, and upon the rates of amortization and net profits allowed by the Sugar Commission. The Chairman and two members of the board of the Sugar Corporation are appointed by the Government, and any benefits secured by the reduction of manufacturing costs will be shared between the Corporation and the Treasury. Sharing with the consumers through reductions of prices is, apparently, not contemplated. Taking the scheme by and large, it seems likely to be better than the worst, but worse than the best that might be done, given more vision and vigour on the part of the Government and less tenderness for private vested interests.

(iii) Oil from Coal

The extraction of motor spirit and "Diesel oil" from indigenous bituminous coal is one of the newest of Britain's new industries. All technical processes for obtaining oil from

---

[1] Since incorporated as the "British Sugar Corporation Ltd" with a nominal capital of £5,000,000.

coal are based upon the application of heat, and the degree of success depends largely upon the nature of the raw coal used, the temperature to which it is raised, the period of heating, the air-pressure, and the methods adopted for removing the products of distillation from the residues. Three oil products are important—motor spirit, Diesel oils, and fuel oils for steam raising purposes; and it is fortunate that many kinds of British bituminous coals are very suitable for the new oil-extraction processes. Since Great Britain, as a great industrial country, has an expanding demand for liquid fuels but no natural supplies of oil, the importance of this new industry in the near future will no doubt be considerable.

Public interest in the possibility of extracting oil fuel from British coal dates back to the Royal Commission on Fuel and Engines for the Navy which sat during 1912–13 and had before it (*inter alia*) a report on the "possibility of a development of a new carbonizing industry, founded on the distillation of bituminous coal at a temperature much below that used in gas retorts or coke ovens."[1] The oil shortage during the war years emphasized the importance of developing, if possible, home sources of fuel oil suitable for use by the Navy and Mercantile marine. A scheme of research into low temperature carbonization to be carried through by the Fuel Research Board was formulated in 1917.[2] Low temperature carbonization was subsequently defined as "the destructive distillation of coal at temperatures round about 600° C.—the main object being to obtain oil fuel and motor spirit together with a solid smokeless fuel that can be burnt in any domestic grate."[3]

Private enterprise also entered the field. A private company called Low Temperature Carbonization Ltd., was registered in May, 1917, and converted into a public company two years later. In 1927 this company opened a new plant at Barugh, near Barnsley, with a capacity of about 1000 tons of coke a

[1] Fuel Research Board, *Annual Report*, 1918–19, 6.
[2] Fuel Research Board, *Annual Report*, 1920–1, Second Section, (1922), 7 ff. The Royal Commission on the Coal Industry (1925) emphasized the importance of perfecting methods of obtaining liquid fuel from British Coal. *Report* (*Cmd.* 2600, 1926) 24–7.
[3] Fuel Research Board, *Annual Report*, 1924, 34 ff.

week. Within the next few years it acquired control of Gas &
Fuel Plants, Ltd., Doncaster Coalite Ltd., and London Coalite
Ltd. The issued capital of Low Temperature Carbonization
Ltd. is £1,275,000, and there is also some £273,000 of
debenture capital.[1] Other companies were formed and by
1929 over £5,000,000 of capital was in course of being
invested in plants for the development of some twenty-six
different low-temperature processes. The majority of these
companies have not yet passed the experimental stage, and
their output is negligible. Also there is a trade association
called the Low Temperature Coal Distillers' Association, which
(inter alia) keeps in touch with research progress and results.

Unfortunately for the pioneers in this field, prices of tar,
coke and imported oil fuels have fallen so much that reduced
costs due to technical progress have been largely cancelled out
by reduced sales revenues. The disposal of the other saleable
product, gas, depends mainly upon local industrial demand. If
the gas it to be sold to a gas undertaking its value cannot
exceed the gas-works cost of producing gas in the ordinary
manner. If it cannot be sold in this way, its value is unlikely
to exceed the cost of the cheapest alternative fuel suitable for
the same purpose. "The difficulties are mainly economic and
the root difficulty is that each single product of the process
competes directly with a material already in the market."[2]
This competition between substitutes forces prices down, quite
apart from the general downward trend due to other causes.
In face of these drawbacks the 1934 Report of Low Temperature Carbonization Ltd., struck a hopeful note. Profits on
trading account, including interest and dividends from the
subsidiary company, Doncaster Coalite Ltd., amounted to
£87,286, an increase of £26,466 over the previous year. After
writing off sundry items and paying debenture interest, the
company was able to pay 3 per cent (less tax) on the whole of
its ordinary share capital of £1,200,334, including £300,000
issued during 1934. The company's new extensions and works

---

[1] *Stock Exchange Year Book, 1936.*
[2] Fuel Research Board, *Annual Report to 31st March, 1931,* 38.

had raised total capacity from 220,000 to 560,000 tons of coal
per annum. The demand for coalite was increasing "at a most
satisfactory rate" and Doncaster Coalite Ltd. had been able
to contribute over £46,500 to the aggregate profits for the year.
The chairman and managing director (Col. W. A. Bristow) also
stated that—

There is a new factor which is having a most beneficial effect
upon the fortunes of the company, and that is the increasing use
of oil in almost every branch of engineering. When the late Mr.
Thomas Parker took out his first patent for low temperature
carbonization, coal was pre-eminent as a source of power. Since
that time the advance of the internal combustion engine using
heavy oil, and the use of oil for steam raising, has revolutionized
engineering practice, and the change-over from coal to oil continues to-day on an extensive scale.

Nor is this all, as since the commencement of the late war the
whole of the defence of this country, and the British Empire in
general, have become dependent upon the supply of immense
quantities of imported petrol and oil. The first line of defence, the
Royal Air Force, must remain immobile without petrol, the Navy
is in the same plight without fuel oil, and the Army is also largely
dependent upon oil for its major operations. . . .

We have for the first time in history produced from coal
aviation petrol and naval fuel oil. Nine home defence squadrons
of the Royal Air Force have been running on coal petrol made by
this company and refined and distributed by Messrs. Carless Capel
and Leonard. At the last Air Force Pageant over eighty of our
finest fighting machines were flying on our coal petrol. In
addition to the fuel oil supplied to the Navy, large quantities have
been used by railways and important industrial undertakings, and
the foundations of this new industry have been well and truly laid.

More recently, Low Temperature Carbonization Ltd. has made
a long-term agreement with Imperial Chemical Industries for
the supply of coal-oil to Billingham for treatment by hydrogenation, and has also formed another subsidiary company to
operate a new plant adjacent to, and in co-operation with, the
Bolsover Colliery, Derbyshire.

The quantity of tar obtained by the low temperature carbonization process (i.e. at temperatures around 600° C.) is
about 20 gallons per ton of coal, against approximately 11

gallons obtained at high temperatures. Moreover, the gas obtained by low temperature carbonization has higher calorific values than that obtained at high temperatures.

Oil can be recovered from the tar and gas by "scrubbing" or "stripping" the gas and distilling the tar, just as benzol is obtained from gas and tar derived from high temperature carbonization of coal. It has been proved that after refining, the product is a motor spirit superior to petrol.[1]

From 55 to 75 per cent of the coal carbonized comes out in the form of coke (now generally called "coalite"), which differs from gas coke because it is more easily ignitable and burns more freely in ordinary domestic grates. "The great advantage (says Dr. Lander) is its smokelessness combined with its free burning properties. There is no doubt that the smoke produced from domestic chimneys causes much damage and expense, but the amount of this is not easily evaluated in terms of £.s.d. A conservative estimate is that the damage amounts to 10s. per ton of coal burned for domestic purposes: some estimates are far higher than this. Could this 10s. per ton be included in the balance sheet there is little doubt that the production of free-burning cokes would soon become a flourishing industry and the benefits to the country would be considerable. The benefits to the mining industry would not, however, be so great as is sometimes claimed. More coal would have to be mined, which would be an advantage, but the demand for household coal would be diminished, and this is the coal which fetches the highest prices."[2]

Low-temperature coke or "coalite" is unsuitable for industrial use, but it has much besides easy ignition and smokelessness to commend it as a domestic fuel. It is cleaner to handle, is lighter bulk for bulk than coal, and its radiant efficiency is 25 per cent greater than that of coal. On the other hand although it glows cheerfully enough, it does not produce flames; and a ton of it takes up more room, and is dearer than

---

[1] *Fuel Research Board Technical Paper No. 34; Light Spirits from the Low Temperature Carbonization of Coal*, by D. Hicks and J. G. King (1931). Cf. also I. Thomas, *Coal in the New Era*, 1934, 78.

[2] Fuel Research Board Annual Report to 31st March, 1931, 39.

a ton of coal, although, since it radiates more heat, it is really slightly cheaper than coal. But as domestic consumers look at the relative prices in £.s.d. and not at relative radiant efficiencies, it will probably be necessary to reduce the price of coalite below that of house coal in order to sell it in large quantities, especially in face of the existing deep-rooted British preference for open coal fires. It has been suggested, quite reasonably, that the domestic burning of bituminous coal should be made illegal, at least in our large cities and towns. This would greatly extend the market for smokeless fuels such as "coalite" and anthracite, and would be of the greatest assistance to the low temperature carbonization companies; but safeguards would have to be devised against any anti-social exploitation by the companies of the position so created. No net decrease in the demand for coal would be likely to result from such a measure; indeed Mr. Ivor Thomas argues very convincingly that demand would increase, and that "if 45 million tons of coal were carbonized, it should . . . be possible to recover 135 million gallons of oil by conventional methods, and 1000 million gallons with hydrogenation. Our total oil imports in 1933 were 2066 million gallons, and towards that 1000 million gallons would be an enormous contribution."[1]

Another method of obtaining oil from coal, destined in all probability to become more important than low temperature carbonization, is known as hydrogenation. Apparently the earliest experiments in the hydrogenation of coal were made in 1868 by Marcelin Berthelot, who obtained a liquid product equal to about 60 per cent of the original weight of the coal by treating the coal with a saturated solution of hydriodic acid at a temperature of 270° C. in sealed glass tubes. But no further important developments occurred until Dr. Bergius began his remarkable researches in 1910. He began by producing synthetic or "artificial" coal, and then by adding hydrogen under pressure he found that liquids of lower carbon/hydrogen ratio (i.e. similar to petroleum oil) were the result. The next step was to apply hydrogen under pressure to natural coal, and this

---

[1] *Coal in the New Era*, 92.

was done with such similar and satisfactory results that Dr. Bergius took out his first patents in 1913, and his first British patent (No. 4574) in 1914.[1] Other pioneer workers in the same field were Dafert, Miklanz, Fischer, Tropsch, Kling, Florentin, Waterman, Hlavica, Varga, Graham, the British Fuel Research Station and the research staff of Synthetic Ammonia Nitrates, Ltd., a subsidiary company of Imperial Chemical Industries, Ltd., who have spent over £1,000,000 upon their investigations.[2]

Dr. Bergius's hydrogenation process consists of mixing suitable bituminous washed and powdered coal into a stiff paste with approximately its own weight of heavy oil or tar produced in a previous operation in the same plant, adding a little iron oxide, and submitting the mixture to the action of hydrogen at temperatures ranging from 350° to 520° C. and pressures varying from 150 to 250 atmospheres.[3]

An option on the rights in this process for the British Empire was secured by the British Bergius Syndicate, and later an agreement was made between this syndicate, the Department of Scientific and Industrial Research, the International Bergius Company and Dr. Bergius, under which experiments were carried out in 1926 at Mannheim-Rheinan under the control of a joint committee of the parties, to test the suitability of the process for the treatment of British bituminous coals. The report of the British Director of Fuel Research for the year 1926, stated that—

The results show conclusively that such British coals as have been examined are suitable for the treatment, and that by this means it is possible to obtain from the coal a far greater proportion of liquid fuel than by any other method at present known. The yields so far obtained from typical bituminous coals are somewhat as follows: crude oil and spirit, 50 to 60 per cent; gas, 20 per cent; partially converted organic matter, 15 per cent; and the remainder water and inorganic matter. This compares with, say,

---

[1] Fuel Research Board, *Annual Report to 31/3/1930*, Appendix V.
[2] I. Thomas, *Coal in the New Era (1934)*, 94–5.
[3] Ormandy and Burns, "Oil from Coal," *Journal of the Institute of Fuel*, December, 1933, 73.

10 per cent, or less, oil-producing tar, which is the most obtainable from similar coals by low temperature carbonization.[1]

The work under the joint committee was discontinued, by mutual agreement, at the end of May, 1927.

During 1927–8 an experimental Bergius plant was working at the Fuel Research Station and obtaining at least six times as much oil as could be obtained by carbonization methods. But the cost was estimated to be much above the current prices for imported oils. Meantime, Imperial Chemical Industries, Ltd., had obtained a controlling interest in the British Bergius Syndicate[2] and had begun to experiment at their own works.

In the opinion of the Director of Fuel Research, Imperial Chemical Industries were extremely well-placed for developing the process, because it "is essential from a commercial point of view that all the products of the process should be utilized to the best advantage, and it seems quite possible that the most economical way of getting the necessary hydrogen and utilizing the gas produced by the process, is to combine the plant with coke-oven plant, and with the manufacture of synthetic ammonia, and possibly with low temperature carbonization plant."[3]

At the end of 1933, Drs. Horton, King and Williams stated that "it is now well known that suitable coals, when treated with hydrogen under pressure, can be converted into a tarry liquid to the extent of 65 per cent or more by weight. By further treatment of this product an overall yield of motor spirit amounting to as much as 165 gallons of spirit per ton of coal substance can be obtained.[4] It is calculated that about $1\frac{2}{3}$ tons of specially selected coal have to be used to obtain 1 ton of liquid products of a petrol nature. Additional coal is

[1] Fuel Research Board, *Annual Report, 1926*, 34; cf. Ormandy in *Journal of the Institute of Fuel*, October, 1931, 61 ff.

[2] *The Times Trade Supplement*, 12th August, 1933—Art. by T. L. Gilmour. The world rights are held by International Hydrogenation Patents Ltd., formed in 1930 at the Hague by agreement between Imperial Chemical Industries, Shell Mex. Co., the Standard Oil Co. and I. G. Farbenindustrie.

[3] Fuel Research Board, *Annual Report to 31st March, 1928*, 40.

[4] *Journal of the Institute of Fuel*, December, 1933, 85.

required to provide the power for drying, grinding, and mixing the powdered coal and heavy oil, for pumping the raw materials into the plant, and for the production of the large quantities of hydrogen used in this process. The total coal necessary for all purposes is between 3 and 4 tons per ton of motor fuel produced. Drs. Ormandy and Burns, taking a middle figure of $3\frac{1}{2}$ tons of coal at an average price of 12s. 6d. per ton delivered to the works, show that "this raw material alone costs £2 3s. 9d. per ton of petrol produced," and assuming 300 gallons of petrol to the ton, "the raw material costs alone amount to $1\frac{3}{4}$d. per gallon. If the process be run for the production of fuel oils, the raw material costs per gallon of oil produced will only be slightly less than in the case of petrol.[1] . . . It has been widely stated that the hydrogenation of coal can only be carried out on a very large scale."[2]

The hydrogenation process can be applied to tar as well as coal. By hydrogenation of tar, the whole of the tar treated can be converted into hydrocarbon oils. Thus, from one ton of coal treated by the low temperature carbonization process 20 gallons of tar (as well as gas, coke, etc.) result, and by hydrogenation of the tar about 14 gallons of motor spirit and 6 gallons of Diesel oil can be produced. Or if treated by a "hydrogenation-cracking" process the tar will produce its own volume of excellent motor spirit; pitch and tar acids being entirely eliminated.[3]

Economically the hydrogenation process stands in sharp contrast at several points to the low temperature carbonization process. As we have seen, the main product of the latter process is not oil, but coalite; and the liquids are by-products which cannot be "made to pay" unless the coalite and gas can be sold to advantage against the competition of raw coal. The products of the hydrogenation process, on the other hand, do not afterwards come into competition with coal (as, for example, does the coalite produced by low temperature

---

[1] Imported petrol could be bought (1935) from store at British ports at $3\frac{1}{4}$d. per gallon.
[2] *Journal of the Fuel Institute*, December, 1933, 74.
[3] Fuel Research Board, *Annual Report to 31st March, 1933*, 59, 76 ff.

carbonization). The oil is the *main* product, and the only by-product not utilized in the process itself is ammoniacal liquor, which is readily convertible into fertilizers. The hydrocarbon gases can be used to make hydrogen; the heavy oil is mixed with the coal to reduce it to paste; and the solid residue is used as boiler fuel. The by-product fertilizers are not difficult to sell and the demand for the main product is constantly expanding. It is estimated that 106 tons of coal and 11 tons of hydrogen will give, on the average, 62 tons of motor spirit, 14 tons of ammoniacal liquor, 29 tons of hydrocarbon gases and 6 tons of solid residue. The operating cost of making motor spirit in Great Britain by hydrogenation of coal fell in the eight years 1926–34 from 2s. 6d. to 7d. a gallon; and it will probably be brought still lower as production on a commercial scale expands.

The capital cost of establishing a low-temperature carbonization plant is estimated to be not more than £1 per ton of annual coal-capacity; whereas a hydrogenation plant of similar coal-capacity would cost, probably, ten times as much to construct. Mr. Ivor Thomas puts the same point in another way when he compares the effects of a capital expenditure of £4,000,000 on (a) a low temperature plant; and (b) a hydrogenation plant. His estimates are—

EFFECT OF £4,000,000 CAPITAL EXPENDITURE

(a) *Low Temperature Carbonization Plant*

Annual demand for coal	4,000,000 tons
Miners put into employment . . .	16,000
Annual value of products—	£
Smokeless fuel—3,000,000 tons @ £1 .	. 3,000,000
Oil—60,000,000 gal. @ 2d. . . .	. 500,000
Petrol—10,000,000 gal. @ 1s. . .	. 500,000
Gas—120 million therms @ 3d. . .	. 1,500,000
Total	£5,500,000

(b) *Hydrogenation Plant*

Annual demand for coal	365,000 tons
Miners put into employment	1,500
Annual value of products—	£
Petrol—30,000,000 gal. @ 1s. . .	. 1,500,000
Ammoniacal liquor	uncertain

All these values are ex-works, and rest upon the assumption that a ready market could be found for the various products. If not, the apparent financial superiority of the low temperature process would be much less marked. Mr. Thomas urges that the two processes should be regarded as complementary, not as rivals, and outlines two interesting alternative schemes, prepared for the South Wales and Monmouthshire Development Council, which suggest that ten low temperature plants of 1000 tons daily capacity and one central hydrogenation plant should be erected in the South Wales coal-field. Under Scheme A the hydrogenation of coal would be direct: under Scheme B the hydrogenation plant would deal only with the tar oils produced by the low temperature plants. It is estimated that Scheme A would involve a capital expenditure of between £6,728,000 and £8,100,000: the combined plants would use over 4,000,000 tons of coal annually, and the annual value of the products—petrol, fuel, oil, pitch, gas and smokeless fuel—would probably be between £5,000,000 and £5,500,000. Interest on capital would absorb from £350,000 to £400,000, according to the actual cost of the plants, and the estimated net surplus after charging wages and all other costs might be between £900,000 and £1,000,000 per annum. Under Scheme B the estimated capital expenditure would be some £2,000,000 less, which would reduce the interest charge by approximately £100,000; while the estimated cost of converting tar oil into motor spirit is 4d. a gallon, against 5d. a gallon for direct hydrogenation of coal.[1]

So far hydrogenation is at an even earlier stage of industrial and commercial development than low temperature carbonization. By the end of 1931 Imperial Chemical Industries Ltd. were operating a Bergius hydrogenation plant, but it dealt with only the small amount of 10–15 tons of coal a day, and the

[1] I. Thomas, *op. cit.*, 111–14. The Germans are preparing to spend between £8,000,000 and £20,000,000 on new Bergius process hydrogenation plants in the near future, with the object of obtaining ultimately an annual output of some 255 million gallons of motor spirit from coal. Their present imports of motor spirit are about 300 million gallons. See *Political Quarterly*, January–March 1935, 40.

costs of the resulting motor spirit and fuel oil were much above the current import prices of petrol and heavy oils.[1]

Less than two years later, encouraged by the results of their own experimental work and that of the concerns with which they are linked in Germany and America,[2] together with the British Government's promise of assistance, as embodied in the British Hydrocarbon Oils Production Act, 1934, Imperial Chemical Industries embarked upon the construction of a new hydrogenation plant costing £3,000,000, and designed to produce some 150,000 tons (or 45 million gallons) of petrol per annum,[3] two-thirds direct from coal and one-third from tar oils. Production began eighteen months after the authorization of the scheme, and the first consignment of 300,000 gallons, equal in quality to No. 1 grade petrol, was ready for marketing (through the Shell-Mex, B.P. and Anglo-American Oil Companies) on 10th April, 1935. The Billingham plant, when in full operation, will directly employ not less than 1000 workers itself, and some 1500 coal miners. At this rate a sufficient number of hydrogenation plants to supply the present motor spirit consumption of this country would give employment to about 70,000 people, three-fifths of whom would be coal miners. Technical progress might, of course, somewhat reduce this potential demand for labour.

The British Hydrocarbon Oils Production Act *guarantees* that there shall be a "preference" (i.e. difference between the import duty and the excise duty (if any) on "light hydrocarbon oils manufactured in the U.K. from coal, shale, or peat indigenous to the U.K. or from products from those substances," of, or not less than fourpence a gallon for nine years. Thus, from 1st April, 1935, the preference given to home-produced light oils may be 4d. a gallon for 9 years, or 6d. a

[1] Fuel Research Board, *Annual Report to 31st March, 1932*, 52.
[2] On the international connexions of Imperial Chemical Industries, see Plummer, *International Combines in Modern Industry* (1934), pp. 33, 49–52, 85, 117.
[3] Report of 8th Ordinary General Meeting of Imperial Chemical Industries Ltd., in *The Economist*, 4th May, 1935, 1043. About 1100 million gallons of petrol per annum are used for all purposes in Great Britain, plus approximately 130 million gallons of fuel oil.

gallon for 6 years, or 8d. a gallon for $4\frac{1}{2}$ years, or any other
arrangement provided that the total preference totals not less
than 36 pence–years. This will give Chancellors of the Exchequer greater latitude when dealing with the "petrol taxes"
from year to year as part of their general budgetary plans.[1]

Besides stimulating the activities of Imperial Chemical
Industries at Billingham, the Act has given a fillip to the
leading low-temperature carbonization companies, such as
Low-Temperature Carbonization Ltd., Shellite Ltd., National
Coke and Oil Co. Ltd., and Motor Fuel Proprietary Ltd.

Mr. Ivor Thomas asserts that the "production of oil from
coal has much sounder arguments behind it in Great Britain
than elsewhere in the world. For coal is our chief natural
source of wealth, and production of oil therefrom is virtually
economic or may be expected to become so in the not distant
future."[2] At present, taking one year with another, we produce
at home only about one-tenth of our total consumption of
motor spirit. As we have seen, the cost of making motor spirit
by hydrogenation of coal is approximately 7d. a gallon. In
1935 the price of imported petrol *ex* store at Thamesmouth
was abnormally low at about $3\frac{1}{4}$d. a gallon, against $6\frac{1}{2}$d. a
gallon in 1930. It is clear, therefore, that a tax-preference of
4d. a gallon in favour of home producers just bridged the
gap at that time. Any subsequent rise of the price of imported
petrol and/or any reduction in the costs of the hydrogenation
process will obviously increase the advantage and improve
the prospects of the home industry.

Looking to the future it is reasonable to anticipate the
erection of hydrogenation plants, and perhaps low temperature
carbonization plants working in co-operation by supplying
tar to the hydrogenation plants,[3] in every coal-field where the

---

[1] If and when home-produced motor spirit begins to displace imported
spirit some decrease of revenue from the customs duties on hydrocarbon
oils may occur; but this will be considerably offset by the saving of the
unemployment pay of the workers directly and indirectly put into
employment by the new industry.

[2] *Political Quarterly*, January–March, 1935, 47–8.

[3] Such an arrangement was made between Imperial Chemical Industries (Billingham plant) and Low Temperature Carbonization Ltd.
in 1935.

coal is suitable. Such a development, if it could be pressed forward rapidly on a large scale, would bring some measure of relief to the miners and other industrial workers of Durham, Cumberland, Lancashire, Scotland, and South Wales.[1]

At to-day's prices, the capital cost of hydrogenation plants (including the manufacture of the necessary quantities of hydrogen) with sufficient output capacity to supply our existing home demand for motor fuel would be in the neighbourhood of £135 millions. This large sum could be raised most cheaply and certainly under a Government guarantee. Since the total British demand for motor fuels is expanding and seems likely to continue to expand, there is little likelihood that a serious and immediate economic problem would arise owing to displacement of imported oil fuels by those of British manufacture. Probably the *net* displacement, when it begins, will be very gradual indeed.

Furthermore, so long as war remains a possibility, the importance to this country of home production of oil fuels for the Air Force, Navy, Army, and Mercantile Marine cannot be ignored. A large number of low temperature and hydrogenation plants should be erected as soon as possible in South Wales, Cumberland, Lancashire, and South-west Scotland, where they would be least vulnerable to aerial attacks.

(iv) FILMS AND CINEMAS

I

Some sixty years ago that versatile inventor, Edison, was at work upon the "kinetoscope," a machine which pro-

---

[1] In West Cumberland the coal is entirely suitable for either hydrogenation or low temperature carbonization, while the local rates are not heavy and there is not an excessive debt burden. From South Wales it has been recently reported that both the coal-owners and the miners' leaders are not enthusiastic about the low temperature carbonization process "because the residual smokeless fuel . . . would compete with natural coal." They hold that hydrogenation would be the best system, but the coal-owners would rather collaborate with Imperial Chemical Industries than establish a plant of their own. Both miners and owners agree that "a Billingham" is needed in South Wales. *Reports of Investigations into the Industrial Conditions in certain Depressed Areas* (*Cmd.* 4728, 1934), 18, 19, 153–4. Cf. also Board of Trade *Industrial Survey of South Wales* (1932), 47.

jected short lengths of celluloid films in such a way as to make
a number of photographed pictures appear to the eye as one
moving image. But the kinetoscope's most serious drawback
was that only one person at a time could see the moving picture. "This limitation," says Mr. Andrew Buchanan, "enabled
the now despised magic lantern to have a last laugh, for it
could at least offer its lifeless views to a vast audience, whereas
its flickering rival could present its magic to one only."[1] At
the end of the 'eighties, however, this serious difficulty had
been overcome by the genius and persistence of Friese-Greene
and Lumière, and improved kinetoscopes were made with
greater powers of projection, capable of showing short moving
pictures on fairly large screens to numbers of people simultaneously. Early in the present century it became possible to
show films, some 1000 feet in length, for about fifteen minutes.

And so, in disused assembly rooms, institutes, barns and other
uninviting places, people would gather together excitedly to
witness the most amazing entertainment of all time. These performances were frequently punctuated by breaks in the films,
which plunged audiences into darkness, sometimes for minutes,
sometimes for ever.

Most of the early productions were of a sensational character—
murderous cowboys galloping up and down dusty streets for no
apparent reason; express trains almost leaping from the screens;
"comic" husbands throwing crockery at astonishing wives who
were made up like circus clowns. The settings, or scenes, were
extremely small, and usually consisted of painted back cloths, as
used on the legitimate stage. The first "stories" . . . possessed no
story, containing neither continuity nor logic. . . . Yet they are
not to be ridiculed for they laid the foundations of the Film Story.[2]

The pioneers, finding that the moving-picture business was
very profitable, built more studios and cinemas; films increased in length, and improved in technical and dramatic
quality. In short, the film industry in Europe (including Great
Britain)[3] and America was just entering upon its second phase

---

[1] Buchanan, *Films, The Way of the Cinema* (1932), 5.
[2] *Ibid.*, 6–7.
[3] The first British film studio was established at Freeman's Cricket
Field, Champion Hill in 1898. See Schonfield (ed.), *The Book of British
Industries* (1933), 151. In 1914 about a quarter of the films shown in
Britain were of British make.

when war broke out in 1914. The chaos created by the war held up production and development in Europe and gave America a great opportunity of securing a virtual monopoly throughout the film world. The Americans, quick to seize their chance, rapidly increased their production of films, in spite of all obstacles, and distributed a veritable deluge of pictures, good, bad and indifferent, to all parts of the globe. In Great Britain, our handful of producing companies saved themselves from ruin and turned losses into profits by buying and renting large quantities of American films. For a time the film and cinema industry in Great Britain and elsewhere became Americanized. ". . . America dominated the world market. In the principal European countries she had interests in producing companies, controlled theatres, and had her own agencies for distribution. . . . Hollywood was soon selling a year's production in advance before the films were made."[1]

During the years immediately following the war "European production began again. Germany made films in 1922–5 which are to the cinema of to-day what the plays of Ibsen are to modern drama—*Vaudeville, Warning Shadows, Metropolis.* But the hold of American money dominated not only production at Hollywood, but the distribution and exhibition of films in countries which were themselves producing films of national significance."[2] The British film industry sank deeper and deeper into depression, until by 1926–7, the position had become so serious that a life-or-death decision could no longer be delayed. Either the British film industry must be finally abandoned and forgotten, or some drastic method of reviving it must be immediately adopted. The die was cast for the latter course, and the Cinematograph Films Act, 1927, was rapidly put upon the Statute Book.[3]

The chief object of the Act was to assure to British films a safe, if limited, market, and so to foster and encourage the

---

[1] *The Film in National Life, being the Report of an inquiry . . . by the Commission on Education and Cultural Films* (1932), 46.

[2] A. C. Cameron in *The Common Room,* June 1935, p. 3.

[3] Import duties were imposed upon cinematograph films in 1915, but the object was to restrict non-essential imports in wartime, not to stimulate the growth of a British film industry.

British film industry. The Act (Section 6) requires the Board of Trade to keep a register of films, differentiating between British and foreign films; and to publish weekly lists (in the *Board of Trade Journal*) of all films so registered. A "British Film," within the meaning of the Act, is a film made by a British subject or company in a studio within the British Empire from a scenario written by a British subject. Any film which does not *fully* satisfy these conditions is classified and registered as "foreign." Subject to certain discretionary powers vested in the Board of Trade under Section 27 of the Act, 75 per cent of the salaries and wages bill must be paid to British subjects, exclusive of the remuneration of one foreign actor or producer. Every renter must acquire, and every exhibitor must show, during normal hours and in the ordinary programme a prescribed quota of such British films.

The statutory quota of British films, measured by the ratio between the length of British films and the length of foreign films rented and exhibited, rises as follows—

	Renters' Quota per cent	Exhibitors' Quota per cent
1929	$7\frac{1}{2}$	5
1930–1	10	$7\frac{1}{2}$
1932	$12\frac{1}{2}$	10
1933	15	$12\frac{1}{2}$
1934 and 1935 .	$17\frac{1}{2}$	15
1936–8 (inc.) . . .	20	20

In order to ascertain the proportion of British films exhibited, the length of the films in feet is multiplied by the number of times they are exhibited during normal hours.[1] The penalties for failure to comply with these quota provisions range from a fine of £50 up to a fine of £500 plus revocation of the renters' or exhibitors' licence "if the offence is a third offence."

The Act prohibits "blind" booking, i.e. the booking of films before registration has been effected or validly applied for. "Block" booking is also made illegal. Before 1927, "a producer might announce a series of, say, six films to be made

[1] G. Alchin, *Manual of Law for the Cinema Trade* (1934), 101.

by Mr. X and to feature the star, Miss A. One film would be made and shown to the trade, and the exhibitors would be required to book the block of six, five of which they had not seen. Or, as a condition of exhibiting a 'super' film, the exhibitors might be obliged to take also two or three inferior films. To defeat these methods the Act limits the period over which films may be booked in advance and requires every film to be 'trade shown' before public exhibition."[1]

The response to the stimulus provided by the Act has been, on the whole, very gratifying. Before 1927 few British films were being made, and our cinemas were, of course, showing practically nothing but foreign films. In the year after the Cinematograph Films Act was passed, no fewer than seventy-eight full-length British pictures were "trade shown," and thirty-three were actually exported to America. To-day the British film makers are producing over 50 per cent more films than the statute requires, while the foreign firms naturally are only concerned to acquire just enough British films to enable them to comply with the Act, and thus to exploit their own imported films. Furthermore, the exhibitors are showing nearly 80 per cent more British films than the law requires,[2] and the average number of times every British film was screened in 1934–5 was 7630, against 6900 times for every foreign film. The table on page 320 shows the numbers and length in feet of British and foreign films registered in this country since the Act came into force.

The British proportion of the total footage rose from 21·7 per cent in 1932 to 24·2 per cent in 1933, and 24·3 per cent in 1934. The proportion of British long films to the total footage of long films has also been on the up grade. In 1928 it was only 15 per cent; by 1932 it had reached 24·5, in 1933 and 1934 it was around 27 per cent., and in 1935, 28 per cent. Mere length, of course, tells us nothing about quality, but there is ample evidence that improvement in the quality of British films, taken as a whole, is by no means lagging behind the increase in their quantity.

---

[1] *The Film in National Life,* 46.
[2] *Report of a Committee appointed by the Board of Trade, Cmd.* 5320, 1936, 16.

BRITISH[1]

Year	Long[2]		Short		Total	
	No.	Footage	No.	Footage	No.	Footage
1928 . . .	91	647,893	111	141,061	202	788,954
1929 . . .	83	558,217	200	149,562	283	707,779
1930 . . .	132	862,090	98	113,104	230	975,194
1931 . . .	145	888,431	49	50,066	194	938,497
1932 . . .	156	949,533	86	99,631	242	1,049,164
1933 . . .	189	1,131,550	64	70,647	253	1,202,197
1934 . . .	190	1,185,668	87	98,173	277	1,283,841
1935 . . .	198	1,277,857	145	165,166	343	1,443,023
1936 . . .	222	1,428,281	196	213,253	418	1,641,534
Totals . .	1,406	8,929,520	1,036	1,100,663	2,442	10,030,183
FOREIGN[3]						
1928 . . .	605	3,660,037	818	1,269,045	1,423	4,929,082
1929 . . .	525	3,436,040	962	1,303,495	1,487	4,739,535
1930 . . .	564	3,693,154	987	1,197,674	1,551	4,890,828
1931 . . .	502	3,223,651	977	1,150,779	1,479	4,374,430
1932 . . .	459	2,926,630	720	854,183	1,179	3,780,813
1933 . . .	476	3,037,557	621	735,938	1,097	3,773,495
1934 . . .	480	3,113,871	690	890,996	1,170	4,004,867
1935 . . .	503	3,304,086	611	786,452	1,114	4,090,538
1936 . . .	530	3,453,473	612	784,943	1,142	4,238,416
Totals . .	4,644	29,848,499	6,998	8,973,505	11,642	38,822,004
Totals: British and Foreign	6,050	38,778,019	8,034	10,074,168	14,084	48,852,187

There are now twenty-seven film studios in Great Britain. During 1933, 145 British feature films were released, and probably a slightly larger number in 1934.[4] The estimated value of the British films made in 1933 has been put at £3,000,000,[5] and at nearly £5,000,000 in 1935.

It may fairly be claimed, therefore, that the Act of 1927 was a landmark or turning-point; for it rescued and stimulated the British film industry, and although it

has not always worked in the way in which it was intended to

[1] Including films made in the British Empire Overseas.
[2] 3,000 feet and upwards.
[3] Films made in the U.S.A. form the great majority of foreign films, but the figures given include particulars of films made in other foreign countries.
[4] *Film Daily Year Book.*
[5] *Journal of the Royal Statistical Society*, Part IV, 1934, 640. *The Economist*, 5th December, 1936, 456.

work,[1] and there are still difficulties to be overcome; . . . within its protection the British film industry has made a sensational advance and is now consolidating the ground which it has gained. . . . Like the films of other countries, British films have varied from the very good to the very bad, technically, artistically and morally . . . It is not enough to say 'Show British Films.' We should add 'Make British films which are good of their kind and can command a market in any company; films which are British in their essence, in the picture, in the subject and in the setting.' All that is best in the British film industry recognizes this need; there is the technical ability and knowledge to build up a school of production (not the affair of a day); it remains to organize the demand.[2]

But the increase in output of British films is not all real progress, because many rather poor films have been made and rented merely in order to satisfy the length requirements of the Act. These are often slightingly referred to as "quota films" or "quota quickies." On the other hand, British producers have been encouraged to make a number of extremely good films, and it is to be hoped that they will go on doing this more and more, for the prospects and prosperity of the British film industry will depend to an increasing extent upon the quality and marketability of its output in Great Britain, the British Empire, and the United States.[3]

II

There are, in the film industry, three main groups of *entrepreneurs*, (a) the producers, (b) the renters or distributors, and (c) the exhibitors; corresponding roughly to the manufacturing, wholesaling and retailing stages in the production and distribution of goods. The producer is the firm or group which makes the picture. It hires the actors and the technicians, and it either owns or hires the studio and the

[1] For instance, many excellent foreign films likely to appeal only to the more intelligent filmgoers do not get registered at all because the limited market for them makes renters unwilling to incur the rather heavy costs of registration, printing, and distribution, *plus* the acquisition of the statutory quotas of British films.

[2] *The Film in National Life*, 41–2.

[3] There are some 8000 cinemas in the British Empire, excluding Great Britain, with over 5,500,000 seats. In the U.S.A., 14,500 cinemas can seat 10,000,000 people.

studio equipment. Not many years ago the producer usually provided the necessary capital and marketed the film when completed; but sometimes the renter assumed some of the financial risk. To-day the renters may be described as the middlemen between producers and exhibitors; they acquire films from producers and hire them out to exhibitors; they take charge of publicity, the arrangements for showing the film to "the trade," and for selling it abroad. The majority of the renters are members of a trade association called the Kinematograph Renters' Society, which exists to protect and promote their interests. The exhibitor owns a cinema or group of cinemas, advertises his programmes and "retails" them.

Production is a costly business, even when carried on with due regard for true economy; and cheap production usually means poor quality.

A good film of any type is a conscious synthesis by the producer of the work of a team of artists and craftsmen, whose control he entrusts to the director of the picture. He has to pay his actors and his production staff, his technical experts, and his artisans; to maintain an elaborate studio with developing and printing plant, carpenters and model shops, property, rooms, etc.; and to transport this multiple company to the "location" where outdoor scenes are "shot." It has been estimated that a feature film costs at least £2000 a week to make. It might be better estimated that a good feature picture cannot cost much less than three pounds per foot of "cut" negative to produce. It can cost much more. Finally, the producer has to pay heavy royalties to the manufacturers of the sound-recording equipment which he employs, in addition to large capital outlay for cameras, recording apparatus and electrical equipment.[1]

It must not be imagined, however, that everybody employed in film production receives a princely salary. The named "stars" certainly do; but what of the small army of "extras" who form the crowds or the choruses, and what of the craftsmen and other workers "behind the scenes"? The total volume of labour employed varies a great deal according to the quantity of film production going on at any particular time, and the nature of the films in hand; and there does not seem to be

[1] *The Film in National Life*, 49.

sufficient information available to enable an estimate of numbers employed to be made, even within wide limits. All film producers employ a permanent executive, and a nucleus staff of craftsmen, such as electricians, carpenters, plaster workers and painters, which can be expanded according to the needs of the moment. The various kinds of craftsmen generally receive the appropriate trade union rates of wages. The number of actors fluctuates a great deal. On certain days only two or three of the principals may be required; on other days several hundred "extras" may be called for. The rates of pay of the latter are usually low, and, since the occupation is, in a sense, a casual one, their average earnings over the year are lower still. The rate of pay for an "unnamed" film actor or "extra" is 21s. per day of 9½ hours (i.e. 8 hours actual work and 1½ hours for meals). The overtime rate is 2s. 6d. an hour or part of an hour. Average earnings over a year are exceedingly difficult to estimate, since the quantity of employment depends partly upon the qualities of the individual actor, but mainly upon the factors mentioned above. An actor may be in continuous employment for ten or fifteen days, but may not be called upon again for two or three months. For the majority an average of one day's work a week is probably not far from the truth. This means average earnings of between £50 and £60 per annum.[1] Only a small minority of unnamed film actors succeed in making any kind of a living by film acting alone.

The Film Artistes' Association includes some 1200 "regulars," i.e. people who are trying to make a living by film acting. The Association is primarily a trade union and is affiliated to the Trades Union Congress and the London Trades Council. It has an employment bureau through which it is able to distribute to its members a large proportion of the total employment available in the studios.

Film artistes do not come within the scope of the unemployment insurance scheme because they are regarded as engaged in a non-manual occupation and remunerated *at a rate* exceeding £250 per annum, although the *actual earnings* may be much less.

[1] Information supplied by the Film Artistes' Association.

Therefore, a "regular" cannot supplement his (or her) earnings by drawing unemployment pay during intervals between engagements unless he has previously been in an insurable occupation and has to his credit not less than thirty contributions.

From the making of films we now turn to their exhibition. When an exhibitor hires a film from a renter he pays not only for the right to exhibit it, but for "exclusivity," which means an undertaking by the renter that no prior or contemporaneous public exhibition of the film shall take place in the hiring exhibitor's area. The price or hiring charge obtainable by the renter depends mainly upon four factors—

1. The estimated "drawing power" or box office value of the film.

2. The number of competitors desiring the film.

3. The number of other suitable films available on the given date.

4. The right of priority or "exclusivity."

The normal method of payment is an agreed percentage of box office receipts, and if too high a percentage is paid, too little may be left to cover the exhibitor's other expenses. An exhibitor's financial success or failure depends largely upon the soundness of his judgment in choosing between alternative films. He must consider not only the film rents but his particular audience or audiences; the "star value" of the various films and the quality of the acting; the suitability of the themes and the dialogues; the treatment of the theme—humorous, subtle, or melodramatic, hackneyed or original.

Having made a provisional selection, the exhibitor has definitely to book the films. But "as several competitors in his area may have similar views as to the suitability of certain films he may find that any or all of several things have happened: (a) the circuits may have stepped in and booked the films, or (b) competing cinemas offer better terms, or (c) the price is too prohibitive, or (d) the renter insists that the exhibitor books other films (which the exhibitor does not consider suitable) in order to obtain those he wants to book.

An independent exhibitor finds that perhaps only half his programme needs are available among the suitable films which he can book at fair rentals. How does he complete his programmes? By having to take films which are not ideally suited to his audience and by booking suitable films at uneconomic prices. But this is complicated by quota requirements. . . ."[1] The remainder of the programme usually consists of news reels and "shorts," i.e. short comedies or short travel, educational or informative films.

In Great Britain there are about 4400 commercial cinemas with a seating capacity of some 4,000,000, staffed by about 150,000 full-time and part-time employees of both sexes. These cinemas, nearly all of which are now equipped with electrical talking-picture apparatus, may be classified as first-run or pre-release houses, second-run, third-run and fourth-run houses. The first class comprises the large London West-end cinemas and a small number in the large provincial towns. The prices of admission are high and can be so because the pre-release cinemas have the exclusive right to show new pictures several months before they are "generally released." This amounts to a limited monopoly, and in the film industry, as in the publishing trade, it gives the monopolist the power to charge different prices at different times. After a picture has been generally released it goes round, first to the second-run cinemas, then to the third-run, and lastly to the fourth-run houses, each class paying a smaller picture rental than the class above, and charging lower prices for seats. Certain of the renters like to own and run a number of well-known, strategically situated, first-run cinemas for use as "shop windows" for the pictures they wish to dispose of, because a highly successful first-run considerably enhances the market value of any given film.

The large picture palace is not yet typical of the cinemas of this country, for half the seating accommodation is to be found in the smaller cinemas containing less than 1000 seats, and nearly 70 per cent of cinemas are of this small size. Or, as Mr.

---

[1] Article by Kenneth A. Ryman in *Sight and Sound* (1934), Vol. 3, No. 10.

Rowson puts it, "Five out of every seven cinemas provide not more than 1000 seats each, and the remaining two-sevenths provide the balance of nearly one-half of the total seating in the country."[1] In rural and depressed industrial areas the small cinema is the prevailing type, while in London and other more prosperous urban centres the larger cinema is predominant. Many of the smaller cinemas are obsolete or obsolescent and need re-conditioning or rebuilding in order to bring them into line with the new "talkie" acoustic standards. But among the more cautious of the *entrepreneurs* in the industry there is some reluctance to sink much more capital at present because the industry seems to be "over-built" already. Taking into account the admissions, the normal number of performances daily in the larger and smaller cinemas, and the total seating capacity, it appears that on the average throughout the year the cinemas are only about one-third full. Yet new cinemas are being built at the rate of approximately 100 a year. Other *entrepreneurs*, however, take the view that the existence of a rather high proportion of old-fashioned cinemas should not be allowed to hinder the construction of new and efficient ones; and that the cinema manager, like the transport manager, needs enough capacity to meet the demand at peak periods.

Cinema attendances fluctuate not only throughout the day and week, but seasonally as well. Normally the highest attendances are in January, April, September, October and December, and the lowest in June and July when—unless the summer is an unusually bad one—outdoor pastimes are powerful counter-attractions to the cinema. Many exhibitors would like to experiment with improved programmes and special attractions with which they believe they could "beat the weather." But they cannot make the experiment because they must select from such films as the renters or distributors are prepared to release, and the latter normally release only a very limited number of attractive films in the summer, reserving the bulk of the best films for release in the autumn and winter.

[1] S. Rowson in *Statistical Journal*, Part I, 1936, 78.

New industries are, on the whole, quicker to adopt new ideas and to make changes than old industries. The film industry like various others, has recently been undergoing "rationalization," which has included the formation of combines, both vertical and horizontal. It has hitherto been a widely accepted maxim in the industry that all but the smallest concerns must have interests in all departments. Thus producers aim to acquire control of a "chain" or "circuit" of cinemas in which they can be certain that the films they make—including "bread and butter" products, as well as their better and more expensive pictures—will be exhibited. As a consequence of financial grouping and industrial integration, large combines are emerging, which cover all three stages mentioned above—production, distribution, exhibition. Indeed it may be said that the British film and cinema industry is dominated by two such combines—the Gaumont-British Picture Corporation and the Associated British Picture Corporation. The Gaumont-British Corporation, for example, has as part of its circuit the cinemas owned by the Provincial Cinematograph Theatres Ltd., Associated Provincial Pictures Ltd., and H. &. G. Kinemas. This combine, which has an issued share capital of £6,250,000, plus £5,000,000 of outstanding debenture stock, is controlled by a Trust Company in which, besides certain British interests, the American company known as Twentieth Century-Fox Films, has very substantial holdings.[1] In 1927 its "circuit" comprised twenty cinemas. In 1935 the number was 331, situated in London and the principal provincial towns; which meant control over $10\frac{1}{2}$ per cent of all the cinema seats in Great Britain. Moreover, through its distributing organization, Gaumont-British Distributors Ltd., the Corporation distributes the productions of many of the leading foreign film producers. In 1933 the Gaumont-British company merged its various distributing companies into one organization, which had the effect of eliminating competition within the group in the buying of American pictures, and a little later a separate department was created to deal with

[1] Klingender and Legg, *Money behind the Screen* (1937), 23–29.

foreign sales.[1] By the autumn of 1936 the combine consisted of the parent corporation and sixty-four subsidiaries, including several "equipment subsidiaries," such as British Acoustic Films Ltd., which manufactures sound-recording and reproducing apparatus, International Acoustic Films Ltd., and G.B. Equipments Ltd.[2]

On the production side the Gaumont-British Corporation seems to have sustained losses of late (1936–7), and has considerably reduced its film-making activities in consequence; while negotiations and "deals" which many people expected would lead to a very close association between the companies of the Gaumont-British group and those of the other leading combine, controlled by Associated British Picture Corporation Ltd., actually ended in controversy and litigation.

Associated British Picture Corporation Ltd., is a holding company controlling assets valued at £10,500,000. Its circuit comprised thirty-two cinemas in 1928; by 1937 the number was 290. The Corporation was formerly British International Pictures, but since 1933 it has acquired Associated British Cinemas Limited as a wholly-owned subsidiary. Thus the whole activities of the group, which also includes British Instructional Films, Pathé Pictures, Wardour Films Ltd., and B.I.P. Export Ltd. are now concentrated in the one holding company. Its Studios at Elstree cover 40 acres.[3]

These two leading combines not only produce and distribute films, but control between them well over 600 cinemas, which means that they control between 18 and 19 per cent of all the cinema seats in this country. Whether they will enter into a close alliance in the near future, or whether certain opposing American interests will be powerful enough to prevent this, remains to be seen.

Another large circuit, numbering some 230 picture houses, is known as Union Cinemas. This growing organization is

[1] *The Times, Annual Financial and Commercial Review*, 6th February, 1934.
[2] Klingender and Legg, *op. cit.*, 23–8.
[3] *The Economist*, 7th October, 1933, 676–7. Klingender and Legg, *op. cit.*, 30–32.

quite independent of the two combines. Several other independent circuits control from twenty to eighty cinemas each.

Numerically, the two circuits (Gaumont-British and Associated British Pictures) are dwarfed by the "independents" but as the latter are not organized for the co-operative booking of films they are compelled to pay what they regard as decidedly high prices for the films, both American and British, shown in their theatres. Moreover, the independents may be forced to take—or leave—the entire output, good or bad, of a film-producing company. Their only measure of "protection" against bad films may be to pay their hire prices and refrain from showing them. This is sometimes resorted to in the case of the British "quota films" produced by American companies to satisfy the letter of the quota Act at the minimum of cost and trouble. The two circuits, on the other hand, can bargain effectively with the film-producing organizations, and in general are able to buy their films from 15 per cent to 20 per cent more cheaply than the independents. There has been a tendency therefore, for the circuits to expand at the expense of the independents, partly by the purchase of theatres which have given up the unequal struggle, and partly by the building of new "opposition" theatres.[1]

The two great combines cannot afford to stand still, because the independent circuits and energetic speculators are always on the alert to secure "key" positions for new picture theatres. This trend has dangers as well as advantages. The Film Commission wanted "to see the British industry strongly organized in corporations, disposing of sufficient funds to plan on a big scale," but thought that the substitution of the circuit for the independent exhibitor has limited the choice of the audience between theatres possessing distinct individuality. If it also strangles the independent producer, much of the most intelligent work being done to-day in Great Britain may be lost."[2] A producer who controls at least one large circuit

[1] *The Economist*, 6th October, 1934, 640.
[2] *The Film in National Life* (1932), 44, 79. "Houses, locally-owned, that used to cater for a public with which the directors were in touch, and which went regularly to the house, knowing the kind of programme it would get, have been bought up by the circuits. This has often altered the character of the theatre, giving more gold braid and glitter on the one hand, but on the other impairing originality in the choice of programme." (A. C. Cameron in *The Common Room*, June, 1935, p. 5.)

has reduced his risks to a minimum; but other people's risks are thereby increased. An independent producer may make a cultural film—

it is hailed by the critics as a very fine film, and has a success both of esteem and of profit in the West End theatres; but it is no longer judged by individual viewers. One man books films for each big circuit, and if he thinks the film against the policy of his company he will not book it. The film, let us say, is booked by some few independents, and in their theatre has as great a success as in London. But it is a financial failure; and a failure, not because the public did not want it, but because the big exhibitors would not give the public a chance to deliver a verdict. It is such films as these which need constructive support.[1]

On the other hand, it is folly to refuse to reckon with the fact that film-making necessarily involves heavy capital outlay, and this means that "box-office" success must weigh with film producing companies above all other considerations. If it did not, they would soon find themselves in "Queer Street"—or, more exactly, Carey Street—financially.

The cost of films produced in Great Britain range from a lower limit of about £6000, up to £80,000 in special cases. Discussing the production activities of the two combines, *The Economist* says that—

the policy of the Associated group has been to produce "economic" films whose comparatively low costs could be recovered from the box-office receipts of the tied houses. Occasionally "super" films have been produced, and lately the quality of the whole output has been raised. In addition to the productions at Elstree, a supplementary output is available from the Welwyn studios of British Instructional Films, now controlled by the group. The Gaumont group, on the other hand, has spent more heavily on its film productions, "super" films being more frequently turned out at Shepherd's Bush than at Elstree.[2]

All companies in the film and cinema industry have suffered reductions of profits during the past five or six years owing to the necessity of installing expensive "talking-picture" equipment and the almost simultaneous slump in trade which, of

---

[1] *The Film in National Life* (1932), p. 45.
[2] *The Economist*, 6th October, 1934, 640.

course, reduced the public's aggregate expenditure upon amusements. But it appears that the companies in the two combines have come through this difficult phase far better than the independent companies.[1]

As to the future, public demand will increase and so, probably, will expenses of production. Until quite recently a great many film-makers have under-estimated the public taste. They have worked upon the assumption that the majority of their public would only pay to see slap-stick tom-foolery and nauseating sham sentimentality. If this was ever true, it is so no longer. Whether the public's standards have risen little by little in the past decade; or whether their standards were always higher than the levels achieved by the majority of films, and they have, in consequence grown tired of "being played down to," one cannot say with certainty. Probably the public's standards have been raised as a result of the glaring contrasts they have observed between the few really artistic films, British as well as foreign, and the many reels of rubbish with which they have become all too familiar. If the public will continue to support good films and, as far as possible, shun bad ones, the producers and financiers of poor-quality films will be forced to raise their standard of work—and incidentally their expenses of production— or go out of the industry. It has been suggested that the exhibition of approved or "hall-marked" films of a certain class such as educational or cultural films, might be further encouraged if the State granted some rebate of entertainment tax, subject, of course, to certain conditions, e.g. as to the minimum length of approved films.

There is, it seems, something to be learned from Russia in this connexion. The Russians have a number of film studios, large and small, in various parts of the country, and at each studio there is a gifted director; "but production is not the affair of a single master mind." Before a Russian film reaches its final form it has been "criticized and recriticized by committees, on which even the stage hand is allowed his opinion.

[1] *The Economist*, 24th November, 1934, 991.

Teachers are now being trained in the studio so that they shall
be competent to assist with producing teaching films. The
taste of prospective audiences, adult and juvenile, is tested in
factories, schools and cinema halls, where discussion and sug-
gestion on finished and unfinished films is encouraged in a
variety of ways. Thus a criterion of public demand, other than
box-office receipts, is being built up and a core of constructive
criticism solidified." Although the political thought exempli-
fied in certain Russian films may not be acceptable to many
of us, "the appeal to the intelligence is undeniable" and "the
artistry of Russian production is unchallengeable."[1]

The film companies in Great Britain are, of course, not
entirely free to decide what films shall be shown, for we have a
somewhat curious triangular censorship of films. The three
sides of the "triangle" are the Home Secretary, the local
licensing authorities, and the British Board of Film Censors.
Under the Cinematograph Act, 1909, which applies to the
exhibition of inflammable films,[2] a public cinema exhibition
may be given only in premises licensed for the purpose and in
accordance with the regulations laid dawn by the Home
Secretary. Such licences are granted by local authorities—
county and county borough councils, and, by delegation,
borough, urban and rural district councils, or local Justices of
the Peace in Petty Sessions. There are over 700 film licensing
authorities in Great Britain, and any one of these may, subject
to the Home Office regulations, attach to the grant of a licence
conditions relating to matters other than the safety of the
audience, provided that the conditions are reasonable and
administered in a judicial manner. It is through this channel
that local authorities can assume the censorship of films shown
in their areas. The Home Secretary issues statutory regulations
dealing with safety, but he only advises on censorship matters.
The Home Secretary has issued Model Rules for the guidance
of local licensing authorities, and most of them incorporate

---

[1] *The Film in National Life*, 22–3.
[2] At present this means *all* films, for the word "inflammable" has
received a wide legal interpretation, and a completely non-inflammable
film has not yet been invented.

into licences issued by them conditions to the effect that—

No film, other than a photograph of current events, which has not been passed for universal or public exhibition by the British Board of Film Censors shall be exhibited without the express consent of the licensing authority; and no film, other than a photograph of current events, which has not been passed for universal exhibition by the British Board of Film Censors shall be exhibited in the premises without the express consent of the licensing authority during the time that any child under or appearing to be under the age of 16 years is therein.

Some authorities add a clause waiving the last prohibition if the child is accompanied by a parent or other adult in *bona fide* charge of the child.[1]

The multiplicity of licensing authorities means that a common censorship policy is quite out of the question; and confusion and lack of uniformity would be much worse than it is, but for the work of the British Board of Film Censors, which is an unofficial body set up and maintained by the cinematograph trade, but entirely independent in its decisions. It is not compulsory to submit films to the Board, and its decisions on films submitted have no legal force unless and until they are adopted by the local licensing authority. A film submitted to the Board is viewed by experienced examiners on whose advice the Board either rejects it or passes it, with or without alteration, for universal exhibition ("U" certificate) or for adult audiences ("A" certificate). But the grant of such certificates is no guarantee that the exhibition of the film will not infringe the law, nor can it in any way extinguish the personal responsibility of the exhibitor. Experience has shown, however, that the latter can confidently rely upon the Board's expert estimates of the probable legal consequences of exhibiting certain kinds of films.[2] The general practice is for the Board to send to the licensing authority a statement of the films passed "U" or "A," and this is usually accepted without question. But by so doing the licensing authority does not

[1] G. Alchin, *Manual of Law for the Cinema Trade* (1934), 18–19.
[2] *Ibid.*, 18.

relinquish its powers or its responsibility, and it may require the licensee to supply a synopsis of a given film and to show it privately to the authority's representative.

In the opinion of the Commission on Educational and Cultural Films, the Board of Film Censors does its work with efficiency and courageous impartiality. The National Council of Women, after a careful inquiry, reached the general con-clusion "that the present voluntary system of film censorship is on the whole superior to a statutory system, since it accords better with the democratic principles and traditions to which British people are accustomed." Since the publication of this opinion, a Home Office Advisory Committee, representative of the licensing authorities has been set up (1931) to promote closer co-operation between the licensing authorities and the British Board of Film Censors.

But censorship is, at best, quite negative. It can guard against the worst, but it cannot encourage or stimulate the best. This highly desirable positive work is now in the care of the British Film Institute, founded, as a result of a recom-mendation of the Commission on Educational and Cultural Films, in October, 1933, "as a means of furthering effective co-operation between those who make, distribute and exhibit films on the one hand, and all who are interested in the artistic, educational and cultural possibilities of films on the other."[1] The Institute has set forth its objects as follows—

1. To act as a clearing house for information on all matters affecting films at home and abroad, particularly as regards education and general culture.

2. To influence public opinion to appreciate the value of films as entertainment and instruction.

3. To advise educational institutions and other organiza-tions and persons on films and apparatus.

4. To link up the film trade and the cultural and educa-tional interests of the country.

5. To encourage research into the various uses of the film.

[1] British Film Institute, *First Annual Report*, 1934, 7.

6. To establish a national repository of films for permanent use.

7. To provide a descriptive and critical catalogue of films of educational and cultural value.

8. To advise Government Departments concerned with films.

9. To certify films as educational, cultural, or scientific.

10. To undertake similar duties in relation to the Empire.

In pursuance of this programme the British Film Institute desires to secure the support of all bodies and individuals that have at heart the encouragement of the best type of film and the full development of the constructive uses of the cinema. Alike in the public cinema and in the schoolroom and lecture room the film has a growing influence upon thought and action. The purpose of the British Film Institute is to encourage the best features of this influence and to draw together all those who are concerned in its exercise.

The Board of Governors of the Institute has been constituted with the idea of giving equal representation to the public interest, the cinema industry, and educational and cultural interests. Many provincial branches have been formed and in order to secure the widest possible contacts the Governors decided to create an Advisory Council of representatives of all the chief interests (technical, commercial, educational, social, scientific, literary, and artistic) concerned with the future development of films. This Council has nine or ten "panels" of expert advisers upon special subjects, such as education, international relations, and entertainment. Thus, the Entertainment Panel considers and investigates such matters as—

1. Securing views from the public as to the type of film required.

2. The setting up of machinery whereby these opinions can be made available to film producers.

3. Special films and programmes for children's performances.

4. Encouragement to the repertory theatre movement.

5. Methods to be adopted whereby public support may be given to films containing some unusual merit, which do not obtain appreciation from the ordinary cinema-going public.[1]

The Institute has embarked and will embark upon many other activities. It was brought into existence at a moment when the quality and prestige of British films were beginning to rise and when producers and exhibitors were evincing greater willingness to try out films of educational value or high artistic merit. The Film Institute's task is to take advantage of this favourable tendency and to give it strength and direction so that it may bring forth concrete and admirable results.

Mr. Rowson estimates that the British public spend about £40,200,000 annually upon cinema entertainment, of which £6,700,000 is entertainment tax. This probably represents some 958 million admissions per annum in Great Britain, or approximately 18½ millions every week throughout the year.[2] In order to meet this huge demand a continuous stream of new films, made in and collected from all parts of the world, must flow out to the exhibitors in sufficient volume to enable the majority to make at least two changes every week in a programme including from three to six items. And all this must be done at very modest prices per cinema seat. The total "admissions" in 1934 were approximately 963 millions, and the average price paid per seat was slightly over 10d.[3] The following figures, taken from Mr. Rowson's article in the *Daily Film Renter, New Year Edition*, 1st January, 1935, show that more than 80 per cent of British cinema-goers, or nearly 15 million persons each week, pay not more than one shilling for their seats, out of which amounts varying from ½d.

[1] British Film Institute, *First Annual Report*, 1934, 15.
[2] Mr. Rowson estimates that all non-cinema entertainments in Great Britain (plays, variety shows, concerts, sports, etc.) serve about 5 million people every week, at an average admission price of 1s. 2·4d. per head (including tax), or 1s. net.
[3] The number of *persons* was, of course, lower than the number of admissions; but although the cinema industry would like to have definite data regarding the frequency of individuals' visits to the cinema, we have at present no means of calculating the numbers of persons.

AVERAGE WEEKLY ADMISSIONS TO CINEMAS IN GREAT BRITAIN
AND CASH RECEIPTS AND ENTERTAINMENT TAX PAYABLE DURING
1934 AT DIFFERENT RATES OF ADMISSION

Price of Admission (including tax)	Estimated Average Weekly No.	Proportion of Total per cent	Total Cash Receipts (inc. Tax)	Total Tax Payable
			£	£
3d. and under .	1,100,000	6·1	640,000	90,000
Over 3d. to 7d. .	6,900,000	37·4	8,880,000	1,485,000
Over 7d. to 1s. .	6,800,000	36·8	15,360,000	2,565,000
Over 1s. to 1s. 6d. .	2,700,000	14·6	9,450,000	1,575,000
Over 1s. 6d. to 2s. .	500,000	2·6	2,370,000	395,000
Over 2s. . .	500,000	2·5	3,500,000	590,000
Total . .	18,500,000	100·0	40,200,000	6,700,000

to 2d. are paid over to the Exchequer in entertainment tax.
Nearly a quarter of the exhibitors' total takings comes from
seats for which the price (including tax) is not more than 7d.
In other words, the British cinema trade caters every week-day
for over 1¼ millions of people at an average admission price of
5½d. per head, of which o·9d. is entertainment tax. Deducting
entertainment tax, the exhibitors are left with approximately
£33,500,000 per annum. Out of this sum the hire of films and
other programme costs, as well as all the running expenses—
rents and rates, salaries and wages, repairs, renewals, and
advertising—must be paid. The amount of rent paid for
films to the distributors varies between wide limits and
depends upon several considerations, of which the chief
seems to be bargaining power and skill exercised more or less
unscrupulously.

"I venture to suggest," says Mr. Rowson, "that in no other
industry in the world, not even in the bazaars of the East, is the
art of bargaining exercised with as great skill as in the selling of
films. It led some years ago to a number of very marked trade
abuses and, when the Bill which became known later as the
Quota Act was passing through Parliament, special provisions
were introduced to regulate and restrict the conditions under
which films could be traded for exhibition. It is rumoured in the
trade, possibly with some justification, that keen salesmanship
has been able to find ways to surmount the statutory barriers, and

the expectations of Parliament in this respect have been defeated."[1]

Total film rents paid probably amount to one-third of the exhibitors' net takings; i.e. in Great Britain, some £11,000,000 per annum. Of this sum, probably £3,700,000 is absorbed by wages, salaries, overhead charges, import duties, prints of films, advertising and trade shows; and some £2,400,000 is paid for British films; leaving about £5,000,000 as the sum available for remittance abroad, chiefly to the United States, for American interests are still powerful in this country[2] and America is still the principal source of imported films.

Out of 476 imported films registered in 1933 for distribution and exhibition in Great Britain, no fewer than 330 were so registered by nine American-owned companies, directly representing the leading American film-producing companies. These 330 films include practically all the most important subjects, and their value in the aggregate must be at least 90 and probably 95 per cent of the total. All the films imported for these American-owned companies are handled by them as agents, and the sums later remitted to their American principals comprise contributions to the cost of the films and also the profits of the renters here in their business of distribution.[3]

American producers have the advantage of a huge home market; and having recovered in their own country the expenses of making the film, all they gain in an export market, such as Great Britain, is almost entirely additional profit. The British film industry has a much smaller home market, yet until exports of British films can be greatly increased, it is here that our film producers must look to recover their production expenses. The potentialities of the Empire as a market for British films are, of course, enormous, and our leading film producers are co-operating in an attempt to understand

---

[1] S. Rowson in *Jnl. R. Stat. Society*, Part IV, 1934, 639.

[2] The Commission on Educational and Cultural Films (1932) were informed that "American producing organizations . . . still own or control about one-tenth of the cinemas" in Great Britain, including some important London pre-release houses.

[3] Rowson, *op. cit.*, 634–5, 639–40. Mr. Rowson argues that there is serious under-valuation of film imports and exports in the Board of Trade Returns.

and supply colonial audiences, both white and coloured, with suitable films of good quality.

The progress made by the British film industry in 1934 is admirably summarized in *The Times Annual Financial and Commercial Review* (12th February, 1935)—

Over the past few years the rise of the British film industry in size, prestige, and financial importance has been impressive. It has gradually overcome the many problems of production necessary to make its finished article technically as good as that of America, while, more recently, the standard of direction, probably the most important factor of all, has risen considerably. The result is that the British film is now taking its place as a serious rival to the American product in world markets. This is the outstanding impression gained from a study of developments during 1934, and its best confirmation is the changing attitude of the American industry towards its British counterpart. . . .

Progress last year (1934) was more marked in other directions than the quantity of production. Total British footage increased further, but the foreign footage was also larger, after showing declines in 1932 and 1933. Thus the proportion of British to the total was almost unchanged at 24·3 per cent. The figures are not an accurate measure of production activities, for the announcement of ambitious programmes of production by the leading groups was a feature of the past year. . . .

The engagement of famous "stars" and the production of films of international appeal have obviously brought about an increase in production costs, but the British industry still has an important advantage over the American in this respect. In order to recoup the larger outlay entailed, however, wide-scale distribution has become more than ever necessary, and this has made the overseas market of major importance. Marked expansion has taken place in the Dominions and Colonies. It is perhaps natural that the industry should continue to eat into America's predominant position in these markets, but success has also attended efforts in other countries. In particular, the great American market—potentially three or four times as large as the British—has been penetrated with good results. Gaumont-British established its own sales organization in that country—the first British company to do so.

A development which provoked much discussion was the revival of interest in colour photography, which has enormous possibilities, but of which no system has yet proved entirely satisfactory from the commercial point of view. Several new processes came into prominence and are to be exploited, but whether any of these is to cause far-reaching alterations in practice is a matter for the future.

The Committee set up by the Board of Trade to

consider the position of British films, having in mind the approaching expiry of the Cinematograph Films Act, 1927, and to advise . . . what measures are still required in the public interest to promote the production, renting and exhibition of such films,

reported in November, 1936.[1] Briefly, the principal recommendation was the continuance, for a further decade, of the main provisions of the Act of 1927, with certain additions designed to strengthen its beneficial effects and to prevent evasions. Thus, it is suggested that the restrictions and penalties for blind and block booking shall be increased, and that, in order to help the makers of British short films, there shall be separate quotas for short, as well as long films, beginning as follows: Renter's quota, long films 20 per cent, short films 15 per cent; Exhibitors' quota, long films 15 per cent, short films 10 per cent. Of outstanding importance among the evasions of the spirit and intentions of the Act of 1927—

is the production of cheap British films, made at the lowest cost irrespective of quality by or at the order of foreign-controlled renters solely to enable them to show formal compliance with . . . the renters' quota. Such films, known as 'quota quickies' from the speed at which they are made, have tended to bring British films into disrepute. . . . It was admitted by the renters in evidence before us that the majority of the films made for them to enable them to satisfy their quota obligations are worthless and remain in their offices largely unsold and unused.[2]

It is proposed that in future, before a new British film can be registered for renters' quota, it shall pass a quality test before a Films Commission of three or five persons having no professional or pecuniary interests in the film industry. This body would have various other duties connected with the administration of the new legislation. Finally, since lack of finance "is a powerful factor enabling foreign interests to

[1] *Cmd.* 5320, 1936.   [2] *Ibid.*, 13–14, 20.

obtain control and is certainly an impediment to the industry's continued and satisfactory expansion," the Government should encourage financial interests to constitute one or more organizations to provide cheap credit for British film producers in approved cases, but always on a commercial basis.

While it is not certain that the Government will accept all the recommendations of the Moyne Committee, the continuance of the British film quota system in a more or less improved form for a further period of ten years can be confidently predicted, and legislation to that end will probably be introduced before the close of 1937.

CHAPTER VII

THE NEW INDUSTRIES AND THE NATIONAL ECONOMY

I

THE ground surveyed in the foregoing chapters represents a large, expanding and varied section of the whole field of British industry. The total number of insured workpeople between the ages of 16 and 64 is at present about 13 millions[1]; of these nearly 2 millions, or over 15 per cent are engaged in the new industries mentioned above.

There seems to be a general impression that an unusually large proportion of the workers employed in new industries are females; but in fact the proportion of females is less than 26 per cent against 27·2 per cent if we take insured workers in all industries. In only two of the twelve industries—rayon weaving and knitting, and films and cinemas—do the females exceed the males. In the manufacture of electric cable, apparatus, lamps, etc., the proportion of females is as high as 42.9 per cent; but in all the other new industries, and in all the other sections of the electrical industry, the males are in a marked majority.

Another popular impression is that the new industries employ a high proportion of semi-skilled workers and that skilled workers are tending to disappear. On this point, unfortunately, it is impossible to apply any satisfactory statistical test because of the difficulty of defining "skilled work." While it is true that the kinds of skill required are changing a good deal in many branches of industry, it is by no means certain that the total volume of skilled work of all kinds is decreasing.[2] The most highly skilled work in connexion with many modern machine or mass-assembly processes is often done not when the machines and plant are running and production is in full

[1] Excluding agricultural workers.
[2] For an illuminating discussion of this question of "new skills for old," see A. Barratt Brown, *The Machine and the Worker* (1934), Ch. 5.

flow, but in planning and preparing beforehand in order to ensure that production shall flow smoothly and without interruption. Moreover, changes of technique and method do not always displace the existing skilled workers. For example, although extension of the uses of press machinery has deprived sheet metal workers of some tasks they formerly had to do, many new types of skilled sheet metal work have arisen, especially in connexion with the manufacture of motors and aircraft.

The rise of a new industry often means the decline of an old one; but usually there is some net gain because the new products, produced and marketed by the most modern methods, find their way to a wider circle of buyers. The effects of this are felt not only directly in the new industry, but indirectly in all the industries, new or old, that supply materials and accessories. For instance, it is beyond dispute that cheaper and more comfortable transport *creates* traffic, just as the advent of cheaper and more efficient motor cars has transformed a very widespread, but generally unsatisfied *desire* to possess one's own vehicle, into *effective demand* on a very large scale. A demand for a motor car is a joint demand for the seven thousand components of which the complete vehicle consists. It is, of course, true that the shrinkage of older industries may throw a great strain, for the time being, upon the whole national economy; but this does not mean that all is lost. As a matter of fact, by no means *all* of our older industries are shrinking. Some are stable; others are still expanding. But the net expansion in this quarter is not sufficient to prevent the growth of a large mass of unemployment, unless supported and augmented by the rise and expansion of new industries. Even if we assume the mobility of labour to be perfect, we are still left with the awkward fact that the development of new industries is usually a slower process than the contraction or decline of old ones. Only by energetic and enlightened public and private enterprise can the evil consequences of this "lag" be minimized.

Reliable statistics covering the past decade show that there

7777777777777

77777777

has been, in British industry, a silent, spontaneous migration from industries which are contracting to those which are expanding. Not all the expanding industries are "new" in the sense in which that term is used in this book,[1] but those new industries which have passed beyond the "infant" stage —e.g. the electrical industry, road motor transport, motor car manufacture, and the rayon industry—certainly stand out. Whether we look at the indices of expansion in the period 1923–36, or at the total numbers of insured workers in 1936, we find these new industries at or near the top of the list of expanding industries.[2]

CHANGES BETWEEN JULY, 1923, AND JULY, 1936, IN THE ESTIMATED NUMBERS OF INSURED WORKPEOPLE IN CERTAIN INDUSTRIES IN GREAT BRITAIN AND NORTHERN IRELAND

Industry	Estimated No. of Insured persons		Index of Expansion (June, 1923 = 100)
	(aged 16 or over) July, 1923	(aged 16–64) July, 1936	
Electrical Equipment, etc.—			
(a) Wiring and Contracting	11,870	38,160	321·5
(b) Cable, Apparatus, Lamps, etc.	72,840	151,830	208·4
(c) Electrical Engineering	62,280	101,700	163·3
Rayon and Silk.	38,140	80,130	210·1
Road Transport—			
(a) Trams and Omnibuses	110,360	194,760	176·5
(b) Other Road Transport	147,240	219,200	148·9
Motor Vehicles, Cycles and Aircraft.	194,420	314,000	161·5

Other industries, not strictly "new," have benefited from the expansion of the new industries. Thus the hosiery and light metal industries (which have expansion indices of 132·7 and 161·8 respectively) certainly owe much of their expansion to

[1] It might well be argued that some sections of the "distributing trades" are quite new.
[2] See *Ministry of Labour Gazette*, December, 1934, 458–9; cf. *The Economist*, 9th and 16th May, 1936; two articles on "The Anatomy of Employment," and 2nd January, 1937, 5–6.

the progress of the rayon, electrical, and motor manufacturing industries.

Many of these workers have been drawn not only into new industries, but into new localities. Owing to the widespread distribution of electric power and the flexibility of road transport, new factories are not so strongly attracted towards the coal-fields and the great ports or railway centres, as were the majority of the industries which grew up in the last century. These modern de-concentrating influences give greater freedom of choice of locality, and new factories tend to be set up at points conveniently central for collecting various raw materials or marketing the finished goods, where land is cheap and relatively abundant, local rates low, and labour "unorganized and tame."[1] Broadly, the "southward drift" into the Midlands and South-east of England, including much concentration in certain parts of Greater London,[2] which has coincided with economic depression and social distress during the last ten or fifteen years, coupled with the concurrent rise of new industries, is not to any appreciable extent a movement of established factories or industries from one place to another, but rather a movement of population out of old industries and industrial areas to seek employment in new industries arising elsewhere. It is a shifting not of plant, but of people.

We must not, however, allow the magnitude of this movement to blind us to the fact that *the majority* of the people have not moved away, even from the most depressed areas, such as South Wales and the North-eastern counties. These distressed majorities are left, without employment and without hope, in the midst of their still useful but partially unused and fast decaying social capital—houses, shops, schools, roads, and public utilities. The argument that a determined attempt should be made to bring new industries into these districts to

---

[1] H. Dalton, *Practical Socialism for Britain* (1935), 299.

[2] For statistical details, see *Preliminary Report of the Population Census*, 1931; Board of Trade *Survey of Industrial Development*, 1933 and 1934; Registrar-General's *Statistical Review of* 1933; D. H. Smith, *The Industries of Greater London* (1933), and Manchester University Economics Research Section, *Re-adjustment in Lancashire* (1936).

compensate for the decline of the old is a strong one on both economic and social grounds. Yet the fact that relatively few new industries have, so far, come into the distressed areas, suggests that on balance the disadvantages outweigh the advantages in the eyes of those responsible for choosing factory sites. But in a great many cases the scales are pretty evenly weighted, so that very little may be sufficient to tip the beam. New industries do not always and necessarily tend to become located in places hitherto untouched by industry.[1] Indeed, the existing industrial districts have various facilities to offer which, in the absence of strong countervailing factors, would always bring new industries into old industrial areas. But in this, as in many other instances, the *entrepreneur* has seldom a clear and simple choice before him. He must weigh carefully the advantages against the disadvantages—"external economies" against high local rates; nearness to his principal market against proximity to his raw materials; cheap electric power against dear land, and so on—before making his final decision. Sometimes, when all is weighed and considered, there is little or nothing to choose between two possible locations: or it may be that some *entrepreneurs* attach greater importance to certain factors than to others; and so we find the manufacturing plants of a new industry not concentrated in one district, but distributed between several, apparently on no particular principle. Here, probably, we have a clue to the solution of the problem before us. Some special, long-period inducement or inducements must be held out to those about to set up new factories, strong enough to attract the majority into those existing industrial areas most in need of new sources of employment. If the matter were handled energetically by the State through a special department, a great deal of information regarding sites in depressed areas, transport and power facilities and costs, local rates, available labour supplies, wage levels, etc., could be collected and made easily accessible to

[1] Thus Lancashire has received a high proportion of the new industrial establishments opened in recent years. Cf. Board of Trade, *Reports on Industrial Development*, and *Social Survey of Merseyside* (1934), II 354 ff.

firms or companies seeking factory sites. Details of any special inducements held out by local authorities and/or the State could be advertised by the same department. Various inducements could be devised and offered by the State in co-operation with the local authorities concerned, such as the grant of cheap loans, guaranteed interest, taxation relief, and the allocation of public contracts to new industrial enterprises settling in selected areas; or land for factories in such areas might be acquired by the State or local authorities and let at low rents. Moreover, "it might be well worth while for the Treasury to make a substantial contribution in aid of new industrial enterprises in the depressed areas."[1] By such means it would be possible steadily to build up a number of areas of *diversified* industry—areas much more like Bristol and district, for instance, and much less like South Wales—with good results for British national economy and social life.[2]

II

The variety of new industries is striking. Indeed, it may be said that we have here, in a sense, a fairly representative section of the whole of British industry; for power, transport, engineering (electrical and motor), the manufacture of metals, textiles and foodstuffs, and amusements are all represented.

Certain of these new industries have already established themselves in the front rank as large industries of great and increasing national importance. This is clearly the case with electricity generation and supply, road motor transport, the manufacture of electrical equipment, and the motor industry. In peace or war the first two are "key" industries; and in case of war, the manufacture of electrical equipment, motors, aircraft and aero-engines, and, possibly, the extraction of oil from coal, become key industries also. Although the making

---

[1] Dalton, *op cit.*, 301. Cf. Sir Arthur Salter, *Letter to the Electors of Oxford University* (1937), 8.

[2] "If I had to choose between being able to put 50,000 people to work in old or in new industries I would choose the latter, because it gives a better industrial balance. The Special Areas have become depressed partly because there has been little diversity of employment." (Capt. D. Euan Wallace in *The Common Room*, March, 1935, 21.)

of films, like the extraction of oil from coal, is still in its infancy in this country, the exhibition of films is, probably, the most wide-spread and popular of all our amusement trades. All large towns, most of the small ones, and even some of the villages now have their cinemas. Films, unlike another highly popular amusement—football, appeal at least as much to the women as to the men.

Variety is noticeable, moreover, not only in the nature of the new industries, but in their organization. For example, the widest differences exist in connexion with collective bargaining and the rates of wages paid. Trade union traditions and organization are usually strongest in industrial areas where new industries have grown out of, or alongside older industries of a similar type. Skilled craftsmen employed in a new industry generally bring their trade union traditions with them, but among the semi-skilled workers, especially among the women and girls, trade union organization in the new industries is, as yet, very weak. Thus it is that we find some employers still fighting bitterly against trade unionism among the semi-skilled workers, while they, perforce, tolerate it so far as skilled craftsmen are concerned, for if they did not they would, in many cases, find it impossible to secure enough craftsmen to keep their plants running. In the electricity supply industry and in several sections of the electrical equipment industry joint industrial councils are well developed, employers and employees are highly organized, industrial relations are good, and the wage rates compare very favourably with those in other trades. The road motor transport industry has only recently begun to emerge from chaos so far as wages and wage-fixing machinery in the goods section are concerned, as a result of an attempt on the part of the State to regulate and limit hours of labour and to set up machinery capable of introducing fair and uniform rates of wages in all undertakings and districts. The passenger section of the industry has, as yet, no such nation-wide machinery, but hours and wages are regulated partly by statute and partly by trade union agreements. The latter are quite common among the larger undertakings, both private and municipal, but among the smaller firms and companies trade union agreements are more rarely found, and wages, in consequence, are frequently low. Wages in the motor manufacturing industry are usually fairly good, though subject to considerable seasonal fluctuations. Trade union organization is weak in certain of the large plants, particularly where they are isolated or situated in a new industrial area. In the rayon industry trade union organization is recognized by employers, but is not strong at present. Wages are rather low, but differ a good deal from plant to plant and place to place. In the canning industry minimum rates for the lowest grades of workers are determined by a Trade Board. Wages in this industry and in the beet sugar industry are, on the whole, low, and employment is highly seasonal. In the film and cinema industry the craftsmen, who are usually members of trade unions, receive fairly good wages according to their grade, but all other workers' wages are low. In the aluminium industry a very unsatisfactory position exists. Wages are low for all grades and the industry is dominated by a single giant capitalistic organization which refuses to negotiate with the trade unions. In striking contrast we have air transport and aircraft construction, in which a high proportion of the workers are highly skilled craftsmen and mechanics earning good wages.

Turning from organization on the labour side to the organization of capital, we again find a great variety of forms, with, perhaps, more distinct marks of modern trends in industrial structure. In various industries—for instance, in the motor industry, in road transport, and in the cinema trade —large and small units are to be found side by side; but usually the industry or section is dominated by a few giant companies or combines. These are sometimes single units that have expanded greatly from small beginnings, like Morris Motors or Austin's in the motor industry, or great combinations of units wielding tremendous industrial power, concentrated in the hands of a few industrial and financial "captains." Such concerns as Tilling-British Automobile Traction, Gaumont-British, Imperial Chemical Industries, Rootes, Courtaulds,

British Aluminium, Electric and Musical Industries, are examples of this feature of the organization of the new industries. Nor does this combination movement stop at national frontiers. Examples of important international combines of various kinds are to be found in the electrical, aluminium, rayon, and dyestuffs industries.

Moreover, most of the new industries are developing in an age more tolerant of State "interference" in economic life. That the consequent extension of State action in the industrial field has not failed to leave its mark upon the new industries is most clearly seen in the regulation of road motor transport, the subsidizing of air transport and beet sugar manufacture, the protection of the motor and electrical industries by high import duties, and the virtual creation, firstly, of the synthetic dyestuffs industry by prohibiting imports of dyestuffs except under special licence; and secondly, of the film-making industry by the quota provisions of the Cinematograph Act. The rayon industry and the extraction of oil from coal furnish examples of State protection and encouragement by way of a tax differential, i.e. customs duty *minus* a smaller excise duty; while the introduction of socialization and the emergence of the Public Corporation is seen in the electricity supply and road transport industries.

It is still an unsettled question in the sphere of modern industrial organization whether unification under public control is preferable to unification under private control; but the more intelligent protagonists of these two policies have recently made certain modifications of their views which, for all practical purposes, seem to have lessened the gulf between them. Thus many believers in private enterprise no longer maintain that all public enterprises must inevitably be costly and dismal failures; while many of the advocates of socialization freely admit that close and successful public operation and control of any industry is unlikely to be achieved either by "civil service" methods, or by subcommittees of democratically elected local authorities. The gradual spread of socialization seems to have strengthened the opinion that the

day-to-day control of public industrial concerns should be in
the hands of special bodies or boards of managers chosen *ad hoc*
for their known fitness to do the particular work required. In
a report, published in 1932, on the public control and regulation of industry and trade the General Council of the Trades
Union Congress put forward the view that in any socialized
industry the board of management should consist of persons,
drawn from any class in the community, and appointed by the
Government, not as representatives of particular interests,
but solely on the ground of their fitness for the positions to be
filled. The authors of the report did not wish to rule out the
representation of various interests, including, of course,
organized labour, but suggested that this could best be done
by setting up in each case an advisory or consultative committee, to work in close co-operation with the Board of
Management. All British trade unionists do not accept these
proposals. Many still hold to their preference for *representative*
boards of management, on the ground that the proposed
advisory committees seem likely to be ineffective bodies, and
that, with regard to the boards of management, it is unwise
to place wide and almost absolute power over the many in
the hands of a non-representative few. But the specially
appointed board of management is gradually finding favour
among people of various shades of political opinion. As
Mr. G. D. H. Cole has said regarding recent legislation
nationalizing the bulk transmission and wholesaling of electrical power and establishing an extensive system of control
over its generation, "we have the startling paradox that the
most socialistic piece of legislation passed since the war has
been enacted, with very little opposition in any quarter, by a
Conservative Government,"[1] The Central Electricity Board,
which is placed, with monopoly powers, in a key position
between the power stations on the one hand, and the distributors or retailers (whether private or municipal) on the
other, is a body of experts appointed by the Minister (for
periods of five or ten years, as he may decide). The Board's

[1] *Economic Tracts for the Times* (1932), 271–2.

capital is raised by borrowing at fixed rates of interest, and the stockholders have no control over the conduct of the industry. The British Broadcasting Corporation is another example of a socialized service controlled by a body of directors appointed by the Government and entrusted with wide powers and a "free hand."

The same principles are followed in the most recent extension of socialization, by which the bulk of the passenger transport services of Greater London has been placed under the control of a specially appointed public body, the London Passenger Transport Board. In this case, as in the others, there is a small central controlling body or board of experts enjoying a large measure of autonomy and freedom of action, untrammelled by decisions of stockholders, but subject in the last resort to parliamentary control. The members of these boards are not the elected representatives of various interests, but paid experts chosen primarily because of their special fitness to "run" the particular public services to which they are appointed. Unlike the members of the Central Electricity Board and the British Broadcasting Corporation, the members of the London Passenger Transport Board are appointed not directly by the Minister or Government, but indirectly by a body of "appointing trustees." The appointments are made for limited periods, ranging from three to ten years, and reappointment of retiring members is permitted. On the question whether representation of various interests should be conceded by means of advisory or consultative committees, the British legislature seems undecided. The electricity industry, for example, has no such committee; the London passenger transport industry has.

So far, socialization of industries in Great Britain is very partial and incomplete. The great majority of our industries are as yet untouched by this new and more rational form of industrial organization; and even where it has been introduced, there is still ample room for its extension and development.

The electricity supply industry provides a very important

commodity for which there is a highly elastic dual demand, (*a*) from final (domestic) consumers, and (*b*) from industrial users. In spite of considerable technical progress, however, the full potentialities of this new form of power have by no means been made available to the whole community. In order to achieve such a result, electricity must be widely distributed and very cheap; but taking this country as a whole it cannot be said that this is so to-day. The fault lies chiefly in our organization; and to the extent to which organization has recently been improved by the socialization of the whole-saling of electricity under the control of the Central Electricity Board, we have clearly begun to remove the major obstacles to the nation-wide distribution of electricity and to lowness and uniformity of charges. But, equally clearly, we have not gone far enough. Further reorganization of the electricity supply industry is clearly overdue and could best be carried out by a small number of public regional distributing boards, which would absorb the company and municipal undertakings and operate under the supreme control of the Central Electricity Board or the Electricity Commissioners, provided of course that appropriate additional powers were granted by Parliament.

Financial reorganization on a large scale would also be involved. The aggregate capital invested in electricity generation and distribution in this country down to the present time has been estimated as follows—[1]

	£ millions
By public supply undertakings on power stations transmission and retail services	450
On industrial and domestic equipment . . .	120
On railway, tramway and private generating plants .	200
	770

Nearly two-thirds of the capital invested in public supply undertakings has been raised by the municipal authorities, either from the general public or from the Local Loans Fund through the Public Works Commissioners; and about two-thirds of the £450 millions of loan and share capital is still

---

[1] Estimate made by Sir Arnold Gridley in *Financial News* Electricity Supplement, 25th March, 1935, p. 8. Some authorities put the first item slightly lower at £430 millions.

outstanding.[1] The aggregate issued capitals of the principal companies amount to some £125 millions,[2] valued in the stock market at approximately £150 millions. Although the private electricity supply undertakings number about 250, the real control is largely concentrated in the hands of about a score of big groups or combines. Some of these "holding" or "management" companies, e.g. the North-Eastern Electric, are concentrated geographically as well as financially, controlling numerous subsidiary companies all in adjacent areas. In other cases the subsidiaries are scattered throughout the country. "One group, the Electric Development and Securities Trust, which controls eleven companies in different parts of Great Britain, is itself controlled by the General Electric Company, an example of the incursion of the manufacturers into the field of supply in order to ensure the maintenance of the markets for their apparatus."[3] The interest of certain groups are mainly in densely populated urban areas or industrial districts, while others, like Edmundson's Electricity Corporation, which has numerous subsidiaries and sub-subsidiaries, supply predominantly rural regions, such as Shropshire, Worcestershire, Cornwall, Wiltshire, Berkshire, Oxfordshire, and Cambridgeshire.[4]

If we include the Central Electricity Board's £50 millions of capital, it is clear that financial concentration has already proceeded some distance. This should now be carried further, especially upon the distributing side of the industry, by reorganizing and consolidating all the outstanding capital into a small number of fixed interest-bearing stocks, very much on the plan of the London Passenger Transport Board stocks.[5]

---

[1] H. G., *op. cit.*, and *The Economist*, 20th October, 1934, 737, 739.

[2] Over 7½ millions of this is accounted for by the distribution of bonus shares from undistributed profits.

[3] *Financial News Electricity Supplement*, 25th March, 1935, p. 11.

[4] Before July, 1936, the control of this large group was for many years in the hands of American capitalists. The issued capital of Edmundson's Electricity Corporation Ltd. is £5,536,000.

[5] See Chapter III, pp. 150–1. Already the electricity supply industry "has firmly established itself in the position once held by the railways, as the most popular industrial medium for investment funds outside the charmed circle of Government and Corporation stocks."

Thus all ordinary shares would be eliminated and with them all unnecessarily high profits.[1] The profit-taking shareholder would disappear and the consumer would come into his own.

After an exhaustive study and discussion of the whole matter, an American authority concludes as follows—

The questions of high electricity prices and of the chaos of distribution (in Great Britain) require a great deal of study, followed by effective action from Parliament. . . . The solution of the distribution problem raises more difficult and important questions than have been dealt with in the planning of generation and transmission . . . national planning of electricity must be applied to the problem of distribution as well.[2]

This unavoidable conclusion was confirmed by the Electricity Commissioners in their 15th Annual Report, and in the middle of 1935 the Minister of Transport appointed a committee of three (Sir Harry McGowan, Sir John Snell, and Mr. John Morison) to—

bring under review the organization of the distribution of electricity in Great Britain, including the control of statutory electricity companies by other companies, to advise on methods by which improvements can be effected with a view to ensuring and expediting the standardization of systems, pressures, and methods of charge, further extending facilities (including supplies in rural areas) and reducing costs, and to make recommendations.

The report of this Committee was a most disappointing document and its recommendations were timid in the extreme. The Committee emphasized the existing chaos of authorities, areas, voltages and systems of supply, criticized the practices of certain companies, and made it clear that there is great need and scope for reform; but they quite failed to take the bold and logical line suggested by many competent experts and by the success of the Central Electricity Board. Instead of recommending the establishment of a National Electricity Board to control both the generation and the distribution of

[1] The ordinary dividends of leading electricity supply companies in 1933 and 1934 ranged from 6 to 15 per cent. (*The Economist*, 27th April, 1935, 966; cf. *Financial News Electricity Supplement*, 25th March, 1935, 10.)

[2] M. E. Dimock, *op. cit.*, 262.

electricity on a national scale purely in the public interests, the Committee recommended a series of half-measures likely to concentrate control of the retailing of electricity mainly in the hands of the large companies for at least another fifty years. On this *The Economist* commented as follows—

If the operation of company undertakings has on the whole fallen short of reasonable standards, both in business efficiency and also in public responsibility, what reason is there for leaving large companies in possession of the field for another fifty years? True, there are a number of companies open to neither reproach. But there is no particular reason to think that the virtues are found rather among the large companies than the small; and the terms proposed for compensation are such that (unless a crushing burden of capital charges is to be imposed on all consumers) District Commissioners will find themselves compelled to hand over the greater part of their districts to the larger companies, whether these are good, bad or indifferent. Consumption of electricity is not likely to streak ahead on this showing.

In so far as the report envisages the transfer to Local Authorities of a substantial district surrounding their own area, there is less ground for criticism. For although the administration of electricity supply by Local Authorities has, on the average, fallen as far short of the ideals of business efficiency as that of the companies, they have given service on much more economical terms—at all events, to domestic consumers. . . . The report implicitly recognizes that the ideal solution of the country's electricity distribution problem would be the constitution of regional authorities. There will be general agreement with this view, particularly when it can be shown that suitable arrangements could be devised to ensure public responsibility and public accountability. They are ready to prepare the way for such a solution—in fifty years' time! . . . One could have hoped that so eminent a Committee, even if they refused the ideal solution, would not have set their seal on temporization and delay.[1]

The socialization of passenger transport by road, rail and tube in Greater London is now an accomplished fact. Is it

---

[1] *The Economist*, 4th July, 1936, 4. The Government proposes to adopt the Committee's chief recommendations, except that schemes of consolidation will be prepared by the Electricity Commissioners and not by temporary District Commissioners, and schemes not agreed to by the undertakers will require the special approval of Parliament.

likely that the socialization of transport in this country will
be carried further in the near future?

The Labour Party statement of the essentials of a *national*
transport policy is as follows—

In considering a national transport policy based on national
ownership and control, it is desirable to lay down certain essentials
which it should be designed to meet—

(a) The provision of transport facilities as a whole should be
sufficient to meet all reasonable public needs. Such provision
must have regard to many and varying factors which, in turn,
differ from place to place and from undertaking to undertaking;
thus reasonable peak, seasonal and other exceptional traffic,
should be met with necessary speed and promptitude. Transport
provision beyond these requirements is wasteful and must in the
long run involve unnecessary costs; so far as possible the capital
should be fully employed.

(b) Public tastes, preferences and even prejudices, especially
in passenger transport, should be catered for within reason, but
not to an extent involving serious economic loss.

(c) The general direction and day-to-day management should
be endowed with a strong sense of initiative and responsibility
and should therefore be freed from unnecessarily detailed
Ministerial and Parliamentary supervision once the broad principles of policy have been laid down by the statute creating the
new machinery. They must not get into a groove; they should
be open to new ideas and be ready to meet and even to anticipate
all reasonable complaints; the managerial mind should become a
transport frame of mind and should as far as possible be lifted
above any specialist training and experience in road, rail, coast-
wise shipping, harbours and docks, or other particular section of
transport.

(d) There should be adequate standards of remuneration and
other conditions for the personnel of the transport system, and a
definite and steady development of co-operation between the
management and the other personnel. [1]

With regard to the necessary machinery of administration
and control, the Labour Party rejects the proposal that the
Ministry of Transport should undertake this work; pointing
out that as transport is only one of several functions, such as

---

[1] Labour Party Pamphlet, *The National Planning of Transport*
(1932), 11.

highways and electricity, which come within the purview of the Ministry, to saddle the Minister with the "full and final responsibility for every transport decision, whether general or detailed," would be to place an unfair burden upon shoulders already well loaded. Even if a new Department were created, it would still be highly undesirable to make a political Minister, who is inevitably liable to Parliamentary and electoral pressures, responsible for settling transport facilities, charges, wages, appointments, etc. The most attractive alternative is the creation of a National Transport Board, appointed by the Minister of Transport and fully responsible for the efficient management, direction and co-ordination of transport services, subject to the general terms of the originating Statute and such specific checks as may be devised in the public interest. Parliament's functions would be to lay down the general lines on which the industry should be run, and to exercise ultimate control; but not normally to attempt to deal with the detailed direction or day-to-day problems of the industry. Such important steps as the raising of new capital or the reconstitution of the Board should require the sanction of the Minister or of Parliament.

This proposed socialization of our transport system would present two main tasks: (a) the "internal" reorganization of each section of the transport industry so as to raise its efficiency in the public interests; and (b) the balancing and co-ordination of each of these sections, in such a manner as to eliminate overlapping and unnecessary duplication of services, while affording a high degree of service in terms of speed, frequency, safety, and low cost.[1]

---

[1] The Salter Conference agreed with the Royal Commission on Transport that further diversion of certain kinds of traffic from the railways to the roads would not be in the national interest, and recommended the Minister of Transport to seek powers to prevent, by regulation, the transference from rail to road of classes of traffic unsuitable for road haulage by reason of the character of the commodity and the distance to be covered. Under such a comprehensive national transport system as is outlined above, co-ordination of road and rail transport could be worked out still more fully. Moreover, railway goods work could be centralized and conducted on a large scale at a relatively small number of large depots, whence motor collection and delivery vans could operate

A transport system composed of two or more competing monopolies is almost certain to result in a destructive battle between giants, followed by a treaty or combination for the relief and benefit of the giants but probably not in the best interests of those numerous unorganized pygmies—the consumers or general public. Already competition between the railways has been reduced to quite small proportions as a result of the grouping of 1921, the subsequent agreements for the pooling of receipts from competitive traffic, the acquisition by two or more railways of shareholdings in the same road transport undertakings, and the pooling arrangement between the London suburban lines of the four main line railways and the London Passenger Transport Board under the London Passenger Transport Act, 1933. It is now suggested that the railway companies should come to be regarded as *transport* companies capable of undertaking a given piece of transport by any means or combination of means which appears to them to be the most economical and, at the same time, most suited to meet the needs of the traveller or trader. This would mean the absorption of all road passenger and goods services undertaken for hire or as public services and not performed by a firm for the transport of its own commodities. In the Irish Free State a movement in this direction, encouraged by the State, is aiming at the reorganization and operation of road transport for both passengers and goods, under a pooling arrangement with the railway companies.[1]

Such a line of development undoubtedly tends in the right direction, for it is not in the national interest that transport by railway should be treated as essentially different from, or the natural enemy of, transport by road.

An "ideal distribution" of traffic would provide for an economically sound division of function between road, rail, and other

over areas four or five times as large as those covered by horse vehicles. This would probably be much less costly than the present, almost traditional practice of carrying goods on the rail to the station nearest to the consignee, irrespective of its size and its facilities for handling the traffic economically.

[1] See *Modern Transport*, 12th January, 1935; and *The Times British Motor Supplement*, 2nd April, 1935.

forms of transport, and would take into account, not only the price to the consumer and the cost to the operator, but also the ultimate real cost to the community. Such an "ideal division" of function would provide that every passenger and every ton of goods would pass by that mode of transport or combination of modes which would provide the most efficient service at the least cost to the community. In this way overlapping, redundant or unnecessary services would disappear, and each form of transport would convey just those passengers and goods for which it was best suited.[1]

Moreover, capital expenditure would be co-ordinated and directed along the channels most remunerative to the community as a whole; which is certainly not the case at present. Sir Josiah Stamp has pointed out that: "Even governmental application of capital to transport itself is quite empirical, especially if it has responsibility for one form and not for another. How much more is the application of capital by a hundred different agencies?"[2] Co-ordination of public transport services is admitted on all hands to be economical and desirable; but opinions differ as to the method most likely to ensure maximum efficiency at minimum cost.

It is, however exceedingly doubtful whether the general operation of Britain's rail and road transport services should be allowed to get into, or having got there, to remain in the hands of the railway companies as at present constituted. As Mr. C. T. Brunner has said—

It is not so much that the railways will deliberately refrain from expanding their road services, but the railway managers, prejudiced as they are already in favour of railway as against road transport, are not likely to explore the possibilities of road transport with anything like the same enthusiasm as people interested primarily in the subject, and, from the nature of their habits and training on the railways, will find it difficult to adapt

---

[1] Presidential Address by Prof. H. M. Hallsworth, before Section F of the British Association, Aberdeen, 1934. *Economic Journal*, December, 1934, 553–4.

[2] *Presidential Address to the Institute of Transport;* quoted in *Economic Journal*, December, 1934, 554.

[3] Cf. Royal Commission on Transport, *Final Report* (1931), 172–4; M. E. Dimock, *British Public Utilities and National Development* (1933), 115–7; and G. Walker in *Economic Journal*, December 1936, 673–5.

themselves to the enterprising, original, experimental frame of mind which managers of road-transport undertakings are trained and accustomed to show. [1]

The most permanent, constructive and far-sighted solution would be the socialization of road, rail and canal transport services and their co-ordination within a single organization. By way of approach to this goal, it will first be necessary to create a psychological transformation; to banish what Mr. Herbert Morrison calls "the biased railway mind and the biased road mind," and substitute "the big transport mind." Unlike the railways, road transport services have neither the exclusive use of the track, nor control of the traffic on it. Therefore they have no direct control over congestion. But road traffic congestion, which is against their interests, since it causes delay and increases running costs, can be reduced indirectly by organizing in such a manner that no unnecessary journeys are made and no unnecessary vehicles are on the roads at any given time. Thus road wear and tear would be somewhat diminished and with it the general burden of the Road Fund upon the road transport industry. This means the organization of road transport on a comprehensive scale, plus centralized control. State regulation and the manipulation of taxes is not enough. The whole process would probably need to be more gradual than the socialization of London passenger transport, for the national scheme in its final form would involve transport of goods as well as passengers, and would include railways and canals as well as all passenger and goods services on the roads, except the "ancillary" transport, i.e. carriage of goods belonging wholly or mainly to the owners of the vehicles in which they are carried.

The exception of this ancillary transport is to be recommended because it simplifies the remainder of the task of socialization and because such transport is much more an integral part of the particular industry it serves than it is of the transport industry at large. There is an important difference between transporters of passengers or goods who hold

[1] C. T. Brunner, *Road versus Rail* (1929), 73.

themselves out to be hired by any member of the public, and those who do not; and it is doubtful whether socialization of the transport at present owned and operated by the latter would result in any appreciable increase in efficiency or reduction of costs. It would mean, on the other hand, that the State, through the Ministry of Transport, would become hopelessly immersed simultaneously in the internal transport arrangements of a vast variety of trades and industries. Given effective State regulation of wages and hours, there does not appear to be sufficient foundation for the assertion that it "would be impossible to establish a really satisfactory national transport system so long as this section of road transport was allowed to continue an independent unco-ordinated existence."[1]

There remains the problem of ensuring the maintenance in the socialized transport industry of a high degree of efficiency and elasticity, so that the ever-changing transport requirements of the community would be satisfied. This might be effected by setting up a special tribunal charged with the duty of seeing that the transport industry was conducted with efficiency and due economy, and that it was meeting the legitimate and reasonable demands of the community and the transport employees. Moreover, there would be an additional check upon the public transport services if individuals, firms, and companies were left free to use their own road vehicles for their own purposes, if they so desired. Thus, the upper limit to road or rail haulage charges is at or near the point at which the haulier's customers will acquire and run their own transport units. So that even if charges showed a tendency to rise after the socialization of the industry, the rise would soon be checked by the elasticity of demand arising from the possibility of substituting an alternative means of transport. This, incidentally, is another good reason for leaving the ancillary users alone.

But socialization can go far beyond broadcasting, electricity and transport. Sir Arthur Salter's opinion is that more than

[1] Labour Party Pamphlet, *The National Planning of Transport*, p. 20.

half the economic life of Britain, including the distribution of the main necessities of life, could, with marked advantage, be brought under public management;[1] and it is most important that the possibility and feasibility of socializing every new industry should be carefully and wisely examined in the early stages of its development.

Probably the boldest, most constructive and far-sighted policy for the British sugar industry would be along the line of socialization. Sugar is an article widely consumed and in steady demand in this country. The refiners of imported raw sugar and the groups of beet sugar manufacturers are few in number, and the largest of the refiners, Tate and Lyle Ltd., already have a stake in the beet sugar industry. There has been overlapping between the two sections of the British sugar trade, and consequent waste; and the possibility of "a closer understanding between the refiners and the beet sugar factories"[2] has been discussed. Such close understandings, however, seldom bring any benefit to the consumers. On the contrary, they tend to develop into monopolies, and the consumer may consider himself fortunate if the State is alert enough to save him from being thoroughly exploited. The surest safeguard against this, and, in the case of the sugar industry, the best way to cut the Gordian knot into which it is now tied, would be to socialize the whole industry, refineries and beet sugar factories alike. All the companies, should be bought out at a valuation based upon the "reasonable maintainable net revenue" of each one. All "water" should be rigorously squeezed out of their capitals, and the purchase prices, whether reached by agreement or arbitration, should be satisfied in cash or public stocks bearing fixed rates of interest. The necessary cash could readily be raised by the State in the open market. All ordinary shares should be eliminated, and with them all shareholders' rights of control over any units or parts of the industry. Control should be centralized in the hands of a public corporation, similar to the

[1] See *The Listener*, 12th December, 1934.
[2] *Report on the Sugar Beet Industry at Home and Abroad* (1931), 226.

London Passenger Transport Board, answerable to a Minister and, ultimately, to Parliament. If this were done soon, while interest rates are low, the socialized industry could be re-capitalized upon very advantageous terms. By pooling the income earned by the refineries and the beet sugar factories, the Sugar Corporation should be able to pay its way without a State subsidy, for, taken as a whole, both sections of the industry have evidently been very lucrative to the private capitalist.[1] If, after having paid all its expenses, including depreciation of plant and the interest on its capital, the Public Sugar Corporation had any surpluses, these could be passed on to the farmers, by paying them better prices for beet; or to the sugar users by reducing the selling price of sugar; or to the workers in the industry by raising wages; or, if and when surpluses were large enough, they could be divided between these three groups. In any case, surplus or no surplus, the State would have entire control, through a Public Corporation, over an important and, indeed, essential industry; and having decided upon a policy, it could carry it through without putting large subsidies into the wrong pockets.

Three other industries ripe for socialization are the aluminium industry (which is already highly concentrated under the control of a large combine), the coal-oil industry, and air transport. In view of the large capital outlay essential to the establishment of any appreciable number of coal-oil production

---

[1] E.g. Manbré & Garton (Sugar Refiners) earned an average profit of 14·7 per cent per annum on their ordinary share capital during the seven years 1929–35. Tate and Lyle Ltd. earned net profits amounting to 18·3 per cent on their ordinary share capital in 1933 and carried forward and placed to reserves nearly £100,000. In 1934 their earnings on ordinary share capital were 33·7 per cent, and in 1935 they earned 38 per cent on the same capital and paid, in addition, a capital bonus of 40 per cent. The following paragraph from *The Observer*, 25th August, 1935, is not without interest: "Tate and Lyle £1 shares at 80s. 3d. are thought to have possibilities. The financial year ends on September 30, and the report is due in November. Last year the dividend was raised from 17 per cent to 22½ per cent, and the interim distribution has been maintained this year at 6 per cent. No doubt the final dividend will be affected by the 40 per cent bonus distributed last year, but it is anticipated that it will be satisfactory." Actually 18¼ per cent was paid in 1934-5 and 1935-6 on the much enlarged share capital. Cf. *The Economist*, 23rd November, 1935; 28th November, 1936.

plants, and also their importance as a factor in national defence, it seems desirable that this very new industry should be planned and socialized *from the outset*, in order to achieve maximum economy and wise localization, and to avoid the expensive and protracted future struggle, which past experience in other industries leads us to expect, between those concerned for the public welfare, on the one hand, and private vested interests, on the other. Much the same may be said of air transport. If Imperial Airways Ltd. is the government's chosen instrument and recipient-in-chief of air subsidies, why should not this company be converted into a public corporation, with the addition, in due course, of the combined internal air transport companies, so that all British internal and external air lines could be controlled and co-ordinated by a single authority actuated solely by regard for the public interest?

Finally we must notice yet another respect in which the new industries bear the marks of their period. The bulk of their output is sold in the home market. It is true that the electrical, motor, rayon, aluminium, canning, and dyestuffs industries— and even the young film industry—have not neglected export markets; but, at least down to the present time, it is the home market which chiefly counts. Nor is this at all surprising when we remember the world-wide vogue of economic nationalism, high protection and "self-sufficiency," and the tendency of many of the international combines to "reserve" to each member his home market.

III

The people of Britain know by recent experience the perils of excessive specialization. To-day no single country or small group of countries can be the world's workshop. In the modern world it is usual for new industries, unhampered by old-fashioned traditional customs, habits and methods, and having at their command unprecedented capital and technical resources, research and marketing facilities, and the latest methods of large-scale organization and control, to spread rapidly throughout several countries simultaneously until, within a short space, they are reaching out towards the ends of the earth. Manufacture is now tending to become almost as wide spread throughout the world as agriculture. Most of the new British industries have never known times of unrivalled supremacy. None of them has ever been like certain British industries in the nineteenth century, a giant among pygmies, and master of the markets of the world. On the contrary, some of them, starting rather late in the day, have had to struggle forward against the competition of strong, energetic and established opponents. All the evidence, therefore, suggests that in this new era British economic policy should aim at industrial diversification by adding new industries to compensate for a certain inevitable measure of contraction in the old. We can face the future with confidence only if we clearly realize that the economic conditions of the twentieth century, at home and abroad, are very different from those of the nineteenth century, and that it is not in our power to change them. Extreme specialization may have been good economic policy for the nation in the past, but henceforth we must have many eggs in many baskets.

The speed and extent of the growth of our new industries, continuing even through times of unprecedented and world-wide economic depression, clearly indicates that Britain is by no means played out industrially. Her people are ingenious and adaptable. They have already shown high powers of adjustment to great economic transformations, and there is no reason to think that they will lose these attributes in the future. So long as the structure of British industry changes with the changing years, always keeping abreast of new scientific, technical, economic and organizational developments, the increase of prosperity in this country, and the enhanced social utility which accompanies greater variety of commodities and consumption, need never become things of the past. The flow of increasing quantities of capital and labour into new industries is not only a natural consequence of economic progress and rising real incomes, but a necessary condition of the continuance of such progress in the future.

APPENDIX A

WAGES

I

ELECTRICITY SUPPLY INDUSTRY

Rates of Wages fixed by the Joint Industrial Council for
Scottish District (No. 13)

GROUPING OF UNDERTAKINGS

"A" ZONE

LOCAL AUTHORITIES	COMPANIES
Ayrshire Electricity Board.	Clyde Valley Electrical Power
Dundee.	Co.
Edinburgh.	Coatbridge and Airdrie Electric
Falkirk.	Supply Co.
Glasgow.	Electric Supply Corporation,
Greenock.	Ltd. (Dumbarton).
Hamilton.	Fife Electric Power Co.
Lanarkshire County Council.	Strathclyde Electricity Supply
Motherwell and Wishaw.	Co., Ltd.
Paisley.	

"B" ZONE

LOCAL AUTHORITIES   COMPANIES

"C" ZONE

LOCAL AUTHORITIES	COMPANIES
Aberdeen.	Arbroath Electric Light and
Alloa.	Power Co., Ltd.
Bo'ness.	Beauly Electric Supply Co.,
Denny and Dunipace.	Ltd.
Dumfries.	Duncan's Electricity Supply
Inverness.	Co., Ltd.
Kirkcaldy.	Electric Supply Corporation,
Linlithgow.	Ltd.
Lossiemouth and Brander-	Fochaber's Electricity Supply
burgh.	Co.

367

"C" Zone (contd.)

LOCAL AUTHORITIES	COMPANIES
North Berwick.	Fort-William Electric Lighting Co., Ltd.
Oban.	Galashiels and District Electric Supply Co., Ltd.
Perth.	North of Scotland Electric Light and Power Co., Ltd.
Stirling.	Scottish Central Electric Power Co.
	Skelmorlie Electric Supply Co., Ltd.
	Strathpeffer and Dingwall Electric Co., Ltd.
	Urban Electric Supply Co., Ltd. (Hawick).

RATES OF WAGES

Switchboard and Sub-station Attendants

Grade	Zone:	Rate in Pence per Hour "A"	"B"	"C"
Switchboard Attendant Class I				
All Operations				
1– 5,000 k.w. . . .		19·50	19·00	18·50
5,001–10,000 k.w. . . .		20·00	19·50	19·00
10,001–20,000 k.w. . . .		21·00	20·50	20·00
20,001–50,000 k.w. . . .		22·50	21·94	21·37
50,001 and over		23·00	22·42	21·85
Switchboard Attendant Class II				
Part Operations				
1– 5,000 k.w. . . .		17·00	16·50	16·00
5,001–10,000 k.w. . . .		17·50	17·00	16·50
10,001–20,000 k.w. . . .		18·50	18·00	17·50
Rotary S/S Attendants				
1–1,000 k.w.		16·00	15·50	15·00
1,001–2,000 k.w.		18·50	18·00	17·50
2,001–4,000 k.w.		19·75	19·25	18·75
Over 4,000 k.w.		21·00	20·50	20·00
Static S/S Attendants				
1–5,000 k.w.		16·00	15·50	15·00
Over 5,000 k.w.		18·50	18·00	17·50
Assistant Switchboard Attendants				
1– 5,000 k.w. . . .		14·50	14·12	13·76
5,001–10,000 k.w. . . .		14·88	14·50	14·12
10,001–20,000 k.w. . . .		15·63	15·25	14·87
20,001–50,000 k.w. . . .		16·88	16·46	16·04
50,001 and over		17·25	16·82	16·39
Assistant Rotary S/S Attendants				
1–1,000 k.w.		11·88	11·69	11·50
1,001–2,000 k.w.		13·75	13·40	13·00
2,001–4,000 k.w.		14·69	14·30	13·92
Over 4,000 k.w.		15·63	15·25	14·87
Assistant Static S/S Attendant				
Over 5,000 k.w.		13·75	13·40	13·00

GENERAL EMPLOYEES

Grade	Zone:	Rate in Pence per Hour		
		"A"	"B"	"C"
Arc Lamp Trimmer . . .		13·77	13·49	12·93
Ash Handler		13·21	12·93	12·37
Attendant—Pump		14·57	14·27	13·70
Attendant—Conveyor . . .		13·21	12·93	12·37
Attendant—Public Lighting . .		13·77	13·49	12·93
Blacksmith		17·50	17·00	16·50
Blacksmith's Hammerman . .		14·50	14·00	13·50
Cleaner—Boiler, etc. . . .		13·21	12·93	12·37
Coal Handler		13·21	12·93	12·37
Coal Tipper		13·21	12·93	12·37
Coal Weigher		31·21	12·93	12·37
Driver—Engine or Turbine . .		15·72	15·15	14·57
Driver (Assistant)—Engine or Turbine		14·57	14·27	13·70
Electrician		17·50	17·00	16·50
Fitter—Iron or Brass . . .		17·50	17·00	16·50
Finisher—Brass		17·50	17·00	16·50
Greaser and Oiler		13·21	12·93	12·37
Joiner		17·50	17·00	16·50
Jointer		18·50	18·00	17·50
Labourer		13·21	12·93	12·37
Linesman (Power) Grade "A" . .		17·50	17·00	16·50
Linesman (Power) Grade "B" . .		16·00	15·50	15·00
Mate (Electrician's, Fitter's, Jointer's)		13·21	12·93	12·37
Meter and Instrument Repairer .		17·50	17·00	16·50
Meter Changer and Fixer . .		15·71	15·43	14·87
Meter Reader		14·71	14·43	13·87
Moulder		17·50	17·00	16·50
Patternmaker		17·50	17·00	16·50
Turner (Iron or Brass) . . .		17·50	17·00	16·50
Stoker		15·15	14·57	14·27
Storeman		13·21	12·93	12·37

II

WAGES AND CONDITIONS IN THE ROAD HAULAGE INDUSTRY,

agreed upon by the National Joint Conciliation Board for the Road Motor Transport Industry (Goods)

(i) GENERAL WORKING CONDITIONS TO OPERATE ON AND FROM 1ST JANUARY, 1935

1. *Higher Wages and Conditions.* Where, either by agreement with employers or with local Associations, wages higher than those hereinafter stated are in operation, and/or conditions superior to those herein provided prevail, there shall be no reduction or variation of those wages or conditions except by mutual consent.

2. *Working Conditions.* The working week shall be a guaranteed week of 48 hours on the accumulative basis, Monday to Saturday, inclusive of garage duties, but excluding meal times.

3. *Overtime.* Overtime shall be paid for the first 8 hours following the completion of 48 hours, at the rate of time and an eighth, and time and a quarter thereafter.

A man may be booked off if away from home, for one period not exceeding two hours (exclusive of meal times) between two driving periods, for which he shall receive an allowance of 1s. for such period or any part thereof. Booking off shall be deemed to mean that the driver shall be away from the vehicle and free from all responsibility and control of the vehicle. This provision shall be reviewed at the expiration of one year.

A man ordered to report and presenting himself for duty shall be paid a minimum of 2 hours. If ordered to report a second time in the same day, he shall be paid a minimum of 4 hours.

A man commencing work on any day shall be paid a minimum of 4 hours. It shall be permissible for a regularly employed man to work for a minimum of 2 hours for the purpose of attending to his vehicle or engine. On Sunday, a man called upon to report and presenting himself shall be paid as above at time and a half.

4. *Casual Men.* A casual man engaged for long-distance or trunk services shall be paid a minimum of 8½ hours on any day from Monday to Friday and 5½ hours on Saturday if he is completing a job which commenced before the Saturday. If engaged for a single engagement for a Saturday he shall be paid a minimum of 8½ hours. Any time worked in excess of 8½ hours (Monday to Friday) or 5½ hours on Saturday, to be paid at time and a quarter.

5. *Sunday Work—All Classes.* Time and a half to be paid for all hours between Saturday midnight and Sunday midnight, with

a guaranteed minimum of 4 hours at time and a half; but it shall be permissible for a regularly employed man to be brought in for a minimum of two hours at time and a half for the purpose of attending to his vehicle or engine.

6. *Subsistence Allowance.* A minimum of 5s. shall be paid for a period not exceeding 12 hours' rest. If the period of rest exceeds 12 hours, a further 2s. 6d. shall be paid. If the period of rest exceeds 18 hours, an additional 2s. 6d. shall be paid, making a total of 10s. Where the employer provides lodging accommodation, as approved by the Area Joint Board, an agreed deduction shall be made for the use of such accommodation.

7. *Statutory and Proclaimed Holidays.* The following holidays to be paid for: Christmas Day, Good Friday, the four Bank Holidays, and all nationally proclaimed holidays. If a man is called upon to work on these days, he shall receive an additional day's pay. Where in any trade or district it is not the custom or practice to observe the normal statutory holidays, a day shall be selected in lieu thereof.

8. *Annual Holidays.* A week's holiday with pay to be given to regular employees provided that the employee has been in continuous service for one year and has not been absent from his employment for more than seven days within any one year without reasonable cause or previous notification, or if a temporary break of service should occur due to shortage of work or other causes outside a man's control, not exceeding one month. The holidays to be taken between 1st April and 31st October, unless otherwise arranged. A man shall be entitled to this holiday at the completion of a year's service.

(ii) WAGES AND CLASSIFICATION OF VEHICLES

1. *General Minimum Rate of Wages to apply to all Road Transport Workers in England and Wales (other than London) engaged upon Long Distance and Trunk Services*[1]—

Drivers of vehicles—   Per week
    Class 1—Under 2 tons carrying capacity   .   .   60s.
    ,,   2—Of 2 tons carrying capacity, and including
        vehicles up to gross laden weight of 12
        tons   .   .   .   .   .   .   65s.
    ,,   3—Over 12 tons and up to 22 tons gross laden
        weight   .   .   .   .   .   .   70s.
Statutory attendants and mates (adults), when
    employed .   .   .   .   .   .   56s.

[1] For wages, etc., applicable to road haulage in Scotland, see *Labour Gazette*, August 1935, 289.

2. *Classifications and Rates of pay operative for all classes of transport in London and the Metropolitan Area—*

Drivers of vehicles—
Under 1 ton carrying capacity . . . . 54s.
Of 1 ton carrying capacity . . . . 58s. and 63s.
Over 1 ton and including 2 tons carrying capacity 62s. and 63s.
Over 2 tons and up to 5 tons carrying capacity 68s. and 69s.
Over 5 tons carrying capacity . . . 72s. and 73s.
Statutory attendants and mates when employed . 57s.
Mates on steam wagons . . . . . . 59s.

The Workpeople's Organization having, on 30th April, and 8th May, 1934, submitted a claim to the respective Employers' Organizations for an increase of the London rates, which claim has not yet been disposed of, the above rates are inserted without prejudice and will operate pending a settlement of the claim in question. When the settlement is effected the agreed rates shall be substituted for the rates above, and will then become the London rates.

3. *Classifications and rates of pay for other than Trunk and Long Distance Services, but not applying to the London and Metropolitan Area—*

	Grade 1 Per week	Grade 2 Per week	Grade 3 Per week
Drivers of vehicles—			
Carrying capacity—			
Under 30 cwt. . . .	52s. 6d.	49s.	45s.
30 cwt. and not exceeding 2 tons	57s. 6d.	54s.	50s.
Over 2 tons and up to and including 3½ tons .	62s. 6d.	58s. 6d.	54s. 6d.
Over 3½ tons carrying capacity up to and including 12 tons laden weight (gross) . .	65s.	61s.	57s.
Over 12 tons gross laden weight	70s.	66s.	62s.
Statutory attendants and mates (adults), when employed .	56s.	52s.	48s.

4. *Rates for Youths and Attendants.* The youths' rate, when employed as drivers, shall only apply to vehicles not exceeding 30 cwt. carrying capacity. On vehicles above that capacity, the adult rate shall apply.

The youths' rates are for an experimental period of 2 years, during which time the whole question of recruitment to the industry will be reviewed by the Board.

	Grade 1	Grade 2	Grade 3
Youths—first year . . .	35s.	32s. 6d.	30s.
second year . .	40s.	37s. 6d.	35s.
third year (until the age of 21 is attained) .	47s. 6d.	45s.	42s. 6d.

The adult rate shall apply in any case where the person is 21 years of age or over.

III
WAGES OF OMNIBUS (PUBLIC SERVICE VEHICLE) DRIVERS AND CONDUCTORS IN GREAT BRITAIN, 1936

Practically all the large omnibus companies now have separate, and by no means uniform, wages agreements with a trade union (usually the Transport and General Workers' Union). The wages are commonly based on a 48-hour week, but the actual hours worked may be, and frequently are, more or less than 48, and the rates of wages paid for overtime, Sunday work and "spread-over" differ a good deal. The ordinary commencing trade union rates of wages for drivers of company-owned concerns vary (1936) from 11¾d. to 1s. 3¾d. per hour, and the maximum rates vary from 1s. 1¾d. to 1s. 6½d. For conductors the corresponding rates are from 8½d. to 1s. 2¾d., and from 9¾d. to 1s. 4d. Most of the company undertakings *not* bound by trade union agreements are small, and the wages they pay are as a rule a good deal below the trade union rates; especially if we remember that men employed by these small concerns work a great deal of overtime which goes entirely unremunerated. Cases have come to light where drivers have received 40s. for a 70-hour week.

In general, the municipalities pay higher wages to bus drivers and conductors than do the companies. An examination of the wages paid by about 120 undertakings showed that, taking the largest or "modal" groups of company and municipal undertakings, the differences were approximately as follows—

	Municipalities s. d.		Companies s. d.	
Wages per 48-hour week.				
Drivers—				
Average commencing rate .	60	9	52	6
Average maximum rate . .	65	3	60	6

	Municipalities	*Companies*
Wages per 48-hour week.	*s. d.*	*s. d.*
Adult Male Conductors—		
Average commencing rate .	53 0	51 0
Average maximum rate . .	62 9	54 6

It must be remembered that these are averages. Some of the
non-trade union companies pay commencing rates to adult male
conductors as low as 27s. 6d. a week. Under trade union agreements with companies adult male conductors receive wages
ranging from commencing minima of 33s. to maxima of 64s. per
week of 48 hours. The corresponding municipal rates of wages
are 48s. and 64s. The time taken to reach maximum wages varies
between one and eight years. In a relatively small number of
cases somewhat higher wages are paid to drivers of one-man
operated vehicles.

The wages paid by the London Passenger Transport Board,
within its extensive district in and around Greater London, are a
good deal higher than those paid in other parts of the country by
either public or private undertakings. Moreover, the overtime
and other special rates paid by the L.P.T.B. compare very favourably with those paid elsewhere.

WEEKLY WAGES (FOR 48 HOURS AT ORDINARY RATES) OF PUBLIC SERVICE VEHICLE DRIVERS AND CONDUCTORS EMPLOYED BY LONDON PASSENGER TRANSPORT BOARD, 1936

	DRIVERS		CONDUCTORS	
	Com-mencing rate	Maximum rate	Com-mencing rate	Maximum rate
	s. d.	*s. d.*	*s. d.*	*s. d.*
Inner London Area .	82 6	88 6	77 6	83 6
Outer London Area . "Limited Stop" Carriages . .	77 6	80 0	62 0	64 0
"Ordinary Stage" Carriages . .	67 6	72 6	60 0	64 0

Notes: In the Inner London Area the maximum rate is paid after 6
months' service.

On "Limited Stop" Carriages the maximum is paid after one
year's service.

On "Ordinary Stage" Carriages the maximum is reached after
18 months' service.

Persons employed on the Board's public service vehicles are
provided with passes entitling them to free travel at any time
on such of the Board's public service vehicles as operate within
the area in which the person is employed.

Free uniforms are allowed as follows: Drivers—one overcoat
every two years, white summer coat, summer cap and two cap
covers every year. Conductors—cloth jacket, serge jacket,
pair cloth trousers, pair serge trousers, cap, and two white cap
covers every year.

APPENDIX B

STATISTICS

I

ESTIMATE OF NUMBER OF PERSONS ENGAGED IN
(a) Road Motor Transport and
(b) Auxiliary Industries
in Great Britain, 1935

(a)

Licensed Bus Drivers	88,786	Annual Report of Area Traffic Commissioners 1934–5.
Licensed Bus Conductors	69,264	
Lorry and Van Drivers	434,720	Ministry of Transport Statistics of Road Vehicles compared with Ministry of Transport Census of Road Vehicles, September, 1933.
Lorry Drivers' Mates[1] and Statutory Attendants	50,000	
Taxi Drivers and Chauffeurs	65,000	

(b)

Motor Mechanics	94,000	Census 1931, Occupational Tables, England and Wales, and Scotland.[2]
Motor Garage Proprietors, Haulage Contractors, Managers, Inspectors, and Foreman	48,000	
Petrol and Oil Refining and Distribution	40,000	Estimated number of garages in Great Britain plus number of workers in Petrol Refining Industry.
Road Construction and Maintenance	100,000	Reports on the Road Fund; Report of Committee on Local Expenditure for Scotland; *Ministry of Labour Gazette.*

989,770[3]

[1] Motor vehicles drawing trailers are obliged by law to carry one man in addition to the driver. On other motor lorries it is not usual to carry a second man, unless he is needed to assist in loading and unloading.

[2] These two figures may be too large, because it is possible that some of these motor mechanics are not working in the Road Motor Transport Industry; and that a small number of garage proprietors and haulage contractors who drive their own vehicles may have been counted also as "lorry and van drivers." On the other hand, the figures have not been adjusted upwards to allow for expansion during 1931–5.

[3] It is probable that the figures overlap, to the extent of about 100,000 workers, with those for the manufacture and repair of motor vehicles.

II

BRITISH PRODUCTION OF MOTOR VEHICLES

(a) Private Cars and Taxis

Year	Home Sales		Exports	Retained Imports	Production
	Private Cars	Taxis			
1923 . .	88,907		4,556	22,067	71,396
1924 . .	121,725		12,875	18,000	116,600
1925 . .	149,971		24,029	42,000	132,000
1926 . .	145,111		25,389	17,000	153,500
1927 . .	161,603	1,174	27,594	26,000	164,553
1928 . .	161,493	1,003	26,180	23,000	165,352
1929[1] .	170,369	1,397	32,915	21,871	182,347
1930 . .	156,460	1,343	26,388	12,048	169,669
1931 . .	144,212	1,217	18,816	4,731	158,997
1932 . .	145,874	716	25,354	1,999	171,244
1933 . .	182,046	1,055	41,358	3,780	220,779
1934 . .	219,510	1,294	45,114	9,629	256,866
1935 . .	271,636	2,240	46,189	13,700	306,365

[1] Year ended September from 1929 onwards.

(b) Commercial Vehicles (Excluding Trolley Buses and Vehicles Exempt from Motor Tax)

Year	Home Sales		Exports	Retained Imports	Production
	Commercial Vehicles	Exempt Vehicles			
1923 . .	26,944		1,698	5,038	23,604
1924 . .	32,962		2,784	5,746	30,000
1925 . .	35,646		5,021	5,667	35,000
1926 . .	42,044		6,999	4,543	44,500
1927 . .	44,104		8,098	5,354	47,227
1928 . .	46,960	3,122	6,360	9,154	46,525
1929[2]	62,873	3,151	8,566	16,444	56,458
1930 . .	61,758	3,164	6,566	3,991	66,859
1931 . .	60,119	2,922	5,475	1,416	67,310
1932 . .	51,917	2,936	7,304	557	61,475
1933 . .	53,227	2,838	9,898	182	65,508
1934 . .	70,816	3,318	12,236	1,458	85,633
1935 . .	74,341	5,095	14,889	1,840	92,485

[2] Year ended September from 1929 onwards.

III

WORLD PRODUCTION OF RAYON

(In thous. lb.)

Country	1929	1930	1931	1933	1935	1936[1]
U.S.A. .	122,375	115,000	140,800	202,400	257,500	278,000
Japan .	30,800	33,330	46,750	89,925	220,000	285,000
Italy . .	71,150	59,700	76,120	82,040	86,000	88,000
U.K. . .	56,900	48,870	54,570	84,080	111,800	113,000
Germany .	55,000	57,880	55,000	68,200	104,000	112,000
France .	37,005	39,160	36,365	57,200	53,000	42,500
Netherlands	17,050	15,840	19,800	23,650	20,000	20,000
Canada .	4,235	4,840	5,565	7,610	12,750	12,000
Belgium .	14,520	10,450	10,395	9,605	13,500	13,500
Others .	31,705	25,155	25,425	31,055	52,310	55,090
Total .	440,740	410,225	470,790	655,765	930,860	1,019,090
Of which—						
Viscose .	386,125	357,500	420,740	563,650	816,360	888,220
Acetate .	25,170	28,105	34,385	62,745	81,000	96,940
Cupra .	18,215	16,040	11,880	23,210	33,350	33,690
Collodion	11,230	8,580	3,785	6,160	150	240

PRODUCTION OF STAPLE FIBRE

(In thousands of lb.)

Country	1933	1934	1935	1936[1]
Italy . . .	11,000	22,000	66,000	100,000
Germany . . .	9,900	18,000	32,000	65,000
Japan . . .	963	2,500	13,500	40,000
Britain . . .	2,750	3,000	10,000	28,000
France . . .	2,200	4,000	8,000	12,000
U.S.A. . . .	2,100[1]	2,200	6,000	12,000
Other countries . .	440	700	1,200	2,150
Total . . .	29,353	52,400	136,700	259,150

[1] Provisional. The figures for 1929–32 include staple fibre.

BRITISH IMPORTS AND EXPORTS OF RAYON YARN AND FABRICS

(i) YARN EXPORTS

1932	5,647,434 lb.
1933	5,289,365 lb.
1934	9,142,324 lb.
1935 [1]	8,410,975 lb.

(ii) ALL-RAYON FABRICS
(Twelve months)

	1933 Thous. sq. yds.	1934 Thous. sq. yds.	1935 Thous. sq. yds.	1936 Thous. sq. yds.
Imports from—				
France	6,663	4,312	2,893	1,459
Italy	7,467	4,154	2,267	100
Switzerland . .	3,093	2,535	2,081	1,417
Germany . .	2,148	2,212	3,759	5,953
Total (all countries) .	21,768	15,719	14,367	14,305
Exports to—				
Australia . . .	1,496	2,632	2,840	7,281
South Africa . .	1,788	2,369	2,621	4,033
New Zealand . .	1,226	2,081	1,441	2,869
Canada . . .	525	456 ⎫		
Other British countries .	3,719	6,197 ⎬	8,043	10,819
Foreign countries .	2,085	2,298 ⎭		
Total (all countries) .	10,841	16,035	14,945	25,002

(iii) MIXTURE FABRICS
(Twelve months)

	1933 Thous. sq. yds.	1934 Thous. sq. yds.	1935 Thous. sq. yds.	1936 Thous. sq. yds.
Imports from—				
France . . .	3,577	2,524	1,820	909
Germany . .	1,871	1,793	1,400	2,013
Belgium . .	1,057	782	—	—
Italy . . .	965	689	586	78
Total (all countries) .	8,214	6,438	4,778	3,804
Exports to—				
India . . .	5,784	8,871	4,990	2,448
South Africa . .	5,450	7,208	6,040	8,401
Australia . .	6,225	7,053	4,417	6,010
Irish Free State .	3,096	4,023	2,767	2,640
Canada . . .	3,643	3,412	1,368	1,808
New Zealand . .	2,617	2,791	2,004	2,101
British West Africa .	1,151	846 ⎫	6,666	8,530
Other British countries .	2,957	3,428 ⎭		
Argentina . .	947	1,464	1,129	1,033
Total (all countries) .	43,372	49,263	36,862	41,804

[1] Includes staple fibre and waste.

IV. SUBSIDIES TO BRITISH CIVIL AVIATION

	To Imperial Airways Ltd.		For Light Aeroplane Clubs, National Flying Services and Gliding	Aerial Routes, Surveys, and Experimental Services	Technical Equipment	Works Services (Mainly Capital Expenditure on Croydon Airport)	Staffing and Maintaining Civil Aerodromes	Headquarters, Meteorological and Miscellaneous Services	Total
	European Services	Egypt-India Services							
	£	£	£	£	£	£	£	£	£
1927–8 .	137,000	93,600	16,400	31,000	16,000	150,000	28,000	16,505	488,505
1928–9 .	137,000	93,600	16,000	29,000	8,000	93,000	29,000	16,364	421,964
1929–30 .	341,500		18,500	15,000	6,000	22,000	29,000	24,160	456,160
1930–31 .	408,000		20,000	23,000	16,000	29,000	29,000	27,500	552,500
1931–2 .	520,000[1]		20,000	31,000	22,000	24,000	32,000	29,400	678,400
1932–3 .	551,000[1]		10,000	22,000	13,000	35,000	33,000	31,364	695,364
1933–4 .	548,000[1]		20,000	22,000	12,000	24,000	34,000	34,047	694,047
1934–5 .	561,000[1]		16,000	11,000		37,000	43,000	37,247	705,247
1935–6 .	473,000[1]		30,000	127,000		53,500	56,000	52,541	792,041

[1] Including the following contributions from Colonial and Dominion Governments, £155,000 in 1931–2; £166,000 in 1932–3; £146,000 in 1933–4; £129,000 in 1934–5 and £120,000 in 1935–6.

SELECT BIBLIOGRAPHY

BOOKS, ARTICLES, AND OFFICIAL PUBLICATIONS

ELECTRICAL AND RADIO EQUIPMENT

Bowden, W., *Technological Changes and Employment in the Electric Lamp Industry*. U.S. Bureau of Labor Statistics, Bulletin No. 593 (1933).

B.B.C. Year Books.

B.E.A.M.A., *Twenty One Years* (1933).

The Broadcaster (Trade Periodical).

Brown, F. J., *Cable and Wireless Communication of the World.*

Committee on Industry and Trade, *Survey of Metal Industries* (1928).

Dimock, M. E., *British Public Utilities and National Development* (1933).

Ford, P., *Work and Wealth in a Modern Port* (1934).

Fourth Census of Production, Final Report, Part II.

Garcke, E., Article in *Encyclopaedia Britannica* (1910).

Hilton, J., and others, *Are Trade Unions Obstructive?* (1935).

Howell, J. W., and Schroeder, H., *History of the Incandescent Lamp* (1927).

League of Nations, *Review of the Economic Aspects of Several International Industrial Agreements* (1930).

League of Nations, *Organization for Communication and Transit* (1934).

Matheson, H., *Broadcasting.*

New Survey of London Life and Labour (1931), Vols. II and VIII.

O'Dea, W. T., *Radio Communication, Part I (Science Museum Handbook*, 1934).

Plummer, A., *International Combines in Modern Industry* (1934).

Radio Yearbook, 1935.

Report on Key Industries (1926).

Schonfield, H. J. (ed.), *The Book of British Industries* (1933).

Smith, D. H., *The Industries of Greater London.*

Sub-Committee on the Electric Lamp Industry, *Findings and Decisions* (1920).

Vyvyan, R. N., *Wireless over Thirty Years.*

The Wireless Trader (Trade Periodical).

The Wireless World (Periodical).

ALUMINIUM

Allen, G. C., *Industrial Development of Birmingham and the Black Country* (1929).

British Aluminium Company Ltd., *Aluminium Production, Properties and Applications*.

Committee on Industry and Trade, *Factors in Industrial and Commercial Efficiency* (1927).

Committee on Trusts, *Report* (1919).

Deville, St. C., *De l'Aluminium, ses Propriétés, sa Fabrication et ses Applications* (1859).

Deville, St. C., "On Aluminium and its Chemical Combinations" (from *Comptes Rendus*, 1854).

Edwards, Frary and Jeffries, *The Aluminium Industry* (1930).

Electricity Commission, *Rural Electrification; Considerations Bearing . . . etc.* (1930).

Findlay, *Chemistry in the Service of Man* (1925).

Fourth Census of Production, Part II, 1934.

Institute of Mechanical Engineers, *Proceedings*, Vol. 125, 1933.

Journal of Political Economy, October, 1920.

Kossmann, *Über die Wirtschaftliche Entwicklung der Aluminiumindustrie*.

League of Nations, *Review of the Economic Aspects of Several International Industrial Agreements* (1930).

Manchester Guardian Commercial, Aluminium Supplement, 3rd July, 1936.

Plummer, A., *International Combines in Modern Industry* (1934).

Statistical Abstract for the British Empire.

RAYON (ARTIFICIAL SILK)

Avram, M. H., *The Rayon Industrie* (1933).

Committee on Industry and Trade, *Survey of Textile Industries* (1928).

De Réaumur, F., *Memoirs pour servir a l'Histoire des Insectes* (1734–42).

The Economist, Commercial History and Review, 1934 and 1935.

Employment of Women, Young Persons and Children Act, 1920, *Report of Departmental Committee of Investigation* (1935).

Howe, *Chemistry in the World's Work* (1926).

Manchester Guardian Commercial, World Textiles Supplements.

Manchester Guardian Commercial, Annual Reviews.

Pilcher and Butler-Jones, *What Industry owes to Chemical Science* (1923).

The Rayon Record (Trade Periodical).

Reinthaler, F., *Artificial Silk* (1928).
The Times Annual Financial and Commercial Review.
The Times Trade and Engineering Review, 1934.
Wilmore, A., *Industrial Britain* (1930).
Woodhouse, T., *Artificial Silk or Rayon, its Manufacture and Uses* (1929).

SYNTHETIC DYESTUFFS

Committee on Industry and Trade, *Factors in Industrial and Commercial Efficiency* (1927).
Departmental Committee on Textile Trades, *Report* (1918).
Dyes and Dyestuffs, *Report* (1921).
Dyestuffs Industry Development Committee, *Report* (1930).
Dyestuffs Industry Development Committee, *Third Report* (1932).
The Economist, Commercial History and Review.
Fourth Census of Production, *Final Report,* Part III (1934).
Manchester Guardian Commercial, Annual Reviews.
New Survey of London Life and Labour, Vol. V.
Papers relative to . . . British Dyestuffs Corporation Ltd. (1925).
Plummer, A., *International Combines in Modern Industry* (1934).

CANNING

Astor and Murray, *The Planning of Agriculture* (1933).
Clapham, J. H., *Economic History of Modern Britain,* Vol. II (1932).
Committee on Industry and Trade, *Survey of Metal Industries* (1928).
Empire Marketing Board, *The Demand for Canned Fruits* (1931).
Financial News, 6th July, 1935.
Hardenburg, E. V., *Bean Culture* (1927).
Imperial Economic Committee, *Canned and Dried Fruit Supplies in 1934* (1935).
Jones, J. H., *The Tinplate Industry* (1914).
Ministry of Agriculture, *Fruit and Vegetable Production for Commercial Canning* (Bulletin No. 45, 1933).
Report on the Import Duties Act Inquiry, Part I, 1935.
Smith, R., *Court Cookery* (1725).
The Times, British Canning Industry Supplement (November, 1931).
The Times, Trade and Engineering Review, 1934.

BEET SUGAR

Agricultural Policy Sub-Committee of the Reconstruction (Selborne) Committee, *Report* (1917).

Astor and Murray, *The Planning of Agriculture* (1933).

Bridges and Dixey, *British Sugar Beet; Ten Years Progress under the Subsidy* (1934).

Cambridge University Dept. of Agriculture, Farm Economics Branch *Report No. 9.*

Cambridge University Dept. of Agriculture *Report No. 19; An Economic Survey of Agriculture in the Eastern Counties of England* (1931).

Committee on Industry and Trade, *Factors in Industrial and Commercial Efficiency* (1927).

Ministry of Agriculture, *Report on the Sugar Beet Industry at Home and Abroad* (1931).

Ministry of Agriculture, *Statements in the form of Balance Sheets . . .* Sect. I, Factories (1934).

Orwin, C. S., on "Agriculture" in *Britain in Depression*, Chap. I. (1935).

Reynolds's Newspaper Supplement, 11th November, 1934.

Sugar Policy (*Cmd.* 4964, 1935).

United Kingdom Sugar Industry Inquiry Committee (Greene Committee), *Report* (1935).

Venn, J. A., *Foundations of Agricultural Economics* (1933).

MOTOR VEHICLES AND AIRCRAFT

Aberconway, Lord, *The Basic Industries of Great Britain* (1927).

Allen, G. C., *British Industries and their Organization* (1935).

Allen, G. C., *The Industrial Development of Birmingham and the Black Country* (1929).

Board of Trade, *Survey of Industrial Development, 1933 and 1934.*

Carpenter and Diederichs, *Internal Combustion Engines* (1908).

Committee on Industry and Trade, *Survey of Metal Industries* (1928).

Duncan, H. O., *The World on Wheels* (1926).

The Economist, Motor Industry Supplement, 7th December, 1935.

Encyclopaedia of the Social Sciences, Vol. II, article "The Automobile Industry."

Epstein, R. C., *The Automobile Industry* (1928).

Epstein, R. C., Article in *Quarterly Journal of Economics*, February, 1926.

Fenelon, K. G., *Economics of Road Transport* (1925).

Fenelon, K. G., Article in *Statistical Journal*, Part II, 1935.

Fleming and Brocklehurst, *A History of Engineering* (1925).

Florence, S., *The Logic of Industrial Organization* (1933).

Fourth Census of Production, Part II, 1934.
Imperial Economic Committee, 3oth *Report; Survey of the Trade in Motor Vehicles* (1937).
London and Cambridge Economic Service, *The British Motor Industry* (Special Memo. No. 18).
Manchester Guardian Commercial, Road Haulage Supplement, July, 1932.
New Survey of London Life and Labour, Vol. II (1931).
Saunders, C., *Seasonal Variations in Employment* (1936).
Schonfield, H. J. (ed.), *The Book of British Industries* (1933).
Smith, D. H., *The Industries of Greater London* (1933).
Society of Motor Manufacturers and Traders, *The Motor Industry of Great Britain* (annual).
Usher, A. P., *A History of Mechanical Inventions* (1929).
Williams, F., *The Sky's the Limit* (Pamphlet, 1935).
Who's Who in British Aviation.

ROAD MOTOR TRANSPORT

Advisory Committee on London Traffic, *Report* (1920).
Area Traffic Commissioners, *Annual Reports.*
British Road Federation, *Road Notes, Great Britain.*
British Road Federation, *The Case for Motor Transport.*
British Road Federation, *The Road and Rail Traffic Act*, 1933.
British Road Federation, *Statement of Policy* (1936).
Brunner, C. T., *The Problem of Motor Transport* (1928).
Brunner, C. T., *Road versus Rail* (1929).
Chester, D. N., *Public Control of Road Passenger Transport* (1936).
Cole, G. D. H., *Economic Tracts for the Times* (1932).
Dimock, M. E., *British Public Utilities and National Development* (1933).
Fenelon, K. G., *Economics of Road Transport* (1925).
Fenelon, K. G., *Transport Co-ordination* (1929).
Fenelon, K. G., Article on "Road Transport in Great Britain since the War," in *Statistical Journal*, Part II, 1935.
Fuel Research Board, *Annual Report*, 1933.
Joint Council for Retail Distributive Trades Section of the Road Transport Industry, *Report*, 1934.
Journal of the Institute of Fuel, June, 1934.
Journal of the Institute of Transport, Various Articles.
Labour Party, *The National Planning of Transport* (1932).
Liberal Industrial Inquiry, *Britain's Industrial Future* (1928).
Licensing Authorities, *Annual Reports.*
Liverpool University, *Social Survey of Merseyside* (1935).

Liverpool University, *Co-ordination of Passenger Transport Services on Merseyside* (1935).
London Passenger Transport Board, *Annual Reports and Accounts.*
Ministry of Labour, *Annual Report* (1932).
Morrison, H., *Socialization and Transport* (1933).
Motor Transport Year Book and Directory.
National Joint Conciliation Board for the Road Motor Transport Industry (Goods), *Reports and Decisions*, 1934–5.
New Survey of London Life and Labour, Vol. VIII (1934).
Paterson, J., *History and Development of Road Transport* (1929).
Road Fund, *Annual Reports and Accounts.*
Road Traffic Census, 1931.
Road Vehicles—Great Britain (Quarterly).
Royal Commission on Transport, *First, Second and Final Reports* (1929–30).
(Salter) Conference on Road and Rail Traffic, *Report* (1932).
Statistical Abstract for London.
The Times, British Motor Industry Supplement, April, 1935.
Traffic Commissioners, *Annual Reports.*

AIR TRANSPORT

Air Ministry, *Reports on the Progress of Civil Aviation* (annual).
Air Transport Manual.
Air Travel (Periodical).
Airways and Airports (Periodical).
Bouché, H., *Economics of Air Transport in Europe* (1935).
Brett, R. D., *History of British Aviation to 1914* (1933).
Brittain, Sir H., *By Air* (1933).
Hallsworth, H. M., Article in *Economic Journal*, December, 1934.
Harper, H., *The Romance of a Modern Airway.*
Harper, H., *Twenty-five Years of Flying* (1929).
Harper and Brenard, *The Romance of the Flying Mail* (1933).
Modern Transport (Periodical).

OIL FROM COAL

Board of Trade, *Industrial Survey of South Wales* (1932).
Fuel Research Board, *Annual Reports.*
Imperial Chemical Industries Ltd., *Annual Reports.*
Hicks and King, *Fuel Research Board Technical Paper No. 34* (1931).
Low Temperature Carbonization Ltd., *Annual Reports.*
Nash and Dowes, *Principles of Motor Fuel Preparation and Application.*

Reports of Investigations into the Industrial Conditions in certain Depressed Areas (1934).
Royal Commission on the Coal Industry, *Report* (1926).
Thomas, I., *Coal in the New Era* (1934).
Thomas, I., Article in *Political Quarterly*, January–March, 1935.

ELECTRICITY SUPPLY

Coal Conservation Committee, *Report* (1917).
Central Electricity Board, *Annual Reports*.
Clapham, J. H., *Economic History of Modern Britain*, vol. II (1932).
Committee on the position of the Electrical Trades after the War, *Report*, (*Cmd*. 9072, 1918).
Committee on Industry and Trade, *Survey of Metal Industries* (1928).
Committee on Industry and Trade, *Survey of Industrial Relations* (1926).
Dimock, M. E., *British Public Utilities and National Development* (1933).
Electricity Commissioners' *Annual Reports*.
Financial News *Electricity Supplement*, March 1935.
Garcke's *Manual of Electricity Undertakings*.
"H.G.," *The Socialization of the Electrical Supply Industry.* (1934).
Labour Party, *The Reorganization of the Electricity Supply Industry* (1932).
League of Nations, *Statistical Year Book*.
Liberal Industrial Enquiry Report, *Britain's Industrial Future* (1928).
(McGowan) *Report on Electricity Distribution* (1936).
Morrison, H., *Socialization and Transport* (1933).
New Survey of London Life and Labour, Vol. VIII.
P.E.P., *Report on the Supply of Electricity in Great Britain* (1936).
Quigley, H., *Electrical Power and National Progress* (1925).
Rather, A. W., *Planning Under Capitalism* (1935), Part II.
Robson, W. A., *Development of Local Government* (1931).
Thomas, I., *Coal in the New Era* (1934).
(Williamson) Electric Power Supply Committee, *Report* (*Cmd*. 9062, 1918).

FILMS AND CINEMAS

Alchin, G., *Manual of Law for the Cinema Trade*.
British Film Institute, *Annual Reports*.

Buchanan, *Films; The Way of the Cinema* (1932).
Cameron, A. C., Article in *The Common Room*, June, 1935.
Commission on Educational and Cultural Films, *The Film in National Life* (1932).
Daily Film Renter.
The Economist, February 6th and 13th, 1937, Articles on the British Film Industry.
Kinema Weekly.
Kinematograph Year Book.
Klingender, F. D. and Legg, S., *Money behind the Screen* (1937).
(Moyne) Committee, *Report* (Cmd. 5320, 1936).
Rowson, S., Article in *Daily Film Renter*, New Year Edn., 1st January, 1935.
Rowson, S., Articles in *Statistical Journal*, Part IV, 1934, and Part I, 1936.
Sight and Sound.
Schonfield, H. J., *Book of British Industries* (1933).
To-day's Cinema.

General

Board of Trade, *Survey of Industrial Development, 1933 and 1934*.
Board of Trade, *Industrial Surveys* (S. Wales, S.-W. Scotland, N.-E. England, Merseyside, and Lancashire), 5 vols. (1932).
Brown, A. B., *The Machine and the Worker* (1934).
Commissioner for Special Areas, *Second Report* and *Third Report* (*Cmd*. 5090 and 5303, 1936).
Dalton, H., *Practical Socialism for Britain* (1935).
The Economist, May 9 and 16, 1936; Articles on "The Anatomy of Employment," and January 2, 1937, pp. 5–6.
Fisher, A. G. B., *The Clash of Progress and Security* (1935).
Jones, J. H. (ed.), *Britain in Depression* (1935).
Levy, H. *The New Industrial System* (1936).
Liverpool University, *Social Survey of Merseyside*, Vol. II.
Manchester University Research Department, *Re-adjustment in Lancashire* (1936).
Marquand, H. A., and others, *Second Industrial Survey of South Wales*, 3 vols. (1937).
Population Census, 1931, *Preliminary Report*.
Registrar-General, *Statistical Review of 1933*.
Robson, W. A. (ed.), *Public Enterprise* (1937).
Salter, Sir Arthur, *Framework of an Ordered Society* (1934).
Smith, D. H., *Industries of Greater London* (1933).
Wallace, D. E., Article in *The Common Room*, March, 1935.

INDEX

MADE IN GREAT BRITAIN AT THE PITMAN PRESS, BATH
C7—(B.251)